The Struggle for the Middle East

The Struggle for the Middle East

The Soviet Union in the Mediterranean 1958–1968

Walter Laqueur

Written under the auspices of the
Center for Strategic and International Studies
Georgetown University, Washington D.C.

The Macmillan Company

Library of Congress Catalog Card Number: 70-95173

First American Edition 1969

First published in Great Britain in 1969
by Routledge & Kegan Paul, London

The Macmillan Company

Printed in the United States of America

This book was researched and written under the first
annual Distinguished Writers Award, granted by the
Center for Strategic and International Studies, Georgetown University,
Washington, D.C.
The Center is a private, non-profit organization that
seeks to advance the understanding of international
policy issues through interdisciplinary study of emerging
world problems. The Center does not take a position on
any policy issue, and the views expressed in works it
sponsors are those of the individual author

Contents

1 Introduction   1

2 Prelude: 1945–58   5

3 The Neutralization of the Northern Tier   14

4 Russia, Zionism, Israel   43

5 The Soviet Union and the Arab World   63

6 Oil for the Lamps of Eastern Europe?   118

7 Trade and Aid   137

8 The Soviet Military Presence   145

9 Communism, Maoism, Arab Socialism   162

10 Conclusion   181

Notes   195

Bibliography   209

Documents   213

Index   352

Documents

            page

1. O. Tuganova: Political Trends in the Arab East (1966)   213
2. Statement on the Situation in the Arab Countries by the Arab Communist Parties (May 1967)   221
3. Egypt and Communism (I). From Speeches by President Gamal Abdul Nasser in Damascus (March 1959)   229
4. Egypt and Communism (II). From Nasser's Speech (May 29, 1967)   235
5. Egypt's Debt to the Soviet Union. From Nasser's Speech (July 23, 1968)   237
6. Soviet Government Statement on the Situation in the Near East (May 24, 1967)   241
7. Statement on the Situation in the Middle East by the East European Communist Parties (June 1967)   243
8. A. N. Kosygin: Speech at the UN (June 19, 1967)   245
9. Decisions of the Israeli Communist Party (RAKAH) (June 1967)   256
10. Moshe Sneh: Our Position (June 1967)   258
11. CPSU: The Policy of the Soviet Union and Israeli Aggression (June 1967)   268
12. L. Brezhnev: The Middle Eastern Crisis (July 1967)   270
13. Soviet Government Statement on the Middle East (March 30, 1968)   274
14. K. Ivanov: Israel, Zionism and International Imperialism (1968)   277

15. 'Baathist Crimes in Syria' (*World Marxist Review*, 1964)   289

16. Khalid Bakdash: The National Liberation Movement
    and the Communists (1965)   292

17. Syrian Communist Party: Our Policy after February 1966   298

18. Soviet Warning to Britain, Israel and the United States
    (May 1966)   302

19. Khalid Bakdash: Syrian Communists Call for Arab
    Unity (September 3, 1967)   304

20. Iraqi Communist Party: 'For the Defence of the
    Republic' (August 1959)   316

21. Documents of the 3rd National Conference of the Iraqi
    Communist Party (1967)   326

22. Reza Radmanesh: The Policy of the Iranian Com-
    munists (1967)   340

23. TASS: Western Interference in the Persian Gulf
    (March 1968)   346

24. Y. Serbin: The Navigation Regime in the Black Sea
    Straits (1966)   348

25. A. N. Kosygin: Speech in Ankara (December 22, 1966)   350

1 Introduction

The present study is devoted to a review of Soviet policy in the Middle East during the last decade and to an analysis of its future prospects. It also deals with developments inside the various Middle East countries in so far as they may influence the outcome of the struggle for the Middle East. It is in some ways a sequel to *Communism and Nationalism in the Middle East* (1956), and *The Soviet Union and the Middle East* (1959). The shortcomings of these earlier books were, and are, obvious to the author. They were written at a time when little source material was available, and when it was just beginning to be realized that the topic itself was a legitimate subject of study. The general outlines of Soviet policy in the Middle East could be only dimly recognized at the time. Since then the situation has changed radically; as far as source material is concerned, the danger now is not of drought, but of drowning, and many new problems have appeared. In the nineteen-fifties Soviet relations with Iran and Turkey were much less complex than they are today; Soviet interest in Middle East oil barely existed, and there was virtually no Soviet interest in Cyprus, Sudan, Algeria, South Arabia, and a great many other places. There was no Soviet fleet in the Mediterranean and, on a different level, hardly any Soviet writings on the Middle East; but as the area assumed growing importance in Soviet policy, so has the volume of literature expanded. I was tempted at times to bring my two earlier books up to date, but refrained for a number of good reasons. They summarized the early stages (the 'prehistory') of the Soviet drive towards the Middle East. It was not simply a question of continuing the historical narrative and adding fresh material; the whole perspective has changed. I believe that the basic assumption of these two earlier books was correct: the Soviet drive towards the Middle East was gathering momentum in the fifties; given the weakness of the area as a whole and the domestic situation in the Arab world, the Soviet Union had an excellent chance greatly to strengthen its position in the Middle East and perhaps even to become the dominant power there. These assumptions were by no means generally shared fifteen or even ten years ago. Soviet pre-occupation with Europe was taken too much for granted, while the prospects of Nasserist Pan-Arabism as an independent political force were overrated.

It was difficult to foresee in the middle fifties exactly what form the radicalization in the Middle East would take in the years to come. The communist camp was still united; no rival centers had arisen to shake the monolithic bloc. We are much wiser now. During this past decade the importance of communist parties has on the whole decreased; there has been a far-reaching *rapprochement* between a number of Middle East countries and the Soviet Union, but it has largely by-passed the official communist parties in the area. Military dictators and new political groups (such as the neo-Ba'th) have been of far greater significance in this context. Even in the nineteen-fifties there were reasons to doubt the relevance of the doctrinal discussions in Soviet writings as a key to the understanding of Soviet policy in the Middle East. These books and articles were of some interest because they helped to explain shifts in policy; occasionally they reflected internal dissension. Today I feel even more sceptical about their relevance, for they shed very little light on the real mainsprings of Soviet policy. The interests of Russia as a great power have played a role in Soviet foreign policy from its earliest days, and this was, of course, inevitable. As the years passed their specific weight has steadily increased and that of Leninist ideology has steadily declined. It has declined, but not altogether disappeared. Official Soviet doctrine still survives almost in its pristine state, but the discrepancy between theory and practice is still growing, and it is now very difficult to ascertain to what extent even those making the doctrinal pronouncements believe in them. The Soviet political and military leaders are, of course, communists, and any attempt to explain their foreign-policy decisions solely on the basis of traditional power politics is ultimately futile. But what does it mean to be a leading communist in the Soviet Union today? The writings of Marx and Lenin alone are unlikely to provide a satisfactory answer. For this reason I have dealt with doctrinal disputations in this book only in passing; it is still a legitimate subject of study, though no longer a very important one. I have had to neglect some other aspects of Soviet policies in the Middle East, and of Middle East reactions, in order to concentrate on the central issues. To treat the issues touched upon fully and exhaustively, each chapter would have to be expanded into a separate monograph.

Key sections of this book were written during the Czechoslovak crisis of 1968. All history is contemporary history, and even Western historians of ancient Rome and Greece are known to have been influenced by the impact of Hitler, Mussolini, and Stalin. There was an almost overwhelming temptation to deal with the prospects of the Middle East in the light of the Czech crisis, a temptation which had to be resisted. The historian knows from his own and others' experience that the danger of distortion is greatest at a time of crisis; that events which loom very large at the moment of writing may appear in a different perspective a few years later. He knows about the cunning of reason: a great triumph may be the prelude to disaster and a defeat may eventually turn into victory. Lastly, he knows that the future is *a priori* unpredictable, that there is no inevitability about it, and that even highly probable events may never come to pass. Nevertheless, with all these reservations, a major crisis such as the invasion of Czechoslovakia has its advantages for the historian: all the quasi-problems suddenly disappear and his perception of the essential issues is sharpened. An event of this kind furnishes a sudden and usually brutal test: it clears away the cobwebs of wishful thinking, of irrelevant theories and spurious explanations. It shows that at a time of decision it is power that matters and the firm resolve to use it.

The Soviet leaders have frequently stressed that the area adjacent to their southern borders is of vital concern to them. They regard it as their legitimate sphere of influence. But the Middle East is not Eastern Europe, and the Soviet capacity to intervene there will probably be limited for a number of years to come. Soviet ties, even with Egypt and Syria, are not nearly so close as those with Poland and East Germany, but Moscow has no intention of giving up the bridgehead established in the Middle East at great cost and with great patience over many years. On the contrary, it will try to consolidate and extend it, and for this reason the critical years are still ahead. The Middle East is not intrinsically one of the most important areas in world affairs. It has long ceased to be a crossroads, its military bases are no longer needed, it has no important natural resources other than oil, but there is no lack of oil elsewhere in the world. And yet, in view of the delicate balance of global power, the Soviet Union attributes great importance to the Middle East, and its presence there may have far-reaching political effects in Europe as well as Africa and Asia. From the Soviet point of view, the area has a great attraction, both because of its nearness to its southern frontiers and because of its internal instability. Among Soviet foreign political priorities the Middle East now takes a high place, not because it is intrinsically important, but because it is so weak. In many ways it seems to present the line of least resistance: in the Far East there is the growing threat of China; in Europe any advance beyond the 'red line' would mean a clash with NATO and the Americans. But the place of the Middle East in the contest between the powers has never been clearly defined, and it is therefore likely to remain one of the main danger zones in world politics in the years to come.

I have received assistance and advice from many institutions and individuals. I am greatly indebted to Dr David Abshire and Professor Alvin Cottrell of the Center for Strategic and International Studies of Georgetown University, who first suggested this study to me and made it possible for me to write it. I owe much to Mr Zeev Ben Shlomo, who helped me in my research, to Miss Diana Langton, my secretary, and to Mrs C. Wichmann and Mr E. Kahn of the Middle East Documents section at the Institute of Contemporary History (Wiener Library) in London, who within a short period have made this a collection of great help to the student of contemporary history.

June 1969   *London/Boston, Mass.*

2   Prelude: 1945-58

Russian interest in the Ottoman Empire, its involvement in what was then the Eastern Question, antedates the revolutions of 1917 by about 150 years. In Tsarist foreign policy, throughout the nineteenth century, in the ideology of Slavophils and Panslavists the question of Constantinople and the Straits played a central, almost mystical, role. Turkey was about to disintegrate, the Hagia Sofia was at last to return to its rightful owners. The Russian mission in the Near East was the dynamic centre of Russian history; there its manifest destiny would be fulfilled. But the first world war brought not only the demise of the Ottoman Empire, it also caused the downfall of the Romanovs. With the Bolshevik revolution such imperialist ambitions were solemnly forsworn: communist Russia, the pioneer of world revolution, was to be also the friend and ally of all national liberation movements. The industrialized countries of Central and Western Europe were expected to play the leading role in the coming stage of the world revolution; the hopes of Marx and Engels had been centred in the West, and the eyes of Lenin and Trotsky were turned there too, although they did not entirely neglect Asia and the East. About a decade before the revolution they had begun to realize that there was a revolutionary potential in the East, that the colonies and the semi-colonial countries of Asia would not forever remain quiescent. Bolshevism tried to assist them in their fight; the Congress of Baku, calling on the toilers of the East to rise against foreign imperialists as well as against native capitalists and landlords, was the first important milestone in this struggle. The Soviet leaders followed with a great deal of sympathy the fight of the Turks under Kemal and the national movements in Persia and Afghanistan. Not much attention

was paid at that time to events in the Arab world. By the standards
of those days, the Arabs were a faraway people; most of their
countries were not yet even semi-independent. Nor was there a
great deal of interest in Zionism, which at that time had just
acquired a Jewish national home. Zionism, in the communist view,
was an anachronistic, reactionary movement. The salvation of the
downtrodden Jewish masses in the East European ghettoes would
come with the victory of world revolution. The Jewish question
could not be solved in a distant country under the protection of
British bayonets. Moscow and the Communist International also
attacked the pan-movements of the day – Panislamism, Panarabism,
Panturkism; these too were condemned as reactionary in character.
Support for 'progressive' movements in the Near East involved
Soviet Russia from the beginning in political and doctrinal contradictions, since they could not be expected to embrace Bolshevik
ideology and practice lock, stock and barrel. Islam, for instance, still
had deep roots in the East, and a frontal attack against it was obviously out of the question, despite communism's unalterable opposition to religion in general.

The existence of Communist parties outside Russia was for the
Soviets, needless to say, a matter of gratification, and in theory their
interests could never collide with those of the Soviet state. In
practice, alas, clashes occurred all too frequently from the very
outset. The policies of Kemal Atatürk, the champion of the Turkish
struggle for independence, were warmly supported in Russia, and
close relations were established between Ankara and Moscow. But
the political and military alliance with Russia did not prevent Kemal
from suppressing the Turkish communists and from having their
leaders assassinated, once they had challenged his rule. Their fate
was deeply deplored in Moscow, but support for Kemal was not
discontinued. Russia could not afford to be particular in its choice of
allies, nor could it ignore the immediate interests of the Soviet
state. This kind of dilemma was to recur many times.

With the ebbing of the first revolutionary wave after the first
world war, conditions in Europe and Asia became more stable and
the hopes for an early victory of the national liberation movements,
let alone of the Communist parties, evaporated. Soviet relations
with Turkey and Persia remained fairly close; there were no other
independent states in the Near East at the time with whom Moscow
could directly deal. Stalin prevailed in the struggle for power in the

Kremlin; the construction of 'socialism in one country' got under way, and foreign policy was relegated to second place. Revolution, it was announced, was not for export. The Comintern underwent strange contortions. After 1928, in response to a new world crisis, it preached an ultra-revolutionary course of action, refusing to co-operate even with the left-wing leaders of the national movements in the East. 'National reformism' was now anathema; Kemalism was re-examined and found wanting. Only the Communist parties could be relied upon, but they, too, had to be severely purged before becoming truly Bolshevik in character. Followed to its logical conclusion, such a policy would have brought about a complete rupture between the Soviet Union and the national movements in the East. But extreme radicalism did not prevail for very long; by the middle nineteen-thirties the orientation was again towards a united front of all anti-imperialist forces. There was less warmth now in the relations with Turkey and Persia than in the early years after the revolution, but this was by no means the fault of the Russians alone, for with the changes on the international scene Turkey and Persia needed Russia less than in the early twenties. The Soviet Union, on the other hand, was deeply absorbed in its domestic problems, while in its foreign policy Europe all but monopolized its attention as both a promise and a danger.

During the first two decades after the revolution and almost up to the end of the second world war, the Near East, once a central preoccupation of Russian statesmen, did not figure high on the list of Soviet priorities. Seen in retrospect, it does not appear that the Soviet Union missed many chances in this part of the world. Of course, the narrow, sectarian approach of the Communist International towards potential allies was not very promising. It was unlikely that anti-religious slogans, with heavy emphasis on the class struggle and on the leading role of the industrial proletariat, would go down well in Turkey, Persia, and the Arab world. But it is doubtful whether Russia would have made much more headway even if Soviet policy had been more flexible and Comintern slogans less sectarian. A revolutionary situation did not yet exist in the Middle East; Britain and France, though facing some unrest, were still firmly in the saddle. Radical Arabs, Turks, and Persians riding the wave of the future were far more likely to opt for nazi Germany and fascist Italy than for Soviet communism.

From time to time the Middle East cropped up in diplomatic

negotiations. When Molotov, then Soviet Foreign Minister, saw
Hitler and Ribbentrop in Berlin in November 1940, the 'general
direction of the Persian Gulf' was mentioned as one of the obvious
spheres of Soviet interest to be discussed at some future stage. But
Hitler had different plans; during the first two years of fighting on
the Eastern front the survival of the Soviet state was at stake, and
Russia's Middle East interests were not energetically pursued. In co-
operation with the Western allies, Soviet troops occupied part of
Iran, and at the end of the war showed great reluctance to withdraw.
But Iran had been occupied primarily to prevent a pro-Axis coup,
as had happened earlier in Iraq, and to safeguard the delivery of
Allied lend-lease supplies at a time when many other routes had been
cut. Turkey was neutral during the war, but as the tide turned the
Soviet Union became more and more critical of Turkish policy.
Towards the end of the war the demand was pressed both for con-
trol over the Straits and for the surrender of certain Turkish
provinces. While Russia's main concerns were still focused on
Europe, and while the political and military problems of absorbing
Eastern Europe preoccupied Soviet leaders, interest in the Middle
East also reawakened. The claim for a Soviet mandate over Tripolitania made at the Potsdam Conference was perhaps not meant very
seriously and was not pressed strongly when it encountered resistance. But it was indicative of the growing awareness in Moscow that
the Soviet Union was now a global power and that there were many
new opportunities to strengthen its position in various parts of the
world.

The Palestine issue came to the fore as the war ended. Almost six
million Jews had been killed in nazi-occupied Europe, and the
struggle of the Jewish community in Palestine for national independence came to preoccupy first the powers, and later the United
Nations. Soviet policy, which had been violently hostile to Zionism,
was modified and favored the establishment of a Jewish as well as
an Arab state in Palestine. This pro-Israeli phase in Soviet policy did
not endure, but while it lasted it was an important factor in the
creation of the Jewish state.

Soon after the war the Arab world entered a period of prolonged
crisis. Syria and Lebanon attained independence, and anti-British
feeling in Egypt and Iraq became far more intense than ever before.
With the downfall of the Axis, many erstwhile supporters of fascism
came to regard the Soviet Union as a potential ally in the struggle

against the West. They were not necessarily willing to embrace the basic tenets of Marxist-Leninist doctrine, but there was considerable sympathy for an ideology favoring radical change – quite apart from the growing prestige of the Soviet Union as the main champion of anti-Westernism. As the war ended there was in the Middle East a growing reservoir of goodwill towards the Soviet Union. At first, Soviet policy made little use of these new opportunities. The intransigence of the Communist parties at the height of the cold war made it all but impossible for them to collaborate with other parties. Soviet political thinking contemplated a sharpening of the global conflict; the independence achieved by many Asian and African countries after the second world war was 'sham', not real, the leaders of these countries, the '*petty-bourgeois* nationalists', were potential traitors – if they had not already betrayed the national interest. Stalin was firmly convinced that in between the Soviet bloc and the camp headed by the United States there was no middle ground; the slogans of positive neutralism, of a 'zone of peace', let alone of peaceful co-existence, were still in the future. In the view of the Soviet leaders communism could make decisive progress only in countries under the direct control of the Soviet army.

There were a few signs of a shift from this rigid position even before Stalin's death, but only after 1953 was there a basic re-orientation of policy. Now Turkey was told that Soviet territorial claims had been dropped, and the attitude towards the Arab national movement became much more friendly. The colonels who had over-thrown King Farouk, and who had at first been denounced as fascist reactionaries, were now reappraised and upgraded. Syria became of considerable interest to Moscow in view of the growing influence of the extreme left in that country. The idea that only an industrial proletariat could lead a national revolution was tacitly dropped, and the progressive character of 'military socialism' was discovered. There was even a certain improvement in Soviet-Israeli relations. At the height of the anti-Semitic purge, during Stalin's last year, diplomatic relations had been severed by Moscow. They were renewed some months after his death, but relations never again became really close, for in the Arab-Israeli dispute the Soviet Union gave increasing support to the Arabs. The discovery of the revolu-tionary potential of the Arab world was the great turning-point in Soviet Middle East policy in the post-Stalin period. The great breakthrough came in 1955 – the year of the Bandung Conference, when Bulganin and Khrushchev visited India, and when, perhaps most significantly, the arms deal with Egypt was signed. The initiative for this deal came at least as much from Egypt as from the Soviet Union. Colonel Nasser was committed to Arab unity under Egyptian leadership, yet the Baghdad Pact, the defensive alliance then sponsored by the Western powers, was splitting the Arab camp and jeopardizing his plans. Arms were needed by Egypt for all too obvious reasons; Nasser wanted to reassert Egypt's strength, to forge an Arab bloc which under his leadership would be a real power in world affairs. He realized that economic development, however urgent, would not give quick results; given the backwardness of the Arab world, it would be at best a long-drawn-out process. The mood both among leaders and the public was not one of patient waiting. Building up Arab military power seemed a short-cut, and the Soviet Union offered arms in much greater quantities and on far more advantageous terms than the West. At this stage the Soviet Union probably wanted to keep out of Middle East internal conflicts; the arms deal, it was asserted, had nothing to do with the Arab-Israeli conflict. For the Russians this was a side issue; their main purpose was, of course, anti-Western. But the arms shipments directly affected the political situation throughout the area; tension continued to grow and the Soviet Union gradually became involved in the Arab-Israeli confrontation as well as in other local conflicts. The Suez crisis of 1956 helped to cement the Soviet-Egyptian alliance. On November 5, 1956, Bulganin sent notes to Britain, France, and Israel announcing that the Soviet Union was firmly resolved to use force to destroy the aggressors and restore peace in the Middle East; the possibility of attacking these countries with ballistic missiles was mentioned. As for Israel, the note stated that its very existence had been put in question. Whether these threats really stopped the war is more than doubtful; they came only after American pressure on Britain and France had made it virtually certain that the 'expedition' would be a failure. But little credit was given to Mr. Dulles in the Arab world, whereas the Soviet Union got all the praise for assisting Egypt in the hour of peril.

The Eisenhower doctrine which was made public several weeks after Suez caused further resentment in the Arab world; the reference to the vacuum that now existed in the Middle East, indirectly stressing Arab military weakness, was bound to cause great offence in the Arab capitals and to make them more inclined than ever to move towards a *rapprochement* with the Soviet Union. What had begun as a 'purely commercial transaction' to break the Western arms monopoly became the starting-point of a political and even ideological reorientation from 'positive neutralism' to 'scientific socialism'. In Egypt this was a more or less orderly process, the licensed infiltration by pro-Soviet elements of a nationalist one-party regime and the gradual change of its character. But the stormy developments in Syria and Iraq threatened to upset for a while the newly established alliance with Arab nationalism. The growth of communist influence in Syria frightened the radical nationalist leaders of the Ba'th and drove them into union with Egypt. In Iraq the overthrow of Nuri Said and Hashemite rule propelled the communists suddenly into a commanding position from which they threatened the pro-Nasserist forces. This challenge could not fail to alarm President Nasser, who sounded the tocsin during the last week of 1958. The communists in the Arab world were separatists, he declared, opposed to Arab unity—an assertion hotly denied by Khrushchev at the 21st Congress of the Soviet Communist party. But Nasser was not easily mollified, and Egypt's communists were again arrested for having deserted the national cause. Although relations with the Soviet Union became for a while markedly cooler, Egypt could not afford an open break. It insisted that the quarrel between the communists and Arab radical nationalism was a purely domestic affair which did not in the least affect Arab admiration for Khrushchev, Mao, Gomulka, and Tito. An Egyptian periodical argued that the Soviet Union would not sacrifice for the sake of the Arab communists the trust and respect it had won from the Arabs as a whole: 'The road to Moscow does not lead via the Syrian and Iraqi Communist parties.' This prediction proved to be surprisingly correct; Soviet policy in the Middle East was not to be deflected from its long-term aims by the temporary suppression of the Communist parties. Soviet patience paid dividends. The United Arab Republic broke up a few years later as suddenly as it had come into existence, and independent Syria again became the most trusted ally of the Soviet Union in the Middle East. The further radicalization of the Egyptian regime, the sharpening of the Arab-Israeli conflict, the end of the struggle in Algeria, and the war in Yemen offered fresh opportunities for consolidating Soviet influence in the Arab world.

The successes of the Soviet Union in the Middle East during the nineteen-fifties cannot be ascribed to any single cause; they certainly cannot be explained by the magic of such words as 'Israel' or 'Algeria' or 'Arab oil'. They cannot be interpreted solely in terms of foreign policies. Russia was not physically involved in the Middle East and thus could refrain from action on occasions and in regions where the West could hardly avoid it. In the Arab world Russia was not tarred with the brush of imperialism. For forty years it had been absent from the area, whereas the Western ('colonial') powers had been very much in evidence. The Western powers sought to 'organize' the Arab world, and established sundry defensive strongholds there, whereas Russia could advocate a neutrality which coincided with the desires of the Arab *élites*. The West, or to be precise Western Europe, was largely dependent on Middle East oil, and believed that its loss would be a catastrophe, whereas the Soviet Union could very well do without it. While Western interests clashed everywhere with the rising tide of radical Arab nationalism, Russia appeared to be a disinterested and benevolent onlooker. Both the Russians and the Nasserists had a vital interest in weakening and ultimately destroying Western positions in the Middle East. At the same time radical nationalists in the Arab world became more receptive to communist ideological influences. The Soviet Union evoked dazzling dreams of speedy modernization and industrialization. The general mood was anti-capitalist and the radical Arab one-party regimes, having decided to nationalize industry, foreign trade, and banking, and having greatly strengthened the State sector, seemed to be moving steadily towards a society that resembled communism in some important aspects.

There was no Soviet advance in other parts of the Middle East in the nineteen-fifties comparable with the dramatic breakthrough in the Arab world. Soviet friendship with Egypt and Syria precluded any closer ties with Israel. Relations with Turkey and Iran remained normal but cool. Ankara and Teheran noted with satisfaction that Soviet territorial claims had been dropped and that Moscow was showing interest in promoting commercial exchanges. But suspicions based on long experience with the powerful neighbor to the north lingered on. In Moscow, on the other hand, Turkey's membership in NATO and Persia's involvement in Western-sponsored defence pacts constituted a major obstacle to any real *rapprochement*.

During the decade between, roughly, 1948 and 1958, between the struggle for Palestine and the creation of the UAR and the revolution in Iraq, the Middle East stood high among the global danger zones. Every year brought new crises, military conflicts, revolutions, and *coups d'état*; at times the Middle East all but monopolized the world's attention, overshadowing events in other parts of the globe – such as the Far East – which were of equal if not greater importance. After 1959 the Middle East figured less frequently in the headlines of the world's press. Internal tensions did not abate by any means, nor was there any dramatic decline in Soviet interest in the area. But the strategic importance of the region was no longer regarded in the West with the same urgent concern, there was an abundance of oil from other sources, and, above all, the Middle East's near monopoly as an area of permanent unrest was broken. Crises in Africa, the Far East, and the Caribbean preoccupied both foreign ministries and newspaper offices to the detriment of the Middle East. This period of relative calm lasted for about seven or eight years, terminating in a new crisis. This lull before the storm is a convenient starting-point for the present study.

3 The Neutralization of the Northern Tier

Turkey

Adnan Menderes' Democratic party, which had ruled Turkey for a decade, was overthrown by a *coup* on May 27, 1960. His regime had alienated a great part of the country's *élite*, especially the urban middle class, many army officers, and the younger intellectuals, who by and large supported the Republican party. Many of the promises made in 1950, when Menderes came to power, had not been kept: political life had not been liberalized, and the government had retreated from secularism, one of the basic principles of the modern Turkish State. The Democratic party had strong roots in the countryside, for the peasants had on the whole benefited from the regime; but ill-considered economic policies had caused galloping inflation and led eventually to an unofficial devaluation which severely affected the urban population. Following widespread student riots, troops were called in by Menderes to restore order, but the army command refused to use force against the demonstrators; instead, a group of officers under General Gürsel, whose declared aim was to restore democracy, arrested Menderes and his closest collaborators and seized power. The new men were politically by no means a homogeneous body; some of them advocated a fully fledged military dictatorship on a Nasserist (or left-wing fascist) pattern. But in the tug-of-war that ensued, the upper hand was gained by those who stood for a compromise with the civilian establishment and for eventual reconciliation with the erstwhile supporters of Menderes. Conditions soon returned to normal; the elections of October 1961 were won by the Republican People's party, whose leader, Ismet Inönü, one of

Atatürk's closest collaborators, became once again prime minister.[1]*

Under Menderes Turkey had collaborated closely with the Western powers; having joined NATO in 1952, it was one of the original signatories of the Baghdad Pact (subsequently CENTO). As the second world war ended, Turkey found itself under great pressure from the Soviet Union, which had demonstratively revoked the 1925 Soviet-Turkish treaty of neutrality and non-aggression; Moscow also demanded a revision of the Montreux Convention governing the Straits and claimed the Turkish provinces of Kars and Ardahan. After Stalin's death the Soviet leaders decided to revise their attitude towards Turkey. The governments of the Georgian and Armenian Soviet Republics renounced their territorial claims and Khrushchev admitted in a speech in the Supreme Soviet that 'we cannot say that this [the deterioration in relations between the two countries] occurred solely because of Turkey's fault . . .'.[2]

No radical changes took place, however, in Turkey's foreign political orientation in the following years, and Soviet attacks on Turkey continued as the Menderes government showed little readiness to renounce its treaty engagements with the West. When the United States decided to send troops to Lebanon in 1958, following a request by the Lebanese government, the expedition started from the NATO base near Adana. At the time of the *coup* against Nuri Said, Menderes at one stage planned military intervention in Iraq; he desisted only after he had been warned by the Americans that the Soviet threats and troop concentrations should not be taken lightly. Towards the end of the Menderes regime relations with Moscow began to improve: the Turkish minister of health visited the Soviet capital, and in early 1960 an exchange of visits was agreed upon in principle between Menderes and Khrushchev.

The *coup* of 1960 was followed in Moscow with much attention and a great deal of sympathy. Though General Gürsel had made it clear from the beginning that there would be no substantial change in Turkey's foreign policy, Soviet observers knew that not all members of the junta shared his views. Inönü, who became prime minister the following year, had always advocated closer relations with the Soviet Union, and Selim Sarper, the new foreign minister, was thought to tend towards neutralism. In the following months there was a good deal of diplomatic activity. Sarper and the Soviet ambassador in Turkey, Ryshov, declared that a marked improve-

* The notes appear at the end of the book, pp. 195–207.

ment had taken place in the relations between the two countries. Admiral Korutürk, the Turkish ambassador in Moscow, made soundings on his own initiative about the Russian attitude towards a new Balkan-Near East pact extending from Belgrade to Cairo. Turkish newspapers, especially those close to Inönü and his party, published favorable articles about the Soviet Union; all this was a far cry from the days of the cold war. Several new political and cultural associations came into being advocating left-wing policies at home and a *rapprochement* with the Soviet Union (the periodical *Yon*, the Peasants Institute, etc.). This ferment on the left produced a reaction on the right;[3] the Turkish public was traditionally suspicious of pro-Soviet activities, a label freely bandied about and often fatal in the domestic struggle for political power.

The diplomatic negotiations had no immediate tangible results, though a few minor economic agreements were concluded, and there was disappointment in Moscow that relations between the two countries did not improve faster and that NATO manœuvres were still taking place in Turkey. Marshal Malinovsky again warned the Turks.[4] Sarper was replaced in 1962 by the pro-Western Erkin. The reaction of Soviet commentators was unfriendly; 'Our Radio', a communist broadcasting station beamed to Turkey from East Germany, asserted that since the progressive elements had been removed from the junta, reactionary policies were again being pursued.

The repercussions of the Cuban crisis in autumn 1962 were felt in the Near East too. When the American government decided to remove its Jupiter missile bases from Turkey, it was generally assumed in Ankara that this was part of a secret deal between Washington and Moscow. If the American government put its own security above the interests of its allies (it was reasoned in Ankara), Turkey, too, should put its national interest first and regain some freedom of manœuvre. Several members of Inönü's cabinet and some senators suggested that Turkey should contribute towards the new climate of coexistence by a gradual reduction of its military and political obligations towards the West and by a neutralist foreign policy.[5] They referred to the friendly relations with Russia which had prevailed in the twenties and thirties, a state of affairs that had changed as a result of Stalin's aggressive demands and threats. Inönü was often quoted at the time to the effect that Turkey had to find its place in the new world that was being born.

Tension between the left and right became more acute throughout

1963. Parliamentary debates and discussions in the press gave the impression that communism had suddenly become a burning issue.[6] Various popular and national front organizations were established, and the right wing reacted by creating associations to combat the spread of communism. Between these claims and counterclaims, it was not easy to form a realistic appraisal about the real power of communism in Turkey. The illegal Turkish Communist party had only a few thousand members, but there were in addition a great many intellectual fellow-travellers in public life, some of them in prominent positions in the mass media. Their doings attracted much attention, the more so since up to 1960 all pro-communist activity had been strictly illegal. The Turkish right prepared new laws to ban communist activities, but in the changed climate of 1963 these encountered strong opposition. The right could not even prevent communists (appearing on behalf of the Turkish Labour party) being permitted for the first time in Turkey's history to broadcast on the occasion of the municipal elections in November 1963. Representatives of twenty-four left-wing organizations, including the Socialist Cultural Society, the Village Teachers Association, and others, in May 1964 established an executive committee to combat Panturanianism, fascism, and religious reaction. Many regarded this as another attempt to establish a pro-communist 'national front' on a broad basis.[7]

The left-wing advocates of Turkish-Soviet *rapprochement* were heavily handicapped in their efforts by the Cyprus problem. The Soviet Union openly supported Makarios, and in September 1964 signed an agreement to supply arms to Cyprus. The Turkish government was firmly resolved to assist the Turkish minority, by military intervention if necessary, but it gained little encouragement for such action among its Western allies. In a letter to Inönü in June 1964 President Johnson gave the Turkish government to understand that it could not count on automatic American support if by its actions it provoked Moscow to intervene. Turkey felt betrayed by its allies and some influential voices suggested that the country should either reduce its NATO obligations or leave the Treaty Organization altogether.[8] Erkin, the foreign minister, went to Moscow in October 1964, and though he talked to his hosts mainly about the promotion of trade between the two countries, the intention was clearly to 'clear up old misunderstandings' and to create a better atmosphere between the two countries.[9] It appeared highly doubtful whether these or other Turkish overtures (such as negotiations with Bulgaria) would induce Moscow to change its policy on Cyprus. Since Inönü could not point to any tangible achievements or even any specific promise, the government's foreign policy was attacked by many critics who felt that it might leave the country during a crisis without any allies at all.[10] The Justice party was among the critics of a comprehensive reorientation towards the East, so were leading army circles, and Erkin advocated a more cautious line than the prime minister.

In 1965 the initiative again passed to the diplomats, with Podgorny's and Gromyko's visits to Turkey and Urgüplü's trip to Moscow; but again there were few tangible results. Inönü's domestic position had progressively weakened; after a defeat in parliament in February 1965, he resigned. Urgüplü was made head of an interim government and after the great electoral victory of the Justice party in October 1965, Demirel became the new prime Minister. After the fall of Khrushchev, Soviet Near East policy, too, was re-examined. Obviously it was not a suitable moment for any far-reaching new departures in Soviet-Turkish relations.

Inönü's policy towards the Soviet Union had been motivated not by any ideological sympathy with communism, but by his interpretation of Turkish national self-interest. The Kemalist tradition had played a great part, and the example set by de Gaulle also had a certain impact. Inönü was firmly convinced that if Turkey was too closely connected with the Western powers it would find it difficult to pursue its own national interests; in addition, there was always the danger of a deal between the two super-powers in which Turkish interests would be sacrificed. Demirel, a much younger man than Inönü and more modern in his outlook, was more sceptical about the prospects of Soviet-Turkish *rapprochement* and the political benefits that Turkey could derive from it. He did not in principle oppose closer relations, but the main purpose of such moves was, in his view, to bring pressure on Washington. His attitude began to change only after Moscow reversed its Cyprus policy.

Demirel's great electoral victory came as a surprise to Moscow. Soviet observers expected that Inönü would continue in office or that the army would again intervene to prevent the accession to power of a party which, in some respects, was in the Menderes tradition. This was, however, a misreading of the Turkish situation: Inönü's position had been precarious even before the acute crisis developed, Demirel was not a new Menderes, and the army seemed perfectly willing to work with him.

With the establishment of the Demirel government and the resulting reshuffle, many left-wingers and fellow-travellers lost their position in the public service. Demirel announced that the country would stay in NATO; his government refused to ratify the cultural agreement with the Soviet Union which had been prepared under Inönü. (This did not prevent a steady stream of cultural exchanges; Soviet literary delegations came to Ankara and Istanbul, the Soviet Union bought several Turkish movies, and an agreement on the promotion of tourism was reached.) Demirel's lack of enthusiasm did not exactly endear him to Moscow, even though the Soviet government preferred not to engage in polemics. But the Turkish communists stepped up their propaganda campaign against the new government: the Justice party, they claimed, was hostile to all the domestic progressive forces; it was enlisting all the extreme re-actionary forces; it was an American puppet brought to power by the American imperialists; it did not want good neighborly relations with the Soviet Union.[11] It was accused of having killed Gürsel with the help of the Americans in a most horrible way, for they regarded him as an obstacle to their plans; did he not return a living corpse from the American hospital where he was to have been cured? Then they had placed Sunay, who agreed to cede new bases to the Americans and to make other concessions, in the presidential mansion, while Tuval, a 'reactionary with fascist views, opposed to the principles of Ataturk', was made chief of the general staff.[12] While the Demirel government denied that there were any new military bases in Turkey, a new base had in fact been established at Sogauli.[13] In an official statement the Turkish CP asserted that Demirel was about to establish fascism and an open military dictatorship in Turkey; it was stirring up anti-communist hysteria which threatened everyone; it had made the country into an Ameri-can and NATO base for military aggression against both the socialist camp and the freedom-loving peoples of the Middle East – all this despite the fact, freely and cynically admitted by the Western imperialists, that in the event of a nuclear war Turkey would be the first country to be obliterated from the face of the earth.[14] Under Demirel the nation was facing economic and political ruin, as well as military disaster; fully implementing the American cold war policy, it was engaging in aggressive military manœuvres directed against the Soviet Union.[15]

The propaganda campaign was extremely violent and it could have created the mistaken impression that Soviet-Turkish relations had reached an all-time low. But there was, as so often, a division of labor; Moscow acted as if the Turkish communists did not exist. There was a definite improvement in relations in 1966, Turkish trade with the communist bloc (about which more below) expanded, and several high-level meetings took place. Demirel and Caglayangil, the new foreign minister, had stated soon after their party came to power that, while they did not feel too sanguine about the prospects of Turkish-Soviet relations, they would do nothing to antagonize Moscow, but would work for a *détente*. By December 1966, on the eve of the Kosygin visit to Ankara, there had already been a definite change for the better; official Soviet spokesmen noted that 'favorable conditions existed for a radical improvement in Soviet-Turkish relations', while the Turks likewise commented on the 'positive changes that evoke satisfaction'.[16]

The gradual reversal of the Soviet position on Cyprus had much to do with this change. In 1964, after the Soviet decision to send arms and equipment to Makarios, the Turkish foreign minister had given warning that open Soviet support for the Greeks would bring the improvement in Soviet-Turkish relations to a standstill.[17] Ryshov, the Soviet ambassador, tried to explain that Ankara was interpreting the Soviet position wrongly. Why would it not trust Moscow as a mediator in the conflict? There were in fact certain straws in the wind that suggested a Soviet retreat from its extreme position; Cyprus was not important enough in Soviet eyes to sacrifice good relations with Turkey. Gromyko had declared as early as January 1965 that the USSR would support an arrangement that would permit Cyprus to continue as an independent state, in which the rights of both the Greek and Turkish communities to live in peace would be observed.[18] This was not incompatible with the Turkish position on Cyprus (independence plus federation). The Cyprus communists noted with regret that the Soviet Union was talking increasingly about 'two communities' in Cyprus, that it was no longer giving all-out support to AKEL – that, in brief, it was moving towards a neutral line, a shift which became even more obvious after the right-wing *coup* in Greece in April 1967.

In Turkey national passions had been running high in connection with the fate of the Turkish minority in Cyprus, and there was deep disappointment when it was realized that Ankara could not muster international support for its position. The Western countries were not sympathetic, while of the Muslim countries only Iran and Pakistan (no Arab country) had voted with Turkey in the UN General Assembly. The signs of a change in the Soviet position were therefore all the more welcome, and there was increasing belief in Ankara that the key to a desirable solution of the Cyprus problem was to be sought in Moscow, not in the West. The Soviet press, in contrast to the propaganda of the Turkish communists, had noted soon after Demirel had taken over that the new regime intended to work 'for the establishment and development of good neighborly relations',[19] and, as a first sign of goodwill, a Soviet Armenian party secretary was removed from his post in May 1966 for having permitted anti-Turkish demonstrations in a border district. Soviet spokesmen, in preparation for Kosygin's visit to Ankara in December 1966, stressed that the Soviet leaders had no ulterior motives in their desire for good neighborliness and that their policy was based solely on the principles of 'equality, respect for territorial integrity, sovereignty, and non-interference. In return for friendship the Soviet Union had not interfered with Turkish relations with other countries, had not burdened the country with unbearable military expenditure, and had not asked for immunity for its citizens on Turkish soil so that they could behave arrogantly and insult the national dignity of the Turks.'[20] *Sapienti sat.* Kosygin's visit to Ankara was the first ever by a Soviet prime minister. There were a great many Turkish and some Soviet flags at the airport, and banners reading '*Hoş Geldiniz*' (Cordially welcome); there was much curiosity and traditional hospitality, neither much hate nor much love. Traditional friendship was invoked incessantly in the after-dinner speeches, but observers noted that the general atmosphere, though polite and dignified, was on the whole quite cool.[21] The Turkish opposition did not exploit the occasion for partisan manœuvres, while Kosygin was exceedingly cautious in his speeches, which were for the most part devoted to the need to expand economic relations. He stressed time and again that there were no longer any questions in dispute between the two countries; statements by Turkish leaders that they were striving for a further improvement in relations had been received with trust in Moscow. Kosygin also emphasized repeatedly that 'we do not consider that such a development should happen at the expense of a worsening of Turkey's relations with any other state'.[22] His trip to Turkey, he said, was not an isolated episode, out of context with what had already happened and without continuation in the future; it was part of a consistent political line which would not be subject to fluctuations: 'The Soviet Union was prepared to take definite steps in order to assure and consolidate this feeling of confidence in our peoples.'[23] It was not quite clear what definite steps he had in mind, unless he meant the non-aggression pact he had suggested in an interview the year before.[24] Views were exchanged about the Cyprus situation, and Kosygin seems to have expressed regret about an arms shipment to Nicosia made shortly before by the Czechs. In the final communiqué reference was made to the Middle East ('both sides expressed the desire that the Near and Middle East should become a zone of peace and security'), as well as to disarmament and European security.[25] Most of the formulations were vague, but the inclusion of a reference to the war in Vietnam was interpreted by some as a Soviet diplomatic victory. However, Kosygin's main intention was not to discuss detailed questions with a view to reaching full agreement, nor would the trade negotiations have made his presence necessary. Above all he wanted to reassure the Turks and to create a climate of confidence, and in this, to a certain extent, he succeeded. One week (some Turkish observers noted) was too short to eradicate the memories of several centuries, but it helped to establish the basis for further agreements paving the way for a general *rapprochement*.

The Soviet leaders did not, of course, expect that Kosygin's visit would solve all problems and prevent future tension altogether. In connection with President Sunay's visit to Washington in 1967, Moscow revived the old issue of American bases. The Soviet press gave a great deal of publicity to appeals by groups of Turkish intellectuals to remove these bases; *Pravda* seemed willing to put the main blame on the Americans 'seeking to keep, by hook or by crook, their rights and privileges'.[26] The Turkish communists, as usual far more outspoken, attacked the 'Demirel-Sunay clique' for accepting the Acheson plan (for establishing new American bases in Cyprus):

During the first phase Cyprus's independence will be destroyed and during the second phase America will establish . . . radar stations, nuclear stockpiles, rocket-launching pads and air and naval bases. . . . The Demirel-Sunay group, which has betrayed the Turkish people and its territorial integrity, is diligently helping the imperialists in the Cyprus question, too.[27]

Official Soviet statements did not, of course, put it so crudely. On the contrary, they went to great lengths to make a success of Demirel's visit to the Soviet Union in September 1967. The communiqué published after the meetings in Moscow mentioned 'positive results brought about by a constructive approach to problems of bilateral relations'.[28] In an interview after his return, the Turkish premier said that his visit had 'eliminated the last traces of hostility from Soviet-Turkish relations'.[29] In 1966, when Kosygin and Demirel had met in Ankara, there had been 'exchanges' on Cyprus; less than a year later, following the deterioration in the relations between Moscow and Athens, the communiqué was more positive. 'The Soviet view on Cyprus is fairly close to ours', Demirel said in his interview.[30] The discussions on disarmament and European security still seemed somewhat academic at the time; but when the Turkish foreign minister again visited Moscow in July 1968 he took with him more specific proposals; moreover, he was also speaking on behalf of his NATO colleagues, who (at their meeting in Reykjavik) had just decided on a common approach to the Soviet Union. Turkey was not willing to accept the Soviet denunciation of Israel as the aggressor in the Middle East crisis, but supported Moscow's call for Israel's withdrawal from the occupied territories. Demirel said that if there were several ways to preserve peace it was irresponsible of the Israelis to insist on one of them. This was a step in the right direction as far as the Soviet Union was concerned, and it was favorably received in Moscow.[31]

Demirel's mission to Moscow and his declarations after his return surprised the opposition at home. The right began to refer to him as 'Comrade Demirel', whereas the opposite camp claimed that his comments on Russia's technical and social achievements were not really consistent with his former style. The man who had once considered closer relations with Russia dangerous and a sign of enmity towards the West had mellowed. After his Moscow trip he had become fair-minded and realistic in his outlook. 'His enthusiastic praise of Russia boosted even Russian pride.'[32] The left was no doubt concerned that Demirel's policy would take much of the wind out of their sails, and the results of the elections of June 1968 seemed to confirm their fears. The Justice party scored minor gains; the People's Republican party, which under Bulent Ecevit had moved to the left, was split: in protest against this trend some fifty of its deputies and senators had broken away from the party in 1967 and established a new group, the Reliance party. The Turkish Labour party, which for practical purposes represented communist interests in the country, had a sizable following among intellectuals, students, and some trade unions, but with its fifteen seats in the 450-member National Assembly it did not constitute a major political force.

What mainly mattered in the elections from the Soviet point of view was Turkey's attitude to NATO; wide publicity was given to demonstrations, appeals, and newspaper comments in Turkey calling for a withdrawal from NATO.[33] Since the NATO treaty was up for renewal in 1969, this had become a topical issue. The Soviet approach seemed to ignore the obvious fact that while there was concern in Turkey about restrictions imposed by the Western alliance and the presence of foreign bases, most Turks were more worried about the growing Soviet presence in the eastern Mediterranean. Military ties with America had been under review since 1965, and while many of the American bases were likely to be evacuated in the near future, the Soviet Union, to quote a highly-placed Turkish commentator, had worked diligently and methodically to eliminate the potential for U.S. military interference, and was successfully filling the vacuum left in the Middle East by the West:

We used to be certain that the walls built by NATO and CENTO would keep Russia in the north. Recently, however, the Soviet Union has with great ease climbed over the walls to the other side. Today we do not feel the threat of her presence. The Soviets are particularly careful not to let Iran, Turkey, and Greece feel such a threat ... leading countries in the West, possibly to avoid additional political and military obligations, look the other way, pretend they are not aware of a threat, and furthermore, try to convince others that there is no threat.[34]

Previously, Turkish leaders had been mainly concerned with the Straits and possible Soviet pressure for a modification of the Montreux Convention. But the provisions of the Convention made it perfectly legal for the Soviet Black Sea Fleet to enter the Mediterranean, whereas it restricted the entrance of ships of third powers into the Black Sea. In the circumstances there was no urgent need from the Soviet point of view to demand a revision of the *status quo*. There were occasional Soviet complaints about alleged violations of the Convention following the visits of American warships in the Black Sea,[35] but the Soviet Black Sea Fleet had meanwhile been built up to such an extent that Moscow could not plausibly argue that the visit of an American frigate endangered the security of the Soviet Union. The reason for Soviet restraint was, as a Turkish commentator noted, that the Straits had lost much of their original importance in the age of ICBMs and nuclear parity.[36]

They had certainly not lost *all* their importance, as the events of 1967 were to show: a record number of Soviet warships passed through the Bosporus and the Dardanelles that year, 167 to be precise, of which roughly two-thirds went through the Straits after the Arab-Israeli war. There was a great deal of sudden concern about the successful Soviet attempt to by-pass Turkey. The pro-government *Son Havadis* asked: 'What are those Soviet vessels looking for in a sea where they have no coast? We should be vigilant and understand once again the importance of the Western alliance against which our leftists are conducting a fierce campaign.'[37] The non-communist left opposition also expressed misgivings: the presence of the Soviet Mediterranean fleet was not a development to be welcomed by Turkey, which preferred the previous balance of naval forces. But there was nothing Turkey could do about it; it had to get used to the idea of coexisting with the Russians in the Mediterranean.

To many Turks, the continuing economic and social backwardness of their country, in a world in which so much depended on technology and productivity, was an even greater menace than the Soviet army or navy. Three out of four Turks were still employed in agriculture, and almost a million citizens were unemployed or underemployed. If Russia had a certain appeal among some sections of the intelligentsia, it was as a once-backward country which had been transformed into a modern power.

The Turkish economy, after many false starts and a great deal of mismanagement, could point to substantial advance in the sixties. The average yearly growth of the GNP in the first five-year plan (which began in 1963) had been 6·4%; in 1966 it reached almost 9%. OECD, in its yearly report, called it a 'good year for the Turkish economy, with fast growth and a high rate of investment'.[38] But it was also a period of major problems: foreign exchange reserves fell to a very low level, capital inflow was reduced, and imports higher than had been envisaged. Optimists argued, not without reason, that if the same level of economic expansion was sustained for a number of years, Turkey would soon attain medium-power status. But fast and orderly economic expansion was threatened by the country's weak financial position. The second five-year plan envisaged investments at a level of 120m. Turkish pounds a year; the country faced an uphill struggle in attracting investors from abroad, and the capacity of the State Bank to finance the expansion of the public sector was also limited. Turkey was already heavily in debt; up to 40% of its exports were needed to cover interest and capital repayments. Severe cuts in imports would have helped to remedy the situation, but would at the same time have caused a substantial decline in economic growth.

In these difficult circumstances the expansion of economic relations with the Soviet Union seemed an obvious way to eliminate or reduce the trade deficit. Negotiations started in 1964 and concerned several major projects, such as the building of an oil refinery south of Izmir with a yearly capacity of 3m. tons, and an aluminium plant near Seydischir with an output of about 60,000 tons per year. Other projects included plants for manufacturing sulphuric acid, fibreboard, glass strip, and an engraved glass factory. Soviet geologists were to help in the search for Turkish oil, and an iron and steel mill was also under consideration. These talks lasted for more than two years and there was hard bargaining. The final offer made by the Soviet Union in this package deal was considerably below the figures quoted originally. Turkey received a credit of $200m. for a period of fifteen years at a 2·5% interest rate to pay for these projects. Most important, the agreement provided for payment in Turkish surplus agricultural products, such as tobacco, raisins, fruit, olive oil, nuts, and cotton, for which it had been difficult to find markets in the West. At the same time Turkey also intensified its trade with the other Soviet bloc countries; this roughly doubled between 1963 and 1967. Seen in a wider context, however, it seemed unlikely that the Soviet Union and East Europe would replace the West in the foreseeable future as Turkey's main source of credit and its chief trading partners. The Soviet credits of $200m. over fifteen years compared with $350m. of loans provided yearly by Western states and private firms. The Soviet Union figured in 1967 only sixth among Turkey's trade partners.[39]

Soviet-Turkish relations during the nineteen-sixties reflected the changing world situation: at the height of the cold war and up to the early sixties Turkey felt directly threatened by Russia and regarded the Western alliance as its main shield against pressure from the north. With the *détente* in West-East relations, the American military presence became much weaker, while the practical value of CENTO in an emergency was more than doubtful. American economic aid, which had totalled $1·9 billion over nearly two decades, was cut to $59m. in 1968 and was to be phased out in 1972.[40] In these circumstances Soviet influence was bound to increase; the fact that Moscow had stopped threatening the Turks, combined with the feeling that the Western alliance no longer sufficed to safeguard Turkish national security, let alone guarantee Turkish interests elsewhere, such as in Cyprus, made for a switch towards neutralism in Turkish policy. Turkey's internal stability made such a reorientation appear less than risky. Close collaboration with the Soviet Union was unlikely to subvert the Justice party and to make it communist in character; even the Republican People's party, further to the left and ideologically committed to a form of neutralism, could not compete with the attractions offered to Soviet foreign policy by regimes such as Nasser's, not to mention the Syrian Neo-Ba'th. The influence of communism in Turkey was small, nor was it always certain what kind of Marxism was preached by its adherents; in the age of Mao and Castro, the Soviet Union had suffered painful experiences with many revolutionary groups in the third world. The realization that communism was basically weak in Turkey and that its future was uncertain no doubt contributed greatly to the Soviet decision that wooing Turkey was preferable to using the frontal-attack approach advocated by the Turkish communists. Friendly relations with a 'reactionary' regime might gravely embarrass communists in Turkey (as well as in Iran and many other countries), but that was the price that had to be paid, in view of the higher interests of proletarian internationalism.

Many Turks were flattered by the attention given to their country by the Russians, and the economic help extended by the Soviets was gratefully acknowledged. Yet there remained a great deal of uneasiness and even fear, which was reinforced by the events in Czechoslovakia in 1968. The Soviet Union had solemnly declared that it would strictly adhere to the principle of non-interference, yet it was not clear whether the Soviet and the Turkish definitions of non-interference were identical. Did it mean that any criticism of things Soviet and of communism was ruled out, and that at some future stage only pro-Soviet politicians would be acceptable to Moscow? The Finnish experience was not encouraging, and Finland was so far the Soviet model of non-interference. What if Turkey should be sucked even more firmly into a new 'southern tier', a Soviet sphere of influence? Would Soviet benevolence still last, or would there be pressure for political change inside Turkey? The Soviet Union had legitimate interests in connection with the security of its southern flank, but how could Turkish independence be maintained against the much more powerful neighbor to the north without support from other quarters? Between the necessity to accommodate itself within reasonable limits to Soviet interests and the strong desire to stay independent, Turkey faced a future fraught with grave dangers. The balance of power in the area and in the world at large had guaranteed its independence in the past. Any shift in the balance was bound to imperil it.

Iran

Almost unnoticed at first, important changes in Iran's foreign and domestic policies were taking place in the nineteen-sixties. After many decades of stagnation the country had entered a phase of accelerated economic growth and social change unprecedented in its recent history. Soviet-Iranian ties became closer than ever before; the *rapprochement* began earlier and was more gradual than that between Russia and Turkey. Official Soviet relations with Persia had never deteriorated as they had with Turkey, and this although Kemalism had always been socially and politically more advanced in Soviet eyes than monarchical Persia. The overthrow of the Mossadeq government and the suppression of the Tudeh party in 1953-4 was deeply regretted in Moscow, but it did not prevent the Soviet Union from discussing with the government of the day outstanding issues, such as border revisions, fishing rights in the Caspian Sea, the problem of Persian gold retained in the USSR, and the Iran Sovneft Oil Company.[41] Persia's defence pacts with Turkey and Pakistan, and above all with the West, were viewed in Moscow with extreme disfavor. In an official note of protest, and unofficially on many other occasions, Persia was reminded that according to the treaties of 1921 and 1927 it did not have the right to join any 'anti-Soviet' pact.[42] The discovery of the big Tudeh conspiracy in the Persian army and air force in 1954 (in which the Soviet military attaché was implicated) did not improve matters. Despite mutual recriminations, the impression remained that Moscow believed Tehran more open to friendly persuasion or pressure than Ankara. The Shah went to the Soviet capital in 1956 for a state visit, a three-year commercial agreement was signed, and the Soviet Union became again one of Iran's best customers; in 1957 21% of Iran's exports went to the Soviet Union.

The year 1959 brought a crisis in Soviet-Iranian relations. The Soviet government had proposed a treaty of friendship and non-aggression, but this was rejected by the Shah and his government, who soon after, in March 1959, signed a bilateral defence agreement with Washington. This provoked bitter Soviet attacks: Iran had been drawn into the camp opposing the Soviet Union; it was being pushed into war and was being made to pay for the aggressive acts of the Americans. At the time of the U2 crisis the Iranian government was accused by the Soviet press of dragging the country down into an abyss and the Shah was personally attacked as a despised puppet, a traitor to Islam, and the oil monopolists' lackey. The Iranian communist broadcasting station based in East Germany summoned 'all true Muslims to follow in the steps of the sons of Ali and to remove the rotten regime'. The emphasis on religious themes was in the circumstances a little surprising; it may not have been unconnected with the conflict between Tehran and Cairo. In 1960 Iran broke off relations with the UAR following a massive and violent anti-Persian propaganda campaign that had been launched by Egypt, and it also extended diplomatic recognition to Israel. Soviet broadcasts warned Tehran that rockets might be used against the take-off bases of aircraft violating Soviet airspace. The execution of five Iranian communists added to Moscow's displeasure.

It seemed while it lasted a dangerous conflict, but towards the end of August 1960 there were the first indications of a lessening of tension. Eghbal, Moscow's *bête noire*, who had signed the treaty with the Americans, was replaced by Sharif Emani. An exchange of messages – six in all – took place between the Shah and Khrushchev in which both parties expressed their desire for a *détente*. The Shah said that Iran wanted friendly relations with the Soviet Union, but this would have to be based on mutual respect.[43] Iran had already proved her goodwill in various ways. Should not the past be forgotten and a fresh start made? The Soviet government in its answer stressed its belief in the principles of peaceful coexistence; but how could there be an improvement unless Iran ceased to be a springboard for the US and other imperialist governments? The Soviet leaders must have realized soon after these first exchanges that their demand was unrealistic; Tehran would hardly give up its defence alliances simply because the Soviet Union objected to them. In a further note they retreated slightly from their earlier stand: the Iranian government was given to understand that a *rapprochement* was possible even without the abandonment of Iran's Western alliances if it made a real step in the right direction.[44] Tehran decided to compromise, and announced in 1962 that it would not permit the stationing of nuclear missiles on its territory.[45] This was surely a step in the right direction. Soviet commentators writing in later years all agreed that it had been the turning-point in Soviet-Iranian relations.[46] When Brezhnev made a state visit to Tehran in November 1963, relations between the two countries had improved to such an extent that he declared they could be an example to all powers. Transit and border agreements were ratified on this occasion, and an economic and technical cooperation agreement concluded for the joint use of the resources of the border rivers Atrak and Aras, and for the joint construction of a dam on the Aras. Other joint economic projects were discussed and the Soviet Union promised a credit of about $30m. A Soviet-Iranian Cultural Relations Society based in Moscow was set up; the parallel Iranian branch of this society was headed by General Djahanbani, a member of the Iranian Senate. The countries of East Europe followed Moscow's lead: Poland and Czechoslovakia, Rumania and Hungary extended credits to Iran and there was a steady flow of delegations between their respective capitals.

This improvement in the relations between the two countries between 1960 and 1963 should be viewed against the background of developments inside Persia. These were years of deep internal crisis; at the same time the decision was taken to carry out far-reaching reforms in Persian society. The elections of 1960 had been a disappointment; the *Majlis* was suspended in May 1961 and not reconvened until October 1963. During the interval the country was ruled by decree; there was not even the pretence of democracy. When Dr Amini took over from Sharif Emani as prime minister in May 1961, he found himself faced with a grave financial crisis and drastic steps had to be adopted to overcome it. Years later he was accused of having quite unnecessarily declared the country bankrupt and thus having played into the hands of the oil companies. With the benefit of hindsight the events of 1961 may appear in a less serious light; at the time it certainly seemed to be a real crisis. On Amini's advice, the Shah promulgated reform proposals to eradicate corruption, improve tax-collection and justice in general, and confer more administrative authority on provincial governors. Above all, land distribution became a firm reality with the Shah's signature on a revised Land Reform Bill.[47] This was the beginning of the 'white revolution'.

The land reform aimed at breaking the domination of the great landowners. It was applied first in north-west Persia, where unrest was rife among the local peasants. During the first stage of the reform, land in almost 15,000 villages was bought up and distributed among more than 600,000 peasants. This land was valued at 13,000 million reals, but the owners were paid only 2,300 million, receiving the rest in the form of shares in State or mixed enterprises. The first stage lasted until the end of 1967, but even before it was concluded the second and third stages got under way: middle and small landowners were instructed to sell or lease their holdings above 30–200 hectares, depending on the fertility of the land and the part of the country. Cooperatives were established and agriculture modernized in every way. These agrarian reforms amounted to a break-up of the traditional social structure in the countryside, the end of the sharecropping system, and the emergence of a new class of small landowners. The redistribution of landownership had far-reaching social and political effects; it had undoubtedly been the original purpose of the Shah and his advisers to gain the support of the peasant majority against the power of the big landowners. In a referendum, there was an overwhelming majority (about 13 to 1) for the royal decree. These figures do not, however, provide a clear picture of the intensity of opposition which the reform schemes provoked. When Amini told the big landowners in 1961 that they had to give up some of their land, for the only alternative facing them was eventually to lose it all as well as their lives, they were not easily convinced. They had the support of the *mullahs*, the champions of Muslim orthodoxy, who claimed that redistribution of land was contrary to the principles of Islam. Some of the tribes, such as the Qashgai, rebelled, and the Arab separatists in Khuzistan used the opportunity to stage an insurrection. The merchants, who had been affected by the new austerity decrees (involving higher customs duties), turned against the government. The intelligentsia was alienated, anyway, and Iranian students abroad protested against decrees which cut off their allowances unless their examination results were satisfactory. This they regarded as a gross interference in their human rights, and it contributed to the spread of radicalism among Persian students abroad. The Tudeh party had not yet recovered from its defeats in 1953 and 1955; it had merged with the Azerbaidjani communists in 1960, but, riddled by internal splits, it did not represent a serious internal challenge to the regime. More serious was the opposition of the members of the National Front, the party headed at one time by Dr. Mossadeq, who, often from within the lower echelons of the civil service, sabotaged the reforms. Riots against the modernization decrees took place in June 1963 in various districts, and the *mullahs* became even more restive when women received the vote; there was growing disaffection among the army command and in the upper reaches of the civil service as the anti-corruption drive culminated in the arrest of several high officials. There was a curious alliance of all the opponents of the reform: big landowners and left-wing students, fanatical *mullahs*, merchants, and separatist tribes. It was a dangerous period, and the assassination of Ali Mansur, the prime minister, in January 1964 was a manifestation of the strong opposition which the reforms of the Shah and his advisers encountered.

It was only natural that the Iranian government should try to reduce all external tension to a minimum during that period of internal upheaval; hence the great efforts to improve relations with the Soviet Union. Russia reciprocated by toning down anti-Persian propaganda, the Soviet assumption being, no doubt, that closer contacts with the Soviet Union would gradually induce the Persians to renounce their alliances with the West and withdraw from their military pacts. There may have been other reasons, such as the growing conflict with China, which caused the Russians to shore up their southern fences. Once the Tehran government had declared that it would not permit the establishment of rocket bases on its territory, the Soviet ideological experts began to modify their attitude towards the domestic reforms carried out by the Shah and his government. Previously they had maintained that the 'notorious reform' was carried out in the interest of the landlords and feudal circles, and that the main intention of those who had framed the law was to strengthen the rotten monarchical regime and to distract the popular masses from fighting for their rights.[48] Once the rocket-base assurance had been given, it was announced in Moscow that

many misunderstandings had been ironed out and that the last
barriers to good relations had been removed.[49] As for the Shah's
reforms, it was now found that there was a real prospect of the
emergence of a new coalition of social forces interested in pursuing a
national policy,[50] that the implementation of the reform programme
would objectively promote social and economic progress, eliminating the most archaic survivals of the Middle Ages, and that it would
raise the material and cultural level of the Persian people.[51] A few
years later comments on the reforms became even more enthusiastic:
Persia was going through a period of serious economic change, a
fundamental break-up of the social structure designed to take the
country into the twentieth century. There were glowing reports
about the striking results of the reforms, the prosperity, the hard-
working young technocrats of the (ruling) dynamic New Iran party;
the people of Iran were facing the future with confidence.[52] The
Soviet leaders seemed willing to accept the monarchy and appeared
indifferent to the entrenchment of a new *bourgeoisie*; so long as it
pursued the right kind of foreign policy, a favorable and optimistic
assessment could be expected of the domestic policies of the Iranian
government.[53] For the Persian communists this line was, of course,
unacceptable, and they continued to attack the 'anti-national, anti-
democratic government': they contended that the White revolution
was an utter failure, that there was deep disappointment with the
Shah's dictatorship.[54] 'The Shah and other leaders know no limit to
their treason to the country.'[55] The Persian communists, like their
Turkish comrades, were given a free hand in their propaganda, but
how effective could it be if it was in such striking contrast to the
Soviet approach? This caused a great deal of heart-searching among
the Tudeh militants and provoked further dissension and splits.
Many left-wing 'deviationists' claimed that Soviet help for the Shah
in his reforms was harmful because, by raising the living standards
of the masses, it would strengthen the hold of the government and
weaken the Communist party.[56] The central leadership of the party
was willing to admit that the reforms were not altogether demagogy,
a sheer political swindle ('such a view could lead to sectarianism and
isolate us from the masses'); their party's uncompromising opposition to the anti-national regime did not mean that it would reject
out of hand every measure taken by the government. But, in the last
resort, revolutionary change was still necessary, for by its violence
and anti-democratic actions the government had ruled out a peaceful

solution of the problems facing the country.[57] Reforms that had no
support among the people were bound to be shortlived and could
not produce the desired and much needed radical changes.[58]

The Soviet approach to Iran after 1962 showed little consideration
for the immediate tactical interests of the Iranian communists. The
overthrow of the Shah and his regime and the emergence of a
communist Iran closely allied with the Soviet Union would have
meant a great victory for world communism, and for the Soviet
Union a breakthrough to the Persian Gulf and the Indian Ocean. It
could have been plausibly argued that Iran was a weaker country
than Turkey and that the overthrow of the Shah and of a relatively
small number of his supporters would open the road to radical
political change. 'Objectively', a subacute revolutionary situation
undoubtedly existed; but such arguments ignore the 'subjective'
factor, the weakness of Iranian communism, its internal splits and
lack of discipline. The fact that the party was so unreliable must
have caused concern in Moscow; in these circumstances a successful
revolution in Tehran might have resulted in the emergence of a
regime less than enthusiastic to cooperate with Moscow. Lastly,
there were the risks involved in an isolated breakthrough in one
country, however important; a victory in Iran might have been offset by negative reactions in the neighboring countries. Soviet
political planning looked towards a more distant future. It was, of
course, obvious that Soviet economic aid would help the present
regime to consolidate itself, but it would also contribute to the
growth of the State sector in the national economy and thus reduce
the influence of capitalism. The young technocrats who had emerged
as the new *élite* had already established cordial relations with their
Soviet counterparts; gradually they would come to realize that they
could manage without the archaic political system still prevailing.
Meanwhile, the advantages of a non-communist Iran well disposed
towards Moscow, and in which Soviet influence was constantly
growing, were not to be belittled. Given the general framework of
Soviet foreign policy, the violent overthrow of the regime with
Soviet support was ruled out, and the Tudeh party alone was not
able to accomplish it.

And so the official state visits continued, agreements were signed,
and praise was heaped on the Shah. After 1963 these exchanges
became so numerous that it is difficult to keep track of them. The
Shah visited Moscow in July 1965; in the following year he went to

five other East European capitals; to Rumania and Yugoslavia in May and June, to Bulgaria, Hungary, and Poland in September. Everywhere he was welcomed as an honored guest with greater pomp and circumstance than was usually accorded to the heads of the neighboring communist states. The Sofia communiqué said that the Bulgarian people had the 'highest praise for the initiative of His Imperial Majesty the Shah in his campaign against illiteracy'. The Rumanians expressed feelings of 'high esteem' for the efforts made in Iran to make economic, cultural, and social progress. The Hungarians also lauded the Shah for his part in the campaign against illiteracy; they were 'following sympathetically the efforts of the Iranian people towards cultural, economic, and social development'. Ochab, the Polish president, praised his guest for his progressive foreign policy; 'we know and value these efforts', he said, and the Polish communiqué ended with expressions of deep appreciation for Iranian progress.

The Iranian communists were acutely embarrassed, and criticised their East European comrades for exceeding the limits of normal diplomatic courtesy; the Shah, after all, was no more than 'a reactionary monarch hated by his people'. Summarizing the significance of the Shah's visits, Soviet commentators stressed their practical value; West Europe and America exported to Iran ten times as much as they bought from her. Requests to increase their imports from Iran had been ignored and the country's foreign trade balance as a result had been constantly negative. The socialist countries, on the other hand, had developed their contacts on a mutually advantageous basis.[59] The statistics were a little oversimplified; they ignored Iranian exports of oil to the West as well as Western financial aid and capital investment. But it could not be denied that for Iranian products other than oil it was not easy to find markets in the West. Iran, to quote an extreme example, imported from West Germany goods valued at $206m. in 1966–7, but German investments in Iran during the period were a mere $2m.[60]

As one result of the Shah's visits to East Europe, and of other trade negotiations, several commercial treaties were signed in 1966–7, providing for exchanges totalling about $380m. (Poland, 159m.; Czechoslovakia, 107m.; Rumania, 104m.; Bulgaria, 15m.). The East European countries showed great interest in oil imports from Iran, in view of the high prices demanded for Soviet oil and their own growing oil consumption. Of particular significance in this context was the 'oil-tractor' agreement with Rumania concluded in August 1966. In return for substantial deliveries of oil, Rumania was to supply Iran with 15,000 tractors, accessories, and spare parts over the next five years, a tractor-manufacturing and a tractor-assembly plant. Rumania was to gain a near monopoly in the supply of tractors to Iran. The agreement ran into difficulties in its early stages because Iranian experts were said to dislike the tractors which Bucharest wanted to deliver; they had originally been destined for China.

The Shah's trips to the Soviet Union and East Europe were followed by other official visits, including one by prime minister Hodeyda to the Soviet capital in 1967 and Kosygin's state visit to Tehran in April 1968. The Rumanian and Iranian premiers exchanged visits, the Shah's sisters went to Czechoslovakia and the Soviet Union, and a great many parliamentary and technical delegations also went to and fro. Not all of these exchanges were outstanding successes; if the Tehran government had hoped to gain Soviet support for its interests in the Persian Gulf, Mr. Kosygin poured cold water on their expectations. A Soviet official statement about the Persian Gulf published one day before Kosygin's intended visit was officially confirmed, made it clear that Moscow was critical of the Iranian attitude.[61] Nor was there any good reason to take at face value the ritual statements published at the end of such meetings; the Soviet press noted after Hodeyda's visit that Iran was 'alarmed by Israel's continued aggression against the Arab states and the escalation of the criminal war of American imperialism in Vietnam'. Both sides were no doubt aware that neither Israel nor Vietnam was a major preoccupation for Iran, and that the Tehran government had no reason to feel particularly unhappy about the defeat suffered by Nasser at the hands of the Israelis. But even the meetings that were only partly successful had a cumulative effect; they contributed towards a reorientation of Iranian policy after years of almost total dependence on the West. Its repercussions were felt in the foreign political and military field as well as in Iran's economy, to which we shall now turn.

The new confidence shown in Tehran in the middle sixties was one of the most striking by-products of the economic progress that had been achieved. After uncontrolled inflation in 1960–1, Iran's economy began to show an upward trend; between 1964 and 1967 there was an annual growth of almost 11 % while the cost of living rose by less than 1%. The wheat and barley harvest rose from 3·1m. tons in 1962–3 to 5·2m. in 1967; for the first time Iran was able to export grain as well as to meet her own needs. Despite the sizable increase in agricultural output, its share of the gross national product steadily declined (from 34% in 1959–60 to 24% in 1966–7) as the result of the rapid pace of industrialization. *Per capita* income, one of the lowest in the world, rose from $197 in 1965 to $220 in 1968; according to the plan, it was planned to reach $307 in 1973 if the 57% growth of the GNP contemplated in the fourth Iranian five-year plan (1968–73) was reached. The three main centres of industrialization were the Isfahan region, where big new steel works were erected, Ahwaz-Abadan, the centre of the oilfields and the petro-chemical industry, and the Tabriz district, where machine industry was increasingly concentrated.[62]

Economic help to Iran in the past had come mainly from the United States; US aid to Iran between 1954 and 1967, including government loans and grants and the US share of aid provided by the UN and the World Bank, totalled $1·9 billion. In 1967 it amounted to $190m., of which $83m. were part of a programme of military aid. The US aid mission to Tehran was shut down at the end of 1967; American representatives had reached the conclusion that, given the rapid economic expansion, aid was no longer needed.[63]

Oil has been the key factor in Iran's economic development. Until nationalization in 1951, Iran was the leading producer in the Middle East; as a result of the upheavals of the early fifties it had fallen back to third place after Kuwait and Saudi Arabia, even though the State income from the sale of oil rose more than three-fold between 1951 and 1965. Oil operations were still wholly managed by an international consortium of fourteen Western oil companies.[64] Successive Iranian governments had insisted on regaining for their country the lead in Middle East oil production and accused the consortium of slowing down production and thus hampering the economic development of the country. Prime minister Hodeyda publicly charged the oil companies with 'provocation',[65] and the Shah threatened that Iran would break the agreement with the consortium if new arrangements were not made. The dilemma facing the consortium was that a 20% increase per year, as demanded by the Iranian government for a five-year period, was bound to cause a substantial fall in oil prices, since world demand was expected to rise by only 9% per year in the near future (7% in 1967). The oil companies argued that there was world overproduction of oil, that additional new markets did not exist, and that the idea that a producer could push up output regardless of whether the commodity could be sold was totally unrealistic.[66] In addition, it would have brought Iran into sharp conflict with the other producing countries, which were equally eager to increase their output. Against this, Iran argued that it needed the income from the oil industry far more urgently than sparsely populated countries such as Kuwait (not to mention Abu Dhabi), and that its entire economic future was in danger unless oil production (and consequently its own income) was increased to about 280m. tons in 1973.

The intricacies of Middle East oil policies are discussed elsewhere in this study, but they deserve at least a cursory mention here, for in Soviet-Iranian relations these issues have played an important part. According to the Soviet view, the international oil cartel not only organized the boycott of the nationalized Iranian oil on world markets between 1951 and 1953, but had also exerted pressure on Iran ever since.[67] The Soviet thesis that the West kept down oil production because it needed an economically underdeveloped Iran as a supplier of raw materials and as a market for industrial goods found some willing believers in Tehran; so did the suggestion that the government ought to pursue an independent policy 'free from the shackles imposed by the consortium'.[68]

The Iranian communists, as usual, went much further in their attacks, claiming that the oil consortium was far stronger than the government, that the Shah and his advisers were in 'secret collusion' with the oil-plunderers, and that they were 'systematically betraying' their country.[69]

For all their complaints about the oil companies, there was no doubt in the minds of the Persian leaders that in the foreseeable future West Europe and Japan would remain by far their best customers. The Soviet Union, as a matter of principle, did not import substantial quantities of crude oil, and the purchases of the other communist states were small in comparison with the needs of the OECD countries. The one advantage of trade with East Europe was that it was conducted on the basis of a clearing agreement, and thus did not involve convertible currency. Iran paid with crude oil for the import of machines, and this was likely to ease the pressure on her chronic balance of payments deficit.

It would be tedious to enumerate in detail the various trade agreements between Iran, the Soviet Union, and the other East European countries. The 1963 deal concerned the joint building of a hydroelectric station and reservoir on the frontier river Aras, and Soviet assistance to Iran in breeding fish. Far more ambitious were the agreements of January 1966 and March 1967. The first provided for the delivery of natural gas from Iran, hitherto unused, to the Soviet Union for a period of twelve years, and a 42-inch pipeline was to be built from the oilfields of Khuzistan to the Soviet border west of the Caspian Sea; the flow of gas, amounting to 10,000 billion cubic metres per year (rising to 20,000 billion later on), was scheduled to start in 1970: its total value was thought to be about $66m. per year and likely to rise.[70] These gas deliveries were to pay for the various Soviet projects executed in Iran, such as the $230m. steel plant near Isfahan (with an annual capacity of 500,000–600,000 tons, and a possible expansion to more than 2 million), a machine-tool factory, compressors and services in building the pipeline, and about $20m. for the Aras dam. In addition the Soviet Union undertook to buy a sizable share of Iran's exports; almost all its wool exports, two-thirds or more of lead ore, karakul skins, and henna – not to mention 40% of Persia's caviar.

Trade expanded by leaps and bounds. In the early sixties the Soviet Union accounted for less than 3% of Persian imports and had taken 13% of its exports; in 1967 total trade turnover exceeded $70m., more than double the figure for 1965.[71] As a neighbor, Russia had traditionally been one of Iran's chief trading partners, and was among its best customers for products other than oil up to the early thirties. Soviet economists were aware that Western firms held a secure place on the Iranian market and that there was still a certain amount of prejudice against Soviet machinery – 'largely inspired by competitors';[72] they had no illusions about the limit of Soviet-Iranian trade expansion. Soviet experts calculated that with the agreements reached the Soviet share in Iranian imports would not exceed 12% by 1974.[73] It came only sixth in the list, behind West Germany, the United States, Britain, Italy, and Japan. Iran receives at present (1968) about $650–680m. annually from its sales of oil to the West and Japan; total Soviet credits are approximately half that sum ($330m.) and extend over several years. A realistic appraisal of the magnitude of Soviet-Iranian trade and its prospects can be formed only by comparing these figures.

Among the Iranian debts to which the natural gas was mortgaged the politically most interesting item was an allocation of $110m. for Soviet military equipment, mainly trucks, half-trucks, and small arms. This arms deal did not cover sophisticated equipment and did not necessitate the presence of many Soviet instructors. The idea that Western officers in charge of Phantom jets and other CENTO weapons would have to rub shoulders with their Soviet counterparts in Iran had at first caused shudders in the Western capitals. The United States had provided virtually all of Iran's armament since the end of the second world war, and the news in July 1966 that Tehran was considering the purchase of surface-to-air missiles in Moscow provoked a minor shock in Washington. The Tehran government explained its need for such sophisticated weapons with reference to the vulnerability of the Persian Gulf loading installations, especially at Kharg Island, to the Arab air forces – equipped by the Russians. 'We do not even have any anti-aircraft guns to protect us in the Gulf,' the Shah is reported to have said.[74] American surface-to-air missiles could be bought only for cash or on short-term credit at $2\frac{1}{2}\%$ interest. The Soviet government, however, showed little enthusiasm for this particular deal,[75] and the Shah eventually accepted an American offer to modernize the Iranian air defence forces.

The Soviet-Iranian arms deal was welcomed, not surprisingly, by the Persian communists, who argued that this proved that there was no Soviet threat, for 'What country contemplates attacking another state while at the same time supplying it with defensive weapons?'[76] The Tehran government's arms policy was to play it safe. A high-level Iranian army delegation under General Bahram Anian, the chief of staff, went to Moscow in December 1967 to negotiate about further arms supplies for delivery in May 1968, while the Shah was seeking $600m. credits in America for the purchase over a period of six years of supersonic fighter-bombers, modern tanks, and other sophisticated weapons.[77]

The heavy preoccupation of the Persian government with military problems (a defence budget of $512m. in 1968) reflected the changed foreign political situation. As the danger from the north receded, as Britain gave up Aden and announced that it would withdraw from the Persian Gulf in 1971, there was growing concern in Tehran about the defence of its vital interests in that area. Bahrain had always been considered Iran's fourteenth province; any advance by pan-Arab forces in either the Persian Gulf area or South Arabia was considered an immediate threat to Iran. In the past the quarrel had centred on such relatively harmless topics as whether the Gulf should be named 'Persian' or 'Arab', or on Tehran's refusal to recognize Bahraini postage stamps. With Britain's withdrawal the whole question was likely to be reopened. Tehran would have favored an agreement with Saudi Arabia and Kuwait, but any alliance with Saudi Arabia was looked upon with great disfavor by Moscow,[78] whereas the Emir of Kuwait was too afraid of radical Arab nationalism to pursue an independent policy. In 1968 diplomatic relations between Tehran and Cairo were restored and the Iraqi prime minister visited the Iranian capital. But it remained doubtful whether there could be a lasting reconciliation between Tehran and the pan-Arab leaders, the traditional animosity between Persians and Arabs quite apart. The Arabs still claimed Persian Khuzistan (a demand pressed in particular by the left-wing Ba'th), and Iran continued to regard Bahrain as part of its territory. The danger of armed conflict in the Persian Gulf after withdrawal of the British forces had been by no means entirely removed.

It is doubtful whether Iran, given a free choice, would really have chosen the Soviet Union as its neighbor, as the Shah once said in Moscow in an after-dinner speech, if only because Russia was so much larger and stronger. Since the question had been decided, not on the basis of free will, Iran had to make the best of it; once the cold war had receded, successive Iranian governments engaged, not unsuccessfully, in a balancing act: they collaborated with the Russians in building various enterprises in the north, while in southern Iran cooperation with the oil companies continued. The building of the big pipeline from the south to the Soviet border was in some ways symbolic: up to Saveh in the centre of the country Western firms were to build it; from Saveh on the Russians would continue the work. American setbacks in Vietnam and the British retreat from Aden and the coming withdrawal from the Persian Gulf strengthened the Tehran government in its belief that it had to accommodate itself (within limits) to the Russians, who seemed reasonable and helpful, had dropped all territorial claims, and no longer gave active support to the Iranian communists. Traditional suspicions had not disappeared, and the idea of a Soviet presence in Aden or the Persian Gulf did not fill Persian hearts with joy. The neutralist policy, moreover, had one serious flaw: it was based on the assumption that the global balance of power and the equilibrium in the Middle East would remain more or less stable. But if it changed in favor of the Soviet Union, there was the danger that the northern neighbors might not be satisfied with mere neutrality. The effects of such a development on Iran's position could not be taken lightly. To a large extent its future depended on the measure of domestic progress, the speed of modernization and industrialization, and the rise in the standard of living. In contrast to some other Middle East states, Iran was a nation with a long national tradition and thus, despite all transient difficulties, great reserves of strength. Progress and stability, to be sure, ultimately depended not only on the yearly rate of growth, but on the government's success in regaining the confidence of an *élite*, large sections of which were still disaffected, in bringing about a community of purpose between the leaders and the people. Accelerated economic growth *per se* would result in greater prosperity, but not necessarily in greater stability. Until these aims were realized, and radical changes within the regime had taken place, Iran was bound to remain doubly vulnerable.

4 Russia, Zionism, Israel

Soviet attitudes towards Israel, unfriendly almost from the beginning, became more hostile as Moscow's relations with the Arab countries improved; but they were also affected by the existence of a 'Jewish question' inside the Soviet Union. The traditional Soviet and communist approach to Zionism before the establishment of the Jewish state was wholly negative. The Communist party in Palestine denied the very principle of Jewish immigration, let alone the idea of a national home, which did not make it exactly popular within the Jewish community. The Soviet decision in 1947 to vote at the United Nations for a Jewish state came as an agreeable surprise to Zionists; the Soviet Union was among the very first to grant the Jewish state full diplomatic recognition. This Soviet-Israeli honeymoon did not, however, last; it was only a brief and, in retrospect, somewhat incongruous interlude. There was at the end of the war a great deal of sympathy for the remnants of European Jewry. However hard-boiled the Kremlin's policy may be, it is not impossible that the Soviet leaders, too, were not immune to this general sentiment. Unwilling to revise their basic attitude towards Zionism, they nevertheless recognized the necessity to find a haven for the survivors of the holocaust. From the point of view of Soviet interests in the Middle East, moreover, a good case could be made for supporting Jewish statehood. The Jewish independence movement in Palestine fulfilled an 'objectively progressive' function, for it helped to weaken Britain's position in the Middle East, and, generally speaking, added to the unrest which in Soviet eyes was a symptom of the unfolding general crisis of capitalism. The Arab world was at the time still ruled by monarchs (Farouk, the Hashemites) and reactionary *élites*; there was not much scope for an active Soviet foreign policy in these countries.

Soon after the establishment of the state, the first unfriendly commentaries began to appear in the Soviet press. This change in attitude was caused mainly by domestic factors. Stalin and his advisers had clearly overrated the extent to which the Jews had been integrated into Soviet society. According to Soviet doctrine, the national problem had long ago been solved: this was one of the triumphs of Leninism-Stalinism. In fact, the situation was a great deal more complicated. While many individual Jews had been prominent Bolsheviks in the early years of the regime, the great majority of them were purged in the thirties. Most Soviet Jews were not party members and their attitude towards the regime was as ambivalent as that of other national minorities. During Stalin's last years they were singled out for persecution; individual Jews were arrested and some were executed, an unofficial *numerus clausus* was introduced, and some professions were closed to them altogether. All this contributed to the alienation of Soviet Jews; there is some reason to believe that but for Stalin's death Soviet Jews would have been hit even more severely by a systematic campaign which was anti-Semitic in everything but name. The establishment of the state of Israel struck a deep emotional chord among many of them, however irreligious and alienated from Jewish traditions. The arrival of the first Israeli ambassador to Moscow turned into a spontaneous popular demonstration without precedent in the Soviet capital. This was a cause of much concern to the Soviet leadership, and within a few months an anti-Zionist campaign was launched. It was to be made clear beyond any shadow of doubt that diplomatic relations with the state of Israel did not entail sympathy with Zionism; Soviet Jews were to have no ties with their co-religionists abroad; the Soviet Union was their homeland and they would not be permitted to emigrate to Israel. As the anti-Jewish purge became more intense in 1951-2, the accusations became louder and wilder. Jewish organizations and individual Jews, not necessarily Zionist, were denounced as inveterate enemies of the Soviet Union.

Soviet-Israeli relations, never particularly close, were naturally affected by this campaign; a few months before Stalin's death diplomatic ties were severed. The campaign ceased after the death of the dictator, those arrested were released, the preparations for show trials were discontinued, and after a brief interval diplomatic relations with Israel were resumed. But there was no dramatic improvement: the Jewish problem in the Soviet Union persisted; while Soviet Jews had no longer to fear for their lives, many anomalies in their status remained, and promotion in many fields remained difficult if not impossible; they were treated as a minority, but did not have the rights of political and cultural autonomy given to other national minorities. According to the official version, Soviet Jews had been completely assimilated; they did not need schools or newspapers of their own, and they certainly did not want to emigrate. But in fact, Soviet society being what it was, full assimilation was very difficult for them. There is little doubt that, given the opportunity, a sizable number would have left the country. Traditional, popular anti-Semitism had by no means been stamped out altogether in the Soviet Union; in addition, suspicion of the Jews persisted on the part of the party and state organs. Unlike other minorities, the Jews, or at least many of them, had relations abroad; their national and cultural centre lay elsewhere, they could not be relied upon in an emergency. Describing a vicious circle, this distrust in its turn caused further disaffection among the Jews. By the late nineteen-fifties only a few Jewish 'technicians' were left in the Soviet political leadership.

The attitude towards Israel was also increasingly affected by the growing Soviet involvement in the Arab world. Once the state of Israel was established, it ceased to be an agent of revolutionary ferment, and thus had no further value for the Kremlin. In the Arab countries, on the other hand, the anti-Western movement gained strength in the early nineteen-fifties. The anti-British demonstrations in Egypt and Iraq, the overthrow of Farouk, the mounting disturbances in Syria – all attracted Soviet attention. With the arms deal of 1955 the groundwork was laid for close political military and economic cooperation with Egypt and Syria. With all its hostility to Israel, however, the Soviet Union had apparently at first no desire to become involved in the Arab-Israeli dispute, which it regarded as a national conflict of no direct concern to itself. But since the struggle against Israel figured very high on the list of Arab priorities Soviet diplomats soon realized that, short of giving substantial assistance to the Arabs against Israel, they would make little headway in the Arab world. While unwilling to accept the more extreme Arab demands (e.g. the destruction of the Jewish state), the Soviet Union began to give full support in the United Nations to all other Arab complaints. A massive propaganda campaign was launched against Israel, where there was growing concern about the large-scale Soviet arms shipments, including many weapons that the Jews could not get from the Western powers. There was little doubt in Israeli minds that these arms would ultimately be used, not against 'Western imperialism', but in that war against Israel which featured so prominently in countless speeches, articles, and solemn declarations issuing from the Arab world. Concern at the growing Soviet antagonism was shared by the left, traditionally pro-Soviet in its outlook, where it was felt that Soviet policy, while on the whole progressive and worthy of support, was blatantly one-sided in the Arab-Israeli conflict, giving full backing to the Arabs, irrespective of the merits of the case in the light of 'proletarian internationalism'. Eventually even the Israeli Communist party faltered; having stoically and faithfully supported Soviet anti-Israel policy for almost two decades, it split more or less on national lines. The extreme left was deeply pained by Russia's attitude, and depressed by its support for the Arabs in the Security Council, which, they thought, made any effective United Nations action for peace impossible. Above all, there was the problem of Soviet Jewry. If Israel was to grow and to develop, it needed hundreds of thousands of newcomers. Immigration from the Soviet Union, to be sure, had been stopped in the nineteen-twenties, but Jews had been permitted to emigrate to Israel from most of the 'people's democracies' (including Poland, Bulgaria, and Rumania). Was it altogether unrealistic to assume that one day the gates of the Soviet Union would also be opened? Soviet anti-Zionist and anti-Israel campaigns were followed in Israel more in sorrow than in anger, and many efforts were made to 'talk' to the Russians, to persuade them to re-examine their attitude. There was a great deal of sympathy for things Russian, not perhaps for the Soviet regime but certainly for Russian literature and music. The old Israeli establishment had modelled itself on the pattern of the radical Russian intelligentsia. The Soviet response, while negative on all basic political issues, was sufficiently vague to encourage the belief (among those eager to believe) that an improvement could be achieved if only Israel would reorientate its policy. An unsentimental analysis would have shown that a basic change in the Soviet attitude was well-nigh impossible. Unlike the 'people's democracies', the Soviet Union could not let any sizable number of Jews go, for this would have been an admission of the failure of Soviet nationalities policy. It would moreover have created a dangerous precedent and caused serious problems with other national minorities. Above all, it would have thwarted political efforts in the Arab world. As between the Arab states and Israel, the Soviet Union never wavered. The Arab world had a great revolutionary potential, in the sense that anti-Western attitudes were deeply ingrained, whereas Israel, having established a reasonably modern state, could not feel the same resentment towards the West, quite apart from its many ties with Jews in the Western world. Above all, and most decisively, the Arabs were the stronger battalions; the few Jews could not resist 60 million Arabs who, with Soviet help, would soon overcome their backwardness. All ideological reservations apart, there was the hard fact that Israel had only 2, not 20 million inhabitants, and even if it had radically changed its policy it would have remained in Soviet eyes far less important than the Arabs. For this reason, if for no other, Israeli attempts to bring about a change in Soviet policy were doomed to fail. The main themes of Soviet anti-Israel propaganda hardly changed between 1955 and 1968; there were merely ups and downs in the intensity of the campaign. After the rise of the Neo-Ba'th in Syria in February 1966, the line became harsher than before, but too much significance should not be read into these variations of the Soviet political barometer: on the whole there was remarkable consistency.

From summer 1957 onwards, the Soviet press and radio gave much publicity to the reports of individual Soviet citizens who, misled by Zionist propaganda, had been deeply disappointed by their bitter experiences in the 'Zionist paradise'. (A few Soviet citizens, mainly from the formerly Polish regions and the Baltic republics, were permitted each year to rejoin their relatives in Israel. The number of permits granted averaged between 50 and 150 a month.) The Soviet press was particularly critical of Israeli claims to have established a socialist society; the *kibbutzim* were described as labour camps in which idealistic workers were exploited by Wall Street bloodsuckers. Israel was attacked for having collaborated with nazism in the past, and for whitewashing the Third Reich by accepting reparations from West Germany. Israel, according to the Soviet version, was a willing tool of American monopoly capitalism, engaging in ugly plots against the progressive regimes in the Arab world. On the subject of Israeli strength (or weakness) there was considerable ambiguity: Israel was described at one and the same time as a puppet and an imperialist power in its own right. Before the war of

1967 the general tendency was to stress its utter dependence on America, whereas after the war there was an inclination to describe it as in itself imperialist, inciting peaceful but gullible Americans against the Soviet Union, sowing enmity and distrust between the two super-powers. The activities of Israeli tourists in the Soviet Union and of Israeli diplomats in Moscow were frequently given attention in the press, and Soviet citizens were warned of the dangers of ideological contamination. Africans and Asians were exhorted not to accept Israeli technical help, for Zion's emissaries were agents of NATO and of world imperialism. They were acting on behalf of the big oil companies, which were eager to provoke a war in order to perpetuate their hold on the area. It was never made quite clear how a new war could help the oil companies, which wanted above all peace and stability. Since they were the first to suffer in any crisis, their feelings towards Israel, whose very existence complicated their relations with Arab governments, were anything but friendly. Israel was accused by the Soviet press and radio of producing poison gas, atomic bombs, and other means of mass destruction, usually in cooperation with West Germany. Soviet arms deliveries to the Arab countries, on the other hand, were not thought to be a matter of public interest.[1] Whenever clashes occurred along the Arab-Israel borders, only the Cairo or Damascus version was reproduced, and the impression gained by the unsuspecting Soviet reader must have been frightening: an aggressive state engaging incessantly in totally unprovoked attacks on its peaceful neighbors, a permanent danger to peace in the area and indeed to the whole world. Israel was furious about the systematic campaign of vilification; it probably underrated the sales resistance of Soviet readers who, given their long experience, had learned to read *Pravda* and *Izvestia* with critical eyes and were not deeply affected by the stream of invective. Occasionally the propaganda overreached itself and had to beat a temporary retreat. One example was the publication of a book, *Judaism without Embellishment*, which drew freely on traditional anti-Semitic themes and contained particularly offensive cartoons.[2] It was withdrawn from circulation, but other books continued to appear, not much less aggressive and mendacious in tone. An article in *Komsomolskaia Pravda* put the number of Zionist followers in the United States at between 20 and 25 millions, and described them as having virtual control of American (59% of all business enterprises, 70% of the law firms, 80% of the mass media).[3] Such crudities caused no little embarrassment to Western communists: 'Where do you get that kind of figure?' asked the chairman of the Communist party of the state of California. 'You get them from one kind of source, the Gerald L. K. Smiths and so forth, the anti-Semites of the United States.'

The question of Soviet motives is an important one. There was a great deal of unabashed cynicism and Israelis were probably ill advised to get over-excited about what was the normal Soviet way to express disapproval of those whom it disliked or with whom it disagreed. There is no good reason to believe that the Soviet leaders were genuinely convinced that Israel had been the aggressor in every clash with the Arabs; Soviet comments after the Six Day War made it clear that the Russians had been unhappy about the extremism of certain Arab leaders and the excesses of Arab propaganda. But in addition to the anti-Israel polemics, normal by Soviet standards, there was an edge of extra hostility that cannot be explained within the framework of Marxism-Leninism, a shrillness and intensity which stemmed partly from traditional antagonism towards Jews and which often ascribed to them both superhuman cunning and inherently evil intentions. The 'Protocols of the Elders of Zion', the concept of Jewish world domination, had, after all, emanated from Russia. Old-fashioned anti-Semitism was contemptuously rejected after the revolution, but the deeper instincts which had, *inter alia*, produced the 'Protocols', were by no means totally uprooted, and conspiracy theories became more fashionable than ever. A Soviet communist was conditioned to see plots everywhere and his task was to unmask them; this, to a considerable extent, determined his approach to Zionism, Israel, and the Jews in general. Those who made Soviet policy did not altogether disbelieve their own propaganda; it is usually not at all easy to establish with any degree of certitude where cynicism ended and conviction began.

Mention has been made of the Syrian *coup* of February 1966 which brought the Neo-Ba'th to power in Syria. From that date on there was a steady stream of Soviet announcements that Israel was about to attack this, the most progressive of all Arab states, alone or in combination with the US Sixth Fleet, or in collaboration with the reactionary forces in the Arab world. There had been such warnings in the past, but after February 1966 they became a permanent feature of Soviet propaganda. During the month of May 1966, to give but one example, there was a strong warning (May 7) by the diplomatic correspondent of *Izvestia*, Kondrachov, claiming that Israel had elevated provocations against neighboring states to the level of official policy; one-third of Israel's army had been moved to the Syrian border. *Pravda* returned to the same subject on May 21; on the following day Radio Moscow announced that the danger of war in the Middle East was now extremely acute. To give additional emphasis to this warning, it was followed by an official statement by the Soviet government on May 27; the Soviet Union would not remain indifferent to attempts to violate peace in the immediate proximity of its frontiers.[4] The next few days brought further articles and broadcasts and an official note on the same lines was handed to the Israeli ambassador in Moscow.

Between May 1966 and the outbreak of war the year after, not a single month passed without at least one such crisis. It is possible that the one in May 1966 was deliberately provoked; it followed the visit to Moscow by Yusef Zuayin, the new Syrian prime minister One could think of a number of reasons which may have induced both Russians and Syrians to create a war scare: it was bound to strengthen the Neo-Ba'th regime internally, deter Israel from retaliating against the guerrilla forces operating from Syrian territory, compel Syria's enemies in the Arab world to give at least verbal support to the Arab sister country threatened by Zionist attacks, induce Nasser to cooperate more closely with the new Syrian regime. It must have seemed a clever stratagem involving no risks, for Israel, utterly dependent on the United States, would not dare to engage in large-scale military action against America's wish. But war scares in the Middle East have a self-generating effect, and in the long run they can be self-fulfilling. If the scare of May 1966 was deliberately provoked despite better knowledge, there is no reason to assume that all the subsequent scares were orchestrated in a similar manner.

The outbreak of war in 1967 and the war scare preceding it were part of a chain reaction which had been started by Soviet leaders in cooperation with their allies in the Arab world, over whom they gradually lost control. Accident, misunderstanding, and misinformation played a great (and growing) role once the train of events had been set in motion. Conjuring up foreign political threats for domestic purposes had been one of Stalin's favorite tactics; in the late nineteen-twenties he invoked the threat of Anglo-French military intervention, when in fact there was no such danger. These war scares always followed a certain pattern; they were never totally implausible. There had, after all, be.n a war of intervention in Russia in 1918–19, and the Israelis had attacked Egypt in 1956. The belief in conspiracy as a main agent in politics has always had a strong appeal in the Soviet Union and the Arab world. Such inclinations are dangerous if coupled with the frequent use of disinformation as a political weapon; it seems to be well beyond human capacity to sow suspicion without ill effects on one's own judgment.

Within the Soviet establishment there was not complete unanimity with regard to Israel. Among the intelligentsia many felt unhappy about the thinly veiled anti-Semitic policy directed against 'rootless cosmopolitans'; they realized that Soviet enmity towards Israel could be explained more easily by the requirements of power politics than by communist ideology. The Russian intelligentsia had traditionally regarded anti-Semitism as morally and intellectually beyond the pale; other parts of Russian society had been more receptive. In theory, anti-Semitism was a crime in the Soviet Union, but the constant anti-Israel campaign was bound to create the impression that Zionism was merely a synonym for the Jews.

For very different reasons, there were misgivings about the wisdom of Soviet Middle East policy among technocrats and even military leaders; they regarded economic assistance and arms shipments on such a lavish scale as a doubtful investment. The Soviet economy was still in need of capital and capital goods, and they failed to understand why priority should be given to foreign countries ruled by non-communists, and not too efficiently at that. Among the foreign political experts, too, counsels were divided: those dealing with the third world warmly endorsed the support given to Nasser and the Syrians; others, dealing with Europe and America, realized that the anti-Israel policy was not popular in the West, even among communists. It also provoked criticism among Russia's East European allies, partly for economic reasons (they had to foot some of the bills of Soviet Middle East policy), partly on political grounds. These then were the doves. The hawks were found mainly among the guardians of party orthodoxy, and those who disliked Jews and were glad to rationalize their feeling in ideological terms; there were not a few in the army, the leadership of the party, and the communist youth organization, the Komsomol, favoring a more dynamic and expansive foreign policy and demanding that Israel be 'taught a lesson'. Between the ideologists who backed the military regimes in Egypt and Syria and those who had strong reservations about them and did not rule out a betrayal on their part, there were the middle-grounders, firmly anti-Israel, who, however, refrained from giving free rein to anti-Jewish sentiments. This is not to suggest that there was a violent tug-of-war among the Soviet leaders; Israel was not of sufficient importance to preoccupy them for long; but the differences of opinion, although not extreme, were sufficiently wide to make it difficult at any given time to talk about a full political consensus; the days of total unanimity in the Kremlin had long since passed. If a war scare was launched at a certain point, this did not necessarily mean that the entire leadership had decided to intensify the conflict in the Middle East. The initiative might have been taken by a group of hawks without any prior consultation and decision at the highest level.

Such seems to have been the case with regard to the crisis in May 1967. The news about Israeli troop concentrations and the impending invasion of Syria which started the scare came from Soviet and Syrian sources. The Egyptians, as it subsequently transpired, re-garded these fears as 'hallucinations',[5] but they decided for reasons of their own to act as if the warnings were justified. This still leaves open the question whether the Russians were acting on the basis of wrong information, a possibility that cannot be entirely excluded. Their whole appraisal of Israel, of its readiness to fight, and of the military capacity of Egypt and Syria were, as later appeared, quite mistaken. It is equally possible that for a variety of reasons the news about Israeli troop concentrations was deliberately fabricated against better knowledge.[6]

It can be taken for granted that the Soviet leaders did not at that time want a war between Israel and the Arab countries; there was genuine surprise and confusion as the conflict escalated after Nasser's closure of the Straits of Tiran. There is reason to doubt whether Moscow had been informed beforehand that Nasser was about to take this step, but once the decision had been taken the Soviet leaders faced a serious dilemma. They simply had to support the Arabs; the Soviet government statement on May 24 made it clear that they would stand by them if they were attacked; but they also made it known directly to Nasser, and by implication in their public pro-nouncements, that they would not support a 'holy war' against Israel such as the Arabs proclaimed. Soviet policy at this stage was to give political help to Nasser and to work for an 'acceptable, just, and peaceful solution' of the crisis – that is, to make it possible for

Egypt to keep the gains it had just made. The Aqaba issue, according to Soviet comments, was not of great importance. Western propaganda, it was said on one occasion, was deliberately inflaming the problem, and on another: 'The impression is created that somebody is ready to take dangerous steps and kindle the danger of war in the Middle East in order to decide whether one or two or four ships will sail through the straits of Tiran.'[7] In the early stages of the crisis the main blame was put on America, which wanted to divert attention from an escalation of the war in Vietnam,[8] and a leading Soviet commentator wrote that the events in the Middle East should not be regarded in isolation.[9] It happened to be a mistaken appraisal of the situation, for the Middle East crisis had nothing at all to do with the bombing of the demilitarized zone in Vietnam. Later the anti-American motif was toned down; clearly negotiations with Washington had got under way and the ground-rules of the dispute had been established for the two super-powers. America and Russia would not intervene and they would work (within narrow limits) for a de-escalation of the conflict. Both Moscow and Washington sent notes to that effect to Cairo and Tel Aviv, but while Nasser privately promised that he would not fire the first shot, his spokesmen announced that war was now inevitable and that the combined might of the Arab armies would crush Israel within a few days.

At this stage Moscow no longer had control over Egypt and Syria. It could not press in the United Nations for a solution that was unacceptable to Nasser (such as a return to the *status quo ante*). Soviet spokesmen complained about the lack of American willingness to restrain Israeli extremists, and contrasted Cairo's 'constructive proposals' with Israeli 'irresponsibility'.[10] But their hands had been forced by the precipitate actions of their Arab allies; the war scare was about to turn into a real war, the political barometer was fast reaching danger-point, 'black crows were circling over the Middle East'.[11] By that time the political picture had become almost hopelessly blurred: according to the original Soviet version, Syria had been threatened by a combined Israeli-Jordanian invasion sponsored by the CIA and the oil magnates. But on May 30 Hussein signed a pact with Nasser and thus joined the anti-Israeli front. What had been described as a confrontation between 'reactionaries' and 'progressives' now became a national conflict, and while Soviet spokesmen were not at a loss for ideological explanations, these were by no means shared by all other communist parties, let alone the non-communist left in Europe and America.

While the Soviet leaders, like the American, preferred not to take any further action for the moment, both Arabs and Israelis tried to anticipate what action the Soviet Union would take in the event of armed conflict. Nasser and the Syrians thought they would not need Soviet military help provided Moscow prevented the Americans from intervening. Of this they were assured by the end of May, and it gave them great confidence, for they were convinced that the war against Israel would be a walk-over if no other powers interfered. In its statement of May 23, the Soviet government had declared that the aggressors would face not only the united strength of the Arab countries, but also a firm riposte from the Soviet Union and other peace-loving states.[12] No one apparently bothered to find out what a 'firm riposte' meant in military and political terms: in the general euphoria it was probably not thought worthwhile to clarify such details. There is no reason to assume that the Arab countries had asked for and received a firm undertaking from the Soviet Union that there would, if necessary, be Soviet military intervention; the complaints by Boumedienne and many Arab newspapers that the Soviet Union had left its allies in the lurch after June 9 were quite unjustified.

The Israelis were naturally deeply concerned about possible Soviet action. Most of them, especially the army leaders, thought Soviet military intervention unlikely, but in view of American uncertainties the unspecified Soviet threats could not be taken lightly; there had been warnings from Washington about the possibility of Soviet intervention. Eshkol and the foreign ministry made a desperate last-minute effort to convince the Soviet Union that Israel had no intention of invading Syria, that there had been no troop concentrations, and that the Soviet attacks on Israel had been altogether unjustified. But the Soviet diplomats were not at that stage interested in historical truth and abstract justice; their task was to threaten Israel with dire consequences if it decided to break the Egyptian blockade. This the Israelis were unwilling to accept, and after June 1, with the danger to the existence of the state increasing daily, it was decided to act as if the Soviet threats had no substance.[13]

As far as can be ascertained in retrospect, it had been the Soviet assumption that full-scale war would not break out in the Middle East, and a quick Israeli victory was thought even less likely. Up to the very outbreak of war the line pursued by Federenko, the Soviet delegate at the UN, was that there was no particular urgency, that Israel and its backers were creating an atmosphere of artificial hysteria, and that no emergency meeting or specific action was needed. His attitude did not change during the first two days of the war; according to Soviet press and radio reports, the Egyptian and Syrian armies continued to advance into Israel and the Arab air forces continued to attack even after they had ceased to exist. As they had done in the past, the Soviet mass media published only the Arab communiqués; it was not until the night of June 6 that Moscow realized the magnitude of the defeat, and on June 7 instructions were given to Federenko to ask for an immediate cease-fire and unconditional Israeli withdrawal. The Soviet representative, who had until then prevented any action by the Security Council, now argued that the Middle East crisis was of the greatest urgency, and accused the United States of sabotaging the work of the Security Council because it was not willing to act quickly enough.

At first the Arab states rejected the Soviet proposal of a cease-fire, whereupon Federenko put the blame on Israel. Meanwhile anti-Israel protest meetings were taking place in Soviet factories and the leaders of the Soviet bloc were asked to come to an urgent meeting in Moscow on June 9; Rumania did not sign the communiqué issued after the meeting, but Yugoslavia, exceptionally, did. It is unlikely that the possibility of armed intervention was discussed at this meeting, if only because Arab resistance had by that time ceased. All the communist leaders could do in the circumstances was to decide on concerted political and economic action to prevent a total collapse of the 'progressive' regimes in the Arab world. It was suggested at the time that the Soviet Union might have decided to intervene had Israeli forces advanced beyond Kuneitra towards Damascus. In retrospect even that appears doubtful, because no Soviet forces were ready for such an expedition at short notice; everything had happened much too fast. On June 10 the Soviet Union broke off diplomatic relations with Israel; the other communist countries (again with the exception of Rumania) followed suit within the next few days. It is not certain whether there was unanimity in Moscow about the wisdom of this step, for it must have been clear that a break in diplomatic relations would from then on limit Russia's freedom of action in the Middle East, and make it even more difficult to bring pressure to bear on Israel in the days to

come. Moscow had warned Israel so often that its very existence was
at stake that Israel had almost become inured to it; short of military
action, the break in diplomatic relations exhausted the Soviet
arsenal, but in view of mounting dissatisfaction with the Soviet
Union in the Arab world, the leaders in Moscow felt they had to
take some action to reassure their allies and a diplomatic break was
the least they could do. Israel, it was said, was flouting world
opinion; if it did not immediately withdraw to the former borders
the Soviet Union and its allies would impose sanctions, 'with all their
possible consequences';[14] what kind of sanctions was not specified.

The full extent of the Arab defeat did not emerge from the Soviet
press even during the first weeks after the war; President Nasser's
'grave setback', itself a euphemism, became a 'difficult moment'.

The Soviet political and military leadership did not, of course, fail
to realize the seriousness of the defeat; immediate measures were
taken to rush arms, military instructors, and economic aid to Egypt
and Syria. Substantial arms shipments and 100 Migs were flown to
Cairo within a few days of the armistice.[15] But for the moment the
main emphasis was to be in the political field. The Soviet Union
asked for an emergency session of the General Assembly of the
United Nations, and when it convened on June 19 Prime Minister
Kosygin appeared as the first speaker. Israel had committed a
perfidy without precedent, he said, by provoking a total war of
aggression against Egypt and Syria. He demanded the condemnation
of Israel, the immediate retreat of Israeli troops, and the payment of
reparations to the Arab states for the damage they had suffered. It
soon appeared, however, that the Soviet proposal would not gain
a majority, and even a more modest Yugoslav proposal reducing the
demands to one (withdrawal of Israeli troops) ran into opposition.
The feeling of the majority, as subsequently expressed in the
Security Council resolution of November 22, 1967, was that the
withdrawal of Israeli forces from the occupied areas should be
combined with the termination of all states of belligerency, freedom
of shipping, and the mutual acknowledgment by all parties of the
sovereignty, territorial integrity, and political independence of every
state in the area.

The Soviet campaign in the United Nations was not very successful; the watered-down Soviet proposal, rejected by the Arab states
as not far-reaching enough, was defeated in the General Assembly.
The Security Council decision, which later on became the basis of

Soviet and Arab policy, at first aroused little enthusiasm among the Arabs; Syria did not accept it and boycotted Gunnar Jarring, the Swedish mediator appointed by the United Nations. It was the aim of Soviet policy after the Six Day War to isolate Israel, to compel it eventually to give up the conquered territories. Less than a week after the end of the war Israel began to feel the full blast of Soviet displeasure, expressed in a sustained propaganda campaign almost unprecedented in its ferocity; seldom had a small country been given so much publicity in the Soviet mass media, which asserted that there had been few examples in history of such treacherous aggression as had been committed by Israel against the Arab states.[16] Israel was accused of barbaric war crimes: 'The aggressors are killing prisoners of war and defenceless peasants. They publicly execute men, women and children. . . . Even Western correspondents compare these crimes to those perpetrated by the nazis.'[17] *Pravda* first used the term 'genocide', which was to be freely used from then on.[18] There were reports that Israeli soldiers had fired indiscriminately on passers-by in Arab villages well after the fighting had ended, that they had used wounded Arabs for target practice, and burnt whole families alive. Many Arabs had been subjected to horrible tortures. The personification of this new Israel was Moshe Dayan, 'a pupil of Hitler and the darling of the nazis all over the world, a man of immense brutality, cowardice, and hypocrisy'.[19] A former lackey of the British, this would-be Napoleon had developed an insatiable appetite, dreaming of an Israeli empire from the Nile to the Euphrates.[20] *Krokodil*, the Soviet satirical weekly, renamed him 'Moshe Adolfovich' and compared his campaign to Hitler's attack on Poland in 1939.[21] At his orders, Israeli soldiers had bayoneted children and raped women; the reports that they had also blown up some houses and that drunken Israeli officers and soldiers had desecrated Arab holy places came almost as an anticlimax.[22]

The campaign was not restricted to Israel; world Zionism figured equally prominently – a pack of gangsters and the tool of Wall Street bankers. Active in more than sixty countries, Zionism was not a political movement, but a criminal conspiracy directed against all peace-loving peoples. Drawing its inspiration from the teachings of Judaism, it had always been racialist in character; it was based on tyranny and slave labour; ultimately it aimed at world domination. But fortunately, owing mainly to Soviet help, these sinister plots had been uncovered in time and would be frustrated. The Israeli triumph had been a Pyrrhic victory, for in their main aim they had failed; the 'progressive' Arab regimes had not been overthrown. There was no doubt that the Israelis would fare as the nazis did before them.

The effects of this massive propaganda campaign could not be ignored. It was hardly likely to appeal to intellectuals and the politically well-informed, but the sheer repetition of atrocity stories was bound to have a certain impact on the public at large. Outside the Soviet Union the campaign proceeded less crudely, but its aims were essentially the same and the political and psychological climate was certainly more favorable than before the Six Day War. Before June 5, 1967, the great majority of left-wing public opinion, including many communist parties, had either supported Israel or at any rate shown misgivings about Soviet policy. Israel had been openly threatened with extinction by the Arab leaders, and the Soviet version that this had been the work of only a few reactionaries and adventurists among them, and that Nasser and the Syrians had never been part of it, was given little credence. Israel's decision to go to war on June 5 was more often than not justified on the left as an act of self-defence. But once the war had ended, the general attitude began rapidly to change. Israel was no longer in immediate danger; it had shown that it could take care of itself. The Arab refugees, on the other hand, became an object of pity, and Israel's failure to provide a constructive solution provoked much criticism. Israel refused to withdraw its troops from the territory it had conquered; it now acted as an occupier. Houses were blown up, Arab civilians exiled or arrested. It seemed only natural that left-wing opinion should become more receptive to anti-Israel arguments.

Propaganda played an important role after June 10, 1967, as it had before the outbreak of the war. But, propagandist accounts apart, the Arab defeat had to be explained, both for Soviet domestic consumption and to answer the critics of the Soviet Union in the Arab world. On June 9 President Boumedienne of Algeria had openly criticized the Soviet Union for being unwilling to take greater risks in its support of the Arab cause. Later on newspapers in various Arab countries, including even Egypt, began to spread 'anti-Soviet' views (to quote a *Pravda* correspondent): the reactionaries, aided and abetted by the Chinese, were making 'dirty accusations'.[23] When President Boumedienne went to Moscow in June 1967 there was some blunt speaking. In answer to his inquiries about Soviet military assistance to the 'progressive' countries in the Arab world, the Soviet leaders asked for his views about the consequences of nuclear war. But Boumedienne, who had temporarily assumed a leading role in the Arab camp, was not put off so easily: an atomic war, after all, was likely to affect New York and Moscow much more than Algiers or Cairo.

Gradually a coherent Soviet version of the origins of the Six Day War and the Arab defeat emerged. The Israelis, of course, remained the chief villains. They had defeated the Arab armies mainly owing to the element of surprise; to believe Belayev and Primakov, who provided the first detailed authoritative comment,[24] the attack had come more or less like a bolt from the blue. The Israelis were better equipped; just before they struck they had received major arms shipments from the imperialist powers. There were also hints of more direct military cooperation between Israel and America, but Soviet commentators preferred not to be too specific about this. They did not give wide publicity to Nasser's allegations (subsequently withdrawn) that the Sixth Fleet and the British had provided the Israelis with air support. This would have immediately exposed the Soviet Union to the charge of not having extended equal help to the Arabs. The Israelis, it was maintained, had been successful because they were fanatical and cruel. Like the Germans under Hitler, the majority of Israelis had accepted the chauvinist, imperialist policy of their leaders.[25]

There was also some criticism of the Arabs: Nasser had been betrayed by the 'military *bourgeoisie*',[26] especially in the air force command. Soviet commentators even mentioned the names of some of these 'reactionaries' who had deliberately sabotaged the Arab war effort because they thought the progressive changes taking place in the UAR a greater danger than Israel. Certain Arab propagandists were also taken to task; Ahmad Shukairy's extremist slogans ('throw the Israelis into the sea') had done great harm to the Arab cause. Nasser and the Syrian leaders (who had been as extreme in their declarations), were, publicly at least, exempt from criticism; their behavior had been statesmanlike throughout the crisis; they had been the victims of calumny spread by the Western press. Not the new, progressive Egypt and Syria had been defeated by the Israelis, but the remnants of the old order, which unfortunately were still quite strong.[27] But given Nasser's (and the Egyptian people's) fervent wish to purge these reactionary and anti-Soviet elements who had thwarted the Arab war effort, they would overcome their present weakness, become much stronger, and eventually regain the lost territories. Such encouragement was, however, frequently mixed with criticism of the Arabs, not only for their ultra-radical slogans in the past, but also for their intransigence in the present, which 'objectively played into Israel's hands'. Some Soviet commentators thought Arab unwillingness to recognize Israel unwise, and were concerned about the 'ultra-leftists' who suggested a new round immediately, even if it meant certain Arab defeat.[28] Arab opposition to the Security Council resolution was also wrong: 'justified though it was, it actually played into the hands of Israel, enabling her to drag out the solution of the main issue – the withdrawal of troops'.[29] On occasion Soviet observers admitted that in a strange way Israel was objectively playing a progressive role: it had been a factor making for Arab unity and for progressive development (that is, radicalization) in the Arab world.[30] This was, in other words, Hegel's cunning of reason, the price that had to be paid both for Arab unity and for the road to socialism. But it was a high price, for it compelled the Arab states to spend large sums on defence rather than economic development, and it provided 'fertile soil for leftist adventurism', which, disregarding the practical position, called for an immediate new round of fighting.[31]

The Arab-Israeli war had political repercussions in East Europe out of proportion to its intrinsic importance, and apparently it also provoked some dissension within the Soviet Union. While Soviet propaganda remained on the whole bitterly hostile to Israel, there were occasional dissenting voices claiming that, after all, there was a difference between Hitler's war and the events of June 1967,[32] and that it should be made clearer that the Soviet people was not anti-Semitic. Soviet statements oscillated between open threats of Soviet intervention and possible annihilation of the state of Israel,[33] and communiqués that were remarkably moderate in tone, omitting even any reference to Israeli aggression.[34] Neutral observers in Moscow reported that there was a good deal of sneaking admiration for Israel's achievement, among both the military and the political leaders, and deep disappointment with the Arabs, even if for obvious reasons it could not be publicly voiced.

In East Europe the Arab-Israeli war was one of the reasons for the further polarization in the communist camp. It helped to trigger off both the Czech thaw and the Polish cultural pogrom in the spring of 1968. Pro-Israel sentiments had been fairly pronounced in some East European countries, despite (or because of) the Soviet line; there was identification with a small country which had successfully resisted the pressure exerted by much stronger forces. In Poland, on the other hand, where the leadership faced an acute internal crisis, the Jews became pawns in the struggle between rival factions: they were made scapegoats for the riots that broke out in March 1968. 'Cleanse the party of Zionists' became the new watchword (as if there had been any Zionists in the Communist Party of Poland). It was a deeply cynical performance, and no one could say what its long-term results would be. It was the first time that a communist regime had openly sacrificed internationalism, hitherto one of the basic tenets of communist ideology, in theory as well as in practice. There were few victims, but the political implications were more far-reaching than those of the Slansky trial in Czechoslovakia. What happened in Poland heralded a movement in the communist world away from traditional beliefs towards a new order in which nationalism (and national enmities), rather than Marxism-Leninism, became the main ideological cement. Polish 'anti-Zionism' found some admirers in the Soviet Union,[35] provoked open resistance in Czechoslovakia and Yugoslavia,[36] and was the cause of acute embarrassment to communist parties in the West.

Some of the smaller European communist parties (the Dutch, Austrian, and Swiss, for instance) had been critical of all-out Soviet support for the Arabs, and there was no blind acceptance among the bigger parties either. Soviet spokesmen found it increasingly difficult to justify the break in diplomatic relations with Israel. Moscow had maintained diplomatic relations with nazi Germany and fascist Italy; it had not severed its ties with Greece, despite the *coup* in 1967; the decision not to maintain relations with Israel was unprecedented and raised awkward questions.[37]

After the end of the Arab-Israeli war a great many diplomatic journeys were undertaken between Moscow and the Arab capitals. The Soviet generals were the first to visit Cairo. Podgorny, President of the Supreme Soviet, visited Cairo, Damascus, and Baghdad in June-July 1967 to reassure the Arab leaders that Soviet help would continue. In January 1968 a Soviet delegation headed by Kyrill Mazurov, a member of the Politburo, visited Cairo; he had been preceded by Marshal Tito. Boumedienne was the first Arab leader to call on the Kremlin; he was followed by Atassi of Syria, Arif, the

Iraqi President, King Hussein of Jordan, and in July 1968 by Nasser himself. Two top-level gatherings of communist leaders, in Budapest in July and in Warsaw in December 1967, were devoted to deliberations on the Middle East situation. The Arabs wanted more arms and economic aid; the Soviet leaders, as far as can be ascertained, expressed complete sympathy with the Arab aim of eliminating the consequences of Israeli aggression. At the same time they made it clear to their guests that a military solution of the conflict was out of the question in the near future. They also tried to put their exchanges with the Arab world on a basis of reciprocity; they could not indefinitely underwrite military and economic aid on an ever-growing scale.

The Arab-Israeli conflict had facilitated Soviet activities in the Middle East in the fifties and early sixties. The Soviet investment in Egypt and Syria had been eminently worthwhile, but after about 1965 returns began to diminish. The defeat of the Arab states had been a blow to Soviet prestige and had necessitated further heavy investment in these countries. But despite this outlay, relations between the Soviet Union and the Arab countries were not markedly closer in 1968 than before the war. It was not at all clear whether the Soviet position in the Arab world had become stronger, or whether Egypt, as a result of the purges, had made much progress on the road to communism.

The Israeli victory in 1967 had come as a surprise to Moscow. The Soviet leaders had underrated Israel because they were convinced that 'Jews do not fight'; the traditional Russian image of the Jew had changed little since the revolution. The realization that Jews did fight if their national existence was at stake did not make the Kremlin any more friendly towards Israel; on the contrary, there was a great deal of annoyance, righteous anger, and the desire to teach the Israelis a lesson. But the war also reopened discussions in Moscow as to how far Soviet hostility to Israel should be allowed to escalate, taking into account both Soviet self-interest and the 'international duty' of the Soviet Union. Hostility towards Israel, both emotional and political, was deeply ingrained in some powerful circles in Moscow, but there were also voices asserting that Soviet support for Arab national aspirations did not necessarily entail full identification with them.

5 The Soviet Union and the Arab World

In the nineteen-fifties conditions in the Arab world favored a radical break with past policies. The new leaders of Egypt were eager to establish closer contacts with the Soviet Union. A new class and a new generation had come to power, and they felt the need for a new and more daring approach in domestic and foreign policy alike. Unlike Turkey and Iran, the Arab world had not preserved its sovereignty in its recent history; there was a great deal of resentment against the West, which had dominated the Middle East for so long and still kept much of its influence through defence pacts and economic links. And, again unlike Turkey and Iran, the Arab world had no common border with the Soviet Union and was not directly exposed to Soviet pressure. The Soviet Union was thought of as a powerful but distant country whose support against the encroachments of the West should have been enlisted by the Arabs long before. Of domination from that quarter the radical Arab leaders were not afraid, for the Soviet Union did not behave like the old colonialist powers. To communist influence they felt quite immune: asked about the danger of communist penetration, Nasser once said: 'All our people are politicians and very smart. . . . I am certain that no communist will, whatever happens, influence Arab nationalism. On the contrary, the ideas of Arab nationalism will finally and forever prevail.'[1]

The Soviet leaders were aware of the mental reservations of their new allies in the Middle East, but this did not worry them unduly, for they were convinced that the logic of events would gradually drive the Arab leaders (or their successors) towards closer political collaboration with the Soviet Union, and that an ideological *rapprochement* would eventually follow.[2]

By 1958 Soviet political, military, and economic ties with Egypt had become very close: it was the honeymoon of the new alliance. The USSR had supported Egypt during the Suez crisis, it had underwritten the first stage of work on the Aswan dam, and was soon to undertake the second, main stage as well. Substantial arms shipments had been delivered to Egypt and a loan agreement totalling $175m. had been signed. Nasser went twice to Moscow in 1958; the second time in connection with the Iraqi revolution and the American landing in Lebanon. Khrushchev promised every possible help; he would issue warnings, but made it clear that there would be no Soviet armed intervention.[3]

Amid these protestations of lasting friendship, careful observers could detect warning signs well before the year had ended. Syria had merged with Egypt in February 1958; the Soviet government did not comment, but for a number of good reasons it was not over-enthusiastic. During 1958 Nasser had become more conciliatory towards the United States; he wanted American wheat and financial support for his economic projects. Above all, events in Iraq precipitated a crisis. The Iraqi revolution, which Nasser had followed with high expectations and not a few designs of his own, had gone sour: the radical nationalists in Baghdad turned against the local Nasserists and entered into a close alliance with the communists. Moscow praised Kassem as a truly democratic ruler; Iraq had suddenly become a more democratic country than Egypt; the Iraqi revolution rather than the Egyptian represented a higher stage of political development.[4]

Nasser accepted the challenge: in a speech in Port Said on December 23, 1958, and in a series of addresses between January and April 1959, he conducted a major propaganda campaign against communism, the enemy of Arab nationalism and unity. Communism was equated with Western imperialism, the communists wanted 'to dominate us and establish a terrorist, bloody dictatorship'; they were foreign agents, and Khrushchev's representations on their behalf was 'intervention in our affairs'.[5] Moscow mildly rebuked Nasser, but preferred at first to ignore his outbursts. The communist press, less restrained, criticized the internal situation in Egypt and Syria, as it had done all along; the suppression of democracy, the persecution of Arab communists, and the murder of one of their leaders were the main targets of attack. The *World Marxist Review* complained about the climate of fear in Egypt, the ruthless dictatorship, Gestapo methods, unbridled terror, unemployment, poverty, and concentration camps.[6] The propaganda war abated a little in February, but reached its highest pitch in late March and early April, after the bloody suppression by Kassem and the communists of the Mosul uprising. Some of the most bitter insults were exchanged in April 1959; these had been preceded by an exchange of letters between Khrushchev and Nasser, of which some details were later revealed: Khrushchev had called the president of the UAR a 'passionate and hot-headed young man' who had 'taken upon himself more than his stature permitted', and had accused him of trying to annex Iraq.[7] Nasser replied that 'but for my hot-headedness our country today would be a Western base for rockets and atomic bombs against the Soviet Union. . . . With the same hot-headedness we shall face the new danger as we have faced enemies in the past. . . . We will also win against the new agents of communism.'[8] Soviet spokesmen had always stressed the decisive part of the Soviet Union in saving Egypt in 1956, but Nasser now disparaged its role during the Suez crisis: 'We did not see the smallest hint of help from a single foreign state, including the Soviet Union.'[9] And a few days later:

We were trying to convince ourselves that the communist parties in our countries were independent of international communism. We found out that they were not, and that was why I called them communist stooges. They carried out orders and instructions to liquidate patriotic and national elements in order to place our country inside the zone of communist influence. We were suddenly faced by flagrant interference in our internal affairs by Russia[10]

and this despite the fact that Khrushchev in his personal notes to the Egyptian president had acknowledged that Cairo's attitude towards communism was a matter of domestic policy which concerned the United Arab Republic alone.[11] Accusing the Russians of trying to establish a 'Red Fertile Crescent', Nasser claimed that the large reservoir of goodwill built up by Moscow in three years of friendship had been lost in less than three weeks after the Mosul revolt. *Pravda* countered by criticizing an unnamed public figure in the Arab world for his policy of immediate and mechanical unification of all Arab states, whether they wanted it or not. All who did not agree with his ideas were declared to be communists, Zionists, and enemies of the Arab people.[12] In April and May further letters were exchanged between Khrushchev and Nasser, and it appears that the former succeeded in mollifying the Egyptian leader. In a speech in India in May, Khrushchev emphasized that 'properly speaking we have no conflict with Egypt', and on another occasion it was said in Moscow that even an anti-communist campaign by a recipient of Soviet aid would not affect the fulfilment of past commitments and the prospects of further assistance.[13]

At this stage the dispute suddenly subsided. Less than a year later Nasser declared that it was his duty to pay tribute to the tact and disinterestedness which the Soviet Union had demonstrated towards Egypt: 'In spite of the divergence of opinions, Moscow never put pressure on us, never threatened to stop her aid.'[14]

Both sides were clearly eager not to burn all bridges. The Soviet Union regarded Egypt as the key country in the Arab world, and it did not underrate Egypt's potential role in Africa. Subsequent events in Iraq seemed to confirm this appraisal. For Iraq began to backslide: the 'progressive elements' were persecuted under Kassem and all but annihilated under his successors. Too much had been invested in Egypt to withdraw support lightly; the impression created in the third world would have been most unfortunate from the Soviet point of view. The communist movement in Egypt was small, split into several factions, and ineffectual; there was no real alternative to Nasser's leadership in Egypt, or indeed in the Arab world. Consequently, Moscow decided to ignore the attacks and to supply the aid that had been promised.

In August 1960 the agreement for the second stage of the Aswan dam was signed. The High Dam was to be the outstanding symbol of the achievements of Nasser's regime: it was to expand Egypt's cultivable area from 6 to 7·3 million acres, provide all-year-round irrigation to another 700,000 acres, facilitate navigation on the Nile, provide cheap electricity for industrialization. It was believed at the time that as a result the national income of Egypt would rise by some 29%. Soviet support for this project ('a symbol', a 'shining beacon of progress' – Mikoyan) was of paramount importance. Nasser was at ease working with the Russians who, he said, had proved loyal partners in all their undertakings; their terms were fair, interest charges low (2½%), and no strings were attached.[15] Soviet comment was that 'in contrast to the West we have not tried to use the High Dam as a means to put pressure on Egypt', and an American observer noted that Russia had now succeeded in assuring herself of close ties with the UAR for at least the next decade.[16]

Further exchanges between Cairo and Moscow took place on all levels: Patriarch Alexius visited Egypt, while Field-Marshal Abd al Hakim Amer led an Egyptian delegation to Moscow to discuss Soviet military aid. When Nasser met Khrushchev at the United Nations General Assembly in New York in October 1960, the hatchet was finally buried; all that remained to do, Nasser said, was to 'review the crisis in a spirit of mutual understanding' in order to strengthen the basis of our friendship'.[17]

From his point of view, a break with the Soviet Union would have been a major calamity; it would have made him dependent on the Western powers, from whom he was unlikely to get the necessary support for both his economic projects and his military ambitions. Relations with America, to be sure, improved in 1960; American shipments provided food for many Egyptians, more help was promised, and John Badeau, well known for his sympathies for the Arab cause, was appointed American Ambassador to Cairo. John F. Kennedy engaged in a prolonged private correspondence with Nasser; the general impression in the Middle East was that America was about to become 'more neutral' in the Arab-Israeli dispute. Yet there were also constant irritations, such as the 'Cleopatra' incident and the Douglas amendment to the Mutual Security Act,[18] both of which Nasser attributed to Zionist intrigues. Above all, his policy continued to clash with American interests all over the Middle East and Africa.

Egypt had increasingly come to support Soviet policies in the United Nations and elsewhere; its proclaimed positive neutrality was gradually wearing thin. The denunciation by the Egyptian press of 'Kennedy's massacre in Cuba' caused no more than raised eyebrows in Washington, but the Congo was a different matter; Cairo, with or on behalf of the Soviet Union, intervened directly in this conflict and there ensued a bitter quarrel with Washington.

Developments inside Egypt made a lasting reconciliation with the West less and less likely and a further *rapprochement* with the Soviet Union almost a foregone conclusion. In July 1961 Nasser undertook a sharp turn to the left 'to protect the revolutionary regime from feudalism, monopolies, and exploiting capitalism'; after the breakdown of the union with Syria further drastic measures were adopted. The aim of the decrees was to stamp out 'capitalist reaction', which Nasser thought had been responsible for the Syrian secession and now threatened his own rule in Egypt. Some 400 banks, factories, and public utilities were nationalized, some private properties were seized, maximum land-ownership was reduced to 100 *feddan*, workers were promised a share in profits, 5,000 political opponents were arrested, and many foreign nationals expelled.

Control over large sectors of the Egyptian economy passed into the hands of the State bureaucracy. It is immaterial in this context whether these measures were indeed 'socialist' in character (as Nasser claimed), or whether it was simply another case of State domination of the economy of which there are many examples in history, from Pharaonic Egypt to Mussolini's Republic of Salò. From the Soviet point of view, the decrees were definitely a step in the right direction, because they were 'objectively undermining the foundations of private ownership and preparing the conditions for the liquidation of capitalist relations'.[19] Egypt was on the road of non-capitalist development, not a third road, a cross between capitalism and socialism, but a road leading to socialism.[20] Nasser in his early days had flirted with fascism; the Free Officers' movement in 1952 had been patriotic and radical in character, without any clear ideological content. It had been in favor of 'socialism', but so was everyone else at the time. The radicalization of the regime took Moscow by surprise. The official Soviet appraisal did not change at once; a leading Soviet correspondent visiting Egypt at the time wrote that the policy was as yet far removed from building socialism, and that the decrees only partly changed the situation in the villages where the '*bourgeoisie*' had consolidated its positions.[21] It is instructive to compare the accounts of the same correspondent published a few years later, when he was to write about the great progress that had been made on the road to socialism, and about the friendship he encountered everywhere.[22]

There were occasional setbacks. Even after the hatchet had been buried in 1960 the Egyptian press continued to attack international communism, and Soviet spokesmen retaliated in kind from time to time. *Pravda* in May 1961 complained that the Egyptian press had opened its columns to the 'vilest anti-Soviet slander' and, recalling the political and economic support that had been given to the UAR, it reminded freedom-loving Arabs of their proverb, 'Cut not the tree that provides the shade'.[23] Was Soviet economic aid after all not altogether unconditional? The Egyptians were not deterred: the Soviet Union, they claimed, was again interfering, challenging the UAR's sovereignty and dignity instead of basing relations on equality.[24] Hostile slogans made their appearance, such as 'Destiny has shown you to be imperialists and also agents of world Zionism, suckled by the Jew Marx'. When Anwar as-Sadat visited Moscow at the head of an Egyptian parliamentary delegation, he was told by Khrushchev that while the Egyptian leaders still understood little of socialism, they would end up as communists 'because life imposes communism on man'. How, he asked, could the Russians have confidence in Nasser, seeing that he was losing his grip, unable to solve his country's problems?[25]

It looked as if a major storm was again brewing, but the conflict subsided very quickly. It was to be the last serious open clash between the two countries for many years; occasionally criticism made itself heard, but there were no more orchestrated campaigns. The new provisions of the National Charter of 1962, which allocated 50% of the seats in parliament to workers and peasants, were noted with satisfaction in Moscow; so was the fact that 'for the first time the workers openly observed their proletarian festival' (May 1).[26] Trade relations, which had tailed off after 1958, again picked up and 1962 was a record year for Soviet economic aid. Long-range TU-16 jet bombers and Mig fighters were supplied to the Egyptian air force and a great many official visits were exchanged.

These were the years of intense ideological discussions in the Soviet Union about the concept of the 'independent state of national democracy' (enunciated in 1960), about socialism of the national type, and the character of the national liberation movement. More and more Soviet Middle East experts came to accept the view, voiced at first only by a few, such as G. Mirsky,[27] that the regime in the UAR (and in some other developing countries) was basically progressive; the world outlook of these revolutionary democrats had undergone an evolution; though they were not representatives of the working class, they were able to change direction and move towards socialism.[28]

It is more than doubtful whether the Soviet leaders decided to modify their policy *vis-à-vis* the UAR as the result of academic disputations of this kind. It is far more likely that the discussions among the experts reflected divided opinions within the leadership. Khrushchev, 'erratic, but tending towards an abandonment of accepted doctrinal compromises', went further than any other Soviet leader in reappraising his attitude towards Nasser;[29] in 1964, without apparently consulting his colleagues in the politburo, he granted

Egypt a new substantial loan and made both Nasser and Abd
al Hakim Amer (as well as Ben Bella) 'Heroes of the Soviet Union'.

In 1964 Nasser had been ten years in power; other third world
leaders had come and gone, but his influence and prestige had
steadily grown. Khrushchev had no more doubts about his pro-
Egyptian policy; the warnings of Arab communists that, some
economic reforms apart, no essential changes had taken place in the
policy and character of the regime were impatiently brushed aside.[30]
When Nasser, in anticipation of Khrushchev's visit in 1964, abolished
the emergency laws under which political prisoners (including many
communists) had been held without trial, *Pravda* hailed it as a
'historical step'.[31] Soviet persistence and patience had been vindi-
cated.

Khrushchev's visit to Egypt was the culmination of this policy.
He was welcomed in Cairo with great enthusiasm, in contrast to the
reception given to Chou En-lai, who had been to Egypt shortly
before. The Soviet leader stressed on every occasion the disinterested
character of the economic help extended by his country, and the
fact that there was full agreement between Moscow and Cairo on all
important international issues. All went well but for the hosts'
constant harping on Arab unity; irritated by the unceasing stress on
nationalism, Khrushchev condemned on several occasions the purely
nationalist approach to unity, contrasting it with the communist
approach, with its revolutionary class basis.[32] Soviet commentators
obliquely referred to these incidents, but tried to avoid giving
offence, claiming that the concept of Arab unity had of late undergone a substantial change; the question of the 'unity of the Arab
working people', they said, was being raised with increasing
acuteness.[33] Soviet arms supplies were also discussed on this state
visit; Marshal Grechko and other high-ranking Soviet officers were
members of the Soviet party. Khrushchev revealed that Field-
Marshal Amer had jokingly turned to him after Grechko's speech
and said: 'Give us more arms.' Remarking wryly that 'apparently all
military men are alike' in constantly asking for more arms, he said
that there would be no difficulties regarding additional arms if that
became necessary.[34]

Ali Sabry's visit to Moscow followed in September 1964. Sabry,
then Prime Minister, wanted to discuss the use of the new loan of
$250m. that Khrushchev had promised the Egyptians. The largest
project covered by the new agreement was an iron and steel complex

with an initial annual capacity of more than a million tons; other projects included a power station, a lubricating oil plant, and twenty training centers for workers.[35] Both sides stressed that Soviet-Egyptian friendship had reached a new peak, largely owing to Khrushchev's personal initiative. In a memorandum written in Yalta a few weeks before his death, Togliatti, the Italian communist leader, described Khrushchev's visit to Egypt as one of the most important victories obtained by the Russians over the Chinese.[36]

A few weeks later Khrushchev was overthrown, and it was at first by no means certain that the new collective leadership would display the same warmth and willingness to support Egypt. The Arab communist leaders who had been greatly annoyed by Khrushchev's excessive enthusiasm for Nasser used the opportunity to stress the need to differentiate between the 'non-capitalist path' and the building of socialism. Soviet ideological experts suddenly decided to give a higher grading to Algeria than to the UAR.[37] Cairo was apprehensive; though Cairo Radio announced that relations between states were not based on the preferences of individuals, one of Nasser's aides was quoted to the effect that the *Rais* had been visibly affected by the report of Khrushchev's dismissal. Haykal, who only a short time before had heaped extravagant praise on the fallen leader,[38] had second thoughts: was it not a fact that Khrushchev was the only Soviet leader with whom the Egyptian revolution had clashed in a 'fearful and intense battle'; he had not been far removed from Stalinism and had committed many mistakes; he had not been the first to call for a *rapprochement* with Egypt; his opponents had preceded him in their admiration for the Egyptian revolution.[39] Haykal no doubt somewhat exaggerated the intensity of the admiration the Soviet leadership felt for the Egyptian revolution; Moscow continued to have serious reservations about the character of the Egyptian regime, even though comment was guarded. What made them opt for Egypt and what precluded a Soviet reorientation at this stage was the growing rivalry with China and the defeat of 'national democracy' in other parts of the world. China was showing at the time a certain activity in the Middle East; Chou En-lai had been to Cairo in late 1963 and paid a longer visit in 1965. A Soviet rebuff to Cairo would have led with near certainty to an Egyptian *rapprochement* with China and this was the last thing the Soviet leaders wanted.

'Grading' the countries of 'national democracy' was in those years a favorite pastime in Moscow. Algeria usually scored higher than the UAR, mainly because the Russians had serious misgivings about the Arab Socialist Union, Egypt's state party which, despite many efforts, had failed to become a real political force comparable to the Algerian FLN.[40] But such Soviet reasoning and the optimistic assessments about the course of events in Indonesia and Ghana had a fatal flaw: Ben Bella, on whom the Soviets had put so many hopes, was overthrown in August 1965; Sukarno and Nkrumah fell early in 1966. Of all the hopefuls in the third world only some minor African countries remained, and of course Castro, but his loyalty to the Soviet Union had always been a little suspect. As a result, Nasser's prestige again soared in Moscow, even though there was a tendency among political observers there to be less sanguine about the prospects of the national liberation movement in general.[41]

There had been differences of opinion between Khrushchev and his colleagues in the politburo, but few of a basic character, as became apparent soon after his fall; the others had objected more to his character and style than to his policy. Within a few weeks after his dismissal, Nasser was given assurances that Soviet policy towards Egypt would not change; Jakob Malik, a deputy foreign minister, went briefly to Cairo to see him, and was followed in December 1964 by a more highly placed leader, Alexander Shelepin, a member of the politburo.[42] Shelepin went out of his way to praise Egyptian foreign policy, especially in the Congo, and promised that Soviet economic help would continue.[43] Field-Marshal Abd al Hakim Amer attended the November festivities in Moscow that year; his visit was hailed as a 'new milestone in the strengthening of friendship and solidarity between the two countries', and he signed a new military agreement with Malinovsky, the Soviet defence minister, details of which were not published at the time.[44] The stage was thus set for a resumption of contacts on the highest level, and Nasser went to Moscow in August 1965. The topics that were discussed ranged widely, including Vietnam, the Soviet-Chinese conflict, Soviet help for the new Egyptian five-year plan. Nasser promised to support Moscow at the forthcoming Afro-Asian conference; it was thought at the time that this conference would witness a Soviet-Chinese showdown, which the Soviet leaders regarded with some trepidation.[45] But the basic aim of the meeting in Moscow was, according to Haykal, the Soviet wish (expressed by Brezhnev) 'to know you better as a human being', to strengthen personal relations and 'establish personal friendships'.[46] The Soviet leaders certainly missed no opportunity to flatter Nasser. Haykal reported that Nasser was asked on one occasion by Marshal Malinovsky why he did not wear the order of Hero of the Soviet Union which Khrushchev had bestowed on him; Mikoyan added that the Soviet Union continued to regard Nasser as a 'real hero of heroes'.[47]

Compelling reasons induced the Soviet leaders to continue the Egyptian alliance and Nasser was at least equally interested in ensuring that Soviet support should not cease. He had by now come to depend on Soviet arms supplies; Egypt's economy, in an uncertain state at the best of times, had been further weakened by the war in the Yemen. His position in the Arab world had deteriorated: he had quarrelled with Syria, and there was open conflict with Jordan, Saudia, and Tunisia. The war in the Yemen was going badly and of his great friends in the third world only Tito was left. He could have worked for a *rapprochement* with the American leaders, some of whom were only too eager to re-establish a working relationship. But they had offended him on so many occasions and he had retaliated by such a deliberate policy of irritating and provoking the Americans that even the patience of the most long-suffering American diplomats began to wear thin. Aware that his isolation, part inevitable, part self-induced, was growing, the Soviet alliance became more important for Nasser than ever.

Two other major visits by Soviet leaders to Egypt took place before the Israeli war in 1967. Kosygin made a state visit in May 1966, and foreign minister Gromyko came for a shorter stay in late March 1967. Kosygin dutifully made the rounds: he saw the land-reclamation projects at Al Tahrir, the industrial complex at Helwan, the Aswan dam. He told the National Assembly that he admired Egypt's social and economic progress and its steadfast anti-imperialist struggle, and promised further economic and military support.[48] There was no need to discuss further credits; the loan of the year before was still only half taken up. The final communiqué dealt with the aggressive activities of the imperialist forces and the growing danger of war.[49] There seemed to be no specific problems of any urgency; Moscow wanted to demonstrate (as two *Pravda* correspondents put it) 'the falseness of the theory that the Soviet Union had cooled towards the third world and no longer attached great importance to the Afro-Asian states'.[50]

Kosygin also had a meeting with Ahmad Shukairy, the head of the

Palestine Liberation Organization, later on denounced by the Russians as a nationalist hot-head whom no one had ever taken seriously. Kosygin gave an impression of militant solidarity with Nasser, but remained in fact a little vague on some essential points, such as the Soviet commitment in the event of an armed conflict with Saudi Arabia or an Egyptian preventive war against Israel (a possibility mentioned by Nasser in a speech shortly before Kosygin's arrival).

The talks between Gromyko and Nasser in March 1967 were shrouded in unusual secrecy. The visit came unannounced; it was suggested that it had to do with the situation in Arabia, or perhaps with Egypt's inability to make the repayments due. But would the presence of the foreign minister have been needed for discussions of this character? The Yugoslavs announced that the question of the UN peacekeeping force in Gaza would also be discussed,[51] a most intriguing piece of information in view of what happened less than two months later.

There were many indications that all was not well in Egypt even before the disastrous war against Israel. Soviet economic aid extended to the UAR since 1954 totalled $740m.;[52] in addition, the communist countries of Eastern Europe had extended aid and grants estimated at $540m. Military aid was more difficult to assess; estimates varied between $900m. and $1·6 billion, far more than had been given by the Soviet Union to any other country. United States economic aid to Egypt during the same period totalled $1·1 billion – mostly in 'Food for Peace' shipments of grain. The US had provided the bulk of Egyptian grain imports, but in view of growing Egyptian hostility towards Washington (Nasser's famous 'Jump in the lake' speech; the burning of the American library in Cairo; the shooting down of an American civilian aircraft), it was doubtful whether aid would be continued, and the Soviet Union faced an additional commitment of exporting to the UAR up to 2·5m. tons of grain a year, worth perhaps $300m., with only a remote possibility of repayment.

Soviet commentators emphasized the 'remarkable successes' in Egyptian industry and agriculture;[53] work on the Aswan dam proceeded on schedule. Under competent management, the Suez Canal functioned reasonably well and had become a major source of income. But despite the enormous investments the strains and stresses in Egypt's economy were more palpably felt every year;

consumption was outstripping production, the cost of living was rising steeply, Egypt was no longer in a position to pay its foreign debts. It owed the International Monetary Fund about $300m. and the total UAR foreign currency reserves were equivalent to only about 8% of her foreign debts. Soviet observers regarded the inadequacy of agrarian reform as the main stumbling-block; a new rural *bourgeoisie* had emerged; the more prosperous sections of the peasantry were going over to a capitalist mode of production.[54] They also blamed the mixed economy; capitalists were still appropriating public funds for private profit.[55] Egypt's three main sources of foreign exchange were the Suez Canal (about $220m. in 1966), the cotton crop (about $336m. in 1966), and, to a lesser extent, tourism. But over half of the yearly cotton crop was already mortgaged for years to come to the USSR and Eastern Europe. The continuing population explosion prevented any real and lasting improvement in the standard of living; the Aswan dam and the other industrial projects were just sufficient to prevent a further decline. Egypt was an unlikely place to serve as a communist show window in the third world, but despite grave misgivings the Soviets had not given up hope, and they advised Nasser to press ahead with his industrialization drive regardless of obstacles. But it must have dawned on some Soviet economic experts by 1966 at the latest that Egypt was even less likely than Cuba (where the Soviet Union had entered into similar commitments) to attain self-sufficiency and economic independence. There was always the chance that one day Egypt would be able to put its hands on the oilfields of Arabia or Libya; seen in this light, the build-up of the army could perhaps be regarded as a productive investment.

Egypt's very weakness was its strength *vis-à-vis* the Soviet Union: it needed immediate and massive help. Had the Soviet Union refused to help, Cairo would have been compelled to turn to another big power; given the world situation in 1966–7, and above all the declining fortunes of its other protégés in the third world, Moscow simply could not afford to lose Egypt. In economic terms the alliance was a major liability, but the Soviet Union had become reconciled to the idea that in the modern world big powers had to pay a high price for political influence.

The original Soviet military agreement with Egypt, periodically reviewed, provided for the delivery of about 150 MiG 15s and 17s, some 40 Ilyushin tactical bombers, several hundred tanks, two destroyers, and three submarines. More and more sophisticated weapons were subsequently supplied, including the most modern Soviet tanks, TU-16 jet bombers, MiG 21 aircraft, Komar and Ossa rocket-vessels. Soviet commanders became frequent guests in Cairo: Marshal Grechko, Admiral Gorshkov, as well as the chiefs of staffs of the Soviet navy and air force. There was close military cooperation, and hundreds of Soviet military experts were permanently stationed in Egypt to maintain liaison and to act as advisers and instructors. There were also reports about secret treaties providing Russia with naval bases in the Mediterranean and the Red Sea, airstrips and other military installations in the Western Desert and Upper Egypt.[56] These were not military bases in the traditional sense, for this would have created political complications; there was no question of surrendering Egyptian sovereignty in peacetime. But the arrangements made it possible for the Soviet navy to refuel, to have repair work done, and to rotate crews far away from Soviet territory.

Over a decade the Egyptian armed forces had been built up by the USSR. We do not know how satisfied the Soviet military leaders were with the results of their work. They certainly regarded Egypt as the strongest military power in the area. True, there had been some warning signs, such as the failure of the Egyptian expeditionary force in the Yemen, but for a number of reasons Moscow seemed to favor Egyptian involvement in South Arabia and, having cooperated with the Egyptian army for so long, they could not fail to identify themselves with it.

Political relations between Moscow and Cairo were bedevilled by an excess of ideological analysis, and this has also, to a certain extent, affected Western writings on the subject. These investigations into ideological similarities and differences created a great deal of confusion, partly because of semantic difficulties, for 'scientific socialism' is far from having the same meaning in Cairo and Moscow. But there was also an inclination to exaggerate the importance of the ideological factor in the relations between the two countries. Soviet commentators are aware of the strong religious and national elements in the new Egyptian ideology, and have, on the whole, taken a more lenient view of these 'remnants of the past' than of the Nasserist pretensions to establish its own Arab socialist ideology. Above all, they have been unhappy about Egyptian reluctance to accept Soviet notions of class (and class struggle) and the rejection of the central concept of the dictatorship of the proletariat.[57] Soviet experts noted more in sorrow than in anger that though their Egyptian friends had somehow instinctively chosen the right path in recent years, they were still ideologically very backward, and had therefore to be closely watched.

The analysis of Soviet-Egyptian relations in terms of the class struggle and the dictatorship of the proletariat does not take one very far, for in the last resort both Soviet communism and Nasserism are two different forms of national socialism, with the former on a somewhat higher level of ideological sophistication. The dictatorship of the proletariat is a central concept in Soviet ideology, but it is hardly a reality in Soviet life. The whole discussion about the leading role of the working class (allegedly existing in Russia) as distinct from leadership by the intelligentsia and the bureaucracy (as practised in Egypt) is sterile. For the Soviet Union, like Egypt, is run by a bureaucracy consisting mainly of party officials, the 'technical intelligentsia', the army, and the secret police. What really bothered the Soviet experts was the absence of an effective state party; they had argued for a long time that the Arab Socialist Union, with its 6 million members, could not be the cadre party which Egypt, like every progressive country, needed. They had suggested that within the ASU leadership should pass to an *élitist* group; Soviet advisers had been instrumental in convening study seminars in Cairo, setting up an ideological training center, and promoting a variety of publications, including the periodical *Al Tali'a* (Vanguard).[58] All to little avail, for the ASU continued to lead a shadowy existence; important political initiatives emanated from Nasser and his inner circle, several high-ranking army officers, some technocrats, a few intellectuals, and the police and secret service chiefs. The absence of a central political party reflected, as the Russians saw it, the 'ideological weakness' of Egypt; Arab radicalism was a mood rather than a doctrine; no one could say with any certainty how it would react at a time of stress. Fifteen years earlier such an unsatisfactory state of affairs would have prevented any real alliance between the Soviet Union and a foreign country, but in the changed world of the nineteen-sixties it seemed to matter less. Egypt under Nasser had chosen the 'non-capitalist way'; the regime was opposed to the West and supported the Soviet Union, and this was the main criterion. The Soviet leaders had learned from bitter experience that ideological unity was of little benefit if the parties concerned did not also give full and active support to Soviet policies. Moscow had not been spoiled by its erstwhile allies from Tirana and Bucharest to Peking. During the Czechoslovak crisis of 1968 they were let down by most communist parties, whereas Nasser and his friends gave them much-needed support. The leaders in the Kremlin, both Khrushchev and his successors, were eminently practical men, and they drew the obvious lesson: what mattered in the last resort was unquestioning loyalty, not ideological conformity. Nasser was one of the main beneficiaries of the new polycentrism in the communist world.

The extent of Soviet responsibility for the war of 1967 and Egypt's defeat will not be altogether clear for a long time to come. It is unlikely that the Soviet Union wanted a war at that stage; on the other hand, it decisively contributed towards its outbreak through some major errors (at best) of judgment: the assumption that Nasser and the Arab leaders were satisfied with the *status quo* with regard to Israel and that therefore their bellicose speeches could be safely ignored; the belief that the great quantities of Soviet arms would be regarded as mere status symbols; the conviction that Egypt under Soviet guidance had gained much strength and that the Soviet Union would be able to control events in case of a major crisis. All these assumptions were proved wrong within a very few days in the summer of 1967; Soviet policy and Soviet prestige were affected by the Egyptian collapse and a basic reappraisal of the whole relationship with Cairo became necessary. An explanation had to be provided for the Soviet public: Egypt had been described for many years in the Soviet press as a progressive country with tremendous achievements to its credit, in contrast to Israel, ruled by a reactionary, anti-popular government and in a state of permanent crisis. Israel, needless to say, was also much the smaller country. The same correspondents and political analysts who had described Nasser's regime in glowing terms, the Beliaevs, Primakovs, and Ivanovs, cannot have found it easy to admit that something must have been radically wrong in their accounts. The official explanation was that Israel had intended by means of a surprise attack to overthrow the progressive regimes in the Arab world, but that this scheme had failed owing to the resolute stand taken by the Soviet Union.[59] Soviet commentators also mentioned the 'complicated internal political situation' in the UAR created as a result of the defeat.[60] The setback was explained by the Russians with reference to 'apostasy and treason' on the part of some high-ranking officers and of the reactionaries in general, the former landowners, sections of the petty *bourgeoisie* and the intelligentsia and, of course, the religious fanatics of the Muslim Brotherhood.[61] But this was not quite convincing. Why had the regime suffered economic and military setbacks in the first place? There were some frank articles, and one can well imagine that comment not scheduled for publication was even more outspoken. The Arab armies, it was said, had been composed largely of peasants, most of them poorly educated;[62] the officers had been self-seeking, using their privileges to improve their personal position.[63] Soviet arms and equipment had not been properly used; 'the surprise attack did not explain everything'.[64] Above all, there had not been sufficient contact between the leadership and the 'popular masses', and the demand was now voiced to purge the State apparatus of all 'reactionaries', to reorganize Egyptian political life, to give greater participation to the 'popular masses' in running the country. Soviet observers welcomed the purge of more than 600 officers and the conspiracy trials, including that of the former minister of war, Shams el Din el Badran, and Radwan, the former minister of the interior. According to the Soviet post-mortem, the Egyptian revolution had failed to change the old State machine radically, for the army officers as a 'class' had been 'susceptible to corrosion'.[65] The participation of the 'popular masses' was not, of course, meant quite literally, nor was the opposition to military men in principle. The Soviet leaders wanted above all more power for the 'Russian party' in Cairo, and the dismissal of all those who, as *Pravda* put it in February 1968, 'spread doubts about the nature of Soviet-Egyptian relations and called for a resumption of friendly relations with the United States'. The call for agreement with America was not confined (according to *Rose el-Yusef*) to the 'secret thoughts of those now behind bars, but was also heard on very different lips which voiced the spirit of defeatism and the secret desire to rob the people of their victories and to strike at socialism'.[66] The friends of Russia, men 'known for their progressive views', were Ali Sabry, Vice-President and subsequently leader of the ASU, Shaarawi Gomaa, minister of the interior, Amin Howeidi, then head of Nasser's private secret service and minister of state, Muhammad Fayek, minister of national guidance, and the Cairo ASU secretary, Abdel Magid Ferid. There were also the communist intellectuals ('progressive elements known for their Marxist views') who had been given prominent positions in press and radio and for whom

Moscow now demanded greater scope in the party apparatus.[67] Nasser's own position between these warring factions was by no means clear. The army, his traditional source of power, had lost face in the war, and he could no longer be quite certain of the loyalty of the new officers who had replaced his old comrades. The demonstrations of workers and students in February 1968 were manifestations of workers and students in February 1968 were manifestations of a serious malaise. Nasser was grateful for the 'resolute help and the tremendous efforts made by the Soviet leadership', as he put it in a cable to the Soviet Presidium.[68] But he was also aware of the growing resentment against the Soviet presence in Egypt, the almost total dependence which had resulted from his policy. Once Lord Cromer, the British Resident, had been Egypt's real ruler; Nasser's agents no doubt told him that the parallel between Lord Cromer and Vinogradow, the new Soviet ambassador, was being freely drawn in Cairo after the war. From time to time Nasser made half-hearted attempts to assert himself and to follow an independent line. The faithful Haykal launched a trial balloon in his weekly column, asking in a cautious and roundabout way for more freedom of manœuvre in Egypt's foreign policy, only to beat a hasty retreat when the Russian party counter-attacked. In an interview with an American periodical, Nasser belittled the number of Soviet military advisers ('less than a thousand' – certainly an understatement) and described his own foreign policy as non-aligned.[69] But it was perhaps symptomatic that only a heavily censored version of this interview was published in Egypt.

As Nasser reviewed the situation of his country one year after the war, he must have decided that he had no choice but to put all his hopes in the Soviet alliance. The decision cannot have been easy; it had been his great ambition to restore real independence to Egypt and for a while, during the late fifties and early sixties, he appeared to have succeeded. But he had always wanted to accomplish too much in too little time: industrialization and a social revolution in Egypt, supremacy among the Arabs, a leading role in the third world, a campaign in the Yemen, and the liberation of Palestine. After the Six Day War Egypt urgently needed economic aid, and above all it needed arms for which it could not pay. Nasser admitted as much: 'We have so far paid not one penny for the arms we obtained from the Soviet Union to equip our armed forces. Actually, were it a question of payment, we have no money to buy arms. . . .'[70]

There was no chance of receiving the aircraft and missiles free of charge from anyone but Russia. He was, of course, aware that by burning the bridges to America he weakened his bargaining position *vis-à-vis* Moscow. But he was no longer concerned about the price that would eventually have to be paid. He still maintained that there were no strings attached: 'Why does the Soviet Union give us all these things? I wish to tell you frankly and clearly that the Soviet Union has never tried, not even in the time of our greatest trials, to dictate conditions to us or to ask anything of us. . . . We went on [in Moscow] asking for hours, but they did not make one request of us. Even when I told them I felt ashamed that we were making so many demands while they had asked nothing from us . . . they told us: We take this stand on the basis of our ideology. . . . We have nothing to ask. . . .'[71] After his state visit to the USSR in 1968 he welcomed the presence of Soviet naval forces in the Mediterranean, the new shield of the 'progressive Arab states'.[72] His old friend Tito, whom he had seen on his way back, disapproved of Moscow's Mediterranean ambitions and warned him of the dangers of total dependence,[73] but Nasser, plagued by illness, was now a man near despair, talking in apocalyptic terms about a new war. He had made concession after concession to the Russians, purging the army and the State apparatus of all people considered undesirable in Moscow. One observer noted that the Arabs must have found it difficult to square these concessions with what used to be their fierce attachment to Egyptian sovereignty and independence.[74] But Nasser was now in a great hurry. His pride had been deeply wounded; everything was now to be subordinated to the coming war against Israel. There was the old problem, as Haykal wrote in August 1967 and again in July 1968, that the Soviet Union wanted to avoid a head-on collision with the United States. But this did not mean that Moscow would refrain from giving help in a coming war; if only the Arabs showed enough self-assertion, they could induce the Russians to attach more importance to the Middle East than to Vietnam. These were almost literally the same arguments the Syrians had used before the Six Day War.[75]

Russian hopes had been dimmed by the outcome of that war. Soviet visitors to Cairo discovered aspects of Egyptian life they had overlooked before: 'Here a string of young girls carrying 30 kilogram baskets of rubble on their heads runs along while an overseer chases them with a stick. Quicker! quicker! quicker! It is unbearable for a Soviet citizen to watch, but you must not interfere.'[76] Nevertheless, the Soviet Union continued to give economic help. Mazurov, a Soviet deputy prime minister, repeated at the opening of the Aswan power station in January 1968 that Soviet aid would continue until all traces of the aggression had disappeared. Moscow undertook to supply within three months 300,000 tons of wheat to help Egypt to overcome a critical shortage. Soviet work on the Helwan complex continued; it was announced that production would meet all the domestic iron and steel requirements and leave about 500,000 tons of steel for export. But the new mills were not to be completed until 1976.[77]

Of the greatest immediate importance was the military help. Even before the end of the war, on June 8, 1967, a Moscow-Cairo airbridge had been established to fly war material into Egypt. A year after the war Western specialists estimated that the Soviet Union had replaced 300 of the 365 jet fighters that had been lost, 50 of the 69 bombers, 450 of the 550 tanks; the stocks of Styx-type anti-shipping missiles were replenished and ground-to-ground missiles of the modified Kennel type with a range of 45 miles were provided for the first time, thus introducing a new element into the Middle East arms race.[78] In October 1968 the value of arms deliveries since the Six Day War was estimated at $2·5 billion.

With all that there cannot have been many illusions in Moscow about Egypt's short-term military prospects. What if, owing to Nasser's impetuosity, yet another situation developed over which the Russians would have no control? There were frequent Soviet warnings against 'rank demagogy and adventurist exhortations', usually attributed to Chinese influence in the Middle East.[79] The Soviet generals asked for, and received, a far greater say in Cairo than before the war; perhaps they thought that the mere presence of 3,000 Soviet military experts and instructors would act if necessary as an effective brake.

The question whether Nasser was expendable must have occurred more than once after the war to those responsible for Soviet Middle East policy. Moody, unpredictable, unable to fulfil his promises, he surely appeared at times a major liability to his Soviet allies. But no other Egyptian leader, certainly no member of the 'Russian party' in Cairo, enjoyed the same prestige in his country, let alone in the Arab world. Nasser was the only charismatic leader, and miraculously his prestige was not irremediably shaken by his defeat – or so it seemed.

Wider issues were also involved: given the assumption that Soviet power was to be asserted in its own backyard, support for Egypt seems in retrospect almost inevitable. But the Soviet endeavour to make Egypt a showcase for socialism was clearly based on a miscalculation; the country was too poor, nor was it well suited for a Soviet-style regime. Egypt's weakness was in some ways an asset, for it made the country permanently dependent on the Soviet Union. A defeated country was more likely to remain a faithful and loyal client than a victorious and prosperous one. With loyalty at a premium in the communist world, this was not a consideration to be ignored.

From Egypt's point of view, the interim balance was almost wholly negative. The alliance with the Soviet Union, from the original arms deal of 1955 on to 1968, was largely the work of one man. Ideologically Nasser was truly uncommitted; he belonged to the generation which, in the case of an Axis victory, would have turned with equal ease to fascism. He was a radical nationalist, not a socialist, let alone a Marxist. He could argue in his defence that Egypt's desperate poverty had left him little freedom of choice, that America made all kinds of conditions that were offensive to an Arab patriot, that Egypt's interests clashed everywhere with those of the West – in Israel, in Africa, in the Arab peninsula. The Russians regarded him as a chosen instrument; for the Americans he was at best an unfriendly neutral. They wanted him to concentrate on economic construction at home, not to make war against Israel, not to intervene in Africa, not to manufacture rockets or nuclear weapons; they tried to restrain him with regard to all the things that were dear to his heart, whereas the Russians had been in every respect far more sympathetic.

In the last resort it was a tragic story of overweening ambition. To achieve his aims, Nasser needed massive foreign help. He was forced to gamble, persuading himself and trying to convince others that they could receive such help without any loss to Egypt's independence. Persistent, clever, but lacking real wisdom and foresight, he grossly overestimated the strength of his country, its immunity to 'foreign ideas', and, in general, the significance of radical Arab nationalism in the modern world. Whenever Nasser suffered a setback during the fifteen years of his rule, he had sought shelter in closer proximity to Moscow. After 1965 many of his plans were frustrated, and the *rapprochement* seemed to have become permanent. Looking back in 1968 on his achievements and failures, and above all on the tremendous discrepancy between promise and fulfilment, Nasser must have had his moments of despair. But there was still the hope that the front of his enemies would crumble, that with one swift, masterful *coup* he would destroy them all and enter history as a great leader and liberator.

Only the future will show whether the trend of Nasser's policy, the ever-growing dependence on the Soviet Union, is reversible. Given Egypt's geographical position and the balance of power in the area which Nasser had tried so hard to upset, it is probably premature to speak about a 'point of no return'. It still depends in the last resort on the scale of priorities of Egypt's leaders. Nasser's priorities are clear and unlikely to change. Those to whom the heavy burden of succession will one day pass are not to be envied.

Syria

Summing up on Syria in 1958, I wrote that this was the most militantly anti-Western of all Arab countries and that it had moved closest to the Soviet Union. Not as the result of 'Soviet propaganda', but as the culmination of an internal radicalization.[80] After more than a decade full of dramatic events – the union with Egypt and its dissolution, *coups* and counter-*coups*, one war and innumerable war scares – there is no reason to revise and little to add to that appraisal. While refraining from open criticism, the Soviet Union had been far from enthusiastic about Syria's union with Egypt. The *World Marxist Review*, more outspoken than the Soviet press on such occasions, had called it a 'deplorable example': Syria had been subordinated to Egypt; the unity that had been imposed from above was artificial in character; Syria was ruled by undemocratic means; the Egyptian *bourgeoisie* had simply extended the sphere of its activities.[81] When Syria again became independent in September 1961, the Soviet Union was the first of the big powers to recognize the new regime.[82] The new Syrian government, headed by Mamun al-Kuzbari, favored a neutralist foreign policy, but was opposed to agrarian reform, let alone communism, which it regarded as hostile to Islam and Arab nationalism. In the elections that took place at the end of 1961 the new leaders received a comfortable majority. It seemed, as a Soviet historian noted, that everything had been put back to where it was before: the 'golden age of *bourgeois* democracy' had returned.[83] But a parliamentary majority meant little in a country lacking a democratic tradition; the new regime had powerful enemies among the intelligentsia and the army officers, especially those of the younger generation. In March 1963 the government was overthrown by a military *coup* headed by Colonel Amin el Hafiz and the leaders of the Ba'th Party. Since then and up to the time of writing the Ba'th has remained in power. But the *coup* of 1963 was by no means the last one, for the party was taken over by a new group of army officers and politicians. All the early Ba'th leaders were ousted; in 1968 that party had nothing in common but the name with the movement that had come to power five years earlier.[84] The year 1963 marked the zenith of its influence and popularity. The Ba'th is a nationalist and socialist party, with members in many Arab countries, whose origins go back to the late nineteen-thirties. In 1963 Ba'th governments came to power in both Syria and Iraq, but their leaders showed little political ability; torn by internal divisions and weakened by the refusal of the military to accept civilian leadership, they suffered almost instant eclipse. A Soviet commentator has provided a vivid, and on the whole accurate picture of conditions in Syria in 1963:

While this political merry-go-round continued, Syria presented an extraordinary spectacle: ministers and senior officials appointed to their posts exclusively on the principle of 'reliability', but often having no idea of the real situation and its economic problems, and interested only in political cabals; officers, each of them thinking that his hour would come at any moment, and that a battalion of soldiers or a dozen armored cars would be enough to seize power; journalists trying to guess who in fact would carry out the next *coup*. Plots, rumors of plots, denial of rumors of plots, suspicious troop movements. No one trusts his neighbor, everyone tries to outsmart his partner; superiors look searchingly at their subordinates: Who will be the next to strike? . . . There was a popular anecdote at the time in Damascus about an officer who came up to the headquarters building. The sentry asked what he wanted. 'To carry out a *coup d'état*.' 'Don't you know the standing orders? Wait in the queue round the corner.'[85]*

The Soviet attitude towards the old Ba'th had never been very

---

* The freshness of the comments of the writer of this account, G. Mirsky, is unfortunately not at all typical of the general level of Soviet political reportage on or analysis of the Middle East. Mirsky's articles and books, however much mistaken on occasion, often display an intelligence and originality sadly absent in most Soviet political writing.

friendly: the Ba'thists were accused of terrorism, adventurism, anti-communist propaganda: their socialism was a sham, they behaved like fascists and Spanish falangists. The frequent professions of friendship for the Soviet Union made by their leaders left Moscow unimpressed.[86] This negative communist appraisal of the Ba'th was no doubt influenced by the fact that Syria, unlike Egypt, had a fairly substantial communist party, and that the Ba'th, in contrast to the Egyptian ASU, was a cadre party with a well-defined political program. It was weaker than Nasserism and at the same time more difficult to infiltrate. The collapse of Ba'th rule in Iraq was welcomed in the Soviet Union and a similar fate was predicted for the Syrian government: 'chaos prevails in any country which the Ba'thists rule'.[87] But the Syrian Ba'th managed to cling on to power; the main struggle was fought out inside the party, between the regional (Syrian) command and its general leadership (the All-Arab National Command). The contest was mainly between the old, civilian leaders of the party (such as Salah Bitar and Michel Aflaq) and a group of young, ambitious, and radical army officers who were steadily gaining influence. The former gradually lost control, and the prime minister Amin el Hafiz, himself a military man, took a middle-of-the-road position between the two factions. Soviet observers were quick to note these developments, welcoming the victory of the 'healthy, honest, energetic, patriotic elements' over the 'treacherous, discredited clique of old-style politicians'.[88] When the Syrian government decided (in January 1965) to nationalize over a hundred companies, and when the communists were released from prison, there was a marked improvement in the Soviet attitude: 'Enthusiasm reigns in the workers' quarters of Syrian towns.'[89] The Ba'th remained 'petty *bourgeois*' as far as its class character was concerned, but it was now noted in Moscow that its slogans ('some directly borrowed from the communists') had many supporters among workers and peasants.[90] In some respects, the Ba'th program did not go far enough for Moscow; the trade unions, the communists claimed, had not been given enough authority. On the other hand, even in 1965, the Syrian communists detected a tendency towards ultra-radicalism among the left-wing Ba'th likely to antagonize the middle classes; lack of understanding of their just demands was bound to play into the hands of the reactionaries.[91]

The internal Syrian crisis reached its climax towards the end of 1965, when the regional party leadership under Salah Jadid, the army chief of staff, demanded the resignation of Amin el Hafiz. Hafiz refused to comply. According to one Soviet source, there had been a quarrel about foreign policies; according to another, Hafiz believed that the ultra-leftists would by their hasty action discredit the idea of building socialism in Syria.[92] Bitar, the main exponent of the civilian leadership, agreed to form a government on condition that the military stayed out of politics. The All-Arab Command dissolved the regional (Syrian) leadership and assumed the functions of supreme political authority in Syria. This was the eighth government since the Ba'th had come to power in 1963. It was to be as shortlived as most of its predecessors, for the military, who still wielded real power, immediately plotted its overthrow. On February 23, 1966, in the bloodiest of all *coups* so far (the eighteenth since Syria had become independent) the left-wing Ba'th returned to power; Amin el Hafiz, Bitar, and the other old party leaders were arrested. Nuredin Atassi became the new head of state and Dr Zu'ayin was made prime minister, while effective power rested in the hands of a small group of colonels. Most of the new rulers belonged to ethnic and religious minority groups, mainly the Alawites and, to a lesser extent, the Druzes and Ismailites. Soviet observers were aware of this fact and expressed some concern; they wrote that people in Syria talked too much and too easily about socialism in various parts of the world,[93] but they were agreed that, by and large, the February *coup* was not a *coup* like its predecessors, but a great progressive event, and that under the new rulers, who had declared their intention of carrying out a policy of socialist transformation, relations between Moscow and Damascus would become much closer than ever before. It was hoped in particular that the Syrian communists would soon be given an opportunity to take a leading part in the new regime.

The communists, who had been in opposition both during the Nasserist period and after 1961, were inclined to take a more critical view of the Ba'th than Moscow, but after the January 1965 decrees they modified their line. The Ba'th policy of nationalization, their Central Committee stated, was an important step forward.[94] Hints were dropped that they were ready to cooperate with the Ba'th, which would need their political know-how and particularly their ability to mobilize the masses. Above all, they could serve as a bridge to Moscow. There were, of course, conditions attached: Khalid Bakdash, one of their leaders, would have to be allowed to return from exile, and some of their representatives would have to

join the new government.[95] Negotiations between the Ba'th leaders
and the communists began in February 1965; the former, despite
their slogans about 'left-wing unity', could not reach agreement
among themselves about the measure of freedom to be given to the
communists. Eventually the Beirut communist press (*Al Nida*,
Al Akhbar) was permitted to circulate freely in Syria, but Bakdash
was allowed to return only after the February 1966 *coup*. The neo-
Ba'th, after purging many of its old members, appointed communists
to cabinet posts, but it was never quite clear how many there were,
because the communist ministers were coopted as individuals rather
than as representatives of their party. The Ba'th was reluctant
to admit that communists were now sitting in their inner councils,
denouncing the news of this fact as yet another 'imperialist provocation'. Soviet and communist spokesmen were less inhibited about
the subject and flatly announced that 'communists and members of
other progressive groups' had at last joined the Damascus government.[96]

Not all Ba'thists were happy about these developments, but they
were told by their leaders that it was a political necessity. The Ba'th
lacked a mass basis; some sources put its membership as low as
2,000, not counting several hundred army officers. It needed all the
outside support it could get. A rebuff to the communists would have
jeopardized the close contacts with Moscow. The Soviet leaders
had reservations about the neo-Ba'th, but these were outweighed
by the opportunities offered by this enthusiastic new ally. Moscow
showed immediate readiness to help : a protective screen was erected
around Syria to shield it from its enemies and detractors. Throughout 1966 and early 1967 the Soviet mass media published frequent
announcements about alleged conspiracies to overthrow the new
regime, hatched from within, in the other Arab capitals, and, needless to say, by Israel. Nasser was advised to establish close links with
the neo-Ba'th, thus ensuring the survival of the regime. The new
rulers of Syria did not make it easy for their protectors. The violent
manifestoes issued by the Syrian government, its incessant attacks
on the 'reactionary forces' in the Arab world, caused a great deal of
concern in Arab capitals and fears about a 'Soviet Cuba in the Middle
East'.[97] During the first weeks and months of the new regime the
Soviet leaders were uncertain about its chances of survival, and there
were great sighs of relief in May and June 1966, when it was reported from Damascus that the opposition was too weak and dis-

united to take any effective action against the neo-Ba'th: 'The tide was running in favor of the new government.'[98]

There was a great deal of coming and going between Damascus and Moscow after February 1966. Military contacts had existed for a long time; Mamduh Jaber, the then Syrian defence minister, had gone on an official mission to the Soviet capital in October 1964. Marshal Grechko had told him on that occasion that the Soviet Union was ready to assist Syria materially and morally to defeat imperialism and its supporters.[99] Naturally, the Syrian generals were above all interested in the material implications of this promise and discussed their shopping list in considerable detail. After the 1966 *coup* the flow of Soviet arms increased; there were unconfirmed reports that the Soviet Union had asked for two bases in exchange for the war material that was about to be supplied.[100]

Several weeks after coming to power, Prime Minister Zu'ayin went to Moscow with a request for Soviet political support. He also wanted help for the ambitious Euphrates dam project, the Syrian equivalent of the Aswan dam. It involved the building of a reservoir lake of about 350 square miles, the irrigation of some 1½m. acres of land, and the building of a huge hydro-electric complex. Politically, the project was far more problematical than the Aswan dam, for Syria had not bothered to consult Turkey and Iraq, the other riparian states. Turkey, with which Syria's relations were traditionally bad, could largely thwart the scheme by building a dam of its own, as indeed it had announced it would do. Iraq, on the other hand, was likely to suffer; a million Iraqi farmers were bound to be affected by the Syrian dam. Disregarding these objections, the Syrians went ahead with the project on the basis of a West German promise to finance and supervise the building of the dam. When Damascus broke off relations with Bonn in 1965, in protest against West Germany's recognition of Israel, it became necessary to find a new sponsor. Zu'ayin's efforts in Moscow were successful; the Soviet Union agreed to step in and to underwrite a substantial part of the project – 'a crushing blow for West Germany and Western Imperialism' as the Damascus newspapers put it.[101] The first Soviet dam experts arrived in Damascus in May 1966 to great official acclaim; the government declared that this project would be the basis of the new Syrian five-year plan: 'We are determined to build the dam, over our own bones if need be.'[102] Russia also agreed to help Syria in extending its railway network, to renovate the Homs-Aleppo line

to build a new line from Qamishli in eastern Syria to Latakia on the
Mediterranean coast, and also to provide new equipment.[103] An oil
agreement with the USSR had been signed in 1965, and in April 1966
a further Soviet offer was submitted to develop Syria's oilfields.

For a little while the Euphrates project was given so much
publicity that the impression was created (to quote a Lebanese newspaper) that the country's entire future depended on whether or not
the dam was built. There is reason to doubt whether this enthusiasm
was ever widely shared: not only was the Euphrates project much
smaller than the Aswan dam, it was also much less vital for the
country's economy. It was regarded primarily as a symbol of political
achievement of the neo-Ba'th, a group of politicians without genuine
interest in economic problems.

The future of the regime remained uncertain and the construction
of the dam was at best several years ahead; more effective slogans
were needed to mobilize the public, to dramatize the achievements of
the new regime against the 'enemies of Syria and socialism'. Soviet-
Syrian cooperation in the field of propaganda and political warfare
manifested itself in the creation and orchestration of artificial crises;
political tension was kept high for weeks on end. Sometimes the
initiative emanated from Moscow, more often from Damascus.
Every few weeks it was announced that the Israeli army, in cooperation with Jordan and Saudi Arabia, was about to attack Syria, that
the CIA and the British oil companies were hatching plots, that
Syrian reactionaries were engaged in sinister intrigues. A state-of-
siege mentality was systematically inculcated and the tone of the
official Damascus press, never a paragon of moderation and sobriety,
became quite hysterical during the summer of 1966: Syria was under
imperialist attack, the reactionaries were trying to isolate it. The
country could rely only on the Soviet Union, and (perhaps) on
Egypt.

It is not easy to establish in retrospect with any degree of accuracy
how much of this was deliberately fabricated and how much was
genuinely believed by the instigators. The apprehensions of the neo-
Ba'th were not entirely unjustified; the hold of the regime was
precarious, the measures taken against the middle classes and the
Islamic clergy diminished what popularity it had. Even the communists admitted that, in hastily nationalizing some small enterprises,
the cart had been put before the horse. Khalid Bakdash found it
necessary to reassure the small shopkeepers: they would be defended

against all those who stood to the left of the communist party.[104] No doubt there were plots against the neo-Ba'th, but the more serious ones came from inside the regime, such as the conspiracy of Colonel Selim Hatoum. He had played the leading role in the February *coup*, but subsequently quarrelled with his colleagues, escaped to Jordan, returned to Damascus during the Six Day War, and was executed by his captors. Hatoum was accused by Damascus and Moscow of having been an agent of both China and the CIA. The truth was less complicated: Hatoum had suffered defeat in a struggle for power in which ideology played only a secondary role.

Among the men who had come to power after February 1966 there were several radical socialists, such as the trade union leader Khaled el Jundi, who was arrested after the Six Day War. But for most of the new leaders, especially the army officers, the fashionable socialist phraseology was little more than a smokescreen behind which an unceasing struggle for power and personal aggrandizement went on. Despite the revolutionary slogans, the attachment of these men to the cause of socialism (let alone 'revolutionary democracy') was more than a little suspect: they were riding high on what they thought was the wave of the future. Arab socialists outside Syria were at first perplexed; by backing the neo-Ba'th, the Soviet Union was pursuing a policy that was not based on either moral or revolutionary principles, for these individuals were 'known opportunists'; in respect to the Ba'th, most of them were transients, who had neither shared in the party struggle nor adhered to its ideology.[105] That the new leaders had been disloyal to the traditional Ba'th ideology was not Moscow's concern; the decisive question was whether they would be loyal to their new partners. There could be no certainty on this count in Moscow, where at times misgivings were expressed about the boastfulness of the neo-Ba'th, its lack of moderation and its instability. But the Russians could not hope to educate their new allies within a short period; at most they could act as a realistic and moderating influence and keep some control by means of frequent consultations and meetings. There were many such contacts between the Syrian and Soviet leaders during the months preceding the Six Day War. Hafiz el Asad, the Syrian war minister, went to Moscow, as did the other strong man of the junta, Salah Jadid, heading a Ba'th party delegation in January 1967. This was a real innovation, for up to that date all contacts between Moscow and the Arab governments had been on the government level. The Soviet representatives noted (to quote the official communiqué) the importance of the progressive measures carried out by the Ba'th party in Syria which opened up socialist prospects for the country's development.[106] But in fact the Ba'th leadership was, not to mince words, less interested in the 'socialist transformation of Syrian society' than in the perpetuation of its own rule and in an activist foreign policy. For a long time Syria had been the most militant Arab country in its attitude towards Israel, outdoing the other Arab governments in its insistence on immediate war. It had been the chief base from which the Arab guerrillas staged their raids into Israel. This, and the dispute about the Jordan waters, had been the sources of permanent tension between Israel and Syria. Successive Ba'th governments had failed to gain the support of the other Arab countries for a combined attack on Israel, and the neo-Ba'th government was even less likely to receive support for the proposal, in view of its violent campaigns against the 'reactionary' Arab countries. But it did not desist from its policy and the Soviet leaders had to decide how far to go in their support. Moscow gave Damascus full diplomatic assistance, making solemn declarations that the Soviet Union would not remain indifferent to any attempt to violate peace in a region in direct proximity to its borders.[107] But such promises, far from restraining the Damascus junta, contributed to further tension in the area. The neo-Ba'th leaders thought that with Soviet backing they could pursue even more militant policies. Nor did the defence agreement with Egypt signed in December 1966 have a salutary effect (Kosygin was said to have helped to bring about this reconciliation between Damascus and Cairo); the new guarantee made them only more inclined to undertake aggressive policies.

The leaders of the neo-Ba'th played a fateful role in the events preceding the Arab-Israeli war: the battle at Lake Tiberias in early April 1967, the new wave of Fatah attacks, the internal crisis in Syria culminating in yet another campaign against the 'reactionaries', and ultimately the war scare, were designed to help the neo-Ba'th junta to overcome their internal difficulties.[108] In this they succeeded, but at what a price! The war-scare made war a reality; the baseless rumor that fifteen Israeli brigades were about to attack Syria precipitated Egypt's mobilization. In the war that followed Syria did not acquit itself very well; after the bombastic speeches of Zu'ayin and the other leaders, the hasty retreat from their impregnable positions on the Golan heights came as a shock. One reason for the defeat was the withdrawal of many units from the front line to strengthen internal security – the Syrian leaders were more worried about the enemy within than about the Israelis. Their caution in a way paid off, for during the first year after the war there was no serious challenge to their power, despite the army's dismal performance. The opposition was still ineffective; the government ruled with an iron hand, giving internal security absolute priority in all its political activities. The Syrian army assumed most of the functions of the political police. As plots from within remained the main danger to the regime, frequent purges were carried out in both the army and civilian circles. Immediately after the war ended the Soviet leaders assured Damascus of their continuing support: Podgorny's visit to Damascus and Zu'ayin's trip to Moscow were part of these emergency consultations. Later, in March 1968, Marshal Grechko went to Syria to coordinate military ties between the two countries, and a neo-Ba'th delegation went again to Moscow for 'ideological discussions'.[109] But while the Soviet press expressed admiration for the brave stand of the Syrians against the Israeli aggressors, the Russians were more than a little irritated with their impulsive allies, who had involved them in an adventure over which the senior partner in the alliance had lost control. Soviet commentators reporting from Damascus complained about the Syrian ultra-leftists with their suicidal plan of a new people's war, even if that involved Israeli occupation of still more Arab territory.[110] On various occasions Syria's unwillingness to collaborate with the other Arab countries was criticized; so was its opposition to the Security Council resolution of November 22, 1967, and the refusal to enlarge the government and establish a popular front. The new appointments made in Damascus inspired little confidence in Moscow. The new Syrian chief of staff was Mustafa Tlas, a theoretician of guerrilla warfare and translator of Che Guevara, not one of Moscow's favorite revolutionary heroes. When the Ba'th leaders met Brezhnev and his colleagues early in 1967, and again in summer 1968, it was stated in the joint communiqué that the exchange of opinions demonstrated that both parties held 'similar or identical views' on world affairs.[111] Yet both sides were no doubt aware that this statement was only half true. Despite all protestations to the contrary, ideology played a lesser role in Syrian politics than, say, in China or Cuba, and Syria found it therefore much easier to accommodate itself to the Soviet Union, provided that Soviet help was forthcoming. It needed a protector and it had something to offer in return. Syria was a country with many natural resources, even though under the rule of Nasser and the Ba'th the Syrian economy had declined. As a field for large-scale Soviet investment and a potential showcase for both the achievements of communism and the advantages of Soviet help, Syria was a somewhat more promising choice than Egypt. But the neo-Ba'th had no real sound basis; the regime was thoroughly unpopular; there was not one leader even remotely comparable in stature and mass appeal to Nasser. Its radicalism, coupled with the traditional Syrian xenophobia, made a reconciliation with the West unlikely, but it did not necessarily make them trustworthy allies. The events leading up to the Arab-Israeli war in 1967 had shown that the Syrian rulers were uncontrollable, their record on the home front had demonstrated that their radicalism was largely verbal, and that under their leadership Syria was unlikely to make much progress. In Syria the Soviet Union had found a promising but highly problematical ally; the problems were different in character but no less grave than those facing Egypt. The regime was ruling through fear; its overthrow was likely to lead to violence and counter-terror, similar to the events in Baghdad in 1963. Deeply committed to the neo-Ba'th, the Soviet Union followed events in Syria with much concern.*

Iraq

The overthrow of the monarchy in 1958 marks the great divide in recent Iraqi history. General Abdel Karim Kassem, the military dictator who succeeded the Hashemites, cooperated closely with the communists; within a few months they became one of the country's strongest political forces. Many key positions passed into their hands, including, to all intents and purposes, the revolutionary tribunal under Colonel Mahdawi, set up to carry through a large-scale purge in the country.[112]

* Within the neo-Ba'th there were differences of opinion about the extent of the collaboration with the Soviet Union. Some leaders favoured total submission; others were for an independent pro-Soviet line. The former, headed by prime minister Zu'ayin, were defeated in October 1968 by the faction led by Hafiz el Asad, minister of defence. The charges against Zu'ayin were that he had removed members of the about it. The demonstrative visit of a Syrian military delegation in Peking in spring 1969 was another manifestation of Syrian dissatisfaction with the extent of Soviet help.

Major and minor public figures suspected of lack of enthusiasm for the new regime were imprisoned, and many were executed, with or without the benefit of a trial. 1959 was later remembered in Iraq as the 'Year of the Red Terror'; the country seemed to be on the verge of a communist take-over. But communist strength was not so formidable as it appeared; the party leadership, as one of its main figures later admitted, was too young, without experience or theoretical training, and the party as a whole had grown too fast.[113] Kassem, while using the communists, had no intention of allowing them to dictate his policy. Gradually the communists' power was curtailed, and once it emerged that they were not after all going to rule the country, the party had to pay the price for the terrorist excesses that had been committed at its instigation. The communists had made a basic political mistake: they had tried to settle accounts with their enemies without being able to carry the job through to the end. After 1959 their fortunes began to decline. Through the new 'Association Law', Kassem prevented the legalization of the Communist party, recognizing instead a totally unrepresentative rival group led by Daoud al-Sa'igh; the real party (*Itihad al Sha'b*) became illegal. The communist press was banned and the many front organizations came under attack in October 1960.[114] One by one the key positions in the various political and social organizations that had mushroomed after July 1958 under communist guidance were lost to the party – the associations of teachers, journalists, peasants, and women, as well as the General Federation of Trade Unions (May 1961); they kept their hold on the students union only for a little longer. Since the communists had acquired their positions not by democratic means, but by packing meetings with non-professional elements, it proved surprisingly easy to replace them with supporters of the regime.[115] Many individual communists were arrested in connection with the terrorist excesses that had been committed. Speaking at the congress of the CPSU in October 1961, Salim Adil (*alias* Husain Radawi), the Iraqi party's first secretary, said that 112 communists or pro-communists had been sentenced to death and 770 to imprisonment by military courts, mainly for their part in the Kirkuk disturbances and other riots in 1959.[116] Two years later Salim Adil was himself executed. By November 1960 the last communist supporters had been removed from the government on charges either of deviationism or of incompetence. Mahdawi's People's Court ceased to function, and by early 1961 there was talk that the communists might again have to go underground.[117]

The gradual decline of communist power was a great disappointment to the Soviet Union. During 1958 and 1959 Iraq had been the most promising Arab country, much more so than Nasser's Egypt. Diplomatic ties between Moscow and Baghdad were restored almost immediately after the revolution of July 1958 and the Soviet Union offered to assist the Kassem regime in every possible way. In March 1959 Iraq was granted a development loan of $500m. for a period of six years, to finance fourteen big industrial projects, including a steel mill and several factories. Soviet engineers were to work on a new Baghdad-Basra standard-gauge railway (involving another $180m. loan). The Soviet Union also undertook to improve lands in southern Iraq and navigation on the two main rivers, and to install an atomic reactor in Baghdad.[118] Soviet military aid given to Iraq was estimated at $120m. by April 1960.[119] The Soviet media refrained from attacking Kassem even after he had turned against the communists, but continued to praise the Iraqi revolution. Baghdad had become an 'important source' from which Arab fighters for freedom were seeking material and moral help: a complete phase in the Arab national movement had ended and a new one had opened.[120] Relations with Baghdad remained cordial even after the communists had been removed from key positions. Anastas Mikoyan, accompanied by the minister for foreign trade, visited Baghdad in April 1960 and announced that the Soviet Union had now both economic and military superiority over the West, and that it was ready to share its achievements with Iraq.[121] In September 1960 the Iraqi chief of staff, General Abdi, went on a prolonged visit to Moscow; so did Mahdawi and the Iraqi minister of education. Kassem declared on many occasions that, though no communist himself, he wanted to be on friendly terms with the communist world and needed its support.[122] Having removed the immediate threat of a communist take-over, he had no desire to destroy the party altogether, for he was aware that he might still need it against his many foes, such as the Nasserists and the Ba'thists. Many of the death sentences imposed on communists by military courts were not carried out.

Up to 1960 Kassem's foreign policy had been orientated towards the Soviet Union; the bitterness of the attacks in the official press against 'Western imperialism' easily surpassed even Egypt's anti-American and anti-British campaign. During 1960 there was a marked change; relations with the Western powers improved, and Kassem and the Baghdad press began to stress Iraq's neutrality; there was occasional criticism of the Soviet Union, even at the time of Mikoyan's visit. The following year the pendulum again swung in the opposite direction: Kassem blamed Britain, not the Soviet Union, for the Kurdish rising (of which more below) and he also invited British resistance when staking his claim to Kuwait. For the difficulties encountered in the negotiations with the Iraq Petroleum Company also Britain was blamed, all of which impelled him to look for a new *rapprochement* with Moscow. Trade between Iraq and the Soviet Union continued to expand: the share of the Soviet bloc countries in Iraq's foreign trade rose from 17% in 1960 to 21% the year after; a new cultural agreement was signed and military collaboration continued.

After two years of Kassem's rule the first flush of pro-Iraqi enthusiasm in Moscow had passed, as the limitations of the regime became painfully obvious. There was growing criticism of the persecution of 'patriots and democratic elements' in Iraq; one Soviet periodical wrote that the streets of Baghdad were 'red with their blood', that a wave of reactionary poison was spreading, that the dregs of society had again crawled out from dark corners and gateways.[123] There was Soviet criticism of the Iraqi agricultural reform, which, it was argued, was proceeding far too slowly, of the hostile attitude towards the Soviet Union on the part of some Iraqi newspapers, of the tendency to appease the Western powers.[124] But on the whole such criticism was still muted and infrequent; it cannot be even remotely compared with the intensity of the attacks directed against Kassem's successors in 1963. The Soviet leaders clearly had not written off Kassem entirely, the tacit assumption being that he was, like Nasser, unpredictable, and that while keeping him at a certain distance, nothing should be done to cause a final break. Kassem's growing isolation, the ridiculous cult around his personality, the nonsensical political schemes emanating from his government, made it virtually certain that the days of the regime were numbered. But the communists, even while persecuted by the government, could not afford to dissociate themselves from Kassem altogether; later on they were to claim that it was a wicked slander to suggest that they had ever supported Kassem: they had been ('as everyone knew') the most consistent fighters against his dictatorship. But in fact they had collaborated closely with Kassem during the early phase of his rule, and they had every reason to be afraid of his overthrow, since they were too weak to succeed him themselves. The massacres of 1959 had left deep scars; many people were only waiting for the hour of retaliation and Kassem's pan-Arab rivals happened to be the communists' worst enemies. Much as they had come to dislike and to despise Kassem, the communists had a vested interest in the continuation of his reign.

The Kurdish Problem

The Kurdish issue made it increasingly difficult for the Soviet Union to persist in its attitude of low-key, distant benevolence *vis-à-vis* the regime. For the Kurds were not just an internal Iraqi problem that could be ignored by outsiders; once open warfare had broken out between them and the Baghdad government, the Soviet Union was bound to become involved.[125] There are substantial Kurdish minorities in Iran and Turkey; more than 1 million of them live in Iraq, mainly in the Sulaimaniya and Arbil districts, but also in the region of Mosul and Kirkuk. Individual Kurds suffered no discrimination in Iraq; indeed, some of them rose to leading positions in the State. But there was marked reluctance on the part of the Iraqi authorities to make concessions to the Kurds as a minority, let alone to recognize them as a separate nation, and the more pan-Arab the Iraqi government of the day, the less likely it was to accede to Kurdish demands. A major Kurdish rising had taken place in 1943 under the leadership of Mullah Mustafa Barazani, the head of the Barazani tribes; in October 1945 he crossed with his men into Persian Kurdistan, where, under Soviet auspices, a Kurdish republic was established at Mahabad. The political basis of this republic was the Democratic Party of Kurdistan (DPK), a popular front consisting of various left-wing nationalist bodies and the Kurdish communists.[126]

After the withdrawal of the Soviet troops from Iran this republic collapsed and Mullah Mustafa, who had established an alliance with the DPK, crossed with his men into the Soviet Union, where they remained for more than a decade. After the revolution of 1958 they returned to Iraq and were warmly welcomed by Kassem, but within a year it appeared that the hopes of the Kurds for national self-determination were not likely to be fulfilled; tension rose and in 1961 sporadic clashes occurred between the Barazani tribes and

Iraqi forces. Kassem at this stage decided to support those Kurdish tribes which resented the ascendancy of the Barazanis, and there ensued a period of intertribal warfare in which the DPK and the Barazanis defeated their opponents. By September 1961 this had turned into a full-scale rising; the insurgents seized many police posts in north Iraq and several cities were firmly in their hands. Government troops staged a counter-offensive and bombed Kurdish villages. But access to the mountainous strongholds of the Kurds, difficult enough in summer, proved impossible in winter, and the main body of the insurgents was undefeated. The government has not succeeded in reimposing full control ever since, and a state of intermittent warfare has continued, involving at times up to two-thirds of the Iraqi army.

The Kurdish rising posed a difficult choice for the Soviet Union, and even more so for the Iraqi communists. Whereas the Kurdish communists gave qualified support to Barazani, Iraqi communists urged Kurds and Arabs to join forces in the struggle against imperialist plots aimed at the disruption of the nationalist ranks. The secession of Kurdistan from Iraq and the scheme to establish a Kurdish government was in communist eyes an imperialist plot. The Iraqi Communist Party announced at the time that while supporting the right of the Kurds to self-determination, it opposed both pan-Arab chauvinism and extreme nationalist tendencies among the Kurds.[127] But this line was by no means clear and consistent; while they were still hoping for a reconciliation with Kassem they tended to cold shoulder the Kurds. When the persecution of the party became more intense they expressed support for the just demands of the DPK and denounced the Baghdad government for 'savagely attacking' the Kurds.[128] In a resolution adopted in March 1962 the Iraqi communists reiterated their support for Kurdish autonomy within the Iraqi state. But, as one commentator added, the realization of this immediate aim did not affect the legal right of the Kurds to press for the establishment of an independent Kurdish state, to include the Kurds of Turkey and Iran as well. Meanwhile, there could be no doubt that autonomy for the Iraqi Kurds would have wide repercussions among the Kurds in the neighboring countries and thus give additional impetus to the struggle against CENTO and other imperialist plots.[129] For years the Iraqi communists tried to steer a difficult middle course between Kassem, Arab nationalism, and the Kurdish independence movement.

Soviet policy followed similar lines; at first the Kurdish rising was not even reported in the press. Kassem exonerated the Soviet Union *expressis verbis* from any complicity in the rising, putting all the blame on Western imperialism. After Kassem's fall in June 1963 a new major campaign was launched against the Kurds, and now, with the total suppression of communism in Iraq and the deterioration in Soviet-Iraqi relations, Soviet reticence gave way to warm support for the Kurdish cause. The Soviet delegation raised the issue in the United Nations; according to the accounts by Soviet observers, the 'fascist clique in Baghdad was perpetrating genocide'; crimes against humanity were being committed in Kurdistan; more than 200 villages had been destroyed, and thousands killed in the napalm bombings.[130] In an official declaration dated July 9, 1963, the Soviet government announced that it regarded the campaign against the Kurds as a threat to peace, especially in view of the fact that the fighting was taking place near the Soviet border, in an area which 'the imperialists would like to use for an attack against our country'.[131]

The Ba'th government which had been responsible for the Kurdish campaign of 1963 was overthrown in November of that year and General Arif stopped the war in February 1964. But not for long; in the spring of the following year fighting broke out again; the Baghdad press, which had first denied these reports as foreign fabrications, then argued that the government was only exercising its natural right to destroy the rebel bands.[132] Soviet commentators noted on various occasions that neither the DPK nor Barazani wanted to secede from Iraq; that they stood for a reasonable and peaceful solution of the Kurdish problem within the framework of a progressive policy for Iraq.[133] 'Even if the Iraqi government asked us to separate, we would not agree,' Barazani is said to have told a Soviet correspondent. On other occasions the Soviet press criticized 'extremist circles' among the Kurds which were stubbornly resisting a peaceful solution, thus 'objectively helping to prolong the war' with their unrealistic demands.[134] The Kurdish issue was a thorny problem for all concerned, and the efforts of Prime Minister Bazzaz in 1966 to find a settlement evoked some sympathy in Moscow. A new truce (the third) was eventually signed in June 1966; Bazzaz solemnly declared that the problem could be solved only by full recognition of all Kurdish national rights. The Soviet Union welcomed this step, stressing that the just demands of nearly a quarter of the country's population had to be fulfilled.[135] But the Bazzaz government was overthrown before it could carry out its promises, and by September 1966 the Iraqi communists were noting that government policy had scarcely changed: the army was still in Kurdistan, economic sanctions had not been fully lifted, many Kurdish nationalists were still in prison.[136] They announced that they were supporting the Kurdish national leadership, despite the fact that they were no longer part of it. When it was clear in March 1967 that the government did not intend to carry out the policy outlined by Bazzaz, the communists called on the democratic forces in Kurdistan and its armed units (known as the Peshmerga Army) not to surrender their arms. Not that the Kurds had intended to do so anyway.[137] Communist influence had decreased among the Kurds over the years, partly because of what Kurdish nationalists considered merely 'lukewarm communist support' for their cause, partly as the result of unending internal splits and dissensions within the communist ranks. Over the years many issues had divided them – whether the party organization in Kurdistan should be dissolved and become part of the Popular Front, how closely they were to co-operate with Barazani, whether they were to keep their ties with the DPK, and what their attitude was to be *vis-à-vis* Bazzaz. The prestige of the party and its political effectiveness was seriously affected by these splits and the quarrels between the communists and the Kurdish leadership.[138]

Iraqi attempts to pacify the Kurds continued both before and after the *coup* of July 1968, but a lasting solution was unlikely to be found under a regime that put Pan-Arabism first. From the Soviet point of view, and for the Iraqi communists, this conflict constituted both a challenge and a source of weakness. As in most other Middle East national clashes (excepting only the Arab-Israeli conflict), the Soviet Union was reluctant to give total support to one side, but anything less than full support was unlikely to reap political gains.

After Kassem

The overthrow of Kassem in February 1963 had been a major set-back for the USSR. His domestic policy was criticized in Moscow more outspokenly after his fall than before: the 'cult of personality', the arbitrary rule, and above all the 'rejection of support by the progressive forces'. But Soviet commentators insisted even after his

fall that in foreign affairs Kassem had on the whole followed an
'anti-imperialist course'.[139] The policy of the Ba'th which had come
to power in February was viewed with grave concern; all those who
had been persecuted in the early years of the Kassem regime welcomed the opportunity to get even with their tormentors, and a new
wave of terror erupted. Leading communists were brought to trial
and sentenced to death, many more were lynched by the National
Guard. The Soviet press denounced the terrorist methods of the
new ('fascist') government, while the Iraqi press retaliated by
attacking 'Muscovite imperialism' and the 'hangmen of the Soviet
people'.[140] The Ba'th regarded this settling of accounts with the
communists as an internal affair; if the Soviet Union chose to interfere in Iraq's domestic politics, relations between the two countries
were bound to deteriorate, but this would not be Iraq's fault.[141]

There is no saying how far this crisis would have gone but for the
new *coup* on November 18, 1963, which brought General Abdel
Salam Arif to power. His regime was far less ideological in character
than the Ba'th; the execution of communists ceased and an attempt
was made to normalize relations with the Soviet Union. In December
1963 the Soviet ambassador was told by the new Iraqi foreign minister that he hoped the strained relations between the two countries
were a thing of the past.[142] The Arif dictatorship promulgated several
nationalization decrees affecting Iraqi and foreign banks and also
certain major industrial enterprises. The Soviet Union and the Iraqi
communists welcomed these steps, while noting that they were less
far-reaching than the Egyptian nationalization policy.[143] There was
faint Soviet praise for the liberal views of Abdel Rahman Bazzaz,
the first civilian prime minister for many years, who promised
elections and tried to reduce the influence of army officers in the
government.[144] The communists were less forthcoming and criticized Bazzaz's 'contradictory and suspect' policies; while the Soviet
Union praised Bazzaz's Kurdish policy, the Iraqi communists continued to oppose it.[145] But with all their criticism and the complaints
about the undemocratic nature of the regime and the fate of arrested
party members, they thought Arif's rule greatly preferable to that of
the Ba'th. They expressed their willingness to cooperate with the
Arab Socialist Alliance (the new state party) despite the fact that
they thought it would 'hold in check the contradictions among the
nationalist forces'.[146] Soviet economic and military support continued: by 1966 economic help was extended to thirty-seven different

projects, including work on the Baghdad-Basra Railway. Under the 1967 cultural agreement fifty Iraqi university graduates were to be trained in the Soviet Union, and Soviet professors and researchers worked at Baghdad University.

Among the many visits of Iraqi politicians to Moscow, that of Prime Minister Bazzaz (July 1966), the Iraqi defence minister, and Adnan Pachachi, the foreign minister (April 1967) deserve mention. The acting chief of staff, Major-General Abdel Rahman Arif, was on a mission to Moscow in April 1966 when the news of the death of his brother, the President, reached him. He returned at once to become Iraq's new chief of state. The second Arif was a weak and irresolute man, always inclined to postpone a decision on important problems and to steer a middle course between radicals and conservatives in the Arab world. Naji Talib and Taher Yahia, his prime ministers, proved equally ineffectual, and there were repeated charges of corruption against the government. The communists soon began to predict a new *coup* and an attempt to get rid of Arif, 'whom even his cronies do not consider fit to be president'.[147] The *coup* came two years later; it was carried out not by the Nasserists (as the communists had predicted), but by Baqr, Amash, and Takriti, the Ba'th generals who had been the stalwarts of the anti-Kassem movement in 1963. There was a growing discrepancy between the Soviet attitude towards the Iraqi government and the stand of the Iraqi communists. Despite occasional criticism, Soviet commentators put the stress on the achievements of the regime, on the fact that almost three-quarters of Iraqi industry had been nationalized, on the curtailment of the monopoly of the Iraq Petroleum Company, and, of course, on the Soviet-Iraq oil agreement.[148] Moscow's attitude was not nearly so warm and friendly as towards Syria and Egypt, but the normalization of relations was noted with satisfaction.

The Iraqi communists, on the other hand, continued to attack the regime with great bitterness, not only because of the continued arrest of some of their comrades,[149] but in protest against the 'reactionary, anti-democratic, treacherous' character of the regime in general. The third Iraqi Communist party conference, meeting in January 1968, denounced the 'evil regime' that had caused the imprisonment, death, or dismissal from army ranks of thousands of efficient officers and soldiers, and had sent only token units into the war against Israel.

It expressed equally strong opposition to the deals with French and Italian oil firms and the arms agreement with France. On several occasions in 1966–7 the communist leaders declared that their party would in future follow a revolutionary policy aiming at the overthrow of the Arif regime.[150] This kind of propaganda shed doubt on Soviet professions of friendship; when challenged on this, the official explanation was that the Soviet Union did not bear responsibility for individual communist parties. But in this particular case the explanation did not stand up to examination, for the communist radio broadcasts (*Voice of the Iraqi People*) from which the revolutionary appeals emanated was stationed in Bulgaria. Early in 1968 it was announced that this station would close down, officially on the ground that the traitors who had carried out the 1963 *coup* had destroyed each other and that the Iraqi Communist party had regained its strength.[151] The real reasons were no doubt somewhat more complicated. It was Soviet policy to remain on reasonably good terms with Arif while he was in power, and even his successors were given the benefit of the doubt; the Iraqi Ba'th party had, according to the Soviet press, improved since 1963; it now included new people among its leaders, and the war against the Kurds had been called off.[152]

Soviet long-term policy *vis-à-vis* Iraq had gradually come to resemble that pursued *vis-à-vis* Turkey and Iran: the main aim was to neutralize what had once been the West's northern tier. This could be best achieved by expanding trade relations with these countries, by cooperation in the military field, and, as far as possible, by refraining from polemics. The Iraqi communists were left to fend for themselves in a political constellation that was not unpromising for them. The weakness of the regime, the frequent changes, and the continuing instability in Baghdad helped to create a political climate conducive to a new and perhaps more effective communist bid for power.

Yemen and South Arabia

At the end of the nineteen-fifties the Yemen was still one of the most backward countries in the world. Its ruler, Imam Ahmad, and a small group of the Sayyids (members of the Zaydi sect) literally owned the country, and the main aim of their despotic rule was to perpetuate the existing state of affairs. The economic situation was slowly deteriorating; religious obscurantism effectively barred any progress. It seemed an unlikely ally for the 'progressives' in the Arab world, but its geographical position at the junction of the Red Sea and the Indian Ocean, and the fact that the old Imam was anti-British, qualified the country for membership in the national liberation movement. The Russians, too, were trying to gain influence there; a treaty of friendship between the Yemen and the USSR was signed in 1955, and a trade agreement the year after. Al Badr, the Crown Prince, visited the Soviet Union in 1956, and the Soviet press waxed enthusiastic about the traditional bonds of friendship between the two countries. The late Imam Yahya was praised as a patriotic leader, and the modesty of the Crown Prince's residence was contrasted favorably with the luxurious palaces of other Arab rulers.[153]

Russian engineers began work on the construction of Hodeida harbor, which was completed in 1961; considerable quantities of Soviet arms were sold to the Yemen by the Soviet Union. These included T34 tanks as well as other armour, old-fashioned (Yak 11) aircraft, field and anti-aircraft guns. Military instructors and advisers were provided to teach the 'Victorious Royal Regular Army' (to give it its official name) parachuting and other arts of modern warfare. Soviet leaders assured the regime of their moral support in the conflict with the British over Aden. Egypt's relations with the Yemen were even closer, and for a brief period the Yemen formally became part of the United Arab Republic.

Intense opposition to the regime was widespread, and it was only the masterful personality of Imam Ahmad – skilled in maintaining a balance between the disruptive forces and inspiring a mythical fear in his subjects – which held together the disintegrating fabric of the archaic body politic.[154] He died in September 1962; his son and successor, Al Badr, was overthrown a fortnight later. He was succeeded by a republican regime headed by Abdullah as Sallal, which carried out some overdue reforms, but remained unpopular and found itself unable to impose its authority on the country. Egypt dispatched both experts and regular troops to help Sallal, and to gain a foothold on the peninsula, but the Egyptian expeditionary corps made a poor showing; it was bogged down in the difficult mountainous regions of the country, where its technical superiority could not be developed, while the loyalist tribes led by the Crown Prince conducted successful guerrilla operations against the invaders. What had begun as intertribal war soon turned into a general offensive against the Egyptian occupation. The republican regime was recognized by Washington, whereas Britain preferred to await the outcome of the struggle. Saudi Arabia provided help for the Royalists, though not on so lavish a scale as Nasser's support for the Republicans. The Soviet Union was among the first to recognize the Republican regime, and a Soviet spokesman later declared that the supply of Soviet weapons as well as the help extended by the Egyptian army had 'played an important part in strengthening the republicans against the forces of reaction'.[155] Soviet engineers were building an airport at Al-Rahaba, and Soviet technicians were maintaining Soviet tanks and jet fighters stationed in the Yemen. There were no official reports from Moscow about the Soviet engagement in South Arabia; while it frequently attacked foreign imperialist intervention in the Yemen, the Soviet press was reluctant to reveal details about Moscow's role in the conflict. Needless to say, claims by Yemeni Royalist forces to have shot down Soviet planes were not confirmed in Moscow. But there could be no doubt about the growing Soviet interest in the Yemen: Prime Minister Sallal returned from a visit to Moscow in March 1964 with an agreement on economic and technical cooperation and an aid program. The reclamation of desert for farmland was envisaged as well as the construction of roads and the building of various factories. As the Republicans failed to assert themselves, Soviet writers, betraying their disappointment, noted that with the exception of a few 'patriotic officers' there was no one who could be relied upon; the masses had no political education, political parties did not exist, and the rich merchants ('more interested in building villas, nightclubs, and swimming pools than schools and hospitals') were still the mainstay of the Republican regime.[156]

The civil war in the Yemen, which petered out towards the end of 1968, claimed hundreds of thousands of victims and caused a great deal of destruction. Despite the use of napalm and poison gas, the Egyptians and the republican forces failed to win a decisive victory against the Royalists. The Egyptian expeditionary corps had to be constantly reinforced to prevent a military catastrophe, and the war gradually became a major burden on Egypt's economy. Its political and psychological effects were equally disastrous. The Egyptians and the Sana government put the blame for their lack of success on 'Saudian gold' and imperialist machinations; the more realistic Soviet writers, on the other hand, held that the continued resistance of the Imam's supporters had to be attributed to the loyalty of the backward Yemeni tribes to their religious leader. For both political and military reasons, the Soviet leaders pressed for the establishment of a strong Yemeni army, but Nasser opposed any such scheme, as well as direct Soviet arms deliveries to Sana, in which he saw a potential threat to Egypt's influence in South Arabia.[157] It was realized earlier in Moscow than in Cairo and Sana that the Republicans could not hope to achieve a decisive victory and the Russians therefore recommended a negotiated peace. A cease-fire agreement was signed in November 1963, followed by peace talks in Alexandria in September 1964 and again in August 1965, when Nasser and King Faisal concluded an agreement covering the settlement of the conflict. But neither this nor the subsequent negotiations at Khartoum and Beirut in 1967–8 brought an end to the civil war. While pledging full support for the Republican regime, Moscow did not refrain from criticizing the 'extremists' in Sana, who by their unrealistic demands and adventurist actions were damaging their cause and playing into the hands of the imperialists.[158] This referred *inter alia* to the refusal of the Republicans to negotiate with members of the Yemeni royal family. Nor did the Russians accept the rosy picture of the military situation painted by Sana as the war went into its sixth year. A juxtaposition of Yemeni and Soviet announcements in December 1967 and January 1968 makes interesting reading. While President Irani announced that calm had returned, Moscow reported a new Royalist counter-offensive. When the Yemeni minister of the interior declared that the situation in the Sana sector was extremely reassuring, Tass countered with a declaration that the situation continued to deteriorate.[159]

After the Six Day War Egypt was no longer in a position to keep its expeditionary force in the Yemen, and the troops were withdrawn. This resulted, not surprisingly, in the fall of Sallal in November 1967. He was replaced by a three-man Presidential Council of moderate Republicans. As the last Egyptians left Sana in December 1967 there was an excellent chance for the Royalists to make good their promise to take the capital within a few days of the Egyptians' withdrawal, but they encountered stiffer resistance than expected, and their assault failed. The Royalist leadership was inept, and in this critical situation the Republican regime received further military help from the Soviet Union, and to a lesser extent from China, Algeria, and Syria. In an emergency airlift in November and December 1967, the Soviet Union ferried about 10,000 tons of equipment to Hodeida airfield within three weeks.[160] It supplied one squadron of MiG 19s, as well as Ilyushins, complete with ground crews and instructors, while Syria provided most of the pilots. There were also volunteers from the National Liberation Front, the party now governing the new South Yemen People's Republic. But once the immediate danger to the capital had been averted, the Republicans began again to fight among themselves. There were artillery duels in the centre of Sana in August 1968, and so far as control over the countryside was concerned, the issue largely boiled down to who paid most, and to whom.[161] After six years of a cruel and destructive civil war which had seen foreign intervention on a massive scale, an uneasy peace returned to the Yemen.

The situation in South Arabia had been confused enough throughout the fifties and sixties; with the retreat of the British from Aden and the South Arabian Federation it became altogether chaotic. Britain began to withdraw its troops in August 1967, and in November of that year Aden and the whole Aden Protectorate became independent as the People's Republic of South Yemen. This had been preceded by a bitter civil war between two nationalist organizations, the Cairo-supported FLOSY and the independent left-wing National Liberation Front (NLF). After the defeat of FLOSY, Qahtan al Sha'bi, the leader of the NLF, became the first prime minister of the new Republic. His party stood for union with Yemen (Sana), but found itself almost immediately faced with more urgent preoccupations. Within six months of achieving independence the country had slipped towards anarchy and civil war. At a party conference in March 1968, the left wing of the NLF raised the banner of rebellion and decided to distribute arms to the 'Popular Guards', intending to create a counterweight to the army and the security forces, which it charged with 'a feudal mentality'. Some army officers were removed by the rebels, while others were arrested. The army, the only stable and certainly the strongest element in the new state, reacted by confronting al Sha'bi with an ultimatum: the officers had to be released and some of the leaders of the extreme left in their turn were to be arrested. Meanwhile, the NLF left wing continued openly to defy the government, seizing the eastern districts of the country and setting up 'popular councils' to administer them. They dismissed civil servants, senior army officers, and members of the security service, confiscated property, and attacked the government for pursuing a *'bourgeois* liberal policy' instead of 'popular democracy'. Led by the former minister of defence, Salem al-Baidh, they called for armed resistance to the army until a regime composed of labourers, poor farmers, and soldiers was established throughout the country.[162] The army and the NLF majority immediately struck back; the 'opportunist leftists' were accused of undermining the economy, torturing political enemies, and a great many other misdeeds. The situation was further complicated by the renewal of FLOSY activities from their base in the Republic of Yemen (Sana), unsuccessful left-wing attempts to seize power in Aden and Hadramaut, and friction between the army command and al Sha'bi, the prime minister. Several further revolts were reported, and the number of unemployed grew as the former main source of revenue, the entrepôt trade through Aden, dried up. Before independence the South Yemenis had received from Britain a yearly subsidy of about $60m. to balance their budget, this sum representing nearly 70% of the total.[163] This subsidy was discontinued after the removal by the South Yemenis of the last British military advisers. The salaries of government employees were cut and the new government faced a desperate economic situation as well as a political crisis.

The Soviet Union had watched events in Aden and South Arabia for years with great interest. Aden, as *Pravda* noted on the day it achieved independence, held a key position in strategic communications and a key port on the route taken by oil-tankers between the Persian Gulf and Europe.[164] The Soviet Union had displayed considerable activity in the Horn of Africa, opposite Aden; Chinese competition in these parts had only added to the Soviet concern. In the struggle between FLOSY and the NLF Moscow had remained neutral; the main thing, Soviet spokesmen said, was that the patriotic organization that came to power shoud serve the interests of the working class and the people.[165] To them the NLF program, which advocated the confiscation of the land belonging to the sultans and opposed a military agreement with Britain, seemed promising. The first Soviet ambassador arrived in South Yemen in February 1968, and was followed by a Soviet military mission. Soon after the establishment of the new state, Soviet ships and aircraft were given facilities in Aden's harbour and airport.[166] The South Yemen defence minister went to Moscow to ask for increased military help; later on there were requests for Soviet financial aid.

As the civil war spread the Soviet Union had to decide whether to support the rebels or the government. The slogans of the NLF left wing were certainly radical, but there was an enormous discrepancy between their program, and what really could be done in view of the backwardness of the country. Its leaders were by no means orthodox communists; some of them had found their inspiration in Cuba, where they had spent a long time, while others received their guidance from Mao's China. Such ultra-revolutionaries were hardly likely to appeal to the Soviet Union, and Moscow made known its displeasure with the ultra-radical resolutions of the Zingibar party congress. Soviet spokesmen claimed that the extremists had been incited by the Mao clique to oppose the legal government; their 'adventurist policy' was very dangerous and had to be decisively rejected.[167]

The Soviet investment in Yemen and South Arabia was not big in absolute terms. But Soviet arms, the biggest export to South Arabia, have played a decisive role at a critical moment in the Yemen's recent history. Despite the distance, the Soviet Union did not hesitate to send in ground-crews, albeit in small numbers. After the British withdrawal, the risks involved were relatively small. The bitter Egyptian experience must have taught the Russians that only massive military intervention would save the 'progressive forces' from defeat and that, in all probability, internal strife in one form or another would continue for a long time to come in Arabia. Western experts who had argued that South Arabia was too distant and unimportant for the Soviet Union to become deeply involved were proved wrong. The Soviet Union was definitely interested in South Arabia as a land-bridge to East Africa, even though the importance of Aden was greatly reduced while the Suez Canal remained closed. It wanted to get a foothold in Aden and Arabia for geopolitical reasons that were not dissimilar to those that had first induced Britain to establish bases there. It is unlikely that the ultra-radical initiative to establish communist rule in the caves of Hadramaut south'. Soviet opportunities were further enhanced as the result of the overthrow of al Sha'bi in June 1969 by a junta advocating even closer relations with the USSR.

Jordan

Jordan has been referred to in the Soviet Union as the kingdom
created by Winston Churchill between cigar and brandy,[168] but its
right to exist has not been questioned. The Nabulsi national front
government, which established diplomatic relations with the Soviet
Union in 1957 and which opposed the Baghdad Pact, was warmly
acclaimed at the time, and political support has been given to Jordan
ever since in its struggle against Israel. That communism in Jordan
was suppressed did not surprise the Soviet leaders and probably did
not weigh heavily in the scales; the situation in the other Arab
countries was not different. The pro-Western orientation of King
Hussein, on the other hand, the fact that the Jordanian army refused
Soviet arms and continued to receive its equipment from the West,
was a black mark against him. For these reasons Soviet attitudes to
Jordan were never truly cordial. When King Hussein declared in an
interview in 1966 that Zionism and communism probably had the
same objectives, *Izvestia* wondered whether the King was not
'looking at the situation from the moon or Mars'.[169] Before the Six
Day War the Soviet press attacked Jordan as a basis of American
imperialism which, in cooperation with Israel, would attack the
'progressive forces' in the Arab world. The situation suddenly
changed when Jordan joined Egypt and Syria in the battle against
Israel, and gave a better account of itself than either of them. Upon
this the Soviet Union made it known that it would be willing to
supply arms and equipment to rebuild the Jordanian army. American
aid had been discontinued after King Hussein had accused Washington of having intervened in the war on Israel's side. The King seems
to have been tempted at one time; he declared in July 1967 that he
would turn to the Soviet Union if the West did not renew its supply
of arms. President Ayub of Pakistan apparently played the role of
mediator; Hussein met him in Karachi on the eve of his visit to
Moscow in September 1967. Following Ayub's intervention,
Hussein received an invitation, and one month later he went on a
state visit to the Soviet capital. According to official communiqués,
his aim was merely to explain Jordan's position to the Soviet
leaders, but Marshal Grechko participated in the talks, and Hussein,
accompanied by Marshal Zakharov, inspected Soviet military
equipment. He said that he would welcome Soviet artists and
scientists to Jordan, but as for the arms, the Soviet negotiators did

not apparently entirely dissipate his fears about the possible strings attached. The Soviet leaders themselves felt a little uneasy about the presence of the monarch, and Podgorny in his welcoming speech made a reference to the effect that the anti-imperialist struggle brought together strange bedfellows, as the great Lenin had already realized many years earlier.[170]

Hussein's visit to Moscow resulted in a cultural agreement and a declaration by the King that the Arab nation was grateful to the USSR for its assistance. But a military pact was not signed; Hussein was aware that this would result, as in Syria's and Egypt's case, in a total break with the West, and this he was not willing to risk. He must have been aware, too, that a refusal was bound to result in greater pressure by the communists and the Nasserists for a government of national unity to 'reorganize the army and to rearm it with supplies from friendly socialist governments'.[171]

The political survival of King Hussein and his regime over so many years is a near miracle, and the stresses created by the Six Day War have further reduced its long-term prospects. The King's overthrow would have reopened the question of Jordan's future; its transformation into a Syrian or Egyptian style dictatorship was one possibility, but there were several others, such as annexation, war, civil war, and perhaps even big-power intervention. Hardly anyone was interested in precipitating yet another Middle East crisis that might have incalculable consequences. But the ferment inside Jordan could not be contained and the King's position and that of his regime remain therefore extremely precarious.

The Persian Gulf

The Persian Gulf area has been for a long time the scene of many conflicts, ranging from feuds among the Gulf sheikhdoms to the hostility between Arabs and Persians. Iraq has claimed Kuwait, Iran regards Bahrain as one of its provinces, and Saudi Arabia wishes to annex Muscat and Dhabi. There is tribal and religious strife, and a struggle between 'revolutionary nationalists' and 'reactionaries' superimposed on it all. These various crises have from time to time over the last few decades reached boiling-point, without, however, causing great alarm outside the area. The situation changed in the late nineteen-fifties with the growing importance of the Persian Gulf as a leading world oil-producer and the danger that oil supplies would be affected. The British decision to withdraw from the Persian Gulf by the end of 1971, announced in January 1968, opened a new period of turmoil.

The importance of Gulf oil in Soviet Middle East policy is discussed elsewhere in this study, but Soviet interest in the area predates the Persian Gulf oil boom by many years. It existed well before Molotov in 1940 informed the German ambassador in Moscow that 'the area south of Batum and Baku in the general direction of the Persian Gulf is recognized as the center of aspirations of the Soviet Union'.[172] The Russian advance towards Kuwait, Bandar Abbas, and the Persian Gulf figured prominently in British calculations from the eighteen-nineties; there were 'endless rumors' of Russian plans to secure from the Persian government a lease of Bandar Abbas, and Russian writers talked freely about various projects in the same area.[173] The railway from Syria to Kuwait planned by the Russian Count Kapnist in 1898 confirmed Lord Curzon's worst fears, and he made it known that the concession to Russia of a port on the Persian Gulf would be not only a deliberate insult to Britain, but a wanton disruption of the *status quo* and a deliberate provocation to war.[174]

The opportunities that opened to Russia in the Persian Gulf after an interval of more than five decades were wider than those before 1914; it was no longer merely a question of access to warm waters and bringing pressure to bear on the British. With the extension of the Soviet sphere of interest into East Africa and South-East Asia, the Persian Gulf acquired new importance as a bridgehead. At the same time renewed Russian interest in the Indian Ocean was probably not unconnected with the fear of China, and the idea that the Indian Ocean could mark the beginning of a line to contain China.[175] 'For over a century Russia had leaned on one side of the Middle East door to the Indian Ocean and Britain on the other', one observer commented, 'and now British power is finally to disappear from the area'. But as the Russians burst through the door they had to cope with a situation that in one essential respect was very different from the days of Curzon and Sazonov: all the countries in the area had become independent; the era of colonialism and semi-colonialism had passed. During the fifties and early sixties the Soviet Union was feeling its way in the politics of the Persian Gulf; its attitudes and comments were frequently contradictory. Soviet writers could not make up their minds whether the United States and Britain were bitter rivals there, or whether they were working hand in glove. Kuwait remained 'virtually a colony' in their eyes, even though it had attained independence, and the same was true, *a fortiori*, of Bahrain.[176] In 1953 a Soviet writer gave full support to Iran's claim to Bahrain, stating that union with Iran was the aspiration of the people of Bahrain.[177] In later years such backing was no longer given, not, perhaps, because the Soviet line on the subject has radically changed, but simply because in 1953 the Soviet Union was not yet deeply involved; before about 1956 there was in fact no official line. When Khrushchev visited Egypt in 1964 he was exceedingly insulting about the Emir of Kuwait, the 'little ruler' who accepted bribes and was 'trading in the riches of his people. He never had any conscience, and he won't ever have any.'[178] The Al Khalifa family, the rulers of Bahrain, fared no better: they were squandering vast sums on their caprices and 'embezzlement was flourishing'.[179] But this did not prevent the establishment of diplomatic relations between the Soviet Union and the Gulf states. The Kuwaiti minister of finance and industry visited Moscow in November 1964, and a little later a Soviet delegation went to Kuwait to sign an economic and technical cooperation agreement. Kuwait was rapidly upgraded in Soviet esteem. By 1966 the Soviet press noted that its 'international authority had grown'; its policy of non-alignment was praised, and the Prime Minister (and heir-apparent) was commended for his willingness to cooperate with the Soviet Union.[180]

Soviet relations with Saudi Arabia, another Arab country with vital interests in the Persian Gulf area, have been uniformly bad in recent years. The USSR had been the first country to recognize King Ibn Sa'ud after he became ruler of the Hedjaz in 1926 – this, a Soviet source said, was 'essential to the independence and free development of the area'.[181] The backwardness of his country did not at that time preclude the establishment of fairly close relations. When Amir Faisal became King in 1964, Moscow noted the reforms carried out by the new monarch, such as the introduction of a balanced budget and the limitation of the expenses of the Court.[182] But the reforms weighed less heavily in the scales than Faisal's opposition to Nasser's designs. The fact that Faisal not merely suppressed communism in his own country, but actively worked for an anti-Nasserist, anti-communist alliance in the Middle East, soon made him in Soviet eyes the 'avowed henchman of imperialism and Arab reaction'.[183] His visits to Iran and various Arab and North

African countries in 1965 were condemned as an attempt to by-pass the Arab League and to establish an Islamic alliance. Such an alliance would have added to the strength of the conservative camp in the Middle East, and it was therefore at once denounced in Cairo and Moscow as an imperialist plot. The assistance given by Faisal to the Yemeni royalists, and to Jordan and the Syrian opposition, added fuel to the campaign against him.

There was a lull in the cold war between Cairo and Riyadh in 1964, and again after the Six Day War, but relations between Saudi Arabia and Moscow remained bad even while there was a temporary reconciliation between Faisal and Nasser. Faisal feared that the Soviet Union would take over from Nasser in the Yemen, using South Arabia as a springboard for expansion into the Persian Gulf. Moscow, on the other hand, accused the Saudi King of far-reaching ambitions: 'It is not just a matter of threatening . . . South Yemen and Aden; he also wants to drive through to the Indian Ocean. Those who reduce Faisal's role to that of a lackey of the Americans are mistaken, for he has his own policy for the South Arabian peninsula.'[184]

But the Persian Gulf imbroglio transcends the West-East conflict. Faisal's championship of Arabism against Iran in the Persian Gulf had, within limits, Nasser's blessing, whereas the Soviet leaders, if faced with a choice between Faisal and the Shah, were by no means willing to support the former. Other elements in this free-for-all in the Gulf were the Iraqi involvement, the new Federation of the small Gulf principalities, and, of course, the various 'progressive forces' on the Arab peninsula. In January 1968 Mr Eugene Rostow expressed the hope that Iran, Turkey, Pakistan, Saudi Arabia, and Kuwait would form a nucleus around which security arrangements could in future be built. This speech was immediately attacked as an attempt to hatch plans for 'knocking together a [Western] military bloc, to strengthen the position of the oil companies, and to combat the national liberation movements';[185] no such defence pact was necessary, since the Soviet Union would protect the Persian Gulf states against any foreign aggressor. There were indications that it was Soviet policy within the area not to become too closely identified with any one side, but to appear as the friend and protector of all (excepting only Saudi Arabia), so as to be able, in the event of a conflict, to play the role of mediator according to the pattern established at Tashkent. But what was the reward of the honest

broker likely to be? Much depended on the development inside the
various states. With the enormous oil revenues from Qatar and
Dhobi (more than $300m. for 350,000 inhabitants), there was no
doubt that a federation of Arab emirates would be economically
viable. It would be a mistake to think, a Soviet observer wrote, 'that
the Sheikhs do not recognize the twentieth century'.[186] But to what
extent would their subjects benefit from the profits? The conflict
between rulers and ruled in the Middle East had not by-passed the
Gulf area. With some exceptions, the rulers have spent their money
wisely, but this alone is hardly sufficient to stem the revolutionary
tide.

During the late fifties and early sixties a number of 'liberation
fronts' came into existence, mostly with Egyptian help. Several such
organizations existed in Bahrain, another in Dhufar and Oman. Most
of these groups were, however, rent by internal ideological and
political strife which inhibited their development. After the Six Day
War Egyptian influence decreased. The Arab National Movement
(ANM), with its headquarters in the Lebanon, which served as a
meeting-place for most of the local liberation fronts, had all along
insisted on its independence of Cairo. Among the militants and
leaders of this movement there were many ex-Palestinians, especially
schoolteachers and trade union officials. After the Arab-Israeli War
of 1967 the Saudi and the Bahrain and Dhufar National Liberation
Fronts gravitated to Damascus rather than Cairo; their presence in
Cairo must have been an embarrassment for President Nasser, in
view of the financial support provided for Egypt by Saudi Arabia
and the oil Sheikhs. Communists have been active within most of
these groups, some of them pro-Soviet, others inspired by Peking.
A Western observer noted in 1968 that the methods of the NLF
which had worked so well in Aden were likely to be successful in the
Gulf too. FLOSY, which had been based on the urban community
of Aden, had been defeated by the NLF, which had concentrated on
operations in the hinterland. It had been NLF strategy in South
Arabia to exploit tribal allegiances in such a way as to gain control
of the countryside and to isolate the towns. But the opposition
offered by the traditional regimes in the Gulf was likely to be tougher
and better organized.[187]

Russian policies in the Persian Gulf have followed a consistent
line over a fairly long period. There have been aspirations, but not
a blueprint, let alone a time-table for conquest. Russia has been

probing the area, and wherever the situation was promising it has taken steps to increase its influence; recent developments have made it a foregone conclusion that the Soviet Union will be drawn even more into the Persian Gulf, and the return of Soviet influence as one of the central factors in Gulf politics does not really come as a surprise. The survival of the Gulf states now depends on their own staying power, the measure of collaboration between them, and their ability to resist pressure. It is unlikely that the traditional structures will survive for very long, but their successors still have a chance to retain their independence with a little luck and if they succeed in finding outside support. Gulf oil will have a great deal of attraction for years to come, and those who own it hope that they will be able to play the Soviet bloc against the West, and vice versa, as Iran has done for many years with considerable success.

6 Oil for the Lamps of Eastern Europe?

Oil concessions represent in the Soviet view the foundation of the entire edifice of Western political influence in the Middle East, of all military bases and aggressive blocs. If this foundation cracks, Soviet writers have argued, the entire structure would begin to totter and then come tumbling down.[1] They refer, in more prosaic language, to the undisputed fact that Western influence in the Middle East is based *inter alia* on the activities of a number of major oil companies, which supply between 50 and 60% (up to 80%, including Libya and Algeria) of the requirements of Western Europe in oil, and that, on the other hand, an enormous part of the national income of the oil-producing countries (88% of the export earnings in Iran, 92% in Iraq, 93% in Saudi Arabia) is derived from this same source. These are impressive figures, but there is an asymmetry between the position of the Middle East oil-producers and the European consumers: while OECD Europe was in the nineteen-sixties the only customer for Arab oil, Arab oil was not the only source of energy for OECD Europe.

One specific aspect of oil politics is of considerable relevance in the context of the present study – the growing Soviet interest in Middle East oil. On Middle East oil in general there is an enormous literature, both on a highly technical level and of the blood-sand-oil-and-intrigue variety, and the present writer cannot hope to compete with either. According to one school of thought, oil and the activities of the Western oil companies are the key to the understanding of Middle East politics; more recently Western experts have pointed to the increasing Soviet (and East European) need for Middle East oil as a major motive for Soviet bloc policies in the area. The present writer does not subscribe to a simplified oil-theory-of-history; in spite of their great economic significance, the oil companies have not during the last decade acted from a position of political strength. While Cuba has been able to resist the United States and Albania has succeeded in defying the Soviet Union, even the smallest Middle East oil producers have not found it difficult to play one oil company against another; the oil companies have been able neither to provoke wars nor to prevent wars. There has been a striking discrepancy between their economic strength and their political power. For individual countries, to be sure, the presence of oil has been a factor of paramount importance. It has had a great impact on their internal politics, as well as on their relations with the outside world. But it has always been a complicated and confusing process, bewildering for the tidy political scientist, and sadly disappointing for the believer in conspiracy theories of history.[2]

Soviet Oil

In the early years of the oil industry Russia was one of the world's major producers; around the turn of the century it held first place: European consumption was to a large extent covered by Baku and Grozny oil. In 1929 Soviet oil exports were surpassed only by those of Venezuela; in 1932, a peak year, more than 6m. tons were exported. With the turn towards autarchy, exports decreased, and during the second world war, with its heavy destruction and dislocation, the Soviet Union had to import substantial quantities of oil products. Once economic recovery had got under way after the war and new oilfields were discovered, oil production more than trebled within a decade (38m. tons in 1950, 129·5m. tons in 1959). The Soviet share in world production rose during this period from 5·5% to 13%, and in 1960, with production at 148m. tons, it moved to second place among the world's producers.[3]

Following the expansion in domestic oil production, the Soviet Union appeared on the world market as a major exporter: exports to countries outside the Soviet bloc rose from 1m. tons in 1950 to more than 20m. in 1960. In 1961 Soviet oil provided 35% of the local demand in Greece, 22% in Italy, 21% in Austria, 19% in Sweden. The British market was closed to Soviet oil, but West Germany received 10% of its supplies from the Soviet Union, and Japan 7%. At this stage leading Western oil companies became alarmed not so much by the actual quantity of Soviet oil that was

exported to the West (less than 10% of the demand of the non-
communist countries) as by the political and economic implications
and the disruption of the highly elaborate pricing system; above all,
the 'Soviet oil offensive' seemed only the beginning of a far more
massive onslaught on Western markets.[4] They asserted that the
Soviet take-over had cost the Middle East and Venezuelan governments $486m., that sales to the West were subsidized (the countries
of East Europe had to pay approximately twice as much for Soviet
oil), and that at the same time East European markets remained
closed to Western firms; it was not only the oil firms and Middle
East governments that were affected: the West as a whole had
suffered, and there was a real threat of Soviet political domination
over buyers.[5] It was argued that the main aim of the Soviet oil
offensive was political, and that it therefore constituted a real danger
to Western security. By disrupting Western oil operations, the
Soviet Union was acquiring a means of exerting influence in the
uncommitted countries, and eventually also in parts of Europe.
Although the Soviet Union could not hope to reap financial profit
by selling oil at cut-rate prices, Western observers assumed (rightly,
as it later appeared) that the hope of obtaining a hold on the business
of oil supply sufficiently large to ensure substantial profits at a later
stage was not absent.[6] Other experts suggested that while political
motives did play a certain part in the Soviet oil offensive, the
exports were profitable business from Moscow's point of view, even
at the low price level. The Russians did not want simply to disrupt
the old price schemes, but to become charter members of a new club
of oil producers, based on a more stable commodity agreement.[7]

The Soviet answer to these attacks was that, far from dumping
oil on Western markets, Russian oil exports to that area between
1956 and 1959 had totalled only 24m. tons, about 4% of its imports.
The USSR was determined to recapture its pre-war place among oil-
exporting nations and would not help to maintain artificially high
prices.[8] This policy brought the Russians into competition with the
other producing countries, including the Arabs. However, on many
subsequent occasions Soviet spokesmen argued that Soviet oil
exports were rising not at the expense of other nations, but because
of the steady increase in the consumption of oil throughout the
world. Between 1925 and 1935 the Soviet share of the West European
market had been about 14%, between 1955 and 1965 it was only
6%; could one in the circumstances really talk about 'flooding the

markets with Red Oil'? 'We sell oil in order to buy goods in return,' the chief Soviet spokesman explained.[9] The period between 1957 and 1961 was one of price-cutting in the oil industry, which eventually led to the establishment of OPEC (the Organization of Petroleum Exporting Countries). Founded in late August 1960 by the Middle East producing countries and Venezuela, its aim was to adopt a uniform attitude to oil companies which reduced oil prices unilaterally and without consultation.[10] Several weeks earlier, Esso had announced a cut in oil prices with special reference to Soviet oil penetration; the Russians had made a four-year contract with Italy to sell crude oil at approximately $1 per ton f.o.b. Black Sea terminals.[11] This was to cover about 20% of the yearly Italian requirements, and the Soviet Union was to receive in exchange much-needed 40-inch-diameter pipe, synthetic fibres, pumps, and other goods. 'At this price,' one American oilman commented, 'it's hardly worth taking oil out of the ground in Texas.'[12] But the Russians maintained that some independent Western companies were offering even bigger discounts, that the Soviet Union was prepared to cut prices only as much as necessary to get a specific sale, and that it was occasionally underbid. Soviet spokesmen complained, in effect, that major American oil companies were waging a cut-throat price offensive against them.[13] They did not deny that the oil-export drive could also be a political weapon. The stoppage of oil to Israel and Soviet operations in Ceylon had shown this; Gurov, head of *Soiuznefteksport*, declared on one occasion that the deliveries of Soviet oil had played a 'major role in the independence struggle of the heroic Cuban people'.[14] Soviet exports of oil continued to rise from about 32m. tons in 1960 to 54m. in 1967, but then began to level off, somewhat to the surprise of most experts (the reasons for this will be discussed later on). As American companies boycotted tanker operators who worked with the Russians, the Soviet Union built up its own tanker fleet; pipelines to East Europe, including the famous *Druzhba* (Friendship) line, were also built during this period. Of the Soviet·exports, a growing proportion went to West Europe and Japan; Russia's best customers in 1967 were Italy, Finland, West Germany, Japan, and Sweden, in that order, with Japan much in appearance as a major new customer. Exports to the underdeveloped countries had never constituted more than a small portion of the total Soviet oil trade.[15] The Soviet Union had been East Europe's chief supplier of oil since the second

world war, but the communist countries had been compelled to pay
$16–20 per ton (Bulgaria 16, Poland 17, Czechoslovakia 18,
Hungary 20), whereas Italy and Japan paid less than $8.[16] This
price differential caused a great many complaints on the part of the
East Europeans.[17] The Soviet standard answer was that their
deliveries to East Europe were carried out on the basis of barter
deals and that the East European countries also overcharged the
Soviet Union for their machinery, which was not of top quality.[18]
The price of Soviet oil in East Europe was somewhat reduced in
1966–7, and this market became less attractive for Moscow. The
bloc countries began to show growing interest in direct deals with
the oil-producers: Rumania and Bulgaria imported Iranian oil; other
East European countries signed agreements with Iraq. After 1965
domestic consumption increased, the whole pattern of Soviet oil
policy began to change, and its interest in Middle East oil became
more pronounced. To understand the implications of these changes
it is necessary at this point to review briefly Middle East oil production and its political and economic significance both for the producer
countries and for West Europe, their leading customer.

Oil in the Middle East

The basic facts about Middle East oil are well known – namely, that
it constitutes by far the most important economic asset of the area,
that it is unequally distributed, that it is exceedingly cheap in comparison with oil produced in other parts of the world, and that there
are seemingly unlimited reserves of it. It is sometimes forgotten,
however, that the Middle East has only very recently assumed its
present importance as one of the world's chief suppliers. The first
important discovery in Iran was made in 1908; oil was found near
Kirkuk in 1927, at Bahrain in 1932, and in Saudi Arabia in 1936, but
up to the second world war the Middle East provided less than 5%
of the world's total output. The striking development of the Middle
East oil industry took place in the nineteen-fifties, with the pheno-
menal increase in output in the known areas and the discovery of
new major oilfields, such as in the Kuwait Neutral Zone in 1953 and
in Libya in 1959. About 130m. tons were produced in 1967 in both
Saudia Arabia and Iran, closely followed by Kuwait with 115m.,
Iraq with 59m., the Kuwait Neutral Zone with 21·7m., Abu Dhabi,
a small Sheikdom on the Persian Gulf, where not a drop of oil had

been produced as recently as 1961, followed with 18·3m. Libyan oil
production rose from less than 1m. tons in 1961 to 83m., and
Algerian production during the same period increased from 2m. to
38m. tons. The year 1967 was not a good one for some of the producing countries. Iraq's production fell in comparison with the previous
year as the result of a conflict between the Iraq Petroleum Company
and the Syrian government, and of the Arab-Israeli war, the Arab
boycott, and the closure of the Suez Canal.[19]

Oil has revolutionized the economy of the Middle East. Kuwait
has fewer than half a million inhabitants, of whom only 150,000 are
Kuwaiti nationals. It has been estimated that its oil revenues are at
present of the order of $710m. per year, about $4,000 a year for each
Kuwaiti national.[20] Kuwait provides free education and health
services; the citizens of Saudi Arabia, whose revenues are of approximately the same order, hardly profited at all from the country's
wealth under the reign of King Saud (1953–64); only since then has
its oil income been used for the economic development of the
country. Most of Middle East oil production is dominated by seven
big companies, Royal Dutch Shell, British Petroleum Company,
Standard Oil of New Jersey, Gulf Oil Corporation, Texaco,
Standard Oil of California, and Socony Mobil Oil – the 'seven
sisters'. Other major companies, though not quite in the same
league, are the French Compagnie Francaise des Pétroles and the
Italian ENI. These companies have doubled in size during the last
decade, but their share of the oil market has shrunk, because total
oil production has grown even faster. Various independent com-
panies from all over the world have been operating in the Middle
East since the late nineteen-fifties. The production of Iranian oil is
in the hands of a consortium of some fourteen oil companies; in
Saudi Arabia Aramco, a cartel of four of the five big American
companies, is the main producer; in Iraq the Iraq Petroleum
Company (IPC) predominates (CFP, Shell, BP and others); in
Kuwait the Kuwait Oil Company (an Anglo-American company).
In addition, there are a number of local government companies at
work, such as NIOC, the Iranian state company which, while co-
operating with the consortium, is also competing with it, and the
Kuwait National Petroleum Company. The newcomers have
received a growing share of the market, among them the (Japanese)
Arabian Oil Company operating off the Kuwait Neutral Zone, and
ENI (an Italian company), which has been active in Iran and

several Arab countries. The whole trend of development in the oil industry has been towards very large units and integrated companies; oil has not only to be produced, but also to be refined, shipped to its destination, and distributed. Consumers have complained about cartel practices and super-profits, whereas the laments of the oil companies and the producer countries have created the impression that cut-throat competition has brought them to the verge of ruin. The enormous revenues earned by the producers show that, despite growing rivalry between companies, competition is still far from complete. Petroleum prices do not necessarily reflect costs,[21] and the days of oligopoly are by no means over. Oil operations in the major producing countries have been on a profit-sharing (50-50) basis; this goes back to a decree by the Saudi government in 1949 demanding 50% of Aramco's income after payment of United States tax. A similar principle had previously been applied in Venezuela, and it meant, in practice, that the governments of the producing countries received roughly 55%–60% of the profits that were actually made. Since then they have been pressing for a higher share of the profits: the Japanese-owned company in Kuwait splits the profits of its operations in the Neutral Zone 57:43 with the Saudi and Kuwaiti governments. Independent companies and some of the 'seven sisters' have offered the governments concerned not only a higher share in the profits, but also shares in the equity (between 10–30%) in the event of oil being discovered.[22] Operating costs have risen steadily as the result of pressure by the oil-producing countries, lower allowances for marketing expenses, and changes in the royalties-expensing agreements. Spokesmen for the oil companies have argued that 'pressure from the producing governments on costs is something we can learn to live with, provided we are not at the same time denied freedom to move prices in the market, so as to maintain a commercial margin of profit'.[23] The governments have also forced the companies to give up most of the original concession areas in which no drillings had been made. In Kuwait and Qatar newly established companies have taken over the relinquished areas; in Iraq, under General Kassem, the IPC was deprived of 99% of its concessions and permitted to carry on work only in the oilfields actually being worked.

Relations between governments and oil companies varied from country to country. It hardly needs stressing that every government wanted a maximum income from its chief natural asset, but whereas

Saudi Arabia and Kuwait, untroubled by the pressure of popular opinion, believed that this could best be achieved by close co-operation with the oil companies, there was a strong belief in Iran, and even more in Iraq, that the country would fare much better if it took over the management of oil operations. Experience with nationalization in Iran had not, however, been encouraging; the main effect of the pressure exerted by successive Iraqi governments on the IPC was that the development of the industry was slowed down and no new exploratory drillings were made. The demand for the nationalization of the oil industry continued nevertheless to grow in the Arab world, while Syria and Egypt claimed that they did not get their due for serving as transit countries. It was Soviet policy to encourage Middle East governments in their demands on the oil companies and to emphasize the advantages of national oil companies free to trade with everyone. The Iraqi government's lack of vigor in its attitude towards the IPC and its alleged failure to engage in an independent oil policy was (to provide but one illustration) the subject of Soviet criticism in 1961–2. It had not passed unnoticed, a Soviet periodical wrote, that the persecution of democratic elements was intensified at the time of the government's negotiations with the oil companies.[24] The 'crimes of the oil companies' remained for many years one of the central themes of Soviet and communist propaganda in the Middle East.

West Europe and Middle East Oil

Since the end of the second world war the consumption of oil and oil products in West Europe has risen more than tenfold, reaching 455m. tons a year in 1967. This figure represents about half of the total energy consumption. Less than 10% of the oil consumed was found in Europe; the rest had to be imported. Almost 80% of these imports came from the Middle East, Libya, and Algeria. Europe has one important indigenous asset to meet its energy requirements, coal, which before the second world war covered almost all domestic energy requirements.[25] Its role has, however, steadily declined ever since, partly on account of the limited reserves and the desire of the European governments to protect and conserve them, but mainly because the price of the cheapest-grade coal in Europe is about $16 a ton, whereas the price of 1 ton of oil has ranged in recent years from $10 to $12.[26] The real price difference is even greater, since

1 metric ton of fuel oil has nearly 1·5 times the heat value of a metric ton of coal; furthermore, coal is subsidized to the extent of about $5 a ton. It has been estimated that West Europe would save about $3·5 billion annually if it switched entirely to oil: 'European coal production is no longer an industry, it is only a means of social insurance.'[27]

These calculations take account only of commercial considerations; they ignore not only the technical and social difficulties involved in such a transition, but also the all-important question of security of supply. How vulnerable West Europe's oil supply really is appeared at the time of the Suez war in 1956: with the blocking of the Canal and the cutting of the IPC pipelines (following the destruction of the pumping stations), two-thirds of Europe's total supply was cut off. Several potential sources existed to cover European requirements and replace Middle East oil, above all in North America and Venezuela; on a considerably smaller scale, liquid oils could be provided from other sources, such as the coal-gas industry.

In the event, the effect of the Suez crisis on the European economy was less grave than at first had been expected.[28] Arrangements were immediately made to re-route the world tanker fleet and additional supplies from the western hemisphere reached Europe within a short time. The price of oil went up for a while, but not by very much; certain European industries were affected by the supply situation, but the overall industrial production of OECD Europe continued to rise. There was a loss in internal revenue as a result of the fall in the consumption of oil products, especially motor gasoline, and the crisis also had an effect on the balance of payments by reason of the increased purchases of American oil and additional dollar freights. It was estimated that during the most difficult period of the crisis, the additional dollar bill was running at the rate of between $300m. and $400m. a year.[29] The crisis was shortlived, but it served as a warning that the disruption of oil supplies from the Middle East at some future date, perhaps over a longer period, could not be ruled out. In order to reduce their vulnerability in any future emergency, European governments decided to consider a number of measures, such as the accumulation of larger reserves, the diversification of sources of supply, and the further development of flexibility in the means of transport by alternative routes, and in refinery operations. It was obvious that in terms of money and material there could not be complete insurance against a future crisis. The provision of a single day's storage capacity in Europe and the oil to fill it was thought at the time to cost about $20m.; but it was generally believed that appropriate planning could at least reduce the immediate impact of a new crisis.

These measures were put to the test at the time of the Arab-Israeli war in 1967, when West Europe's oil supply was again cut. The Suez Canal was blocked; Kuwait and Saudi Arabia, Libya and Iraq, stopped oil production with the outbreak of the war. In Libya and Saudia this was the result of a strike of oil workers, whereas in Kuwait and Iraq the government decided to ban supplies to a number of countries, including the United States and Britain.[30] The Arab foreign ministers' conference in Kuwait decided after the cease-fire to continue the boycott. The non-producing countries and Iraq (which suggested stopping all oil production for three months so as to deplete Europe's reserves) were the most extreme in their demands; the others had misgivings from the very beginning about the effectiveness of the boycott. In the event, their fears proved justified: the Saudi minister of Petroleum Affairs, said that in retrospect it had been a wrong decision taken on the basis of false information: 'It hurt the Arabs more than anyone else.' The non-Arab producers, including Iran, stepped up their production, and the smaller Persian Gulf principalities continued their supplies; Kuwait and Saudi Arabia boycotted only the United States (which does not depend on Middle East oil) and Britain; Libya (under strong pressure from Egypt) also in theory boycotted West Germany, but in fact tolerated exports to that country. The official boycott lasted altogether three months; as a result, Iraq's production fell by $11\frac{1}{2}\%$, while Iran's went up by 23%. The Arab countries lost several hundred million dollars in royalties. No European country went short of oil, despite the fact that the Suez Canal remained closed; at one stage, in early autumn 1967, stocks were down to about ten days' supplies, but after a little while they were back to seasonal level.[31] It had appeared at first that the 1967 stoppage would be far more serious than the Suez crisis, for in 1956 actual oil production had never been suspended. The quantity of oil shipped from the Middle East to Europe was much greater in 1967 than it had been eleven years earlier, and it was thought that Europe was therefore more dependent on Arab oil. Radical leaders in the Arab world, as well as the communists, had maintained for years that oil was their most effective weapon; to cut it off would very quickly paralyse European industrial production and thus force West Europe to yield to Arab demands. By means of oil, Cairo and Damascus radio had argued, the Arab countries could dictate their conditions to the West.

Between 1956 and 1967 efforts had been made to diversify West Europe's sources of supply, but these had not been altogether successful, for oil production in Nigeria ceased as the result of the civil war, Algeria agreed to supply only France, and Libya, which was not affected by the closure of the Suez Canal, joined the Arab League boycott. Yet, despite these setbacks, there was no real crisis and price increases were relatively small. The oil industry showed great elasticity: it proved only too easy, as in 1956, to increase oil production outside the Arab world and there was sufficient capacity available to move the volume of oil that was needed. The oil companies had certainly learned one lesson from the Suez war: they were not going to be dependent on the Suez Canal. The oil flow through Suez, almost entirely in the south-north direction, had more than doubled in the decade since 1956; it accounted for about 70% of the total traffic through the Canal. But there had been a movement towards larger tankers (of the 150,000–200,000-ton class), which in any case could not pass through the Canal. These super-tankers operated more cheaply on the Cape route, and after the war of 1967 (in the words of one observer) the movement towards super-tankers turned into a stampede. The number on order increased from 70 to 140, and even bigger tankers were already under construction.[32]

The crisis of 1967 had several important side effects: the extra strain on the balance of payments contributed to the devaluation of sterling; certain oil companies dependent chiefly on the Middle East showed losses in their annual balance sheets, while others, mainly American-based, showed substantial gains. But overall the boycott caused few tremors on the European industrial scene. It demonstrated that oil was not, after all, the deadly weapon some had believed. The dependence of the Arab governments on their royalties, their inability to sustain a long-term stoppage or boycott, seemed to show that Europe's oil supply was still secure. The oil insurance introduced after the Suez war – 60–65 days' stocks of normal consumption and 80–90 days' for OECD Europe as a whole – had proved its worth.

But there remained some nagging questions: what if, as the result of political instability in the Middle East, the oil supply should one day be cut off for a longer period, or perhaps even permanently? The additional cost of supplying West Europe had not been insignificant; the United Kingdom had to spend some $200m., West Germany $90m., Italy $80m., France $40m.[33] What if these extra costs were to continue or even increase in future? The oil companies and their advisers, and above all the West European governments, soon began to consider how to cope with future emergencies. Some, arguing that oil was for the time being irreplaceable, advocated stockpiling on a scale sufficient to provide (at an annual cost of some $870m.)[34] reserves for nine months' oil consumption and for one or two years' electricity supply. Others, looking ahead to the more distant future, pointed to alternative sources of energy that would become available. The discovery of major new oilfields in Europe was thought to be unlikely, and while American reserves may be far greater than is at present thought, it was assumed that the cost of production there would always be considerably higher than in the Eastern hemisphere. Experts pointed to the increasingly important role of natural gas; in the United States it already covers about 30% of the total energy demand; in Europe, too, the consumption of natural gas is likely to grow at a faster rate than oil, even though it is unlikely to catch up with oil in the near future. Within the general framework of the energy balance, electric power has steadily grown in importance, and it has been estimated that around 1980 it will cover almost half of the total energy requirements. After an uncertain start, there has been rapid progress in nuclear technology. It is no longer in doubt that with the advent of the fast-breeder nuclear power is becoming economic, that in the not too distant future it will provide energy at prices competitive with all but the cheapest crudes, and that in the seventies it will be an important source of energy for generating electricity in Europe. Before the Arab-Israeli war it was generally thought that the switch from oil to uranium in generating power would take longer, not because of technological or economic considerations, but because of the innate conservatism of the public utilities. However, the uncertainties of the Middle East oil supply may well embolden them to take the plunge sooner. The main factor so far inhibiting the use of nuclear energy in ways other than generating electricity has been the absence of a rival to the petrol engine and the high cost of small nuclear reactors – those below 500-megawatt capacity. But in this field, too, a technological breakthrough cannot be ruled out. Given the necessary challenge, such as the danger of a breakdown in oil supplies, it may come earlier than now expected.

West Europe's dependence on Middle East oil must be considered in the general context of its future energy requirements. It will remain the natural market for Middle East oil provided that there continues to be a secure supply of cheap oil. The transition towards the wider use of sources of energy other than oil, which in the long run is inevitable anyway, would be accelerated by political instability in the Middle East. It would no doubt for a number of years entail heavy financial investment and major technical problems. But West Europe's energy supplies would seem to be assured (admittedly at high cost) except in the unlikely event of a total Middle East oil embargo, and future technological progress will make it less dependent still.

The Soviet Union and Middle East Oil

The remarkable growth of Soviet oil production has been noted; it is expected to continue, to reach about 350m. tons in 1970 and in 1980 between 600m. and 700m. tons. The original targets were even higher, but have been slightly lowered. A number of reasons have been suggested for these cuts. It is much easier to boost the flow of oil than to increase refining capacity and to expand the petrochemical industry, which requires heavy financial investment. No new major oilfields have been found in the European part of Russia, drilling costs are increasing, transport costs have become higher, and the cost of oil production (on which we have no exact data) probably compares unfavourably with that of the Middle East.[35] Natural gas plays an increasing part in the Soviet energy balance:[36] enormous quantities of gas have been found in Siberia and Sakhalin, but to carry gas fixed installations are needed and the cost/unit of energy is about double that of crude oil: to pump Sakhalin and East Siberian natural gas to Europe does not seem to be a sound economic proposition.

Soviet energy consumption, too, is growing rapidly, at least by 7% annually, possibly even faster. Oil is likely to provide 40% of the total Soviet energy demand, and most observers expect that in 1980 the total demand for oil will be between 600m. and 700m. tons, i.e. equal to, or at any rate not much less than, the expected production. In particular gasoline consumption in road transport is likely to rise very fast during the next decade, and there will be a much higher demand by industry as production increases.

According to these estimates, the Soviet Union will have sufficient oil to cover its own needs, and there may be a certain surplus for export. Whether Soviet oil exports to West Europe and Japan will continue to grow as in the recent past seems far more doubtful. The Soviet Union has in the past all but monopolized East Europe's oil supplies; of a consumption of about 40m. tons per year (1966) only 15–16m. tons have been produced locally, mainly in Rumania. It has been calculated that by 1980 East European demand will rise to 190m. tons or even more,[37] while local oil production will increase only to about 30m. tons a year. For a number of years the coming oil shortage has been freely discussed by Soviet and East bloc economists. A Polish economist writing in 1966 noted that even at the optimistic figure of only 90m. tons to be imported, the countries of East Europe would be paying out $1·4 billion a year of their scarce foreign currency.[38] As far as oil supplies are concerned, the Soviet Union is not interested in giving East Europe first priority; it wants above all to improve its own terms of trade, either by earning foreign currency or by selling its raw materials to the industrialized non-communist countries in exchange for machinery and equipment.[39] The exportable quantity of Soviet oil is not likely to grow in proportion to the increasing demand in East Europe; on the contrary, the share of it sold to customers outside the bloc is likely to increase. East European economic planners have been given to understand on various occasions that to lessen the pressure on Soviet oil they would be well advised to look for alternative supplies in the third world, mainly in the Middle East. After the Czechoslovak crisis of 1968 higher priority was again given by the Soviet Union to East European needs, but it is too early to say whether this is a temporary palliative or a major policy shift. East Europe thus faces a fuel situation not altogether dissimilar to that of West Europe; its capacity to make massive oil purchases cannot be rated very high in view of its limited foreign-currency earnings. There are several possibilities of dealing with this shortage – namely, the investment of capital in the Soviet oil industry and/or the development of nuclear and other alternative sources of energy. Parts of East Europe are rich in coal, but concentration on the use of coal and lignite would mean a high-cost economy and backwardness in transport; for the next decade nuclear energy will not be available in East Europe in sufficient quantity. Heavy investment in the Soviet oil industry would make East Europe both politically and economically more dependent on Russia, and may for that reason be considered undesirable. It seems most likely therefore that East European states will prefer direct barter agreements with the Middle East producers, such as the deal (already mentioned) between Rumania and Iran in 1966. It has been estimated that if East Europe were to satisfy all its additional requirements for oil in the Middle East, goods worth between $1 and $2 billion would have to be supplied to Iran and the Arab countries.[40] Deliveries of goods on such a scale would be, to put it cautiously, difficult for the recipients to absorb.

The growing need for oil in the Soviet Union and East Europe has gradually brought about a change in the oil policy of the bloc in the Middle East. Before 1966 the Soviet Union did not appear as a buyer of Middle East oil or natural gas, nor did it display any interest in participating in any way in the production of oil. It was mainly in Soviet and communist propaganda that Middle East oil played an important role: oil, it was argued, had for decades enslaved the peoples of the Middle East; was it not high time for them to be liberated from these shackles? Had not the people a better title to the huge revenues than the company shareholders?[41] 'Arab oil for the Arabs', a *Pravda* headline at the time of the Syrian conflict with the Iraq Petroleum Company in 1966–7, introduced an article which quoted with evident satisfaction the slogans seen on the wall of the oil refinery in Homs: 'Oil in the hands of the working people spells a weapon in the fight against imperialism! The battle for oil spells continuation of the struggle for the strengthening of our independence.'[42] The militant policy of the Syrian government was favorably contrasted with the relative moderation of the Iraqi government: 'The popular masses and national forces [in Iraq] look forward to freeing their oil wealth from the grip of the imperialist monopolies, abolishing the unjust conditions in the present concessions, and amending these concessions to serve Iraq's interests.'[43] It is interesting that this appeal of the Communist Party of Iraq did not demand outright expropriation of the foreign companies but merely (as first steps) the establishment of a national oil industry, the amendment of current agreements, and an approach to the 'socialist world to secure the necessary equipment and technicians for the National Oil Company'.[44] Countless statements in similar vein appeared in the Soviet and communist press throughout the nineteen-fifties and sixties; the communists concentrated their organizational efforts, not without some success, on oil workers in the Arab world. At the same time Soviet and East European commentators stressed in their writings West Europe's dependence on Arab oil, asserting that, since there was no way to replace it, the obvious political conclusions should be drawn.[45] Up to the middle sixties the Soviet Union's interest in Middle East oil was on the whole negative. It attacked the Western oil companies, but did not itself need any outside supplies. Some Western observers saw in these attacks an exercise in political warfare calculated to deny West Europe its oil supplies, but it is doubtful whether Soviet policy had in fact such a grand design. The position of the oil companies *vis-à-vis* Arab and Iranian public opinion was in any case precarious, and Soviet experts regarded them as a perfectly legitimate target for a propagandist onslaught.

After 1965, with the changing perspective on oil, Soviet interest in Middle East oil became far more active. During and after the war of 1967, Soviet spokesmen continued to reassure the Arabs that they were not seeking to increase their sales of oil in markets which had formerly belonged to the Arabs. (The Soviet Union had supported the Arab oil boycott; but had not joined it, and there were rumours that Moscow had exploited the situation.) The Soviet argument was that its own share in the international oil trade had remained steady at around 4 or 5%;[46] there was no talk (as there had been in 1960) about recapturing the Soviet Union's pre-war position as one of the world's main exporters of oil.

The Soviet deal with Iran in January 1966 for the supply of natural gas was the major turning-point in Soviet oil policy and an indication of its new interest in supplies; a similar, much smaller, contract was signed with Afghanistan. The year before the Russians had entered into a service contract with the Syrian government to develop the Suwaidiyah oilfield, which in March 1968 began production at the rate of 1m. tons a year. More ambitious was the exploration service contract with Iraq in late 1967, which was to be paid for in crude oil. It was not clear for a while whether this agreement affected the important North Rumailan field which the Iraqis had also promised to France, and the change of government in

Baghdad in July 1968 added to the confusion.[47] This had been a political gesture by the Iraqis; the head of the state National Oil Company declared that the agreement was significant because it 'followed the [Soviet] political backing given the Arabs in the Middle East crisis'.[48] The details of the Iraqi deal are of no great significance in this context, for Russia made a similar proposal to assist Iran in the quest for oil, also to be paid for in crude oil. But it did indicate the new general direction of Soviet oil policy; for the first time since the war the Soviet Union began to import Middle East oil.

Some of the underlying reasons for the oil offensive have been discussed; first among them was the wish to secure energy supplies cheaply in order to meet the growing needs of the Soviet Union and its allies. The economic and political implications were less simple. It had been traditional Soviet policy, wherever their teams prospected for oil or built refineries, to appear as agents of the local government, to lend money, but not to invest capital. For this reason some Western oilmen were as afraid of French and Italian as of Soviet competition.[49] The Soviet intention was, no doubt, to avoid arousing the jealousy and ill will that the presence of the Western companies had often aroused. Its agreements did not really clash with Western deals, which offered large revenues to the host country at no outlay, whereas Russian help cost money, barter goods, or oil.[50] Nowhere but in Spitzbergen had the Soviet Union appeared before as an explorer seeking concessions, but this policy was now likely to change because of its own growing needs and the desire of the host governments for joint-venture contracts, with the Soviet Union putting up most or all of the risk money. The Arab governments, needless to say, did not, as some Western observers had suggested,[51] want their oil industry to come under Soviet domination because of the Arab belief that America and Britain had supported Israel. They wanted maximum profits, and they thought the best way to achieve this aim was to diversify their concessions in the same way that West Europe diversified its supplies. It was thought at the time that these new developments in Soviet oil policy in 1966–7 foreshadowed yet another major initiative: the establishment of large marketing organizations which would make the Soviet Union a leading force in the international oil business, thus providing a successful alternative to the 'stranglehold of capitalist monopolies'. This would involve a great outlay of capital, but it had much to recommend it.

For political as well as economic reasons, the Soviet Union was vitally interested in continuing to supply oil to both East and West Europe; the plans for the delivery of natural gas to Italy by way of a giant pipeline were indicative of its desire to keep its external markets. If there was not sufficient Soviet oil available for such operations, handsome profits could be reaped from marketing Middle East oil. Whether such a policy would meet with the approval of both producers and consumers, who might prefer to deal directly with each other, was a different question. But, as a major producer with great marketing experience and financial backing, the Soviet Union was potentially in a strong position to act as middleman.

Soviet interest in Middle East oil, it is often argued, has been political rather than economic. Political considerations are, of course, never absent from Soviet economic policy, but a good Soviet case could be made for increasing its trade with the oil-producing countries of the Middle East irrespective of political interests. The growing need for additional oil supplies for East Europe has been mentioned; the cheapness of Middle East oil in comparison with that produced in the Soviet Union is an additional attraction. The purchase of oil from Middle East countries seems a logical way to balance trade relations and to recoup the Soviet credits that have been extended to them. In the past there was marked reluctance in the Soviet Union and East Europe to import oil from non-communist countries, because of the danger that supplies would be cut off at a time of crisis. But this argument has been gradually discarded: Soviet imports would be quite small and for that reason the question of security hardly arises. East Europe is far more vulnerable, but it has been emphasized there of late that the communist bloc countries would not have to depend on Western oil monopolies, but on companies sponsored by governments well disposed towards the communist bloc. Moreover, it would always be possible to obtain Russian oil in case of an emergency, just as in a crisis West Europe could fall back on Western hemisphere oil.

The growing importance of Middle East oil and natural gas for the Soviet Union and the Soviet bloc is undisputed, but it is un-likely that this will be a factor of decisive importance in shaping Soviet policy in the area. From the Arab and Iranian point of view, the outlets offered by the Soviet bloc are (and will remain) small in comparison with the great consumer markets of West Europe and Japan. If the Soviet Union desperately needed Middle East oil for its industrial development there would no doubt be far greater pressure to bring the enormous reserves of the Middle East under its control. But this is not a question of life and death for the Soviet Union, which has so far been able to afford a policy of autarchy.* The primacy of politics over economics has been one of the unwritten laws in the Soviet code of conduct. This may change one day, but it is unlikely that the Middle East will be the first exception to this rule.

* It ought to be noted however that the trends indicated in this chapter became even more pronounced during 1968/9. Soviet exports of oil to the West fell from 34m. in 1967 to 32m. in 1968. The target for Soviet oil production in 1980 originally (i.e. in 1961) set at about 700m. has now been reduced to 'over 500m.' Since Soviet oil requirements that year will be in the range of 600m. according to most Western experts it can no longer be taken for granted that the Soviet Union will be able to cover all its domestic needs from internal sources by the late nineteen seventies.

7 Trade and Aid

The impact of Soviet trade and aid on Middle East politics is usually overrated. Economic relations between the Soviet Union and most Middle East countries have greatly expanded during the last decade, but with a few important exceptions they are still on a substantially smaller scale than Middle East trade with the West. Soviet development aid is still less than $\frac{1}{10}$ of one percent of the national income of the Communist country. Commercial transactions *per se* have not yielded a marked increase in Soviet political influence. The one important exception is the supply of arms, which both in monetary value and in political significance has been the most important Soviet export. From 1954 to 1966 the Soviet Union provided about $2 billion in arms and military equipment to Egypt, Syria, Iraq and the Yemen; between June 1967 and October 1968 deliveries reportedly totalled $2·5 billion. During the same period (1954–1967) credits totalling $2 billion were extended to the Middle East, of which, however, it is thought only between one-third and one-half has actually been drawn by the recipients. Soviet military aid, in other words, has been from four to five times greater than economic assistance. While a great deal has been written in Russia during the last decade on the theory and practice of Soviet aid, Soviet arms supplies are never discussed and there are no official figures. The following outline deals only with non-military Soviet aid, politically and economically the less important aspect of trade relations.

Trade with the third world is frequently considered by communist spokesmen as a form of aid. True, Khrushchev and other Soviet leaders can be quoted to the opposite effect ('We are not a charitable institution. We give aid on fair commercial principles'[1]). On other occasions Soviet spokesmen have claimed that the Soviet Union is guided in developing trade and extending aid by the desire to accelerate the revival of the countries concerned, and to speed up the development of their productive forces. At the same time it is politically important as a means of helping them to break out of the imperialist system and to advance their transition on to a non-capitalist road of development. Sometimes the official explanations contradict each other. For instance, it is argued that the Soviet Union does not act primarily from considerations of commercial advantage and the profit motive, but 'from the standpoint of humanity and solidarity with all mankind'.[2] But equally often it is maintained that Soviet trade, especially with neighboring countries, follows a natural and traditional pattern and is based on sound commercial principles. It is always denied that the Soviet Union is guided by tactical political considerations, that there are strings attached to Soviet aid; Soviet motives in extending aid and developing trade are described as absolutely unselfish and disinterested, in contrast to that of non-communist countries.

The real motives, needless to say, are more complex. Not all Soviet trade is politically motivated: Soviet commercial relations with Europe and America have on the whole fewer political implications than those with third-world countries. It is the Soviet intention to demonstrate to the developing countries that they can achieve real progress only by pursuing an economic policy similar to that of the Soviet Union. Within this general scheme, Soviet aid and trade usually concentrate on certain key countries which for political reasons are of particular importance. In the Middle East there has been a marked orientation towards Egypt and Syria, and, to a lesser degree, towards Algeria and Iraq. Up to 1966, when Moscow made substantial pledges in support of India's fourth five-year plan, Egypt, as the recipient of more than $1 billion in credits, was first in the list of countries receiving Soviet aid. Syria, too, has received substantial help ($233m.), more than either the UAR or India on a *per capita* basis. The selection of these two countries makes it clear that political objectives were of paramount importance; Moscow's aid commitments have often fluctuated with the change in the political climate, as trade relations with Syria show. Aid was restricted when the Ba'th took over in Syria in 1963, but restored in 1964 when the Damascus government modified its anti-communist line. During 1965 and after the neo-Ba'th coup of February 1966, there was a further dramatic rise in Soviet grants. The deterioration

in relations with Israel, on the other hand, resulted in the cessation
of Soviet oil shipments to that country and the cancellation of all
other contracts.

Under Stalin the Soviet Union had shown little interest in the
development of trade relations with the countries of the Middle East.
During the nineteen-thirties and forties trade was actually declining,
a trend which was reversed only after 1953. Between 1953 and 1957
some fifty trade-and-payments agreements were concluded between
the Soviet Union and the countries of the Middle East, and the value
of trade doubled. The Soviet Union has always shown a preference
for bilateral trade agreements: it bought Egyptian and Syrian
cotton, Iranian animal and fish products, Yemenite coffee, and
Israeli citrus fruits in exchange for Soviet-produced capital goods.
At the same time, foreign-aid programs were initiated, partly no
doubt under the influence of the success of programs operated by
the United States. But the Soviet programs were usually far simpler
in structure; aid consisted mainly of low interest credits (usually $2\frac{1}{2}\%$
per annum) repayable over twelve years and tied to the execution of
mutually agreed projects. (Western official aid, on the other hand,
consisted to a large extent of free grants or long-term loans carrying
a repayment period of twenty years or more.) Soviet interest rates
were lower than those normally charged by Western lenders and the
various international financial agencies.

Economic cooperation between the Soviet Union and Turkey and
Iran has grown only in recent years.* In 1965 both Turkey and Iran
received substantial Soviet credits ($210m. and $330m. respectively),
but this did not cause a radical reorientation of the trade pattern of
these two countries. The development of trade relations between
the Soviet Union and the Arab countries has been more complex and
politically more significant. Trade with Egypt grew from $15m. in
1954 to $184m. in 1961; Soviet exports rising from $7m. to $97m.,
imports from $8m. to $86m. By 1966 the volume of trade had
reached $314m., by 1967 $380m.[3] Trade with Egypt was based on
the agreements of 1958, 1960, and 1964, which concerned the Aswan
dam and many other projects, including an atomic reactor, industrial plants, and irrigation systems. The 1958 agreement envisaged
a five-year industrial expansion plan of $750m. There were certain
difficulties: Egypt paid the Soviet Union mainly with cotton. But

---

* In 1968 Iran became the third largest recipient of Soviet aid behind India and the
UAR.

Russia produces sufficient cotton for its own consumption in Central Asia, and the Egyptians objected to Soviet reselling of their chief product on the world market, for this was bound to depress the price. It was doubtful from the very beginning whether Egypt would ever be able to repay its loans. Its balance of trade with the Soviet Union became increasingly unfavourable: — $11m. in 1963, — $21m. in 1964, — $45m. in 1965, and it fell steadily behind in its credit repayments, despite the fact that it had drawn only a little over $500m. of the $1,500m. credits extended by the Soviet Union and East Europe. After Nasser's visit to the Soviet Union in 1965 it was reported that the Soviet government had written off some $460m. of the Egyptian debt, and that only some $35–40m. had actually been paid by Cairo. There were further negotiations with Kosygin (in 1966), with Gromyko (in March 1967), and again with Kosygin after the Six Day War, about a further easing of repayment conditions. The Soviet trade figures do not make it clear to what extent its imports from Egypt are in payment for military equipment, how much is in payment for regular credits, and how much constitutes normal sales. Commercial considerations cannot have been uppermost in Soviet minds in the trade with Egypt; over the years they have lost a great deal of money in that country.

Economic relations between the Soviet Union and Syria developed rapidly on the basis of the trade and technical cooperation agreements of 1956 and 1957. After 1958 the volume of trade fell off, but picked up again in the early sixties. By the end of 1964 total Soviet bloc aid to Syria was about $193m., of which the Soviet Union had provided $50m. The Soviet commitment made in 1966 to finance the construction of the Euphrates dam was the biggest single item; other projects included power stations, the building of railway lines, and machinery for factories. Economic relations between the Soviet Union and Iraq had been insignificant under Nuri as-Said, but took an upward turn soon after Kassem came to power. The trade agreements of October 1958 and March 1959 covered a loan of $550m., and envisaged the establishment of metallurgical works and fertilizer plants, and the improvement of the Iraqi railway network. Up to 1965 Soviet aid to Iraq totalled about $184m. Kassem's fall caused a temporary slow-down in some of these schemes, but a new agreement concluded in March 1965 announced plans for a large dam and a hydro-electric station on the Euphrates.

All these technical aid programs provided for the dispatch of

Soviet and East European specialists. In 1957 it was reported that there were 350 non-military technicians in Egypt, about 180 in Syria, and 55 in the Yemen. Their number rose to about 3,000 in 1968; their salaries were usually charged in full to the credits extended. The Soviet Union also undertook to train local technicians; about 19,000 skilled workers were given instruction in special schools in Egypt between 1959 and 1967; some 11,000 are said to be in training at the present time.[4] About 20,000 students and technical trainees from third-world countries received part of their training in the Soviet Union between 1955 and 1965, but there are indications that their number is now declining.

The Soviet aid program to the underdeveloped countries has taken an uneven course. The most rapid expansion took place between 1958 and 1961; 1958 was the peak year in the Middle East, with commitments totalling $278m. There was a sharp decline in 1961, when not a single new credit was extended to any Middle East country, perhaps as a result of the many commitments entered into by the Soviet Union in Africa in 1961–2. In 1963 economic aid to the Middle East began to increase again and reached a new peak in 1964 and 1965 – $530m. and $574m. respectively, most of it to Egypt.[5] Altogether, out of a total of $5 billion in economic credits and grants extended by the Soviet Union between 1954 and 1966 to underdeveloped countries, the Middle East received about 40%, $2 billion; of Soviet exports to developing countries the share of the Middle East was also about one-third of the total, clearly indicating the importance Moscow attached to that trade in comparison with other parts of the world.[6] However, even after this expansion, Soviet bloc trade with the Middle East accounted for only 11–12% of the area's total trade.* The one major exception is Egypt, which has mortgaged a substantial part of its annual cotton crop to the Soviet Union. A considerable part of the burden of the communist economic aid effort has in the past been shouldered by the countries of Eastern Europe. Between 1954 and 1965 they extended credits totalling $725m. to the area. East European exports to the Middle East have been considerably higher than those of the Soviet Union, again excepting Egypt; imports, on the other hand, were considerably smaller. This resulted in a substantial loss for them, and despite

---

* The net outflow of Soviet aid has fallen in recent years; it was about $155m. in 1966 and $125m. in 1967. In 1967 Communist aid offers were 45% lower than in 1966; there had been decreases also during the two previous years.

Soviet pressure there has been growing reluctance in East Europe to continue to engage in such unprofitable trade.

It is pointless to discuss Soviet economic relations with the Middle East without referring again to the one item of export which has had by far the greatest political impact. The Soviet Union provided the complete equipment for the Egyptian and Syrian armies, and has delivered substantial quantities of weapons to Iraq (estimated at $300m. before the Six Day War), the Yemen, Algeria, and the Sudan. There were small Soviet arms shipments to the Middle East even before the famous deal with Egypt in 1955, when Britain had been the main supplier to the area of tanks and jet aircraft. Since the recipients had to pay for their purchases in hard cash, there were narrow limits to these sales.[7] The Soviet Union, by offering barter deals, broke the Western monopoly, and made possible far larger purchases. It supplied some 2,000–3,000 tanks to the Arab states, as well as missiles, missile-firing vessels, Ilyushin and TU-16 tactical bombers, the most recent MiGs, and other sophisticated equipment. After June 1967 new deliveries were made on a very big scale to replace the material that had been lost or damaged; some 4,000–5,000 Soviet military advisers supervised the reorganization of the Arab armies and the establishment of new munitions industries. By its willingness to deliver modern arms at low cost or even free of charge, the Soviet Union established a special position for itself in the Arab world. The West could match the commercial offers and the aid schemes proposed by the Russians, but no Western government could have become the chief arms supplier to Egypt and Syria, Iraq and the Yemen. All these countries were ruled by military men who, much as they needed financial aid, valued the supply of arms even more highly.

In trying to develop trade with the Middle East (and the third world in general) the Soviet Union labored under various handicaps. It is not one of the great trading powers: having recently been overtaken by Japan, it now ranks sixth in the world. Its share in world trade has in fact declined in recent years. According to OECD calculations, Western public development aid disbursements up to the middle sixties were ten times as much as that of the Soviet bloc and China. If Western private investment is added, the ratio is even higher. Leaving arms aside, the Soviet bloc aid commitment to the Middle East has been about $2 billion since 1954, of which, as we said, not much more than one-third has actually been disbursed.

Western official aid in 1960 and 1961, on the other hand, has been almost equal in volume; it is estimated at about $670m., not counting private investment.[8] Again in 1966 the non-Communist countries provided $10·562 million worth of resources, exceeding in one single year total Communist deliveries over a period of twelve years. The Soviet Union has faced great problems in carrying out its promises: 'For many aid recipients the phase of actual project implementation has proved much less glamorous than the initial announcement of large-scale lines of credit.'[9] Very often the signing of an agreement was followed by time-consuming studies and pilot projects; delays and inefficient implementation also had a detrimental effect. Occasionally the goods supplied were not suited to local needs, or they were found deficient in design, quality, and spares. Bulgarian silos built at Latakia in Syria, to give but one example, were found so defective that compensation was asked for. Mention has been made of the resale of raw materials by Soviet and East European buyers; this has concerned Egyptian and Syrian cotton and other produce.

A comparison of trade and aid figures shows that up to 1966 the Soviet effort in the Middle East has been heavily orientated towards Egypt and Syria. This is not to imply that all Soviet trade in the Middle East has been politically motivated; Moscow has shown considerable eagerness to expand its trade wherever this could be done profitably. But the figures also show that it has been willing to lose substantial amounts of money in order to gain political influence. Investments have been made with an eye to long-term gains rather than immediate successes; they have been concentrated on certain strategically chosen projects, such as the Aswan and Euphrates dams, which for obvious reasons were likely to receive far more publicity than food shipments or other, more prosaic, forms of trade or aid. Soviet economic support, furthermore, was always given with an eye to strengthening the State sector of the economy in such a way as to prove the advantages of the Soviet model for the developing countries. The military and technical programs have been designed to create a new Soviet-trained *élite* on the assumption that those who receive their training in the Soviet bloc will be orientated towards the East in the same way as earlier Western-trained generations were, broadly speaking, pro-Western. It is by no means certain that such assumptions are correct: prolonged exposure to life in the Soviet Union and the other East bloc countries does not necessarily convert foreign residents to communism.

The idea that the development of trade relations and the extension of economic aid makes friends and influences people still has many advocates in both East and West. Yet it is certainly incorrect in the short view, and only partly true in a longer perspective. Economic penetration helps to establish positions of strength, but it also extends the area of friction and creates discontent and resentment. Measured in terms of political influence, the results are usually meagre. Even the smallest and weakest countries are not often entirely swayed by considerations of economic loss and profit when facing important political decisions.

8   The Soviet Military Presence

The presence of a Soviet fleet in the Mediterranean attracted a great
deal of publicity during the Arab-Israeli war of 1967, but it had not
come into being overnight; its creation was part of an overall policy
aimed at strengthening the capability of the Soviet Union for
military action in various parts of the world. An appraisal of the role
of the Mediterranean fleet should therefore start with a review,
however brief, of the general development of Soviet military
doctrine and policy over the last decade.

According to classical Marxist-Leninist doctrine, capitalism leads
to war as surely as the clouds bring rain; violence is the midwife of
history and the future is envisaged as a series of terrible clashes
between the Soviet Republic and the *bourgeois* states. The nuclear age,
however, introduced a new dimension: the relation between ends
and means, between the prospective gains and the effect of the use
of the new weapons, rendered the Clausewitz thesis doubtful if not
completely obsolete. For the West, with its defensive mentality, the
bomb posed the dilemma of relying on it, without wanting to use it,
to preserve the *status quo*. The Soviet bloc faced an even more
difficult dilemma. It wanted to change the *status quo*, but it gradually
came to understand that in the nuclear age revolutionary violence,
the midwife of history, could easily become its grave-digger. The
Soviet leaders were ideologically committed to revolutionary action,
but they also realized that this could trigger off a nuclear chain
reaction. The cardinal question then was how to reduce the risk
without abandoning revolutionary ideology altogether. This discussion, which has now lasted for several years, has involved the
very essence of the communist movement, its destiny and historical
justification: how to preserve a revolutionary dynamic despite the

danger of world war? 'Just wars' of national liberation have by no means been ruled out, but there is no guarantee that such 'limited wars', even in the remoter parts of the world, will not escalate into something far more threatening. The new situation gave birth to the doctrine and policy of the limited risk, essays in brinkmanship, based on the assumption that the other side, for reasons such as national parochialism, shortsightedness, lack of nerve, internal resistance by unilateralists, and so on, would not be ready to take equal risks.

Since 1953 Soviet leaders have shown from time to time that the basic policy dilemma was quite clear to them. Malenkov announced soon after Stalin's death that a new world war, given the present means of warfare, meant the destruction of world civilization. A leading Soviet military theoretician wrote in 1960 that a global war would probably mean the end of half of mankind, and the more active and cultured half at that.[1] These were isolated statements at the time, and sometimes had to be withdrawn because of their excessive 'defeatism', but it is known that the problem continued increasingly to preoccupy the Soviet leaders. The Chinese, in their dispute with Moscow, maintained that coexistence was untenable because war as a revolutionary solution in the international class war was inevitable. This policy was unacceptable to Moscow, where it was argued that Peking wanted to instigate a nuclear holocaust because it would result in the destruction of both America and Russia and thus open the way to Chinese world domination.

Western students of Soviet military policy during that period were frequently puzzled. They overrated Soviet strength, miscalculating the number of Soviet ICBMs deployed. The 'missile gap' was exposed as a myth in 1961; up to that date it had been used by the Soviet Union to make political gains and to keep the initiative in international affairs. On the theoretical level, many Western observers failed to understand that for the Soviet leaders 'peaceful coexistence' and 'cold war' were not contradictory policies, but two sides of the same coin. There was a curious air of unreality in Western discussions about strategic calculations and the arms race. The arms-control approach, with its arguments about first strike and second strike, pre-emption and escalation, missile and deterrent gaps, seemed almost completely to ignore the political element. It was an attempt to abstract Soviet military and foreign policy into a strategic formula, in which flesh-and-blood Soviet leaders appeared as mechanical brains, infallible in their reasoning and completely divorced from any psychological, social, or ideological context. To strengthen the surrealist feeling even further, the debate began to look like a game of chess without a chessboard, its mental constructions and strategic anticipations made in a world in which Kafka met Lewis Carroll, in which the employment of nuclear weapons and the avoidance of their use were envisaged at one and the same time, while 'generations' of such weapons were obsolete before they reached the production stage.

Under Stalin no effort had been made to bring the new weapons into the general framework of Soviet foreign and military policy. His successors – Khrushchev in particular – had almost unlimited confidence in nuclear arms: they would not just deter an aggressor; massive nuclear retaliation, the ability to hit the United States, would make it possible to regain the manœuvrability and political initiative which for several years had been impaired by American nuclear superiority.[2] The hardening of Soviet long-range missile sites (i.e. making them less vulnerable to enemy attack) and progress in anti-missile defence reduced the danger of surprise attack. It also caused a partial shift from the concept of massive retaliation to a more flexible strategy. Politically it had contradictory consequences; Khrushchev embarked on a policy of rising risks, vigorous diplomatic campaigns coupled with nuclear blackmail, committing Soviet policy and prestige to dangerous situations, culminating in the attempt to place offensive missiles in Cuba. At the same time he realized that the Soviet Union was not likely to prevail over the West in a major armaments race. With the massive increase in American missile production the strategic balance swung against the Soviet Union. As late as autumn 1961 its leaders declared that the number of American missiles was offset by the superior quality of Soviet weapons, but America, with better intelligence than previously, was not impressed. The Soviet leaders, unwilling to give up their ambitious economic development projects and to concentrate on a crash programme of missile production, drew the obvious conclusion and began to work for a *détente* with the West. This was, above all, Khrushchev's line, but his successors did not radically reverse the policy, although there was a gradual shift in emphasis. Soviet military spokesmen argued that under Khrushchev the all-round strengthening of the armed forces had been neglected; the military lobby claimed that they had not sufficient money at their disposal to ensure Soviet defence. Brezhnev and Kosygin accepted these arguments and decided upon a reallocation of resources; the military budget went up by 5% in 1966 and by 8% the year after. These were the published figures; the real increases were probably higher. The Soviet leaders justified this by referring to the worsening world situation and to the more aggressive character of 'imperialism'. Some military spokesmen even began to question the thesis, generally accepted during the Khrushchev era, that war in the nuclear age had become obsolete as an instrument of policy. Colonel Rybkin, writing in 1966, argued that the Soviet Union could not accept the doctrine that victory in nuclear war was impossible; to do so would spread fatalism, even defeatism.[3] He and other hard-liners were criticized by some of their colleagues, and the party leaders stressed that such fundamental decisions would in any case be taken by the political leadership, not by the military, in view both of the political objectives of a future war and of the destructive properties of modern weapons. But Brezhnev, Kosygin, and some of their colleagues were clearly impressed by the arguments of the hawks, in particular that a formal rejection of the political utility of nuclear war was bad for morale, quite apart from the fact that it ran counter to certain basic ideological tenets of Leninism. A policy of *détente tout court* was likely to erode the ideological cohesion of the world communist movement and undermine Soviet prestige in the third world. They did not question the necessity of great prudence in their relations with the United States, but they refused to accept the policy of *détente* as a constraint on political or military initiatives in areas presumed to be of less than vital interest to the Americans.[4] Such initiatives were to proceed according to the rules of the game, but these rules were fairly vague, and as far as the Russians were concerned they were bound to change as Soviet military capability continued to grow.

The post-Khrushchev leadership undertook a substantial build-up of Soviet strategic forces. In summer and autumn 1966 an accelerated program of ICBM construction got under way, and by the beginning of 1967 the number of operational ICBMs was about 400–50, increasing at a rate of more than 100 a year, compared with the total deployment of fewer than 200 ICBM launchers during the entire Khrushchev period.[5] By 1968 it was thought that the number of land-based ICBM launchers had risen to 750, and Russia was expected to achieve parity with the American total of just over 1,000 in 1969 or 1970. In numbers of warheads (including obsolete manned bombers) the American advantage was still 3 : 1 or more in September 1967, but it was thought that it would be reduced to 2 : 1 if not less by 1970.[6] In addition, a massive research and development effort was undertaken in the Soviet Union after 1958 to ensure military-technological superiority. This program, unlike the American, did not aim mainly at improvement and follow-on of existing weapons systems, but stressed the importance of new break-throughs and new weaponry.

While Soviet military leaders discussed Western intentions and the best ways and means to develop Soviet military power, there was a similar discussion about Soviet aims in the capitals of the West, where some observers argued that there was a danger in taking American superiority for granted and in underrating Soviet ability to push through priority programs and to produce an effective and flexible scientific-technological military base; while America and its principal NATO allies were under great internal pressure to reduce their military budgets, the Soviet Union was forging ahead. In addition to the build-up of its strategic forces, steps were taken in Moscow to obtain a capability for direct intervention in future third world conflicts. The 1968 Soviet military budget for the first time earmarked special funds for arms deliveries to 'national liberation movements'. To a greater extent than before, Soviet military spokesmen discussed the possibility of non-nuclear warfare, even in Europe.[7] Previously it had been assumed that a new war, especially in Europe, would witness immediate strategic nuclear escalation.

Basically, of course, the debate was political, not military. Those Western observers who were convinced that the Soviet Union had undergone a process of *embourgeoisement*, contended that with the rising standard of living and the increasing destructiveness of the new weapons, the dynamism has gone out of the communist states in East Europe, though perhaps not of the communist movements in the third world; proletarians now had more to lose than their chains, and had, as a result, become far more responsible, i.e. less revolutionary in character. Soviet doctrinal declarations were not taken at face value:

Although Soviet propaganda continues to give to the Soviet people a distorted picture of the outside world, and some of the Soviet military still propagate the view that 'imperialism' is actively preparing to launch a war against the 'socialist countries', the Soviet government continued to behave throughout 1967 like a great power concerned to optimize its position within the existing system, rather than like a revolutionary regime out to create a new system. . . .[8]

It followed that Western policy should promote the spread of these trends by working for a *détente* with the Soviet Union and that the common security interests of the two super-powers should be stressed (as in the non-proliferation treaty). Nothing should be done to provoke the Russians. It did not really matter if they caught up with the West in the output of ICBMs, for once a certain level was reached, 'strategic superiority' lost its meaning. Exponents of this school also argued that the emerging threat to both the super-powers from the more militant Chinese was drawing them together.[9] These views found their reflection in continued American hopes for a real *détente* with the Soviet Union in 1967–8, and in the assumption that Soviet action in Czechoslovakia was only a temporary aberration and that, even if it was not, it should not be permitted to affect the overriding necessity for Soviet-American understanding.

A more pessimistic view of Soviet intentions was also represented; this, while not denying that the Soviet regime had become more conservative and nationalist in character, questioned whether it had necessarily become less aggressive. The quasi-Marxist argument that greater wealth would manifest itself in the Soviet bloc in a genuine desire for peaceful coexistence was not accepted; East Germany, it was pointed out, was the communist country with the highest living standards, but was also the one closest to Stalinism within the bloc. According to this school of thought, it was for a variety of reasons more likely than not that the Soviet Union would pursue a more aggressive policy in the years to come, and it was doubtful therefore whether much importance could be attached to the various American-Soviet treaties for which the doves were willing to make concessions. The Soviet Union was gradually catching up with America in the strategic balance; if it had followed a hard line in the past, on a basis of relative military weakness, was there any reason to doubt that it would assert its interests in various parts of the world with even greater emphasis once it reached parity, let alone superiority? It was irrelevant whether Soviet pressure was interpreted with reference to traditional revolutionary ideology or on the basis of the nationalist-totalitarian character of the regime, in geo-political terms or in terms of big-power policies. All big powers have the tendency to expand, until they encounter resistance. Such expansion can always be explained with reference to defence and security; a glacis, or sphere of influence, is clearly needed to defend the Soviet Union against its enemies. But then the sphere of influence itself has to be defended against enemies, real or, more often, imaginary; the allies of the Soviet Union will be secure only if their neighbors, and preferably their neighbors' neighbors as well, are at least neutralized. It may not always be possible to achieve such optimal security, but it is clearly the long-term political and military aim. The weaker the neighbors, the greater the temptation to extend the sphere of influence, and the greater also the chances of success.

During the last years of Khrushchev's rule a determined effort was made to improve the reach and the mobility of Soviet conventional and general-purpose forces. Much of the emphasis was on the development of the naval forces for both 'blue-water' and amphibious landing operations. At the same time large transport aircraft were built to reinforce Soviet long-range air-lift capability. This was one of the lessons from the Soviet setback in Cuba in 1962, strengthened by the growing conviction that Soviet involvement in the Middle East, Asia, and Africa made the existence of a long-range task force a matter of vital importance. In pursuance of this policy, the underseas fleet was expanded; together with the naval air arm (a land-based force of some 850 aircraft), it was given the leading place in the build-up of Soviet naval power.[10] Soviet nuclear-powered submarines began to undertake regular patrols in distant oceans, and made a round-the-world cruise in 1966. Aircraft and troop-carrier construction and the building of helicopter carriers was stepped up to make intervention with local landing parties possible.[11]

The decision to station Soviet ships permanently in the Mediterranean, taken in 1963 or early 1964, was also part of this policy. The existence of these units had been known to experts, but it was only after Brezhnev's call for the withdrawal of the American Sixth Fleet in April 1967 and the Arab-Israeli war that the general public began to take note of the presence of the Soviet fleet and to ponder its implications. There was little the Western powers could do about it: the Mediterranean is open to all seafaring nations and the Soviet naval presence there was not unprecedented. There had been Russian naval units in the area during the Napoleonic wars; Paul I had wanted to occupy Malta, but the British had forestalled him; the Russians fought a naval battle near Mount Athos in 1807, and took part in the battle of Navarino in 1827. The Crimean war marked a setback to the Russian fleet, but towards the end of the century, within the framework of the French-Russian alliance, Russian units began again to appear in the Eastern Mediterranean. After the revolution Soviet destroyers and later on whole flotillas visited Italy, calling at Greek and Turkish ports on their way. These regular calls came to an end only in 1935 with the *rapprochement* between Hitler and Mussolini. In the nineteen-fifties Soviet submarines were stationed in Albania, but these bases ceased to function with the break in Soviet-Albanian relations.

In some important respects the Soviet naval presence of the sixties was different: it was permanent, far more substantial, and part of an overall political and military design. In Stalin's days the main role of the navy was to support the army; there had been a big postwar naval construction program (including aircraft-carriers), but it received low priority and was time and again postponed.[12] Under Khrushchev, too, Soviet admirals faced an uphill struggle in their efforts to convince the political leaders that the navy's activities should not be limited to coastal waters, but that it should be given the capability to engage in independent action on the broad oceans. The access of both the Baltic and the Black Sea fleets to the high seas is by way of straits, not under Soviet control, while the Northern fleet is located far from the political and industrial centers of the Soviet Union. To overcome these geographical handicaps, the admirals suggested greater strategic mobility, using techniques which would enable them to keep their ships away from port over long periods.[13] In the early sixties they had no port facilities in the Mediterranean, but employed instead sheltered, shallow coastal waters as permanent holding grounds: near the Greek island of Cythera, in the south-eastern Cyclades, south of Malta, at the Alborran islands east of Gibraltar, and in the Gulf of Hammamet, off Tunisia. There was a steady procession of oil-tankers, repair-ships, ammunition-barges, submarine-tenders, and other naval auxiliaries to and from these holding grounds. But as the Mediterranean fleet grew in size, the floating bases became inadequate and Soviet warships began to call more and more often at Port Said, Alexandria, and Latakia for refuelling and refitting. From 1961 the Soviet naval commander-in-chief, Admiral Gorshkov, visited Egypt regularly almost every year. The Soviet Union received permanent bases in Egypt in all but name; at almost any given time there were Soviet men-of-war in the Egyptian ports or in Latakia. Officially this remained an *ad hoc* arrangement only because any formal pact would have smacked of traditional imperialist practices. It was Soviet policy to run these bases as unobtrusively as possible, and both the Egyptians and the Syrians had their own reasons for not giving undue publicity to these arrangements.

The role and growing importance of the Soviet fleet was described by its commander in a programmatic article in 1963:

Formerly our warships and naval aviation were a junior service concerned mainly with supporting the ground troops. Now . . . we must be prepared through broad offensive operations to deliver crushing strikes against sea and ground targets of the imperialists on any point of the world oceans and adjacent territories.[14]

Four years later, on the occasion of Soviet Navy Day, 1967, Gorshkov wrote that the big imperialist powers had long lost complete supremacy at sea and that sooner or later they would have to realize that they had no supremacy at all. 'The Soviet navy's ensign is now proudly flown in all the seas and oceans.' On another occasion Gorshkov revealed details about the decision taken in the nineteen-fifties to construct an ocean-going navy capable of carrying out offensive tasks of a strategic nature, in response to the expansion of Western sea power in the decade after the second world war.[15] This decision implied the development of a Soviet task force, including Polaris-type submarines, as well as missile-carrying forces and nuclear weapons capable of engaging in limited war.

Among the Soviet ships regularly deployed in the Mediterranean before the Arab-Israeli war were two cruisers of the *Sverdlov* and *Kirov* class, armed with six-inch guns and guided missiles. There were also *Kynda* and *Kaskin* class guided-missile frigates, with surface-to-surface and surface-to-air missile-launchers. These ships were highly rated by Western observers. An American commentator noted that the *Kyndas* in particular represented an effort by the Soviet navy to close its gun gap, to gain a high level of fire-power, doubly necessary in view of the lack of carrier-based aircraft. The absence of aircraft-carriers has been adduced as proof of the absence of Soviet offensive aims in the Mediterranean. But the building of such carriers would have involved heavy expenditure; the construction of helicopter-carriers represents a compromise. Furthermore, given the growing Soviet influence in Egypt and Syria and the possibility of stationing aircraft in those countries, it was not so certain that the Soviet Union actually needed aircraft-carriers in the area.

The small Soviet Mediterranean Fleet, the '*Eskadra*', also included before May 1967 a number of conventional submarines, among them at least one carrying guided missiles, nine destroyers, several intelligence vessels, as well as survey ships, submarine-tenders, etc., altogether about half that of the American Sixth Fleet, which consisted at the outbreak of the war in June of forty-six ships. Later on as many as sixty Soviet ships were counted, including fifteen destroyers, but their number fluctuated from day to day.[16] In September 1968 the new Soviet helicopter carrier *Moskva* joined the Mediterranean fleet. The Soviet Union had an edge of more than 3 : 1 over the American fleet in the number of submarines, but the presence of two aircraft-carriers, the *Saratoga* and the *America*, made the US fleet more powerful than a comparison of mere numbers would indicate.[17] Some Western reports about growing Soviet strength in the Mediterranean were alarmist, 'inspired by naval lobbyists and patently exaggerated; missiles with a range of ten miles are equated with those of hundreds, and aged cruisers are presented as fierce new contenders for naval supremacy';[18] inferior in numbers and lacking air cover, the Soviet Mediterranean fleet (it was argued) was no match for the Sixth Fleet; it was a political weapon rather than a war fleet. According to C. Gasteyger, the greatest effect of the build-up was psychological, at least during the early stage. But the strategic position of the West was likely to deteriorate in the years to come, whereas the Soviet Mediterranean fleet was to be increased in strength; the Soviet merchant and oil-tanker fleets are also expanding rapidly. The Eastern Mediterranean was, to a certain extent, hostile waters for the Sixth Fleet; the Soviet missiles had a far greater range than any naval guns, perhaps more than 100 miles. The British decision in 1968 to retain in the Mediterranean two frigates and a Canberra reconnaissance squadron was not sufficient to restore the former balance. Admiral Griffin, commander-in-chief of Allied Forces, Southern Europe, commented in 1967 that the Soviet fleet could now project military power at a long distance from home into areas 'where it can hurt us seriously', and predicted the building of further helicopter-carriers (similar to the American assault ships) and the build-up of the Soviet Marine Corps.[19] Admiral Rivero, his successor, on the other hand, said he was not convinced that the Soviet fleet would be substantially increased in the future: 'even a stronger Soviet fleet would be threatened by our aircraft'.[20] His optimism may have been connected with the plans to establish an inter-Allied Mediterranean fleet advanced in summer 1968.

The presence of a permanent Soviet Mediterranean fleet gave rise to much speculation about its military and political purpose. It was thought that the actual combat value of a relatively weak naval force was strictly limited. It could act within limits as a deterrent to nuclear strikes from the American aircraft-carriers and Polaris submarines; this was, no doubt, part of the intention behind the Soviet decision to keep a fleet in the Mediterranean.[21] American naval commanders frequently complained about Soviet harassing tactics and extensive surveillance; the Soviet fleet was clearly collecting intelligence on the Sixth Fleet's capability for both nuclear and limited warfare, and the Soviet government must have immediately known in June 1967 that there was no truth in the charges made by President Nasser and King Hussein about the intervention of the Sixth Fleet in the Arab-Israeli war. The military importance of the Soviet presence in the Mediterranean was, however, seriously reduced and Soviet strategic mobility restricted by the closure of the Suez Canal as the result of the war, and it was clearly in the Soviet interest to try to bring pressure on Israel to withdraw from the Canal. Its closure prevented Soviet access to the Persian Gulf and the Indian Ocean, and as a result the Soviet Far Eastern, not the Mediterranean Fleet, was called in to show the flag in such distant places as Basra and Mogadishu.

Although the military purpose behind the build-up of the Soviet Mediterranean fleet should not be underrated, the overriding considerations behind the decision were clearly political in character. It reflected the desire to make effective political use of sea power, to strengthen the Soviet position in the Middle East, to give fresh courage to Egypt and Syria, to bring pressure on all other countries in the area. While unable to stand up to the American fleet if it came to war, the Soviet naval presence meant nevertheless that the Western naval monopoly in the Mediterranean had come to an end:

The Russian squadron there does for Russia's Arab friends what the American troops in Germany do for America's allies in Europe: if it gets involved in a fight it could bring Russia's full weight in after it. Its presence will make the Western powers step just that more gingerly in any future crisis.[22]

The Soviet naval presence thus acted as a factor inhibiting any Western military move, even though its main immediate impact was no doubt meant to be psychological. A Soviet naval visit to Egypt four weeks after the defeat in 1967 was intended to reassure President Nasser, but Admiral Molokhov's declaration on that occasion, that the Soviet vessels were ready to cooperate with Egyptian armed forces to repel any aggression,[23] was toned down in the Soviet press. Throughout 1967 and 1968 Soviet cruisers and escort ships showed the flag in the Persian Gulf, in Mogadishu, in Madras, Bombay, and Karachi. These visits gave rise to much speculation about possible Soviet intentions to acquire naval bases in the Indian Ocean (in South Arabia and in the Andaman and Nicobar Islands), following Britain's withdrawal from East of Suez in 1971; they also reflected growing Soviet concern with Chinese intentions in South-East Asia, suggesting their connection with long-term plans rather than immediate policies. For, despite its striking growth, the Soviet navy during the late sixties was clearly not yet in a position to undertake all the military and political tasks which some Western observers thought had been assigned to them.

During the Khrushchev era a Soviet project for an atom-free zone in the Mediterranean had from time to time been mooted. With the build-up of the fleet the idea was dropped on the ground that the presence of Soviet ships was a reassurance to the progressive forces in the area and protected the independence of the small nations. When asked at a press conference in Sofia whether the Soviet plan to turn the area into a 'zone of peace' could be combined with the Soviet naval presence, Gromyko said that Soviet ships in the Mediterranean were serving precisely the interests of European security and peace. As a Black Sea power, the Soviet Union was also a Mediterranean country, and it was therefore only natural that it should be interested in the peace and security of a region close to its southern borders.[24] These views were shared by Egypt and Syria, whose representatives declared repeatedly that they regarded the Soviet fleet as their shield against the aggressive designs of the American Sixth Fleet. Similar opinions were voiced by the majority at a conference of 'progressive movements in the Mediterranean', which took place in Rome in April 1968. Among those present were representatives of the Syrian Ba'th and the Egyptian ASU, the Algerian FLN, the Communist parties of France, Italy, Cyprus, Greece, and Morocco, and the Turkish Labor Party.[25] But there were significant differences in the attitudes of the various parties and countries; the Yugoslavs argued that American Atlantic policy was the main threat to peace and demanded the withdrawal of the Sixth Fleet, which was a 'constant danger to the freedom and independence of the Mediterranean countries'; with its removal the main reason for the presence of the Soviet fleet would disappear.[26] The Yugoslavs thus ultimately wanted both fleets to withdraw, an attitude which, needless to say, did not please Moscow and which, incidentally, prevented the adoption of unanimous resolutions at the Rome conference.[27] Yugoslavia's past experience with Soviet foreign policy had not always been fortunate, and when Admiral Gorshkov, on the occasion of an official visit to Belgrade in April 1967, asked for naval bases (to replace the Albanian base at Valone), the Yugoslav government is said to have rejected the demand on the ground of its country's neutral policy.[28]

Non-communist countries had even graver misgivings. Italy felt threatened by the presence of the Soviet fleet, although (a fact usually forgotten when comparisons are made between the Soviet fleet and the Sixth Fleet) the Italian navy was superior to the Soviet '*Eskadra*' in conventional fire-power. After the occupation of Czechoslovakia, the Italian Communist party, too, opposed the presence of the Soviet fleet in the Mediterranean. Spain had justified the Soviet naval presence in 1965, mainly no doubt because it resented its exclusion from NATO. Moscow had reciprocated on various occasions; in August 1967, during the UN debate on Gibraltar, the Soviet bloc had given full support to the Spanish demands. At the same time the build-up of the Soviet fleet was also used by the Spanish government to ask for greater political and military help from the United States. Castiella, the foreign minister, declared in the Cortes that the Soviet naval presence had greatly increased the strategic significance of the Spanish coastal areas.[29] In France concern was expressed about the relatively weaker American position and the delivery to Algeria and Egypt of Soviet missile-carriers.[30] But fears about the possible consequences were felt most acutely in the Eastern Mediterranean, in Greece, Turkey, and Israel. A Turkish government newspaper asked: 'What are those Soviet vessels looking for in a sea where they have no coast? The Russians are trying to establish a net throughout the Mediterranean to control the area.'[31] Early in 1968 the Turkish Foreign Ministry published figures showing that during the previous year, 1967, a record number of Soviet warships had passed through the Straits, 107 of them after the Arab-Israeli war. In the Turkish view, there was nothing the country could do to lessen the danger; a revision of the Montreux Convention was certainly out of the question. The age-old Russian dream of getting a firm foothold in the Mediterranean had finally come true not by overrunning, but by by-passing Turkey.

Above all, Israel had reason to feel concern. Advanced Soviet missiles had been used in the sinking of the Israeli destroyer *Eilat* in October 1967.[32] After this incident a number of Soviet warships were immediately dispatched to Port Said on the mistaken assumption that Israel intended to take reprisals against that city, and that the presence of Soviet units would deter it. This move, unpublicized in the Soviet press, was in some ways a symbolic act, a classic case (to quote an American observer)

of how a major power with nearby conventional forces may feel obliged to respond when an important state with which it is developing close relations, feels itself in danger. It showed that commitment to a certain regime, an investment of national prestige, could lead towards military protection of that regime and through the presence of conventional forces, towards a higher risk of combat involvement, even though this may not have been the original intention.

The Port Said incident may have foreshadowed in some ways the shape of things to come: what if in future a Soviet warship or aircraft stationed in Egypt were hit in the course of a battle? Would the Soviet forces retaliate by a strike against Israel, and would Israel hesitate to fire back? Would it be possible to halt the escalation? The Israeli military were not overawed by the Soviet presence; they felt that the Soviet Union did not have the capacity to engage in any major action in the near future, and they tried to leave no doubt that any Soviet attack would be resisted. It was the Israeli assumption that while Soviet ships could fire rockets at targets in Israel from some distance, a landing operation was ruled out for years to come. Soviet commentators had admitted that it might be five years before Soviet forces were capable of executing and supporting even a lightly opposed landing in that part of the world.[33] Above all, Israel assumed that the Russians would not want to overstep the line, which could involve them in a dangerous confrontation with the United States.

The long-term perspectives were less clear. Khrushchev's policy in the Cuban missile crisis had been foolish in the eyes of his successors, not because it had been too daring, but because the Soviet Union did not have sufficient strength to back up its initiative when challenged. Brezhnev and Kosygin therefore gave priority to a swift build-up of the strategic missile forces and nuclear-powered missile-launching submarines as the 'principal means of deterring an aggressor and decisively defeating him in war'.[34] The Soviet objective was to achieve parity with the United States in the number of launchers by 1970 or at most a little later, and ultimately superiority.[35] (Whether 'superiority' still made sense in the age of MIRVs and other new weapons, and whether parity had not in fact already been reached, were different questions.)

At the same time great efforts are now being invested in strengthening Soviet non-nuclear long-range strike forces. The construction of helicopter-carriers capable of carrying 30–5 helicopters, and the reactivation of the Soviet Marine Corps, are part of this scheme. The marine force counted only 6,000–8,000 men in 1968 (compared with 280,000 American marines), and it was dispersed over four fleets; there was an airborne force of 50,000 and long-range transport aircraft capable of lifting tanks and artillery and up to three divisions. The supply operation on short notice to Cairo after the Six Day War, to the Yemen in November 1967, and the deployment of Soviet troops in Czechoslovakia in August 1968, showed that the Soviet Union had made progress in mastering the requirements of long-distance military intervention, but so far these forces have not encountered opposition, or have been deployed in countries contiguous to the Soviet Union. In the Middle East the Soviet Union is not in full control of the lines of sea and air support and military intervention would present far greater difficulties. It is unlikely that it would be undertaken with small forces in the hope that the adversary would be too stunned to offer serious resistance. The availability of overwhelming force would be, in Soviet eyes, a precondition for success; no one wants to repeat Stalin's mistake in Finland. Such overwhelming force will not be available for long-range intervention for at least a number of years. The Soviet Union will therefore be reluctant to become directly involved in military operations in the Middle East in the near future – certainly not by committing ground-combat units. In the more distant future the Middle East remains for political and strategic reasons the most likely direction in which Moscow's capability in the use of limited military power might be applied.

Long-term Soviet aims in the Middle East cannot, of course, be discussed in isolation from the relations between the two super-powers. Since, at latest, 1963, the date of the test-ban treaty, there has been general agreement between Russia and America about global spheres of influence. While the *détente* gave the world several years of relative peace, its limitations are obvious. It reflected the strategic and political balance of power in 1963, internal develop-ments in Russia and America, as well as the situation in other parts of the world. Any major change affecting one of these factors is bound to upset the balance and thus affect the *détente*. The world situation of 1963 cannot be frozen; there is no good reason to believe that the Soviet leaders regard it as a permanent arrangement. Total war is ruled out but the rules of the game and the division of spheres are considered subject to modification with the growth of Soviet military power and its ability to exploit Western weaknesses and conflicts in the third world.

The place of the Middle East in the West-East *détente* has never been clarified. It had been a British and French sphere of influence until the nineteen-forties. In the fifties and sixties Western influence was greatly reduced, whereas the Soviet Union acquired a dominant position in several Arab countries and succeeded in neutralizing others. Whether Soviet influence will increase now depends on the intensity of internal conflict, domestic developments in the countries of the area, the attitudes of governments, and public opinion. In this struggle for influence, the Soviet Union, like other big powers, is using various means to assert its position, of which the military presence is certainly not the least important. But the future of the Middle East also depends to a large extent on American capability and American intentions, which are less clear than Soviet aims. It depends on the general trend of American policy between the extremes of globalism or isolationism, on the decision as to how high the Middle East ranks in American global priorities and commit-ments. While Soviet military power is likely to grow within the next decade, and to lead to a higher risk policy, it is by no means certain that, even with Soviet supremacy established, the Middle East would necessarily turn into a Soviet sphere of influence, similar to East Europe. The further growth of American isolationism, a conse-quence of the Vietnam war and of a latent trend on both the right and the left of the American political spectrum, would make it, of course, much easier for the Soviet Union to achieve its aims. The disappearance of the 'American threat' would open up many possibilities in the area, ranging from mere neutralization (on the Finnish or Afghan pattern) of Middle East countries to satellization or even territorial annexation. An American retreat from the Middle East and the Eastern Mediterranean may not be likely at present, but the possibility, either as a result of a shift in the global balance of power or as the consequence of some major political miscalculation, cannot be altogether dismissed. The prospects for a united Middle East defence effort in the foreseeable future are nil, for internal conflicts run far too deep; the countries of the Middle East, even if united, are in any case too weak to resist a super-power bent on dominating the area.

These are the worst prospects facing the Middle East; there is, needless to say, no certainty that they will come to pass. The Soviet regime may mellow in time and become more peaceful in character; it may be satisfied with the territorial advances made under Stalin after the second world war. Its growing capability to intervene in other parts of the world, including the Middle East, must not necessarily lead to further conquests in that undefined no-man's-land between Russia and America. Moscow may have to face more urgent preoccupations, both at home and abroad, during the years to come, and the Middle East may receive a further respite. All these possibilities exist, but a realistic appraisal of the situation has to be based on the probability of limited war in the Middle East. In such a situation, the Soviet decision to intervene, and the extent of its intervention, will depend on the wider risks involved; and on the resolution and the military capability of the countries likely to offer resistance.

9 Communism, Maoism, Arab Socialism

The beginnings of communism in the Middle East can be traced back almost fifty years, but nowhere did it attain any political significance until well after the second world war. Before that an objectively revolutionary situation (to use Leninist terminology) did not exist, and the sectarian-dogmatic approach of the Stalin era narrowly circumscribed the freedom of action of communist parties. Conditions changed only after 1945, when communism became fashionable among the intelligentsia and occasionally gained influence among the trade unions. The communist parties shed their hostility to Islam, and tried hard to accommodate themselves to Arab, Turkish, and Iranian nationalism. In the early years the ethnic and religious minorities had provided most of their leaders and a high percentage of their rank and file, especially in the Arab world; during the nineteen-fifties this too began to change. The general ferment in the Arab world opened up possibilities for a popular-front policy or even a communist bid for power. But in retrospect the balance sheet has been disappointing; individual communists and fellow-travellers have been members of the government at one time or another in Iraq and Syria, Egypt and the Sudan. But the parties as such have not benefited; they do not even have legal status in any Middle East country other than Israel. In contrast to South-East Asia, in this region communism has not so far succeeded in capturing the leadership of the nationalist movement.

In Turkey and Iran, too, the internal ferment favored the growth of radical movements. But for these countries Russia was the main foreign threat, and a party so closely identified with the Soviet Union could not have a great appeal. For similar reasons (Soviet opposition to Zionism), communist prospects in Israel were less than bright. In the Arab world and North Africa the breakdown of traditional social structures and ideologies had opened many opportunities to communism, but there, too, the growth of Soviet power did not necessarily enhance the influence of the local communist parties. The military dictatorships that seized power in these countries were in varying degrees friendly towards the Soviet Union. In Egypt, Syria, and Algeria there was also a growing ideological affinity with communism, but the regimes there did not call in the local communist parties (as Cuba was to do later); they set up their own state parties and the orthodox communists found themselves excluded from positions of power. Thus while communist ideas became popular in the Arab world in the nineteen-fifties, the official communist parties were largely by-passed, and, as Soviet strength grew, the Soviet brand of communism lost much of its earlier ideological appeal. With the spread of polycentrism, radicals now looked to China, Yugoslavia, or Cuba for inspiration, or advocated some form of national communism. The Soviet Union no longer exercised monopolistic control of the anti-imperialist and anti-capitalist forces; every self-respecting leader in the Arab world now subscribed to these doctrines, but this did not necessarily induce him to join the communist party; he could with equal justification be a member of the neo-Ba'th or a left-wing Nasserist. In this way his *bona fides* as an Arab nationalist remained unsullied, for the official communists, despite their demonstrative patriotism, were always somewhat suspect in view of their close ties with the Soviet Union; he could if necessary outflank the official communist parties from the left, for they were bound by certain rules of the game (such as Soviet unwillingness to risk a nuclear war on behalf of the Arab world) and could not compete with the ultra-radical slogans of Maoists and the local equivalent of the Castro-Debrayists. The position of the communist parties was further weakened by the ambiguities of Soviet policy towards the Arab world. It was not easy for a communist in an Egyptian concentration camp to defend the 'objectively progressive character' of Soviet help given to Nasser. It was even more difficult for an Iranian communist to explain to the militant rank and file that it was perfectly legitimate for Soviet leaders to praise the Shah while Tudeh denounced him as a criminal and traitor and preached violent revolution. Such conflict situations existed in most Middle East countries, and they contributed to the internal disunity by which the communist parties have been plagued throughout their recent history. The disputes which affected all these parties resulted in many splits on political as well as on personal grounds, with rival cliques competing for the leadership. It was a dismal picture, but it would be wrong to draw premature conclusions about the final decline of communism in the Middle East, for while the communists failed to make headway, the parties in power were no more successful and an acute (or subacute) revolutionary situation continued to exist in many places. The communist failure was relative, not absolute.

The fortunes of the Iranian (Tudeh) Party (TPI) reflect the dilemma that has faced communism all over the Middle East. The TPI, illegal since 1953, has throughout its recent history been torn between the 'revolutionary path' and the possibility of 'peaceful revolution', between collaboration with the national *bourgeoisie* and 'orientation towards the working class', between ignoring and recognizing the economic advances made in recent years.[1] Some of its members bitterly criticized the Soviet Union for helping to stabilize the Shah's regime, while others attacked the party leadership (stationed in East Germany) for not giving emphatic enough support to the *rapprochement* with the USSR on the state level.[2] Throughout the late fifties and early sixties the party was rent by internal strife, and in 1965 two of the seven members of the party leadership, Ahmed Qasemi and Gholam Hussein Forutan, broke away and, with Abbas Shaqai, formed a pro-Chinese communist party, keeping the name Tudeh Party of Iran. Dr Forutan and Qasemi were Stalinist oldtimers who had been involved in a previous inner-party crisis in 1948; Shaqai adhered to the Tudeh line in so far as the condemnation of the 'cult of personality' was concerned. But all three 'entirely accepted the Chinese leaders' position', to quote the resolution that announced their exclusion from the party.[3]

It was not the only such split, as the TPI leadership sadly noted; the party had previously experienced 'many incidents of this nature'. After the attempted assassination of the Shah in 1965, one of the principal accused, Nik-Khah, declared that he, too, thought that a new communist party should be established, since the TPI had in practice lost all its revolutionary potential.[4] The publications of the Persian students in Germany also betrayed strong influences of the European new left rather than orthodox communism.

In Turkey the tradition of nationalist deviation has been engrained right from the earliest days of the communist movement. Kemal Atatürk and his successors suppressed communism, and only after the overthrow of the Menderes regime in 1960 did it for the first time receive opportunities to act in a semi-legal framework. Various socialist study groups and journals came into being, most of them advocating a planned state economy and a return to the progressive principles of Kemalism, which, they argued, had been neglected by his successors. This was a time of great social and intellectual ferment, and some of these radical groups attracted many followers among the intelligentsia, and particularly among the students; among the workers they were on the whole less successful. The most extreme of these groups was the Labor Party of Turkey (*Türkiye Isci Partisi*), founded in 1961 and led by Mehmet Ali Aybar, a Paris-educated Marxist. The TIP was a revolutionary party, but for tactical reasons its program was social-democratic in character, with heavy emphasis on free parliamentary elections.[5] With all its attachment to Marxism-Leninism, the TIP was by no means uncritical of Soviet policy. These manifestations of independence reached a climax in 1968 when Cetin Alton, one of the TIP leaders, openly criticized Moscow economic aid to the Demirel government. In return for this aid, he argued, the Russians could impose their aims on the Turkish government, but these 'were more to their advantage than to that of the Turkish working class'.[6] Shortly after, Aybar, the leader of the TIP, condemned the Soviet Union for reverting to Stalinism during the Czech crisis. The TIP declared that it had from the beginning of the crisis feared that the Soviet Union might act 'out of big-power mentality'.[7]

Israel

In Israel the Communist party (MAKI) split along national lines in June 1965. The old leadership under Mikunis had loyally followed the Soviet party line for many years, but in the end it reluctantly reached the conclusion that Moscow's policy in the Arab-Israeli conflict was opportunistic, and despite its Leninist phraseology based on big-power interests. MAKI realized that the supreme Soviet aim was not the restoration of peace in the area, but the strengthening of its position by giving support to Arab regimes which were often far from progressive. (During the early period of the split the main bone of contention was ostensibly the appraisal of the character of the Arab regimes rather than Soviet policy *vis-à-vis* Israel.) All Arab members of the party (including Tawfiq Toubi, Emil Habibi, and the former 'nationalist deviationist', Emil Touma), in collaboration with a few Jews, split away from MAKI and continued to defend Nasser and the Soviet line. The leaders of the two rival factions (MAKI and RAKAH) were summoned to Moscow in 1965 and several attempts were made to heal the breach, but these were unsuccessful, and two Israeli communist parties had to be invited to the 23rd Congress of the CPSU. The basic communist principle that there could be only one communist party in each country was ignored for the next two years. Of the two communist lists, RAKAH, not surprisingly, emerged as the stronger during the elections in 1965 to the Israeli parliament (with 27,000 votes to MAKI's 13,000). Most of the electoral appeal of the Israeli communists had traditionally been in the Arab districts, such as Nazareth, where, in the absence of a legal Nasserist or Arab nationalist opposition to the state of Israel, it acted as a lightning conductor.

The Six Day War made the split between MAKI and Moscow absolute. The Soviet leadership announced that the pro-Arab RAKAH was truly internationalist and therefore the only representative of the Israeli working class. The Sneh-Mikunis group, on the other hand, had supported Israel's 'aggressive war', thus betraying the basic principles of the working-class movement.[8] MAKI accused the Soviet Union of deviating from the policy of non-involvement which it had followed in the conflicts between India and Pakistan and India and China. The Soviet Union had identified itself with the Nasser-Hussein-Arif camp, and 'as for Israel, found nothing to compare it with except nazi Germany'.[9]

From July 1967 RAKAH was recognized as the official Israeli Communist party by the Soviet bloc and by most major communist parties outside it. MAKI was recognized only by Rumania and several smaller European parties, including those of Holland, Switzerland, and Scandinavia. But there was still some uneasiness among other parties about the unconditional support given by Russia to Arab nationalism, and these misgivings (among the Yugoslav, Italian, French, Austrian, and other parties) increased as, at the time of the Czech crisis, traditional anti-Zionist propaganda gave way to openly anti-Semitic attacks in Poland, the Soviet Union, and, to a somewhat lesser degree, in East Germany.

The struggle between MAKI and RAKAH became very bitter indeed after the Six Day War. RAKAH demanded the unconditional surrender of all Israeli-occupied territories, and regarded the MAKI line (against annexation of occupied territories, but demanding a withdrawal only against guarantees) as a 'chauvinist deviation'.[10] But RAKAH, despite its identification with Arab nationalism, had to fight a struggle on two fronts: most Arab 'progressive' parties refused under any circumstances to cooperate, let alone appear in public with, Jews (or Israeli Arabs). The Israeli communists, on the other hand, unlike their comrades in the Arab countries, did not altogether deny the right of existence of Israel. Arab communist leaders (such as Fuad Nassar, the head of the Jordanian party) came out in favor of the Arab guerrilla organizations[11] even before the Six Day War, whereas RAKAH was opposed to 'individual terror' and dissociated itself from the policy of a 'people's war' against Israel. Soviet policy on guerrilla warfare against Israel was ambiguous and RAKAH and the Arab communists could interpret it in different ways.

Iraq

The history of the Iraqi Communist party with its sudden ups and downs during the last decade is an uninterrupted series of splits, of left-wing and right-wing deviations. Communist influence reached its peak under the Kassem government in the spring of 1959, but, as Soviet spokesmen later said, 'serious leftist political errors' were committed, undisciplined elements had resorted to acts of violence, i.e. established a reign of terror.[12] This referred above all to the Kirkuk riots on July 14, 1959, in which communists played a leading role. But soon the tide turned against them. Kassem preferred to establish a local communist party of his own, headed by Daud al Sa'igh, which, though lacking any mass support, made it impossible for the real communist party to be legally recognized.[13] One section of the Iraqi party called for a 'radical revolutionary course' in response, meaning armed struggle, whereas the majority under Soviet guidance condemned this 'dogmatic and sectarian approach'. The communists continued to support Kassem, even though their party remained illegal and was subjected to sporadic persecution.[14] Several party leaders were excluded when they persisted in their deviation and those remaining complained about baleful Chinese influences in their party. When Kassem was overthrown in 1963, Moscow without much success called for an armed uprising against his successors, whereas Peking justified the *coup* carried out by the Ba'th, which it described as progressive in character.[15]

The fall of Kassem was a heavy blow for the Iraqi communists; thousands of members and fellow-travellers were arrested by Arab nationalists thirsting for revenge for the persecution they had suffered under the Kassem regime. The communists who escaped arrest reorganized in an illegal party, but were harassed by police action even after the Ba'th had been overthrown and General Arif seized power.

The conflicts between 'activists' and 'moderates' in the party continued; there were differences of opinion on the Kurdish issue and with regard to the appraisal of the Arif regime and the Bazzaz government. Kurds had always constituted a high percentage of both the party leadership and the rank and file; at the third party conference in 1968 (to give but one illustration), 31% of those present were Kurds and 62% Arabs.[16] The Iraqi party had long insisted that the ultimate goal for the Kurdish nation was self-determination, including the formation of an independent state for the whole of Kurdistan, whereas Moscow suggested that the Kurds should be satisfied with self-government. The Iraqi party leadership believed that the Kurdish problem could be solved only by a National Front government with communist participation. Meanwhile, the continuation of the war in Kurdistan was likely to weaken the Baghdad government, which was the communists' main enemy. Ideological issues quite apart, there was a great deal of internal strife on purely personal grounds. The 'Ramsi-Walid faction' and the 'Nadjm group' were accused in 1967 of having established a 'splitting center hostile to the party'. They were charged with sectarian opportunism, anti-internationalism, liberalism, and, on top of it all, physical assaults against other party leaders, kidnappings, and an attempt to take over the party leadership by force.[17]* The Iraqi

---

* There was a 'Central Committee of the ICP' under Amer Abdullah and Bahaeddin Nuri in which Chinese influence was said to be strong. The 'Central Command of the ICP' under Aziz al Haj, a communist journalist domiciled in Prague between 1963 and 1968, was probably nearest to the Soviet line, and in 1968, after the Ba'th *coup*, it expressed willingness to cooperate with the regime. Lastly, there was a smaller faction, the 'Struggle Organization', led by Selim Fakhri. The three groups resorted to violence to gain control of party funds and printing presses (*Al Anwar*, June 17, 1968; *Information Bulletin*, 10, 1968).

communists supported the Soviet leaders against Peking[18] and welcomed the occupation of Czechoslovakia. But on domestic problems they remained a house divided.

Syria and Lebanon

The Lebanese Communist party split in 1964; the minority faction led by Yussef Mubarak and Mustafa Shaker claimed that the majority had gone too far in support of Nasser. Without identifying itself fully with Maoist policies, it refused to accept the Soviet position in the conflict with China. In its journal, *Ila al Amam*, it accused Khalid Bakdash, the leader of the Syrian communists, of various revisionist deviations, of being insufficiently militant in the struggle against Israel, and of 'having forced many true revolutionaries to resign from the communist party'.[19] This group also claimed that Bakdash's policy of calling for joint action by all Arab countries to eliminate the 'traces of Israeli aggression' was basically 'Pétainist' in character.[20] Israel could be defeated not by an alliance with the reactionary Arab states, but only by means of a people's war as defined at the Havana Tricontinental Conference. If these were Chinese concepts, they were not necessarily anti-Soviet in character, *Ila al Amam* argued. Objective circumstances in the Arab world made it impossible to choose the peaceful road; the Arabs would have to sacrifice 20, 30, 40 million of their 100 million in order to rid themselves of Israel forever.[21] The best-known convert to this group was the Syrian General Afif al Bizri, a former chief of staff, who was permitted by the neo-Ba'th to return to Syria after the Six Day War and who, much to Bakdash's chagrin, preached 'positive neutralism' in the dispute between Moscow and Peking.[22]

The Syrian party did not have to cope with as many splits in its ranks as the other Arab parties, but on the other hand its relations with the neo-Ba'th were far from satisfactory. Bakdash and Abdel Samad Saker, his second in command, had for years resisted Soviet pressure to cooperate more closely with the neo-Ba'th, which they asserted was unwilling to establish a common progressive front; as a result, cooperation between the communist party and the neo-Ba'th was, as one of their leaders stated on the eve of the Six Day War, 'small and limited'.[23] The basic weakness of the Syrian communists was their failure to infiltrate the army to any large extent. While the mass basis of the neo-Ba'th was exceedingly weak, certainly inferior to that of the communists, its influence among the officer corps made its political position almost unassailable.

Egypt

The ups and downs of communism are more difficult to follow in Egypt than in any other country, for there was never, for any length of time, a central, Moscow-supported, official party. There were a great many *Marxisants* among the intellectuals of Cairo and Alexandria in the nineteen-fifties; most of the young army officers also toyed with communism at one time or another, but they joined at most one of many discussion clubs. A well-disciplined, united party did not come into being until the experts of the Italian Communist party took the initiative in 1957.[24] Following their efforts and long talks between the various factions concerned, a unified Egyptian Communist party was established in January 1958. All but a few dissenters joined this new organization and President Nasser for a while turned a blind eye. Officially communism in Egypt was still illegal, but since the new party promised loyal support to the regime it was not at first harassed. This interlude lasted, however, only a few months; with the merger of Syria and Egypt and the rise of Kassem in Iraq, the Egyptian communists faced a new and complicated political situation. Their Syrian comrades bitterly attacked the enforced union with Egypt, and the Iraqi communists were, if possible, even more hostile. The Egyptian party again split; the majority advocated collaboration with Nasser, the minority bitterly opposed it.[25] Meanwhile Nasser, provoked by communist attacks from Baghdad and Damascus, turned against communism at home without discriminating between sympathizers and enemies in the Egyptian party. Almost all leading party members were arrested or fled abroad. The only organized communist activity in Egypt between 1958 and 1964 took place in prisons and concentration camps.

As relations between Cairo and Moscow improved, discreet Soviet pressure was exerted on behalf of the Egyptian communists; Khrushchev made it known that much as he wanted to visit Egypt it would be most embarrassing for him to do so while so many Egyptian communists were still in prison. Nasser took the hint and the communists were released. Haykal published an article in which he argued that communism in Egypt had failed because of its isolation from the national movement, but at the same time he advocated greater freedom for Egyptian communists on condition 'that their activities do not endanger the principles and basic values in which the overwhelming majority of the society believes'.[26] In view of growing cooperation between Moscow and Nasser's regime, the continued existence of an Egyptian Communist party became a cause of real embarrassment for the Soviet Union. In April 1965, again after intervention by the Italian party, the Egyptian communists announced the voluntary dissolution of their move- ment. It had in fact led a mere shadow existence after the release of its leading members from prison; strict supervision by Nasser's secret police had made any political action on their part impossible. The former party members were instructed to join the ASU, Egypt's state party, but a small group ignored this order and con- tinued to oppose the government. Its leaders were arrested in November 1965 and brought to trial. *Pravda* washed its hands of these 'political adventurers', whose leader, Hussein Ara, had allegedly acted under Chinese influence.[27]

This was the end of Egyptian communism as an independent force. Under the new policy of licensed infiltration, several dozen party members attained positions of some importance within the state and party apparatus. They gradually took over the ideological secretariat of the Arab Socialist Union, founded the 'Institute of Socialist Studies' and the periodical *Al Tali'a*, and through their friends in the press, the radio, and television exerted a considerable influence on Egyptian domestic propaganda and the ideological training of young cadres. Lotfi el-Kholy, editor of *Al Tali'a*, organized an ideological seminar in Cairo in collaboration with leading communist experts from abroad. With Nasser's blessing, they propagated 'scientific socialism' (i.e. a mixture of Leninism and Nasserism), as distinct from 'Arab socialism', which Nasser himself said was a mere invention of the newspapers. But there remained differences of opinion as to the interpretation of 'scientific socialism', especially with regard to such questions as the dictatorship of the proletariat, the class struggle, and Islam. *Al Tali'a* performed a fascinating but awkward tightrope act between the doctrines emanating from Cairo and Moscow, Peking and Havana. The Nasserist left showed itself receptive to the ideas of the European new left and Che Guevara, partly no doubt because Soviet ideologi- cal orthodoxy had become so much less fashionable. The romantic figure of an authentic revolutionary had a far greater appeal to young Egyptians than the time-honored Leninist texts. After the Six Day War the *Al Tali'a* faction was the first to suggest giving military bases in Egypt to the Russians and establishing joint arms factories.[28] It also demanded the further promotion of the 'revolution' in Egypt, meaning above all the promotion of its own members to positions of greater influence. This they achieved to a certain extent in the course of the reorganization of the ASU in 1968. But while *Al Tali'a* enjoyed Soviet sympathy, there were indications that it did not have its full trust and that, above all, it was not considered strong and influential enough to be a serious contender for political power. In the struggle for power that unfolded after the war of 1967, Soviet support was clearly for men like Ali Sabry and the 'centrists' in the ASU (as represented by the periodical *Al Kateb*) who were pro-Soviet in their foreign political orientation, but, unlike the *Tali'a* group, had no pronounced ideological interests and commitments.

Sudan

The achievements of Sudanese communism in recent years have remained largely unnoticed by most outside observers. Sudan, unlike Egypt or Algeria, is not a key country and not much attention has been devoted to its domestic affairs. The communists played an important part in the *coup d'état* of 1964, and dominated the 'Front of Professional Organizations', including the influential Sudanese Lawyers Association. In the provisional government that took power the communists held over a quarter of the portfolios, a share-out of proportion to their real strength in the country, but they continued to harass the government from within, asking for an even greater share of power for themselves and their various front organizations (such as the Gezira Tenants Association). In a government reshuffle the communists lost all their posts but one, and when the SCP refused to accept this, they found themselves excluded from the government coalition altogether.[29] In December 1965 the SCP was banned, but it almost immediately reappeared as the Sudanese Socialist party and continued its activities through an elaborate network of front organizations. At the same time the Communist party insisted on its legal rights and brought an action in the courts to compel the government to recognize it. The Sudanese government countered by arresting some of the party leaders on such charges as possession of arms. Increased communist activity in recent years made the non-communist parties in the Sudan more aware of its real aims, and it thus became more difficult for the communists to infiltrate other political and professional groups and to apply the united front technique. Abd al-Halik Madjub, the party leader, pondering the reasons for the 1965 defeat, declared that his party should have been more aware of the importance and the delicacy of the religious factor in the political and social struggle; it should have made use of religious belief, as the Algerian comrades had done with some success.[30] This referred to Bechir Hadj Ali, the secretary-general of the Algerian party, who in a series of articles had maintained that there was no contradiction between socialism (as a political aim) and Islam as a state religion, that religion had a considerable revolutionary potential, and that philosophical discussions which would only result in dissension among the progressive national forces should be eschewed: 'The Algerian masses will advance towards communism with the Koran in one hand and *Das Kapital* in the other.'[31]

In May 1969 following yet another military coup a dictatorial regime was set up in which the Communists were prominently represented. The established political parties were dissolved and their leaders arrested.[32]

The Role of the Party

Among the many problems facing communists in the Middle East during the fifties and sixties, the one overriding in importance all others was the question whether the party was still necessary, or whether in the higher interests of the cause they ought to renounce independent party propaganda and to present themselves as advisers and assistants of the nationalist leaders, but not as their rivals. Suggestions on these lines were made with increasing frequency in the Soviet Union. This strategy of 'licensed infiltration' by individual communists into the leadership of mass parties in one-party states was nothing less than the 'deliberate renunciation of independent communist parties publicly acting as such'. It certainly was an innovation in Soviet policy and the world communist movement.[33]

The beginning of this new strategy can be traced back to the years after Stalin's death, the time of the Bandung Conference and the Khrushchev-Bulganin trip to India in 1955. It was then that the new Soviet leadership first realized that the national liberation movement in the third world opened up new prospects for communism and that it could substantially change the global balance of power. While the 'national *bourgeois* leadership' in the underdeveloped countries had been ridiculed and attacked during the Stalin era, emphasis was now put on the progressive nature of their movements, even if their ideology was often 'petty *bourgeois*' or 'utopian' in character.[34] From 1954 onwards the Soviet Union began to give massive support to countries of the third world – economic aid and arms as well as political assistance. There was no attempt yet to work out a systematic approach to the problems of the third world, apart from a few propositions which were applied indiscriminately to national liberation movements in general without taking account of the great dissimilarities between them. Only after 1959, under the impression of Castro's victory in Cuba and the rise of Kassem in Iraq, but also of the persecution of communists in Egypt and in Kerala, did a new approach find favor in the Kremlin. It was realized then that aid alone was not sufficient to influence the general trend of political development in the third world, and that it would have to be coordinated with greater communist pressure from inside these countries.[35] In the 1960 declaration of the eighty-one communist parties and, more specifically, in the 1961 Draft Program of the Communist Party of the Soviet Union, the new concept of the 'independent state of national democracy' was formulated. This was the first systematic attempt to shape doctrine to catch up with the facts and to coordinate Soviet and Chinese views on the subject.[36] Above all, it was a more activist approach than the classical communist thesis that ex-colonial countries would all have to go through a *bourgeois* revolution, and that the best policy for communists was to work through various popular and national fronts. But since there was only, at best, a small industrial proletariat in most of these countries, and since the number of communists was even smaller, the old approach had usually condemned the small communist parties to inaction. According to the new line, the state of national democracy ('based upon a strong peasant-proletarian alliance with petty-*bourgeois* support') was able in certain conditions to prepare the road to non-capitalist development, provided that certain preconditions existed. The new regimes would have to be anti-imperialist in character, well disposed towards the Soviet Union, and ready to implement radical social and economic reforms and to give local communist parties full freedom of political action.[37] The new approach justified economic and political support for the new nations, but ideological endorsement at the expense of the local communists was withheld.

This ingenious new formula was, however, soon found wanting. Only in Indonesia did a national-democratic front develop as foreseen in the Soviet concept, a coalition of nationalists and communists initially under nationalist leadership, but with growing communist influence. Cuba omitted the national democratic stage altogether; Castro declared his regime 'socialist' under the leadership of a Marxist-Leninist party. All other Asian and African countries in which the Soviet experts had detected left-wing trends turned into one-party states in which no communist competition was tolerated.[38] After the communist party had been banned even in Algeria (1962), a country on which Moscow had put such high hopes, a revision of the whole strategy became clearly necessary.

The reconsideration of the situation in the third world and its implications for the world communist movement played an important part in the Sino-Soviet dispute, and was the subject of a great many articles, speeches, exchanges, and seminars throughout 1963–6. According to the official Soviet view, cooperation with the third world was to continue in so far as it was 'objectively progressive'. Some of the third-world leaders might establish reactionary political regimes and subject communists to persecution, but such regimes were likely to be shortlived. The Chinese stated that they were willing to collaborate even with kings, princes, and aristocrats, but only if the communists were able to retain their independence; these must always insist on retaining the leadership of the revolution; on no account must they become the 'tail of the landlords and the *bourgeoisie*'. But the Chinese line was impractical because it shirked the most important political issue facing the communists: should they turn against non-capitalist regimes which were carrying out far-reaching social and economic reforms because these were unwilling to give full political freedom to the local communists and come gradually to accept their leadership?

Some Soviet observers began to advocate a new approach. G. Mirsky wrote in 1964 that the national liberation movement could immediately break out of the framework of *bourgeois* revolution and begin the transition to socialist revolution: 'If the conditions for proletarian leadership have not yet matured, the historic mission of breaking with capitalism can be carried out by elements close to the working class. Nature does not suffer a vacuum.'[39] Such unorthodox opinions were at first subjected to criticism, but within a year most experts had come to subscribe to these views, and, more important, Khrushchev himself declared that Egypt had 'embarked on the road to socialist development', an unprecedented compliment that meant breaking with all previous doctrine. According to this analysis, the actions of the new leaders in the third world mattered far more than their words; the ideologies of the developing states were not the most important factor in evaluating their progressive nature.[40] Another writer noted that 'social and economic reforms in these countries were often deeper and more radical than the theories elucidating them'.[41] The young officers, the students, and the lower ranks of the bureaucracy in the new countries were now described as essentially progressive elements, whose often quaint and contradictory ideological pronouncements should not be given excessive weight, for even *bourgeois* leaders would gradually go over from nationalism to the positions of socialism and the working class.[42] If so, the role of the communist parties was bound to be downgraded. 'Life demands the formation of a bloc of left forces, in which the most consistent and best trained Marxist-Leninist elements should play the role of friend and assistant of the national democrats, ideological beacon of socialism and vanguard fighter.'[43] This was a substantial retreat from the doctrine of national democracy and it encountered resistance from the Chinese (who argued that belief in the possibility of a non-capitalist way of development in the third world was meaningless talk), from part of the Soviet apparatus (especially among the guardians of doctrinal orthodoxy), and, not surprisingly, from among the Afro-Asian communists directly concerned.

After Khrushchev's fall the brakes were applied. Economists and ideologists continued their disputes about the class character of the new countries, the bureaucratic *élites*, their self-styled socialism, their foreign policies.[44] Could the dangers of *bourgeois* nationalism be ignored? Would not the ideological initiative be lost if the downgrading of the communist parties went too far? Under Khrushchev's successors there was a general shift of priorities away from the national liberation movement towards communist construction in the USSR.[45] It was not a radical break; the first indications had already been detected during the last months of Khrushchev's rule; the change was caused *inter alia* by the growing strain on the Soviet economy of the many commitments to the new nations. The setbacks suffered by many 'national democratic' regimes (Indonesia, Ghana, Algeria) also contributed to the general disappointment, and as a result the national liberation movement was given a low rating in Soviet world strategy. Some new ideological modifications were made: the non-capitalist path of development was defined as not synonymous with the socialist path, but merely a stage towards it. The concept of the 'state of national democracy' was supplemented by the new formula of 'revolutionary democracy' which was to apply above all to Algeria and Egypt, where communist parties were enjoined to infiltrate state parties and the government in order to bring them over gradually to the communist position.[46]

Many leading Arab communists were indignant about the lowly role assigned to them by Moscow, arguing that the possibility of the restoration of capitalism in Egypt was by no means excluded, that a one-man dictatorship and a bureaucratic state machine was no guarantee for the gradual transition towards socialism. It could not be taken for granted, they said, that the 'Arab socialists' would gradually become adherents of 'scientific socialism'. Concessions to the nationalist *bourgeois* leaders would weaken the proletarian basis of the communist parties and limit their influence. No other social group, certainly no individual, could take over the historical mission of the working class and the communist party. 'Arab socialism' was a mere conglomeration of scientific and utopian socialism, petty-*bourgeois* ideas, narrow nationalism, religious prejudices, and subjective idealism; it did not aim at abolishing the exploitation of man by man.[47] This, in brief, was the line taken by the Syrians and their leader, Khalid Bakdash. Fuad Nassar, the head of the Jordanian party, was closer to the Soviet view. He believed that it was a mistake to regard the national liberation movement merely as a reserve or an auxiliary of the socialist revolution; any attempt to limit its role to the anti-colonial and anti-feudal struggle could only harm the movement and weaken its alliance with the world socialist system. If the national liberation movement was given sufficient support it would turn against capitalism even before the proletariat took a leading role in it. A communist *rapprochement* with this movement involved no dilution of Marxist-Leninist ideology; ideological contradictions and disagreement would continue to exist, but these could be resolved peacefully.[48] Nikola Shawi, the leader of the Lebanese party, took a position in between the two extremes in this dispute. He did not agree with the view held by some of his allies (presumably the pro-Nasser party in Moscow) that it was necessary immediately to merge the socialist parties and organizations into one political movement. On the other hand, he agreed with the Russians that some countries could develop from colonial and semi-colonial regimes to socialism as the non-proletarian strata of the population were joining the struggle against capitalism and setting themselves socialist aims.[49] The Iraqi party in principle supported the idea of a united front, but stressed that it would be difficult, if not impossible, to pursue such a policy wherever the non-communist leaders of the national movement insisted on a one-party system.[50] All Arab communists agreed that the seizure of power by their parties remained the final goal; disagreements concerned the period of transition, and no one could know how long this would last.

The dispute lasted for several years; eventually each party devised its own tactics, adjusting itself to the different conditions prevailing in its own country. In Egypt, where State power was strong and communism relatively weak, the Communist party was dissolved; in Iraq the party remained in isolation; in Syria there was limited cooperation with the neo-Ba'th. Fairly close contacts were established between the CPSU and the Egyptian ASU and the Syrian neo-Ba'th, whereas relations between Moscow and the Algerian FLN remained more formal and distant. In a series of meetings between leaders of the Arab communist parties in Prague, Vienna, and elsewhere between 1964 and autumn 1967, an attempt was made to work out a common platform with regard to current problems.[51] The parties agreed to support Moscow in its dispute with the Chinese, and in 1968 they gave their blessing to the Soviet occupation of Czechoslovakia. (The Moroccan party was the only one to strike a note of dissent.) There was unanimity with regard to Israel: the struggle against imperialism and Zionism had to be intensified, but, according to a communiqué published in 1968, it was wrong to rely entirely on guerrilla war against Israel 'such as suggested by the Mao Tse-tung clique'. The same communiqué emphasized the necessity to step up the campaign against the rightist trend in the Arab national movement, according to which nationalization and other socialist measures had not worked and should not be continued.

Lastly, the dangers of closer cooperation with 'French monopoly capitalism' were stressed.[52]

The attitude of the Arab communist parties with regard to the Arab-Israeli conflict did not substantially differ from that of Nasser and other 'revolutionary democrats'. This made their position in the Arab world much easier than in 1948, when they had the unpopular task of defending the Soviet stand in favor of the partition of Palestine. Now they were swimming with the current. But this raised again the question of the very *raison d'être* of the parties: if they agreed with the 'progressive leadership' of the national movement on all essential points during the transitional period, how was the continued separate existence of the communist parties to be justified?

From the Soviet point of view, the Arab communist parties are of limited use. True, Moscow can rely more on them than on Nasser and the neo-Ba'th, but this is a question of degree, not an issue of principle. Proletarian internationalism has given way to loyalty to the Soviet Union, *tout court*. The Czechoslovak crisis, and before that the dispute with China, have shown the Soviet leaders that they can no longer take the loyalty of many communist parties for granted, whereas non-communist regimes like Egypt and Syria have given them full support. 'Material interest' and political dependence make far more reliable allies than ideological conviction – this is the lesson of the last decade as regards relations between the Soviet Union and outside regimes and parties. With the transition from Bolshevism to a nationalist-socialist policy, the Soviet Union can invoke 'proletarian solidarity' less and less frequently with any hope of success, whereas there are no such problems in its relations with its clients. The links with Arab communism will not be cut, but wherever the respective party is not a factor of major political importance, and whenever its existence constitutes an obstacle to Soviet policy in the Middle East, it is bound to come out second best in this conflict of interests.

The Arab communists can have no illusions about their prospects in the years to come. Popular opinion groping for radical solutions to the crisis in the Arab world does not on the whole favor the Soviet brand of communism. The communist parties have to resist growing pressure on the left as well as on the right. They have to cope with the growing disillusion in Russia and communism that has been spreading in the Middle East, and to compete with various other radical ideologies. They still have their faithful cadres and, though a minority, it is not impossible that they may come to power in one or two Arab countries within the framework of a national front. But past experience has shown that these are not likely to be lasting successes: the communists have no chance of becoming popular mass parties in the Middle East unless they adjust themselves to a much greater degree than in the past to the specific conditions in the Arab world. For an independent radical party of the left there are good prospects in the Middle East, but the communists are not yet an independent party and they would have to pay more than lip-service to Islam, to disavow dialectical materialism, and to give up any idea of nationalizing the land. In other words, it would involve their ceasing to be communists and turning into a national-socialist party. This is by no means impossible; they have already gone a long way towards it. Perhaps this is the road on which they may one day succeed, provided, of course, that they prevail over the many competitors who have already staked their claims in this promising field.

10   Conclusion

The Soviet position in the Middle East is stronger today than it was ten years ago. This was not the result of invasion, nor of infiltration by stealth: the Soviet Union became a Middle East power by invitation. It has seized no military bases, but was offered the facilities it wanted by the governments of Egypt and Syria, Algeria and the Yemen, of their own free will. Soviet progress has been gradual, unlike its advance into Eastern Europe after 1944. Not one country has been taken over, no attempt has been made to impose from above the communist political and social system. There have been changes in some countries, but they were the outcome of internal ferment, not outside pressure. Soviet influence has grown not because of the spread of communist ideology, but as the result of efforts made on different levels to make friends and influence people: loans, arms supplies, political assistance, support of the Arab countries against the West and Israel. It has always been Soviet policy to stress that this assistance, in contrast to imperialist aid, is selfless and free of ulterior motives; neither bases nor oil nor political conformity are expected in return. The Soviet Union has been willing to cooperate with kings and sheikhs as well as ultra-radical revolutionaries. The fact that some of these leaders were militantly anti-communist was no obstacle; it complicated relations in some cases, but on the whole Moscow showed great moderation and patience in the face of Egyptian tantrums (in 1959–61), and turned a blind eye to the suppression of communism in Turkey and Iran. Israel was the only exception, but in this instance, too, the reasons for Soviet hostility were not primarily ideological. Having to choose between the Arab states and Israel, Moscow opted for the bigger battalions, which it thought were also the stronger battalions.

The anti-Jewish prejudices of the Soviet leadership should not be underrated, but what in the last resort prevented a *rapprochement* between Moscow and Jerusalem was not anti-Semitism, but the simple fact that Israel was so small. Size has always been of great significance in shaping Soviet attitudes to other countries; more than once this has been the source of political mistakes.

Soviet objectives in the Middle East are easily defined: to remove Western influence in the area and to strengthen the Soviet position there as much as possible. Turkey and Iran have been to some extent neutralized; with the *détente* in world politics, the conviction grew in Ankara and Tehran that the military danger from the north had passed and that the Soviet Union had given up its old annexationist aims. Soviet policy impressed on both countries the benefits that would accrue from closer economic relations. Suspicion of the powerful neighbor did not fade away completely; it emerged again with the appearance of the Soviet fleet in the Mediterranean and Soviet intervention in East-Central Europe in 1968. The change in Turkey's and Iran's foreign policy was not caused by resentment of the West, though this motive was not altogether absent; it was largely due to the shift in the global balance of power and the proximity of these countries to the Soviet Union.

In Syria and Egypt the Soviet Union found more fertile ground, providing scope for closer political collaboration. Anti-Western feeling was, and is, for historical reasons more intense in these Arab countries, the inclination towards extreme political solutions more pronounced. Ideological affinity played a certain role; Western support for the 'reactionary' Arab states was an aggravating factor, and Moscow's hostility to Israel was greatly appreciated in the Arab world. While the emphasis in relations with Turkey and Iran was mainly on economic collaboration, Soviet political and military help was the great attraction for the Arab world. What started in the nineteen-fifties as a 'strictly business transaction' later became a fairly close political alliance. Following the deterioration of the Egyptian economic situation and the Arab defeat in 1967, the dependence of the 'progressive' Arab countries on the Soviet Union markedly increased. Radical Arab leaders were firmly convinced during the nineteen-fifties that while the West and Israel constituted a mortal threat to Arabism, the Soviet Union for a variety of reasons did not. By the middle sixties they were so deeply immersed in the fight against Israel (and in the struggle for their own political survival) that they had little time or energy to ponder the long-range perspectives, an inability compounded by their capacity for self-delusion and their lack of political experience. While not unaware of their weakness, they felt almost unlimited self-confidence: once having coped with the threat of Zionism, they would successfully defend their independence against all comers.

Soviet successes in the Arab world were striking, but not without their problems. Much money and great efforts were invested in Egypt and Syria, yet the loans and the arms have been used in ways that were not always to Moscow's liking. Egypt and Syria became client states, but not satellites; even after the Six Day War Russia was unable to exert full control in Egypt. It had accepted responsibility, albeit reluctantly, without being always able to impose its will. Soviet help had been provided to make the radical Arab regimes showcases for the superiority of socialism, but their economic achievements were certainly no more striking than those of the 'conservative' countries. The weakness of the radical regimes had some indirect advantage, for it strengthened their dependence on the Soviet Union, but it was hardly a good advertisement for the efficiency of communism.

When the Western powers were the dominating force in the Middle East, they had the monopoly of committing mistakes, whereas the Soviet Union, not being involved in Middle East affairs, enjoyed a great deal of prestige precisely because of its apparent position as a dispassionate, seemingly remote onlooker without any specific interests in the area. But as it became involved in Middle East politics, it had to make choices: it could no longer please everyone, and the aura of disinterested altruism began to disappear. It was Soviet policy to extend its influence without provoking a frontal clash with the United States. Frequently this proved only too easy; there was nothing the United States could do about the internal politics of Syria and Egypt, or a *coup* by radical forces in other Arab countries. Time and circumstances seemed to be working for the Soviet Union in the Middle East, but not always. Whenever the Soviet protégés ran into trouble, direct Soviet intervention became necessary, and this naturally involved risks. Notwithstanding Soviet reservations about its client states, a major setback suffered by any one of them was almost automatically interpreted as a Soviet defeat, and reluctance to come to the help of the 'progressives' was regarded as an admission of weakness. The establishment of client states had a logic and a momentum of its own. It is difficult to get out of obligations and cut losses; having gained footholds in the Middle East, the Soviet Union became increasingly involved in crisis situations it could not fully control; having provided considerable economic assistance to Egypt for more than a decade, Moscow could not discontinue its aid, however costly the venture and however unpromising the long-term prospects. In the past, a substantial part of this burden had been borne by the other East European countries, but they were increasingly reluctant to shoulder this load indefinitely. The complications arising from the supply of arms are even more serious. Arms deals were from the Soviet point of view the most effective way of undermining the Western position in the Middle East and winning friends in the Arab world. But the arms were not delivered as a straightforward business transaction; they gave the Soviet Union a vested interest in the fortunes of Egypt and Syria, the Yemen and Algeria, and it became identified with them. The Arab defeat in 1967 thus adversely affected Soviet prestige. The re-equipment of the Arab armies became necessary, regardless of cost, and has thus involved Soviet prestige even more than in the past. Yet another Arab defeat by Israel must appear well-nigh intolerable in Soviet eyes, but since it has no full control over the armies of the UAR and Syria, and since its capacity to intervene in a war is probably still limited, the Soviet position is not without hazards.

The build-up of a Soviet Mediterranean fleet entails similar problems. The absence of a striking force has served in the past as a plausible reason for refraining from direct if limited military intervention, comparable to the landing of American troops in the Lebanon in 1958. With a substantial fleet in the Mediterranean, the Soviet Union can make its presence felt more directly by showing the flag not only in the Mediterranean, but eventually in the Persian Gulf and the Indian Ocean as well. It has raised Soviet prestige and forced all Mediterranean and Middle East countries to recognize the growing Soviet strength in the area. At the same time it enhances the risks: in the event of a conflict, Soviet policy-makers face the choice of backing down or of escalating a local conflict into a much wider confrontation.

There are other problems, some of them caused by the uneven advance of Soviet influence in the Middle East. The very fact that Syria had moved so far towards a radical political system frightened

Syria's neighbors, and made them more aware of the dangers involved. The Soviet Union would have preferred to encourage Syria without antagonizing its neighbors, but this was not possible. The decision would have been less painful had it been a straightforward choice between 'rising' and 'declining' forces. But in reality the state of affairs is far more intricate: the basis of the national-socialist regimes in Syria, Egypt, and Algeria, not to mention the Yemen, continues to be fragile; their overthrow from within is by no means excluded. National rivalries further complicate the situation: the Soviet Union wants to be on good terms with Greece and Turkey, with Turkey and Syria, with Iran and Iraq, despite the conflicts between these respective pairs. It would like to support Tudeh and the Shah, the Turkish communists and Demirel, the Iraqi opposition and the Iraqi government. The list of policy dilemmas is long, covering every Middle East country, both on the domestic level and in its relations with other states. In most cases a choice has to be made, and this usually implies antagonizing someone.

There is also the eternal problem of priorities. The Soviet Union has had to pay for its new status as a Middle East power $4–5 billion in military aid alone. In a war the cost in terms of money is hardly ever counted, let alone disputed. In peacetime, on the other hand, the cost of economic and military assistance is open to scrutiny and comparison. Few questions are likely to be asked while the going is good, but when there are setbacks the value of the investment is liable to come up for debate: would the cause of socialism not have been better served by using the billions of rubles given to Egypt for domestic economic purposes? The Soviet Union is a big country, but can it go on providing for a growing number of destitute client states? Financial considerations rarely figure in the discussion of decisive political issues, but there are priorities, and the place of the Middle East in the scale of Soviet political aims is likely to be re-examined from time to time in terms of loss and gain, especially if there should be unforeseen difficulties.

What, then, are the short-term Soviet aims in the area? The rapid transformation of the radical-nationalist regimes into fully fledged satellites is certainly not among them. It would give the Soviet Union few benefits it does not already possess. Further nationalization in the 'progressive' countries would not necessarily bring them more securely into the Soviet orbit, whatever the ideologists may claim. It would be desirable from the Soviet point of view if power in the radical Arab countries came to rest in the hands of a disciplined and ideologically trained *élite*, but this is unlikely to happen in the near future. The present *élites* are on the whole pro-Soviet; Oriental communism is unlikely to be affected by the liberal and democratic deviations of Western communism. The danger of national communism, on the other hand, is equally strong in East and West, and no cure has so far been found for it. There is also the constant temptation for communists in the third world to play Peking against Moscow and vice versa. These are real problems and the Soviet Union will have to live with them for a long time.

The present state of affairs has many advantages for Moscow, and its perpetuation seems to be the aim of Soviet policy in the Middle East. Important positions have been gained during the last decade and it seems wiser to consolidate them than to press for full satellization of the pro-Soviet regimes. Whether the Soviet Union will have things all its own way is less certain, for Middle East politics have a life of their own; sooner or later outside powers find themselves confronted with situations they did not envisage in their political planning.

The Soviet Union owes its successes in the Middle East in the final analysis to a number of happy coincidences. It did not have to work very hard to realize its aims. The key to success was not a 'correct Marxist-Leninist' appraisal, nor the triumph of the local communist parties; not loans or credits, nor very cunning diplomacy. Moscow did not gate-crash; it was invited to become a major Middle East power by Egypt and Syria. In many respects the Soviet Union was an ideal ally for the radical Arab leaders – powerful, but not so wealthy as to provoke feelings of envy. Ideologically it was far better suited to the radical mood prevailing in the Arab world than Western democracy or liberalism. The Soviet Union became a leading Middle East power because it was militarily strong and geographically close, and it is therefore idle to speculate whether its advance could have been prevented. With the West in retreat, the Middle East became a power vacuum, bound to be filled by the most powerful neighbor. Arab enmity towards Israel was certainly important, but it was an aggravating circumstance, not the decisive factor. The inroads Moscow has made in the Yemen and Algeria, in the Sudan and Somalia, show that it has improved its position even in countries where Israel was not a major issue. But was not the Arab decision to tie their fortunes to the Soviet Union extremely shortsighted? What if victory over Israel could be achieved only at a formidable price – namely, growing dependence on Russia? In a long-term view, the Arab leaders need the West more than the West needs them, simply because nature has placed them in the vicinity of the super-power with the greater appetite and the fewer scruples. Their chances of remaining independent without the support of an outside power cannot be rated very high. Many Arabs are uneasily aware of the grave problems they face, but their leaders reassure them: the Soviet Union is totally different from the Western imperialists, asks for nothing in return, nor does it aspire to dominate the area. All fears are therefore misplaced.

What direction is Soviet policy likely to take in the years to come, and how are the Middle East countries likely to react? There are no certainties, only trends and possibilities, and about these, too, it is now more difficult to speculate than before. The Middle East political scene is forever changing; it cannot be analysed in isolation from all other major political and military problems in the contemporary world.

Seen from the present, the future of the Middle East depends above all on internal developments in the Soviet Union and, to a lesser extent, on the United States. Essentially, the Soviet Union has become a conservative society with a superstructure of revolutionary ideological phraseology; its appeal as the home of communism scarcely extends beyond its own borders; the idea of world revolution was abandoned long ago. But the Soviet leaders still feel they have to expand their sphere of influence, their own *cordon sanitaire*. Once a sphere of influence is established there is a temptation to look for yet another beyond it, to make it quite secure: empire-building is a self-generating business. They know that, as a Russian eighteenth-century statesman said, 'that which stops growing begins to decay'. As the Soviet Union reaches strategic parity with the United States, there is greater readiness to follow a high-risk policy in areas thought to be non-vital to America. It has entered a stage of transformation, but not, as was widely assumed after Stalin's death, into a more liberal and democratic system. The Soviet leaders cannot dissociate themselves altogether from the old beliefs because this would undermine the legitimacy of their rule. In competition with China for leadership over the camp, if for no other reason, they are under strong pressure to keep up the revolutionary posture and to pursue a militant foreign policy.

The paradox of Soviet development is that while militarily the country has become so much stronger during the last twenty years, politically it is far weaker than under Stalin, when no opposition was tolerated inside Russia or the Soviet bloc. Power has passed into the hands of bureaucrats, men without any marked interest in ideas or theories. They have no clear concept of the future, but take the existing order of things for granted and want to prevent any major change. The political weakness, the many conflicts inside the Soviet bloc and within the Soviet Union itself, are not necessarily conducive to a policy of *détente*; there is many a historical precedent for escape into activism.

At the present time Soviet foreign policy seems closer to that of Ivan Kalita and Ivan the Terrible than to that of Lenin. The emergence of one supreme leader is a distinct possibility, but there are a great many others besides. While orthodox Marxism-Leninism was the guiding principle, it was not too difficult to understand and sometimes to predict Soviet attitudes, despite the distortions of the 'cult of the individual'. It was relatively easy to imagine how a well-disciplined Marxist-Leninist would behave in a given situation, but it is becoming more difficult each year to anticipate the reactions of the latter-day Bolshevik, whose ideology is a mixture of many strange elements, and whose attitude fluctuates unpredictably between extreme caution and surprising recklessness. During the sixties there was an understanding with the United States about spheres of influence, and certain rules of the game are still observed. But with strategic parity the question of the rules of the game and of a re-division of spheres of influence is bound to be reopened. The Soviet Union has pursued a foreign policy that even from a position of relative weakness did not lack drive or self-confidence; how far will it go in a position of strength? The Middle East is in geopolitical terms Russia's back garden; this at any rate is how Soviet leaders see it. They seem to believe that an area so close to their borders should become their sphere of influence.

The stability of the sixties and the rules of the games were based on the credibility of the American deterrent. As strategic parity is reached, some American commitments are bound to be re-examined in the light of a new world situation. It will be asked to what extent American national interest is involved in the defence of the Middle East. Less, no doubt, than Russia's; much less than Europe's. The Middle East has long ceased to be geographically important; there are no cross-roads in the air age. Military bases in the area are desirable, but by no means essential; the ICBM has changed all that. The United States is not a major importer of oil; less than 3% of the oil consumed in America comes from the Middle East, and this could easily be replaced. True, the production cost of Middle East oil is among the lowest in the world; but this concerns above all the oil companies. As far as American national interest is concerned, Middle East oil does not figure high. There are ties of friendship between the United States and some Middle East nations: Turkey, a NATO member, Israel, and a few others. Neo-isolationists will no doubt argue that their fate is not a matter of life and death for America. Yet the fate of the area as a whole will remain a matter of supreme concern to all American policy-makers, for if it were to become an exclusive Soviet sphere of interest the repercussions on the world situation would be immediate and far-reaching. It would decisively shift the balance of power and would have incalculable consequences all over the world.

It was generally believed in Washington during the sixties that, given a strong military presence in the Middle East, the Soviet Union would not deliberately enter on a course of action that would bring about an escalation of the conflict on to the global scale. Despite the traditional Russian interest in the Middle East, the Soviet Union has no vital economic stake in the region, nor does the Middle East constitute a military threat. The Soviet drive to the south is basically a forward political-prestige operation, potentially rewarding, but not essential. Hence there is a good chance in Washington's view that due caution is likely to be exercised in Moscow with regard to the risks involved. But there remain several major question-marks. Centrifugal forces have been at work for a long period in both West and East, but the process has not been symmetrical: whereas in the Soviet Union the feeling of political weakness may well lead into an escape into action, it is strengthening neo-isolationism in the United States. As the Soviet leaders realize that it is becoming more and more difficult to hold the empire built by Stalin, their methods are likely to become more repressive rather than more tolerant. There is not the slightest doubt that they want to keep what they have, and this can be achieved only by extending their spheres of influence. The feeling of weakness adds urgency to this belief.

In America, on the other hand, the Vietnam war has strengthened latent isolationist feelings, to which is added the fear of over-commitment and a growing belief, not only among the pacifists and the New Left, that America should attend to its domestic problems and stop playing the world's policeman. Since the White House, the State Department, and even the Pentagon do not take their decisions in a vacuum, but are influenced by public opinion, it will depend in the last resort on domestic developments whether and how vigorously America will defend its interests in the Middle East.

As Soviet pressure grows, the call for a more active American policy is likely to emanate from Europe, Asia, and the Middle East. In the view of many Europeans and Asians, American interventionism and the cold-war mentality used to be the main threat; in future they may come to regard American isolationism as the main danger. Soviet foreign policy is likely to concentrate on the areas adjacent to the Soviet Union in Europe, on the Middle East and Asia. As a result, Americans now feel less concerned about Soviet policies than those geographically nearer to the Soviet Union who have begun to realize that the roles are about to be reversed and that an immediate threat will affect them far more than the Americans.

The inability of West Europe to overcome its internal divisions, to develop a political will and a policy of its own, and its political and military impotence, is the great tragedy of the post-war period. West Europe still has far more vital interests in the Middle East than America, but it has found itself totally incapable of asserting its influence and pursuing an active European policy in the area. Twenty years after the end of the war, West Europe has abdicated in the Middle East, and this despite the fact that it is economically stronger than the Soviet Union and in most other respects potentially its equal. The resistance to European unity, first by the British, later by de Gaulle, has virtually reduced Europe's influence to nil; and nowhere is the decline more palpable than in the Middle East.

A small country, however stable internally, is not normally able to resist prolonged and determined pressure by a superior power; Czechoslovakia in 1938 and again in 1968 is an obvious illustration. The advent of the atomic bomb changed this, at least for a while, creating a unique constellation from which the small countries benefited. The global equilibrium and the overriding threat of nuclear war tied the hands of the big powers and made it possible even for small countries to retain their independence, sometimes in open defiance of their much stronger neighbors. But it is by no means certain that this particular constellation will last forever. It is already argued that real independence has become impossible in the long run without a nuclear capacity. The smaller countries are likely to become vulnerable once more; they will be able to resist a super-power which is firmly resolved to impose its political will and has the power to do so only if they are united and internally stable. On both these counts the Middle East scores very low. Its internal problems are immense. Peace and stability seem to be as far away as ever, and further violent upheavals appear almost inevitable in the Arab world. There will be more revolutions and quasi-revolutions, but the experience of two decades has created scepticism about the effects of revolutionary action: so far it has produced no achieve-ments which arouse marked enthusiasm. Economic progress and the rate of modernization in Iran has been impressive, and substantial advances have been made by Turkey during the last decade. But the starting-point was abysmally low in both countries, and the time needed to catch up has to be measured in decades rather than years. Economic progress by itself will not, moreover, solve the political problems; on the contrary, it will probably aggravate them and pre-cipitate social change, non-violent or violent. It is doubtful whether the Middle East monarchies will survive for very long; they are too much out of tune with the *Zeitgeist*, although they are not necessarily less efficient or more currupt than the radical *élites*; the transition from monarchy to military dictatorship will not by itself resolve many problems. No Middle East junta has been strikingly successful so far. Only Turkey and Irael have democratically elected govern-ments. So, within limits, has the Lebanon. Whether the multi-party system will be able to weather the coming storms in these countries is a question that cannot be answered with confidence.

No solution is in sight for the crisis of the Arab world. The con-flict with Israel overshadows at present its deeper problems. There is growing bitterness and frustration, and as the destruction of Israel does not seem near, the Arab masses are likely to turn sooner or later against the Arab governments of the day which have been unable to fulfil most of their promises. The economic prospects of some Arab countries are not as unpromising as Egypt's, but most of their energies are sapped and their resources squandered on the military build-up. Egypt's long-term economic prospects would no doubt improve if it gained control over the oilfields of Libya (having so far failed to do so on the Arabian peninsula). But in view of the heavy emotional involvement in the Israeli issue, it is not at all certain how public opinion would react to such a deflection from a war of revenge. Even an Arab victory over Israel would immediately create new problems. It might lessen Arab dependence on the Soviet Union, but the struggle for domination in the Arab world would become more intense; there are many candidates for ruling Palestine and Jordan. The fight between 'radicals' and 'conservatives' (and among the radicals themselves), submerged at the present time, would immediately enter a new and more bitter phase. Since no one leader and no one country is strong enough to unite the Arab world, all indications point to a long period of internal strife. Future wars between the Arab states and Israel seem almost inevitable, but a total Arab victory is unlikely. Meanwhile, the drift towards anarchy in the Arab world seems to be continuing. All immediate political problems apart, there is a deep-seated malaise throughout the area, dissatisfaction with established ideologies and institutions, with governments and society, 'conservative' and 'radical' alike. Among the intelligentsia both Islam and communism are losing ground, democracy is unattainable, planned economy has not worked, military dictatorships have been strong on propaganda, but on little else besides. Nor is Arab nationalism much of a guide to the perplexed. This breakdown of old, established beliefs and values, and the absence of new ones to replace them, is producing a crisis deeper and more intractable than the transient political problems now plaguing these countries, and the growing sense of despair leads them to seek ultra-radical solutions, resulting in incessant changes of government, stagnation, and decline. Perhaps one day the vicious circle will be broken by a new idea or a new leader or movement of national and social renaissance. Today no such saviour is in sight. This drift towards anarchy may not cause undue concern among the Russians. For Israel it would remove the immediate danger; whether it would be a blessing in the long term is more doubtful. It would mean that Israel would not be able to talk to anyone in authority in the Arab world. But negotiate at some future date they must. The only alternative is a permanent struggle in which they cannot afford to lose a single battle and cannot gain a lasting, decisive victory. Zionism had two basic aims: to restore dignity to the Jewish people and to give it security. It has succeeded in the first part of its program, but security is as far away as ever. Immigration remains the cardinal problem, but a mass influx of

American or Soviet Jewry, the two great remaining reservoirs, is highly unlikely in the foreseeable future. That being so, the historical mission of Zionism has come to an end and the state of Israel will have to come to terms with its new function, not on the basis of some ultimate goal, but in its present shape and prospects.

The Arab-Israeli conflict has all but monopolized public interest in Middle East tensions. But there is also the Yemen and the struggle for South Arabia, the Persian Gulf, the unsolved problem of Cyprus, and a great many other equally explosive issues. Nowhere are the problems of the area near a solution, and the internal weakness of the Middle East is bound to make it an easy prey. But as the Soviet military presence becomes more palpable, and its political implications more obvious, America (and the West) may find itself in greater demand than at present as a counterforce to Soviet pressure. The Soviet Union was welcomed in the fifties and sixties as a counterforce against 'Western imperialism'. Since then the political scene has radically changed, and it is gradually coming to be understood that the domination of the Middle East by one great power is not in the best interests of any country in the area. In some capitals it will no doubt take a little time to grasp and digest this, and no radical change in attitude can be expected in a few months or years. But there is a good chance that self-interest and the instinct of survival will eventually make most, though perhaps not all, of these countries recognize these basic facts and act accordingly. If this analysis is correct, the political (in contrast to the military) problems facing the West in the Middle East will ease in the years to come.

Meanwhile, there is the constant danger of local military conflicts escalating into a wider conflagration. Lasting agreement between the two super-powers seems a distant possibility despite the temporary meeting of minds in the talks in New York in 1969 about the Arab–Israeli deadlock. The drive to the south is one of the traditional directions of Russian foreign policy; with the retreat of the West the Middle East has become a power vacuum, and the emergence of China as a great power, hostile to the Soviet Union, has given additional impetus to Soviet activities there and in the Indian subcontinent. Yet it is unlikely that the Soviet Union will be in physical control of the area in the foreseeable future, and there remains a strong element of uncertainty in all these calculations. Moscow may be drawn more deeply than it wants into the problems of the area, whose objective importance is limited. It has been said about Vietnam that it became important mainly because the Americans decided to send an army there. The same applies to the Middle East: the Soviet advance now gives it a significance it would not otherwise have. It is an unfortunate by-product of this advance that it aggravates most of the internal problems of the Middle East. Montesquieu once said: 'Happy the nations whose annals of history are boring to read.' The boring years in the Middle East were always the happy ones. It would be a great contribution to peace in the area if the world's attention was not permanently focused on it. There may be no cure for its sicknesses, but it would alleviate them if the problems were reduced to their real size: Middle East conflicts flourish in the limelight and begin to wither when ignored. Unfortunately, the Middle East is unlikely to be ignored in the years to come; it will probably get more than its share of attention. There are no certainties: the Soviet Union may be deflected from its preoccupation with the Middle East by increasing unrest in Eastern Europe, by the growing menace of China, or by internal problems that cannot even be foreseen. The struggle for power among the Soviet leaders may sooner or later again enter an acute phase. But all this will rather contribute to instability than to peace. The permanent Middle East crisis will in all probability be further aggravated, and the whole area could be one of the main zones of conflict in the turbulent years that seem to lie ahead.

Notes

Chapter 3

1 On recent developments in Turkey and Turkish-Soviet relations: Gasratyan, M. A., *Turtsiya v 1960–63 godakh*, Moscow, 1965; Mango, Andrew, 'Turkey in the Middle East', *Journal of Contemporary History* (July 1968); Kannapin, Hans Eckhardt, 'Die türkisch-Sowjetischen Beziehungen seit 1960', *Osteuropa* (1967), 2; Fernau, F. W., 'Nachbarschaft am Schwarzen Meer', *Europa Archiv* (1967), 17; Eren, Nuri, 'Die türkisch-sowjetischen Beziehungen', ibid. (1965), 9; a series of eight articles in *Yeni Gazete* (December 19, 1966 et seq.); Vdovichenko, D. I., *Borba politicheskikh partii v Turtsii*, Moscow, 1967; Rozaliev, Yu. N., *Klassy i Klassovaia borba v Turtsii*, Moscow, 1966.

2 *Izvestia*, December 30, 1953.

3 *Cumhuriyet* (Ankara), December 5–15, 1961.

4 *Krasnaia Zvezda*, December 14 and 28, 1961.

5 Kannapin, loc. cit., p. 119.

6 *Yeni Istanbul*, March 12, 1963.

7 For subsequent appeals of similar character see *Sosyal Adalet*, December 1965; Kannapin, loc. cit., p. 124. On the Soviet appraisal of socialist and pseudo-socialist forces in Turkey, Gasanova, E. Yu., in *Narody Azii i Afriki* (1965), 1, (1968), 3.

8 Including *Vatan*, *Milliyet*, and *Cumhuriyet*. See also Kannapin, loc. cit., p. 121.

9 *Pravda*, December 10, 1964.

10 Kannapin, loc. cit., p. 123.

11 Our Radio (broadcasting station in Eastern Europe of the Turkish Communist party), June 25, 1966.

12 Our Radio, February 4, 1967.

13 Ibid.

14 Statement of the Central Committee of the Turkish Communist party dated February 25, 1967, broadcast over Our Radio, March 13, 1967.

15 Our Radio, March 17, 1967.

16 Tass International Service, December 19, 1966.

17 Reuter, March 3, 1964.

18 *Izvestia*, January 25, 1965.

19 *Novoe Vremia*, August 19, 1966.

20 Moscow Radio, December 19, 1966.

21 *Neue Zürcher Zeitung*, December 22 and 23, 1966.

22 *Izvestia*, December 24, 1966.

23 Ibid.

24 *Akis*, June, 1965.

25 Tass, December 27, 1966.

26 Ugolkov in *Pravda*, April 5, 1967.
27 Our Radio, April 7, 1967.
28 Tass, September 29, 1967.
29 *New York Times*, October 11, 1967.
30 Loc. cit.
31 *Sovetskaia Rossiya*, September 19, 1967.
32 Tanju, Sadun, in *Ulus*, October 5, 1967.
33 *New Times*, April 17, 1968; *Izvestia*, June 1, 1968; *Za Rubezhom*, May 30, 1968.
34 Orkunt, Sezai, in *Cumhuriyet*, November 9, 1967.
35 *Krasnaia Zvezda*, September 3, 1966.
36 Ulman, Haluk, in *Cumhuriyet*, December 20, 1966.
37 Quoted in *Christian Science Monitor*, May 27, 1968.
38 OECD: *Turkey* (Paris, July 1967), p. 29.
39 *Neue Zürcher Zeitung*, February 10, 1967.
40 *New York Times*, June 9, 1968.
41 Laqueur, W., *The Soviet Union and the Middle East*, London, 1959, pp. 207–8; on Soviet-Iranian relations in the nineteen-fifties; Alekseev, L., *Sovetskii Soyuz i Iran*, Moscow, 1963; Agakhi, A., *Rasprostranenie idei Marksizma–Leninizma v Irane*, Baku, 1961; Ivanov, M. S., *Noveishaia Istoriia Irana*, Moscow, 1965.
42 *Pravda*, July 2, 1954, March 16, 1955.
43 *Middle East Record*, 1960, p. 65.
44 Ibid.
45 *Pravda*, September 16, 1962.
46 Kasatkin in *International Affairs* (Moscow) (April 1968); Tuganova, O. E., in *Mezhdunarodnie otnosheniya na blizhnem i srednem Vostoke*, Moscow, 1967, 268.
47 Avery, Peter, in *The World Today*, July 1965.
48 Konstantinov, G., in *Aziia i Afrika Sevodnia*, June 1962, 58.
49 *Izvestia*, September 16, 1962.
50 Volodarsky, M. I., in *Narody Azii i Afriki* (1966) 3, 154.
51 Ivanov, M. S., op. cit., p. 246
52 Shatalov, I., in *International Affairs*, May 1968.
53 *Mizan Newsletter* (September 1966), 214–15.
54 National Voice of Iran (Communist broadcasting station in Eastern Europe), January 24, 1967.
55 Ibid., January 23, 1967.
56 Statement of the CC, People's Party of Iran, in *Information Bulletin* (March 31, 1966).
57 Eskandari, Iraj, in *World Marxist Review* (May 1965), 45–54.
58 Radmanesh, Reza, in *World Marxist Review* (November 1967), 21.
59 Paklin, N., in *Izvestia*, September 21, 1966.
60 Meyer-Ranke, Peter, 'Iran's neue Rolle: Ordnungsmacht in Mittelost', *Aussenpolitik* (May 1968), 300.
61 *Pravda*, March 4, 1968.
62 For a recent Soviet analysis of Iran's economic development, see Ivanov, M., 'Tendentsii razvitiia Ekonomiki Irana' in *Mirovaia Ekonomika i Mezhdunarodnie Otnosheniya* (December 1967). See also Kasatkin, loc. cit.
63 *New York Times*, March 15, 1968.
64 Hartshorn, J. E., *Oil Companies and Governments*, London, 1967, 324–5.
65 *Christian Science Monitor*, March 15, 1968.
66 *Petroleum Press Service* (April 1968), p. 127.
67 Rachkov, Boris, in *International Affairs* (April 1966), 15.
68 Kasatkin, D., in *International Affairs* (January 1967), 94; Soskin, B., in *Bakinskii Rabochii*, December 8, 1966.

69 Radio Peyk-e Iran, January 18, 1967, and other broadcasts in December 1966 and January 1967.
70 Arabadzhian, A. Z., in *Narody Azii i Afriki*, (1968), 2.
71 Moscow Radio, February 17, 1968.
72 Spandarian, V., in *New Times*, March 29, 1968.
73 Arabadzhian, loc. cit.; see also *New York Times*, March 15, 1968.
74 Ibid., July 14, 1966.
75 Ibid., September 19, 1966.
76 Radio Peyk-e Iran, March 4, 1967.
77 *Christian Science Monitor*, December 8, 1967; *New York Times*, May 22, 1968.
78 Radio Peyk-e Iran, December 16, 1965; National Voice of Iran, December 16, 1965.

Chapter 4

1 See Ivanov, K., and Scheinis, Z., *Gosudarstvo Izrail, evo Polozhenie i Politika*, 2nd ed., Moscow, 1959; Leonidov, A., *Za Kulisami izrailskoi politiki*, Moscow, 1959. Almost all articles in Soviet newspapers and periodicals on Jewish topics and Israel have been reprinted in *Evrei i evreiski Narod* (1959–in progress) and (selectively) in *Jews in Eastern Europe* (1959–in progress).
2 Kichko, T. K., *Iudaizm bez Prikraz*, Moscow, 1964.
3 *Komsomolskaia Pravda*, October 4, 1967.
4 For the war scare of May 1966: *Al Ba'th* (Damascus), May 1–5, 1966; *Izvestia*, May 7, 1966; *Arab World*, May 9, 1966; *Pravda*, May 21, 1966; Tass statement, May 27, 1966; Moscow Radio interview with Ibrahim Makhus, Syrian Foreign Minister, May 29, 1966; *Jewish Observer*, June 3, 1966; *Washington Post*, May 28, 1966.
5 *New York Times*, March 3, 1968, referring to the trial of Shams al Badran, Egyptian minister of war during the crisis.
6 The various possibilities are discussed in some detail in my *The Road to War*, London, 1968, Chapter 3.
7 *Izvestia*, May 30, 1967; Mayevsky in *Pravda*, June 1, 1967.
8 *Izvestia*, May 20, 1967.
9 Mayevsky in *Pravda*, May 21, 1967.
10 *Pravda*, June 1, 1967.
11 *Izvestia*, June 3 and 4, 1967.
12 *Pravda*, May 24, 1967.
13 Laqueur, *The Road to War*, 138–9.
14 *Pravda*, June 10, 1968.
15 Tanjug, June 15, 1968.
16 Radio Moscow, June 16, 1968.
17 *Izvestia*, June 15, 1968.
18 *Sovetskaia Rossiya*, June 23, 1968.
19 *Krasnaia Zvezda*, June 17; *Pravda Ukrainy*, June 18, 1967.
20 *Trud*, June 23; *Krasnaia Zvezda*, July 4, 1967.
21 *Krokodil*, June 19, 1967.
22 *Komsomolskaia Pravda*, August 8, 1967.
23 Primakov in *Pravda*, June 13 and 14, 1967.
24 In a series of six articles in *Pravda* between July 27 and August 9, 1967. See also Astakhov, K., in *International Affairs* (October 1967).
25 Ivanov, K., in *Mezhdunarodnaia Zhizn* (June 1968), 16.
26 Volsky, D., in *Mirovaia Ekonomika i Mezhdunarodnie Otnosheniya* (August 1967), 24.
27 Beliaev in *Pravda*, July 3, 1968.
28 Beliaev and Primakov in *Za Rubezhom*, September 22, 1967.
29 Mirsky, G., in *New Times*, June 5, 1968.

30 Ibid.
31 Ibid.
32 *Nedelya* (Moscow), June 18, 1967.
33 *'Obozrevatel'* in *Pravda*, April 13, 1968.
34 Such as the resolution adopted by the Warsaw meeting of the East European Foreign Ministers. *Soviet News*, January 2, 1968.
35 Ivanov, K., loc. cit., 18–19.
36 For instance, Davico, O., in *Komunist* (Belgrade), March 28, 1968.
37 Soviet books about Israel and the Six Day War include Beliaev and Primakov, *Golub spushchen*, Moscow, 1967, and Demchenko, P., *Arabskii Vostok v chas ispitanii*, Moscow, 1967.

Chapter 5

1 *Egyptian Gazette*, April 26, June 11, 1960.
2 Laqueur, W., *The Soviet Union and the Middle East*, London, 1959, *passim*.
3 Haykal, Muhamad Hasanain, in *Al Ahram*, January 22, 1965.
4 On the Soviet-Egyptian crisis of 1959 see Smolanski, Oles M., 'Moscow-Cairo Crisis 1959' in *Slavic Review* (1963), 713–26; John H. Burnett's dissertation, Chapter 5.
5 Nasser's speech on December 23, 1958, in *Al Gumhuriya*, December 24, 1958. See also his speeches in Damascus on March 11, 12, 13, 15, 20, 22, and at the Officers Club, Cairo, April 25, 1959, translated in Khalil, Muhammad (ed.), *The Arab States and the Arab League*, Beirut, 1965, 946–82.
6 Hafid, Karim, in *World Marxist Review*, June 1960. See also the editorial in *World Marxist Review*, August 1960, and Mahmud, Faruq, ibid., March 1960.
7 *Pravda*, March 17, 1959; *Al Gumhuriya*, March 23 and 31, 1959; *New York Times*, March 20, 1959.
8 Ibid., March 23, 1959.
9 *Pravda*, March 30, 1959.
10 *Mideast Mirror* (Beirut), April 5, 1959.
11 *New York Times*, February 22, 1959.
12 *Pravda*, March 30, 1959.
13 *New York Times*, May 21, 1959.
14 *Al Ahram* (Cairo), May 9, 1960.
15 Ibid., May 19 and 20, 1960.
16 *New York Times*, January 22, 1960.
17 Cairo Radio, October 12, 1960.
18 On the Douglas amendment and the 'Cleopatra' incident: *New York Times*, April 22–May 1, 1960; *Jerusalem Post*, April 21–May 6, 1960; *Al Gumhuriya*, April 18–May 10, 1960.
19 *Mirovaia Ekonomika i Mezhdunarodnie Otnosheniya*, June 1964, p. 75.
20 Beliaev and Cheprakov in *Kommunist*, June 1964.
21 Mayevsky in *Pravda*, August 24, 1961.
22 Mayevsky in *Mezhdunarodnaia Zhizn*, July 1966.
23 *'Obozrevatel'* in *Pravda*, May 31, 1961.
24 *Al Gumhuriya*, June 5 and 6, 1961.
25 *New York Times*, June 8, 1961.
26 *Pravda*, May 2, 1962.
27 Mirsky, G., in *New Times*, 1962, 4.
28 Mirsky, G., in *Mirovaia Ekonomika i Mezhdunarodnie Otnosheniia*, February 1964, 22.
29 Ra'anan, Uri, 'Moscow and the Third World' in *Problems of Communism*, January 1965.

30 Nassar, Fuad, 'On Arab Unity', *World Marxist Review*, February 1964, p. 22.
31 Beliaev, I., *Pravda*, March 27, 1964.
32 Khrushchev's speeches in Cairo (May 10, 1964); Aswan (May 16, 1964); Cairo (May 20, 1964); and Moscow (May 27, 1964).
33 *Pravda*, May 24, 1964.
34 Khrushchev at the banquet on May 18, 1964. In the Radio Moscow version this became 'should it become necessary to repel the schemes of the aggressor'.
35 *Mideast Mirror*, September 26, 1964; Tass, September 23, 1964; *Al Akhbar*, September 23, 1964; Cairo Radio, September 29, 1964.
36 *New York Times*, September 5, 1964.
37 *World Marxist Review*, November 1964, 71–80; *Pravda*, December 11, 1964; Tiagunenko in *Krasnaia Zvezda*, October 11, 1964.
38 *Al Ahram*, May 29, 1964.
39 Ibid., October 23, 1964.
40 *Pravda*, December 11, 1964.
41 Simoniia, N. A., in *Narody Azii i Afriki*, 1966, 6.
42 On Malik's mission see Middle East News Agency (MENA), Cairo, November 13, 1964.
43 On Shelepin's visit see *Mideast Mirror*, January 2, 1965.
44 *Al Ahram*, November 6, 1964; Tass, November 11, 1964.
45 Mikoyan's and Nasser's speeches, Radio Moscow, August 31, 1965; joint communiqué, MENA, September 1, 1965; see also *Arab World*, August 31, September 2, 3, 1965.
46 *Al Ahram*, September 3, 1965.
47 *Arab World*, September 6, 1965.
48 *Pravda*, May 18, 1966.
49 Ibid., May 19, 1966.
50 Ibid., May 20, 1966.
51 Tanjug in English, March 29, 1967, quoted by Kimche, D., and Bawly, D., *The Sandstorm*, London, 1968, 51.
52 *Ekonomicheskaia Gazeta*, 1967, 21, 45.
53 Smetanin, N., in *International Affairs*, July 1965, 39.
54 Primakov in *Pravda*, August 8, 1966; Beliaev in *Pravda*, July 23, 1966.
55 Beliaev and Primakov in *Pravda*, October 29, 1966.
56 *Jewish Observer and Middle East Review*, December 31, 1965, March 11, 1966; Smith, Hedrick, in *New York Times*, April 5, 1966; Hottinger, Arnold, in *Neue Zürcher Zeitung*, May 2, 1967.
57 Grishechkin, K. I., in Goncharov, L. V. (ed.), *Ekonomika Afriki*, Moscow, 1965; Garshin, I. I., in Zhukov, Y. M. (ed.), *Sovremennie Teorii Sotsializma*, Moscow, 1967; Kiselev, V., in *Mirovaia Ekonomika i Mezhdunarodnie Otnosheniia* (1963), 10. These discussions have been conveniently summarized in *Mizan Newsletter*, April 1964, 'Differing Views on the UAR', March 1966, 'The UAR and Proletarian Dictatorship', and January 1968, 'UAR and USSR: The Dialogue of Socialism'.
58 On the Cairo Seminar, October 1966, on 'National and Social Revolution in Africa' see *Problems of Peace and Socialism*, December 1966, *International Affairs*, January 1967, and *Mizan Newsletter*, March 1967.
59 Repin, A., in *Novoe Vremia*, July 5, 1968, 5.
60 Beliaev and Primakov, *Pravda*, July 31, 1967.
61 Ibid.
62 *New Times*, 1967, 26, 7.
63 *Za Rubezhom*, 1967, 27, 7–8.
64 Moscow Radio (in Arabic), July 8, 1967.
65 Primakov, Tass, April 26 and 28, 1968.

66 Quoted in *The Guardian*, March 1, 1968.
67 Primakov in *Novoe Vremia*, February 16, 1968.
68 In a cable to Brezhnev, Kosygin, and Podgorny, United Press report, July 26, 1968.
69 *Look* interview, *New York Times*, March 12, 1968.
70 Nasser's speech at the ASU National Congress, Cairo Radio, July 23, 1968.
71 Ibid.
72 On Nasser's visit to Moscow in July 1968, the official communiqué in *Pravda*, July 11, 1968; see also *Daily Telegraph*, July 2, 1968, *Neue Zürcher Zeitung*, July 8, 1968.
73 On the Yugoslav attitude to the presence of the American and Soviet fleets in the Mediterranean see *Za Rubezhom*, 1968, 5, quoting *Vjesnik; Le Monde*, April 13, 1968; *Cumhuriyet*, April 18, 1968; *Guardian*, July 25, 1968.
74 *The Guardian*, July 5, 1968.
75 Laqueur, W., *The Road to War*, 183.
76 Vera Ketlinskaia in *Znamia*, March 1968.
77 *New York Times*, May 16, 1968.
78 *Times*, April 25, 1968; *New York Times*, October 22, 1968.
79 For instance, Repin, A., in *Novoe Vremia*, July 5, 1968.
80 Laqueur, W., *The Soviet Union and the Middle East*, New York, 1959, 247–8.
81 Plishevsky, I., in *World Marxist Review*, July 1961; also *Noveishaia Istoriya Stran Azii i Afriki* (Moscow, 1965), 399, 441; a summary of Soviet attitudes to the union in *Mizan Newsletter*, January 1966, 29 et seq.
82 *Izvestia*, October 10, 1961.
83 Mirsky, G. I., *Arabskie Narody prodolzhaiut Borbu*, Moscow, 1965, 74 et seq.
84 On the history of the Ba'th see *Nidal al Ba'th*, Beirut, 1963–5; Jaber, Kamel S. Abu, *The Arab Ba'th Socialist Party*, New York, 1966; Saab, Edouard, *La Syrie ou la révolution dans la rancoeur*, Paris, 1968; Torrey, Gordon H., *Syrian Politics and Military*, Columbus, Ohio, 1964; Ben-Tzur, Avraham, 'The Neo-Ba'th Party of Syria' in *Journal of Contemporary History*, July 1968.
85 Mirsky, G., in *New Times*, 1963, 34.
86 *Pravda*, March 12, 1963; Vishnevski in *Izvestia*, June 7, July 20, 1963.
87 Moscow Radio, April 11, 1963.
88 Primakov in *Pravda*, November 14, 1963; *Pravda*, February 26, 1965; Demchenko in *Pravda*, January 28, 1965.
89 Muliukov, Seiful, Moscow Radio, February 26, 1965.
90 *Izvestia*, February 20, 1965.
91 as-Samadin, Zahir Abd, in *World Marxist Review*, July 1964.
92 Shimmel, N., in *New Times*, 1966, 6.
93 Vishnevetsky in *Izvestia*, March 14, 1966; Primakov in *Pravda*, March 18, 1966.
94 *Nidal, Al Shaab*, early April 1966, quoted in *Information Bulletin*, July 8, 1966; *Al Akhbar*, January 17, 1967; see also Bakdash, K., in *World Marxist Review*, December 1965.
95 *Al Anwar*, February 5, 1965; *Al Jaridah*, February 20, 1965; *Al Hayah*, February 20, 1965.
96 *Al Nahar*, April 13, 1966; *New York Times*, April 14, 1966; Novosti news agency quoted in *Al Anwar*, April 21, 1966; *Al Hayah*, April 23, 1966.
97 *Al Hayat*, May 29, 1966, quoted in *Arab World*, May 30, 1966.
98 Beliaev and Primakov in *Pravda*, June 2, 1966; Medvedko, L., in *International Life* (Moscow), July 1966; Demchenko, P., in *New Times*, 30, 1966.
99 *Al Thawra* (Damascus), October 30, 1964.
100 *Al Hayat*, June 1, 1966.

101 On Zu'ayin's trip to Moscow and the Euphrates dam project: *Arab World*, April 19, 25, 26, 27, 1966; Moscow Radio, April 19, 25, 1966; joint communiqué, Tass, April 20, 23, 1966; *Al Thawra*, April 24, 26, 1966; *Al Ba'th*, April 23, 25, 26, 1966; *Mideast Mirror*, April 23, 30, 1966; Damascus Radio, April 30, 1966

102 *The Arab World*, May 30, 1966.

103 Ibid., April 29, 1966.

104 Tuganova, O., in *Izvestia*, September 3, 1966; *Le Monde*, quoted in *Atlas*, September 1966, 43–4.

105 *Al Ahrar* (Beirut), April 23, 1966.

106 *Pravda*, January 21, February 12, 1967.

107 Moscow Radio, May 27, 1966.

108 See Laqueur, *The Road to War*, 71–108.

109 *Izvestia*, March 28, 1968.

110 Medvedko in *Pravda*, April 16, 1968.

111 Quoted in *International Affairs*, May 1967, 115.

112 On communism in Iraq, 1958–61, see *Middle East Record*, 1960, 239–44; 1961, 266–76.

113 Aziz el Haj in *World Marxist Review*, November 1963, 36 et seq.

114 Including *Ittihad al Sha'ab, Sawt al Ahrar, Al Shabibah, Al Insaniyah, Al Hadara, Al Siyasi al Jedid, Al Thabat*, and others. Some of them were temporarily closed down even before October 1960; a few continued sporadically during the first half of 1961.

115 On the purge of the Journalists Union see *Iraq Times*, March 3, June 2, 1961, and *Al Zaman*, June 2 and 4, 1961.

116 *Pravda*, October 25, 1961.

117 *Iraq Times*, December 23, 1960; *Al Fajr al Jadid*, December 22, 1960.

118 Grishin press conference, Baghdad Radio, March 14, 1960.

119 *New York Times*, May 8, 1960.

120 Moscow Radio, July 14, 1960.

121 *Izvestia*, April 16, 1960.

122 *Al Bilad*, April 1, 1960.

123 Donskoy, P., in *Aziia i Afrika sevodnia*, July 1961.

124 Ibid., March 1961; Andreev, Y., in *Voprosy Vostokovedeniia*, January 1961.

125 For Soviet views on the Kurdish campaigns and the Kurdish problem in general, Demchenko, P., *Irakskii Kurdistan v ogne*, Moscow, 1963; Kamel, M. A., *Natsionalno-osvobozhditelnoe dvizhenie v Irakskom Kurdistane*, Baku, 1967.

126 *Middle East Review*, October 21, 1961.

127 *World Marxist Review*, October 21, 1961.

128 Radio Peyk-e Iran, October 21, 1961.

129 Jabar, Ali, in *Al Waqt*, 1962, 8, quoted in *Neue Zürcher Zeitung*, January 10, 1962.

130 Demchenko, Pavel, *Irakskii Kurdistan v ogne*, 3–5.

131 Ibid., 60.

132 Demchenko, P., in *New Times*, 1966, 7, 18.

133 Primakov, E., in *Pravda*, January 18, 1967.

134 Pogodina, I., ibid., July 6, 1966; Potomov, Yu., ibid., February 2, 1966.

135 Seiful-Mulyukov, F., in *New Times*, 1966, 28, 20.

136 Voice of the Iraqi People, September 20, 1966, quoting *Regay-e Kurdistan*, July, 1966.

137 Voice of the Iraqi People, March 23, 1967.

138 See, for instance, *Regay-e Kurdistan*, July 1966; *Tariq al Shab*, February 1967; quoted in Voice of the Iraqi People, February 24, 1967.

139 *Pravda*, February 25, 1963.

140 *Neue Zürcher Zeitung*, April 12, 1963.
141 *Al Jamahir*, February 21, 1963.
142 *Pravda*, December 21, 1963.
143 Ibid., July 18, 1964.
144 Primakov in ibid., July 13, 1964.
145 Voice of the Iraqi People, June 21, July 6, 1966.
146 Resolution of the Central Committee of the Iraqi Communist party (August 1966), Voice of the Iraqi People, September 29, 1966.
147 Ibid.
148 Stupak, A., in *Izvestia*, July 13, 1968.
149 *Problemy Mira i Sotsializma*, July 1968, 93.
150 *Neues Deutschland*, April 23, 1967.
151 Voice of the Iraqi People, February 24 and 26, 1968.
152 Demchenko, P., in *Izvestia*, August 3, 1968.
153 Sultanov, A. F. (ed.), *Sovetsko-Arabskie Druzhestvennie otnosheniia*, Moscow, 1961, 114–17.
154 *Middle East Record*, 1961, p. 694.
155 Radio Baku, November 1, 1963.
156 Primakov in *Pravda*, February 2, 1966; Volsky in *Novoe Vremia*, May 12, 1967.
157 *Nouvel Observateur*, April 26, May 3, 1967.
158 *Pravda*, January 19, 1967.
159 Tass, January 2, 1968.
160 Smith, Hedrick, in *New York Times*, December 15, 1967.
161 *Economist*, September 14, 1968; for other Soviet comments on developments in the Yemen in 1967: Medvedko, L., in *Mezhdunarodnaia Zhizn*, 1968, 2; Demchenko, P., in *Aziia i Afrika Sevodnia*, 1968, 2; Volsky, D., in *Novoe Vremia*, April 28, 1967, and in *New Times*, March 27, 1968.
162 *Arab World*, March 24, April 11, 1968; *Neue Zürcher Zeitung*, February 24, May 10, June 8, 1968; *New York Times*, April 16, 1968.
163 *Economist*, April 27, 1968.
164 *Pravda*, November 29, 1967.
165 Radio Peace and Progress (Moscow), November 17, 1967.
166 *Al Hayat*, January 24, 1968.
167 Radio Peace and Progress, April 24, 1968.
168 *Izvestia*, March 28, 1959.
169 *US News*, December 26, 1966; *Izvestia*, December 24, 1966.
170 *Pravda*, October 3, 1967.
171 *Taqadum* (organ of the Jordanian Communist party), February 1968, quoted in *Al Ittihad*, March 8, 1966.
172 Sontag, R. J., and Beddie, J. S. (eds.), *Nazi-Soviet Relations 1939–1941*, Washington 1948, 259.
173 Langer, W. L., *The Diplomacy of Imperialism*, New York, 1956, 752.
174 Curzon, G. N., *Persia and the Persian Question*, London, 1892, II, 456.
175 I have drawn in this section on a number of papers on the situation in the Persian Gulf submitted to conferences in England in June and September 1968, under the sponsorship of the Institute for Strategic Studies (London) and the Institute for Strategic Studies (Washington) respectively, especially those by Mr. D. A. Schmidt, Brigadier W. F. K. Thompson, Professor B. Lewis, Mr. C. Tugendhat, Mr. T. Stauffer, Major General J. L. Moulton, Professor P. J. Vatikiotis, and Mr. Desmond Wettern.
176 Leonidov, A., in *Sovremennii Vostok*, October 1958; see also *New Times*, 1958, 43; a survey of Soviet literature on the Gulf States before 1959 in *Mizan Newsletter*, January 1959.

177 Andreasyan, Y., in *Vokrug Sveta*, April 1953.
178 Cairo Radio, May 20, 1964.
179 *Mirovaia Ekonomika i Mezhdunarodnie Otnosheniia*, February 1965, 137–8.
180 *New Times*, 1968, 11, (editorial).
181 *Novy Vostok*, Vol. 20/21, 400.
182 *Izvestia*, November 29, 1964; *Pravda*, November 4, 1964.
183 Ibid., May 27, 1966.
184 *International Affairs*, March 1968, p. 44; see also Ivanov, K., in *New Times*, 1968, 8, 18.
185 Tass statement, March 3, 1968; see also *International Affairs*, March 1968, 75–6.
186 Medvedko, L., in *New Times*, March 20, 1968, 16.
187 Schmidt, loc. cit., note 173, 48.

Chapter 6

1 A Soviet writer in *International Affairs* (July 1960), quoted in *The World Today*, July 1964, 313.
2 Hartshorn, J. E., *Oil Companies and Governments*, 2nd ed., London, 1967, provides a general introduction.
3 Ebel, Robert E., *The Petroleum Industry in the Soviet Union*, Washington, 1961; Judy, Richard, *Die Bedeutung der Sowjetunion für die Weltölwirtschaft von 1960 bis 1975*, Hamburg, 1963.
4 National Petroleum Council, *Impact of Oil Exports from the Soviet Bloc*, Washington, 1962; Lubell, Harold, *The Soviet Oil Offensive and Inter-Bloc Economic Competition*, Rand Corporation paper RM 2182–PR, December 1961; Hoskins, Halford L., and Herman, Leon, *Soviet Oil in the Cold War*, Washington, 1961; Hoskins, Halford L., *Problems raised by the Soviet Oil Offensive*, Washington, 1962; *Soviet Oil in East-West Trade*, U.S. Senate 86868, July 3, 1962, Washington, 1962; Saylor, John P., in *Congressional Record*, February 18, 1963; Dirksen, E., in ibid., April 11, 1963.
5 Huttlinger, Joseph P., in *World Petroleum*, November 1962, 52–5.
6 Hoskins and Herman, op. cit., 9.
7 Adelman, M. A. Clawson, Marion (ed.) in *Natural Resources and International Development*, Baltimore, 1964, 96.
8 *Petroleum Press Service*, November 1960.
9 Gurov, Y., in *Ekonomischeskaia Gazeta*, September 1967; *Financial Times*, June 6, 1966.
10 *Middle East Mirror*, October 1, 1960.
11 *Petroleum Press Service*, September 1960.
12 Getty, G. F., in *Washington Post*, March 31, 1963.
13 *Platt's Oilgram News Service*, February 15, 28, 1963.
14 Gurov, loc. cit.
15 *Petroleum Press Service*, June 1968.
16 *Neue Zürcher Zeitung*, April 19, 1968.
17 *Prace*, May 17, 1968.
18 Bogomolov, in *Voprosy Ekonomiki*, February 1966.
19 *Petroleum Press Service*, January 1968.
20 Hartshorn, op. cit., p. 321.
21 The literature on oil-pricing is vast and bewildering. See, for instance, Ovens, David, *Crude Oil Prices*, London, 1958; Leeman, Wayne A., *The Price of Middle Eastern Oil*, Ithaca, 1962; Issawi, Charles, and Yeganeh, M., *The Economics of Middle Eastern Oil*, New York, 1962; Frank, Helmut J., *Crude Oil Prices in the Middle East*, New York, 1966.

22 On oil concessions see Mikdashi, Zuhayr, *A Financial Analysis of Middle East Oil Concessions 1901–1905*, New York, 1965; 'Oil in the Persian Gulf' in *The World Today*, July 1964.

23 Barran, D. H., in *Petroleum Press Service*, July 1964.

24 Andreev, Yu. N., in *Problemy Vostokovedeniia*, January 1961.

25 'Problems and Objectives of Energy Policy' in *OECD Observer*, October 1966.

26 European Coal and Steel Community, *Annual Report, 1967*, Statistical Appendix, Table 13.

27 Adelman, M. A., *Security of Eastern Hemisphere Fuel Supply*, MIT Working Paper 6, Department of Economics, December 1967.

28 *Europe's Need for Oil*, OEEC Publication, Document C (57) 234, January 1958, 39.

29 Ibid., 42.

30 *Neue Zürcher Zeitung*, August 19, 1967.

31 Hartshorn, J. E., 'Oil and the Middle East War' in *The World Today*, April 1968, 155.

32 Tugendhat, Christopher, in an unpublished paper on 'Oil in the Persian Gulf', July 1968.

33 OECD estimates, *Petroleum Press Service*, March 1968, 83.

34 Adelman, M. A., loc. cit., 7; see also *Petroleum Press Service*, January 1968, 3.

35 Ibid., November 1967.

36 Ibid., May 1968.

37 Wasowski, Stanislaw, *The Fuel Situation in Eastern Europe*, Research Paper 366 (September 1967), Institute of Defense Analysis (Washington, 1967), 18–24.

38 Albinowski, Stanislaw, in *Polityka* (Warsaw), September 24, 1966; see also *Independent Petroleum Monthly*, February 1967, and B. Rachkov in *The New Middle East*, May 1969.

39 Wasowski, loc. cit., 34; see also Dudinsky, I., in *Voprosy Ekonomiki*, May 1966.

40 Wasowski, loc. cit., 49.

41 El Salloum, Abdel Wahab, *The Problems of Oil in Iraq*, published by the Permanent Secretariat of the Organization for Afro-Asian Peoples Solidarity, Cairo, n.d.

42 Medvedko, L., in *Pravda*, March 6, 1967.

43 Voice of the Iraqi People, April 13, 1967.

44 Ibid.

45 See, for instance, Ascher, Konstantin, in *Deutsche Aussenpolitik* (East Berlin), June 1968.

46 Gurov, Y., in *Ekonomicheskaia Gazeta*; quoted in *Soviet News* (London), October 10, 1967.

47 *Petroleum Press Service*, February 1968.

48 *New York Times*, December 31, 1967.

49 Ibid., May 5, 1968, December 31, 1967.

50 *Petroleum Press Service*, February 1968.

51 *New York Times*, January 8, 1968.

Chapter 7

1 Quoted in Kocharian in *Sovremennii Vostok*, July 1959, 4. For Soviet trade and aid to underdeveloped countries see Berliner, Joseph S., *Soviet Economic Aid*, New York, 1958; *The Sino-Soviet Economic Offensive in the Less Developed Countries*, Department of State Publications 6632, May 1958; Goldman, Marshall I., *Soviet Foreign Aid*, New York, 1967; Müller, Kurt, *Über Kalkutta nach Paris?*, Hanover, 1965; US Congress Joint Economic Committee, *New Directions in the Soviet Economy*, Part IV; 'The World Outside: Soviet Foreign Aid to the Less Developed Countries', by Leon Tansky, Washington, 1966.

2 Rymalov, V., in *International Affairs*, September 1959, 24.

3 Merkulov, V., in *Vneshnaia Torgovlia*, April 1968.

4   Smirnov, V., and Matiuchin, I., in *Vneshnaia Torgovlia*, January 1968.
5   Tansky, loc. cit., 951–3.
6   Department of State Research Memorandum RSB-80, July 21, 1967; *Communist Governments and Developing Nations: Economic Aid and Trade*.
7   Sutton, John L., and Kemp, G., *Arms to Developing Countries*, Institute for Strategic Studies Paper No. 28, October 1966.
8   OECD, *The Flow of Financial Resources to Developing Countries in* 1961, Paris, 1963.
9   Tansky, loc. cit., 969.

Chapter 8

1   Laqueur, W., and Labedz, L., 'On Thermonuclear Coexistence', *Survey*, October 1961. The best introduction to the subject is Wolfe, Thomas W., *Soviet Strategy at the Crossroads*, Cambridge, Mass., 1964.
2   Gasteyger, Curt, 'Modern Warfare and Soviet Strategy' in *Survey*, October 1965, 46.
3   Kolkowicz, Roman, *The Dilemma of Superpower; Soviet Policy and Strategy in Transition*, IDA Research Paper P-383, Washington, 1967; see also Wolfe, Thomas W., *The Soviet Military Scene: Institutional and Defense Policy Consideration*, Rand Corporation Paper RM-4913-PR, 1966.
4   Kolkowicz, op. cit., 12–13.
5   Wolfe, Thomas W., 'Soviet Military Policy' in *Current History*, October 1967, quoted from *Survival*, January 1968, 4.
6   *The Economist*, July 6, 1968.
7   Jonas, Ann M., in *Air Force Magazine*, January 1968.
8   *Strategic Survey 1967*, published by the Institute for Strategic Studies, London, 1968, 25.
9   'Additional Dimensions of Soviet Strategy' in *Air Force Magazine*, February 1968.
10 Gorshkov, Admiral, quoted in Wolfe, Thomas W., *The Soviet Quest for More Globally Mobile Military Power*, Rand Corporation Memorandum RM-5554-PR, December 1967, 8.
11 Ibid.
12 Herrick, Robert Waring, *Soviet Naval Strategy*, Annapolis, 1968, Chapter IV.
13 Murphy, F. M., 'The Soviet Navy in the Mediterranean' in *US Naval Institute Proceedings*, March 1967, 39–44; see also Mason, Ph., and Couhat, J. Labayle, 'La Présence Navale Sovietique en Méditerranée' in *Revue de Défense Nationale*, May 1968, 858–73.
14 In *Kommunist Vooruzhonikh Sil*, July 1963.
15 Gorshkov's article in *Morskoi Sbornik*, Moscow, 1967.
16 Cleveland, Harlan speech at the National Press Club, Washington, DC, on August 23, 1967, 'The Resurrection of NATO'.
17 Kelly, Orr, in *Evening Star* (Washington), June 22, 1967.
18 Martin, Laurence, in *Spectator* (London), May 10, 1968, and October 4, 1968.
19 *US News and World Report*, December 11, 1967.
20 *Der Spiegel*, 1968, 20.
21 Herrick, R. W., op. cit. pp. 154–55; on the Soviet Mediterranean '*Eskadra*' see also Gasteyger, Curt, in *Foreign Affairs*, July 1968; Griswold, L. (ed.), *Background for Tomorrow*, August 21, 1967; *Jane's Fighting Ships, 1967–8*, introd.
22 *The Economist*, May 18, 1968.
23 *Christian Science Monitor*, July 12, 1967.
24 *Borba*, February 17, 1968.
25 *Unitá*, May 21, 1968.
26 *Internationale Politik* (Belgrade), April 5, 1968.
27 Ibid., March 5, 1968.

28 *Le Monde*, June 6, 1967.
29 Welles Benjamin, in *New York Times*, April 17, 1968.
30 *Revue de Défense Nationale*, January 1968.
31 *Christian Science Monitor*, May 27, 1968.
32 Ferron, James, in *New York Times*, October 23, 1967.
33 Mackintosh, Malcolm, in *The World Today*, April 1968, 150.
34 *Kommunist*, January 1968.
35 McNamara's statement to Senate Armed Services Committee, February 1, 1968: *Strategic Survey*, 1967, 22; Long, John, *The Soviet Armed Forces in the 1970s: Daily Information Bulletin* (Radio Liberty), May 2, 1968.

Chapter 9

1 For the history of the TPI in the nineteen-fifties see *The Evolution of Communism in Iran*, Tehran, 1959.
2 Eskandari, Iradig, in *World Marxist Review*, May 1965, 54–5.
3 Radio Iran Courier, January 3, 1966; see also 'Statement of the CC People's Party of Iran on the activities of the splinter group', December 1965, in *Information Bulletin*, March 31, 1966.
4 *Kayhan International* (Tehran), June 24, 1965.
5 Karpat, Kemal H., 'Socialism and the Labor Party of Turkey' in *Middle East Journal*, spring 1967.
6 Article in *Aksam* quoted in *The Times*, July 12, 1968.
7 Ankara Radio, August 21, 1968.
8 *Kommunist*, No. 11, July 1967; *Pravda*, August 8, 1967.
9 Sneh, Moshe, in *Kol Ha'am*, June 25, 1967; see also *Information Bulletin* of both Maki and Rakah, 1966–7; *Kol Ha'am*, November 12, 1967.
10 *Rakah Information Bulletin*, August 1967; *Maki Information Bulletin*, December 1967; *Al Ittihad*, October 27, 1967.
11 Nassar, Fuad, in *Voprosy Istorii KPSS*, 1967, 2, 23.
12 *Kommunist*, 1959, 12; *Iraqi Review*, September 6, 1958.
13 Uri Dann's book, *Iraq under Kassem* (NewYork, 1969), provides the fullest analysis of this subject.
14 Shevliagin in *Sovetskaia Rossiia*, June 10, 1960.
15 Muliukov, Seyful, in *Trud*, September 26, 1963.
16 Voice of the Iraqi People, January 6, 1968.
17 Ibid., September 30, 1967; *World Marxist Review*, April 1968, 41.
18 *Tariq al Sha'b*, February 1967.
19 *Ila al Amam* (Beirut), September 10, 1967; also Marjan, Badr, and Nimr, Nasib, ibid., September 3, 1967.
20 This is part of a polemic against a report by Bakdash on the August 1967 conference of the Central Committee of the Syrian party, published in *Nidal al Sha'b*.
21 Nimr, Nasib, in *Ila al Amam*, September 10, 1967.
22 *Al Siad* (Beirut), December 12, 1967.
23 *Al Nahar*, April 5, 1967; *Al Hayat*, April 7, 1967; Faysal, Yusuf, at the SED Congress, Voice of the Iraqi People, May 6, 1967.
24 Spano, V., in *Unità*, December 5, 1967; Berner, Wolfgang, *Die KP Italiens und die aegyptischen Kommunisten 1956–58* (*Berichte des Bundesinstituts für ostwissenschaftliche und internationale Studien*, No. 28, 1967); Berner, Wolfgang, '*Nasser und die Kommunisten*' in *Europa Archiv*, 1965, 15; Malek, Anwar Abdel, *Egypte, Société Militaire*, Paris, 1962.
25 Barat, M., in *France Observateur*, January 8, 1959.
26 *Al Ahram*, January 29, 1965.

27 *Al Gumhuriya*, January 10, 1966.
28 See *Al Tali'a*, August, November, December 1967, *passim*.
29 A communist account of the events of 1965 is provided by Abdallah H., in *World Marxist Review*, February 1966.
30 Tanjug, March 11, 1965.
31 *Unità*, June 30, 1964.
32 *Economist*, June 1, 1969.
33 Lowenthal, R., in *Survey*, January 1966, 46–7.
34 For accounts of the changes in Soviet attitudes on this subject see Ra'anan, U., in *Problems of Communism*, January 1965; Lowenthal, R., in *Survey*, April 1963; Kanet, Roger E., in *Russian Review*, January 1968; Yellon, R. A., in *Mizan*, March and July 1967.
35 Lowenthal, R. (ed.), in *Entwicklungsländer zwischen nationaler und kommunistischer Revolution*, Hanover, 1965, 16–17.
36 Ra'anan, U., loc. cit., 23.
37 Ibid.
38 Lowenthal, R., *Entwicklungsländer* . . . p. 17.
39 Mirsky, G., in *New Times*, 1964, 18.
40 Ivanov, K., 'National Liberation Movement', *International Affairs*, 1965, 5, 65.
41 Tiagunenko, V., in *Mirovaia ekonomika i mezhdunarodnie otnosheniia*, 1965, 8, 85.
42 See the contribution by Avakov, R., in the discussion on 'Socialism, Capitalism and the Underdeveloped Countries' in *Mirovaia Ekonomika i mezhdunarodnie otnosheniia*, 1964, 4 and 6; English abridged version – special issue of *Mizan Newsletter*, November 1964.
43 Ulianovsky, R., in *Kommunist*, 1966, 1.
44 Brutents, K., in *Kommunist*, 1964, 17; 'At the Cairo Seminar', *World Marxist Review*, 1967; see also note 42 and the literature quoted in Ra'anan, Yellon and Kanet, loc. cit.
45 'The Ebb Tide?' in *Mizan*, September 1966.
46 Mirsky, G., in *Pravda*, January 31, 1965; Ulianovsky, R., ibid., April 15, 1966; Yellon, loc. cit., 168.
47 Bakdash, Khalid, in *World Marxist Review*, July 1964, and December 1965; Sawaja, in ibid., February 1964.
48 Nassar, Fuad, in *World Marxist Review*, September 1966.
49 Shawi, Nicola, in ibid., July 1966.
50 Voice of the Iraqi People, July 5, 1966.
51 Reports on these meetings were published in *Foreign Report*, January 14 and June 24, 1965; Voice of the Iraqi People, June 1, 1967, and *Al Nahar*, November 21, 1967. The authenticity of these reports cannot always be taken for granted.
52 *Al Akhbar*, quoted in *The Arab World*, August 8, 1968.

Bibliography

The most important single source used is the *Mizan Newsletter*. Since its publication in 1959 under the editorship of Colonel Geoffrey Wheeler and later of David Morison, it has been invaluable to all students of the Middle East and of Soviet policies in that part of the world.

Unpublished Sources

I have read with profit the doctoral dissertations of John H. Burnett and Oles Smolanski on Soviet policy in the Middle East in the nineteen-fifties; Mr. John Baker's substantial and stimulating paper on Soviet policies in the Middle East (Harvard, 1968); Professor John Armstrong's essay on the same topic; Professor Uri Ra'anan on the background and the wider implications of the arms deal of 1955; Professor Adelman, Dr. St. Wasowski, and C. Tugendhat on oil policy; Thomas Wolfe and Roman Kolkowicz on strategic problems; Hans Bräker on Islam and Communism; Wolfgang Berner on communism in Egypt; Joseph G. Whelan on The Soviet Union and the Middle East; Messrs. Desmond Wettern, Standish, Brigadier W. F. K. Thompson, Professor Vatikiotis, Major-General J. L. Moulton, and Mr. D. A. Schmidt on the Persian Gulf.

Books

The essential literature used in the writing of the present study is quoted in the notes (pp. 195–207). The following list includes books that were referred to only on one or two occasions or not at all, but are nevertheless of relevance for the study of the subject.

AL AQQAD, ABBAS MAHMUD, *Ash Shuyu'iya wa'l Islam*, Cairo, 1959.
AL FAKIKI, ABD AL HADI, *Ash Shuyu'iya wa'l qaumiya al Arabiya*, Beirut, 1963.
AL GUNDI, ANAM, *Ila aina yasir ash Shuyu'iya bi'l Iraq?*, Beirut, 1959.

AL MUNAJJID, SALAH, *La Bolchevisation de l'Islam chez les Marxistes et les Socialistes Arabes*, Beirut, 1967.

ALEKSEEV, L., *Sovetski Soiuz i Iran*, Moscow, 1963.

ALITOVSKY, S. N., *Agrarny vopros v sovremennom Irake*, Moscow, 1966.

ANDREASIAN, R. N., and ELYANOV, A. Y., *Blizhnii Vostok; Neft i nezavisimost*, Moscow, 1961.

Ash Shuyu'iya al yaum wa radan, Cairo, n.d.

BADI, S. M., *Rabochiy Klass Irana*, Moscow, 1965.

—— *Agrarniye otnosheniia v sovremennom Irane*, Moscow, 1959.

BASKIN, V. S., *Neftianie monopolii na Blizhnem i Srednem Vostoke*, Moscow, 1957.

BELIAEV, I. P., *Amerikanskii imperializm v Saudovskoi Arabii*, Moscow, 1957.

BINDER, LEONARD, *The Ideological Revolution in the Middle East*, New York, 1964.

BLACK, CYRIL E., and THORNTON, THOMAS P. (eds.), *Communism and Revolution: the Strategic uses of Violence*, Princeton, 1964.

BOLTON, A., *Soviet Middle East Studies* (annotated bibliography), London: Central Asian Research Centre for the Royal Institute of International Affairs, 1959.

CREMEANS, CHARLES D., *The Arabs and the World*, New York, 1963.

DANTSIG, B. M., *Irak v proshlom i nastoiashchem*, Moscow, 1960.

DEMCHENKO, P. Y., *Kurdistan v ogne*, Moscow, 1963.

DRUZA, AL HUKM, *Ash Shuyu'iya al mahalliya wa maraka al Arab. al qaumiya*, Beirut, 1963.

ELLIS, HARRY B., *Challenge in the Middle East: Communist Influence and American Policy*, New York, 1960.

FISHER, S. N., *The Military in the Middle East and Problems in Society and Government*, Ohio State University Press, 1963.

GASRATIAN, M. A., *Turtsia v 1960–1963 godakh: ocherk vnutrennei politiki*, Moscow, 1965.

—— and MOISEEV, P., *Turtsia zhdiot peremien*, Moscow, 1963.

GATAULLIN, M. F., *Ekonomika OAR na novom puti*, Moscow, 1963.

IMHOFF, CHRISTOPH VON, *Duell im Mittlemeer, Moskau greift nach dem Nahen und Mittleren Osten*, Freiburg, 1967.

ISSAWI, CHARLES, *Egypt in Revolution, an Economic Analysis*, London, 1963.

JABER, KAMEL S. ABU, *The Arab Ba'th Socialist Party, History, Ideology, and Organization*, Syracuse, 1966.

KOTLOV, L. N., *Iordania v noveisheie vremia*, Moscow, 1962.

LABIB, FAHRI, and MUSTAQAWI, MAHMUD AL, *Al Itihad al Suvyati wa Misr al Mustaqilla*, Cairo, 1957.

LAQUEUR, WALTER, *Communism and Nationalism in the Middle East*, London, 1956.

—— *The Soviet Union and the Middle East*, London, 1959

LEBEDEV, YE. A. (ed.), *Sovremennaia Iordania (Spravochnik)*, Moscow, 1964.

MALEK, ANWAR ABDEL, *Egypte, Société Militaire*, Paris, 1962.

MALIUKOVSKY, M. V., and others (ed.), *Sovremennyi Irak (Spravochnik)*, Moscow, 1966.

MARQAS, ILYAS, *Tarikh al ahzab ash Shuyu'i al Arabi*, Beirut, 1964.

—— *Al Marksiya fi asrina*, Beirut, 1965.

MEYER-RANKE, PETER, *Der Rote Pharao*, Hamburg, 1964.

'The Middle East and the Arab World', Adelphi Paper No. 20, London: Institute for Strategic Studies, July 1965.

MIOVANOV, I. V., and SEYFUL-MULIUKOV, F. M., *Irak vchera i sevodnia*, Moscow, 1959.

MUHSIN, MAHDI, *Die geistigen und sozialen Wandlungen im Nahen Osten*, Freiburg, 1967.

NASIM, MAHIR, *Ash Shuyu'iya wa'l Sahyuniya*, Cairo, 1959.

PALIUKAITIS, I. I., *Ekonomicheskoe razvitie Irana*, Moscow, 1965.

PEGOV, S. S., and ALITOVSKY, S. N., *Irak*, Moscow, 1966.

PROSHIN, N. I., *Saudovskaya Aravia (Istoriko-ekonomicheskii ocherk)*, Moscow, 1964.

QALUGI, QADIR, *Tagriba arabi fi'l Hizb Ash Shuyu'i*, Beirut, 1960.

RUINDEZH, D. B., *Borba Irakskovo naroda protiv Bagdadskovo pakta (1954–1959)*, Baku, 1966.

SAGER, PETER, *Kairo und Moskau in Arabien*, Berne, 1967.

SAID, ZAKI HAIRI, *Al Mitaq al watani wa'n nizam ad dahili li'l Hizb Ash Shuyu'i al Iraqi*, Baghdad, 1960.

SAINT-MARIE, FRANCOIS DE, *Irak Rouge? Kassem entre Moscou et le Caire*, Paris, 1960.

SEYFUL-MULIUKOV, F. M., *Irak v borbe za nezavisimost i progress*, Moscow, 1959.

SHAMSUTDINOV, A. M. (ed.), *Problemy sovremennoy Turtsii*, Moscow, 1963.

SSSR i Arabskie Strani (published by the Soviet Ministry of Foreign Affairs, Moscow, 1960.

SULTANOV, A. F. (ed.), *Sovetsko-Arabskie druzhestvennie otnosheniia*, Moscow, 1961.

TUGANOVA, O. E., *Mezhdunarodnie Otnosheniia na blizhnem i srednem Vostoke*, Moscow, 1967.

ULE, WOLFGANG, *Bibliographie zu Fragen des Arabischen Sozialismus, des Nationalismus und des Kommunismus unter dem Gesichtspunkt des Islams*, Hamburg, 1967.

VATIKIOTIS, P. J., *The Egyptian Army in Politics: Pattern for new Natons*, Bloomington, 1961.

VATOLINA, L. N., *Ekonomika obedinionnoi Arabskoi Respubliki*, Moscow, 1962.

VDOVICHENKO, D. I., *Natsionalnaya burzhuazia Turtsii*, Moscow, 1962.

VERNIER, BERNARD, *L'Irak d'aujourd'hui*, Paris, 1963.

VOCKE, HARALD, *Das Schwert und die Sterne. Ein Ritt durch den Jemen*, Stuttgart, 1965.

La voie Egyptienne vers le socialisme, Cairo, 1966.

WESTEN, KLAUS, *Der Staat der nationalen Demokratie: Ein kommunistisches Modell für Entwicklungsländer*, Cologne, 1964.

ZVEREVA, L. S., *Kuwait*, Moscow, 1964.

Documents

The following section includes essential documents concerning Soviet-Middle Eastern relations. It also gives excerpts from articles by Soviet authors (such as O. Tuganova and K. Ivanov) which are fairly typical for both level and flavour of Soviet comment on Middle Eastern topics. For reasons of space, cuts had to be made which in the text are indicated by dots. The documents are mostly given in official translation and the spelling of Arab and other names is not therefore always identical with the transliteration in the body of the book.

I

O. Tuganova: *Political Trends in the Arab East*

. . .

Compared with what is going on in South-East Asia and Latin America, the situation in the Arab East seems to be quiet and to some extent even stabilised. But a closer look shows that there, too, the main NATO Powers, above all the United States, are trying to mount an offensive against the national-liberation forces.

Imperialism is still casting a sombre and sometimes bloody shadow on Middle East politics. What is its effect on the foreign policy and further development of the Arab states? How are these states going to co-operate among themselves and with the Socialist countries? How is the whole of the Arab East to be released from the grip of NATO's nuclear-rocket strategy? These questions are of more than theoretical interest, because not only the security, progress and future of these states, but the arrangement of forces on a world scale depend on the answers the Arab peoples and their leaders give.

At the turn of the 1950s, imperialism worked out new tactics. Its chief elements are: resistance to the emergence of non-capitalist trends; concentration of efforts on establishing and promoting stable contacts and alliances with the big bourgeoisie; wide use for that purpose of economic, ideological and political ways and means of pressure, such as 'aid' and 'co-operation' between monopoly and national capital; anti-Communism and reactionary nationalism; and 'recognition' of the neutralism of the Arab countries and efforts to give it a pro-West twist.

However, the application of the new tactics has produced no appreciable results. The imperialist Powers have become increasingly nervous and are inclined to fall back on the tough policy.

.   .   .

In late 1963 and in 1964, the United States presented the U.A.R. with the demands: not to make nuclear weapons and to give the United States the right to control fulfilment of this demand; to stop making rockets and equalise the number of rockets in the hands of the U.A.R. and Israel (once more with U.S. right of inspection); and to freeze the numerical strength of the armed forces of the U.A.R. at the existing level.[1]

These demands were made at a time when the Western Powers blocked positive steps at Geneva designed to eliminate the threat of nuclear war, outlaw nuclear weapons and bring about general and complete disarmament. They came at a time when the Western Powers were accelerating their supply of modern weapons to Israel and helping it to organise nuclear research for military purposes.[2] The *New York Times* reported that as early as 1963 the United States authorised the sale of Hawk missiles to Israel (the first country outside NATO).

The U.S. demands on the U.A.R. were deliberately separated from the problem of liquidating imperialist military bases, including rocket ramps, in the Middle East. The West ignored the demand made by the U.A.R. and backed by the Arab League, that the foreign military bases on the territory of all Arab countries and in Cyprus should be dismantled. Meanwhile, American bases in Turkey and British bases in Cyprus continue to exist; imperialist military bases are maintained in southern Arabia and the Persian Gulf.

The problem of not allowing nuclear-rocket weapons in the Mediterranean, which is patrolled by American Polaris submarines and the nuclear-armed U.S. 6th Fleet, is also closely bound up with the task of reducing international tensions and strengthening peace in the Middle East.

[1] See *Egyptian Gazette*, July 23, 1965, p. 6.
[2] The Communist Party of Israel demanded that the atomic reactor at Dimona should stop working for military purposes and that the Middle East should be declared a nuclear-free zone.

It has become something of a tradition with the imperialists to try to strike first at the U.A.R., whose people are in the vanguard of the liberation struggle in the Arab world. The U.A.R.'s foreign policy is vigorously anti-imperialist. The country's peaceful transition to a non-capitalist way of development is accompanied by a complicated and acute internal political struggle, which imperialism is trying to influence with all the means at its disposal. Imperialist circles are working hard to isolate the U.A.R. from the rest of the Arab world.

. . .

The case of the U.A.R. shows that the imperialists are joining forces with the reactionary and nationalistic elements. Relying on their stooges they are resuming their assault on Arab solidarity.

Until recently, the war in the Yemen was the imperialists' trump card in their dirty game of splitting the Arab countries. The intervention against the Yemeni Republic was inspired by Britain and the United States, and Saudi Arabia found herself in the same camp with imperialism and the royalist forces.[1] The republican Government of the Yemen relied on the support of the United Arab Republic and some other Arab countries.

That was not the first time the imperialist Powers had tried to use Saudi Arabia as an instrument against the national-liberation movement in the Arab East. Washington deftly played up the ambitions of former King Saud, who laid claim to leadership in the Arab world.

Decrepit British imperialism would not mind shelving or temporarily forgetting its conflicts with Saudi Arabia,[2] provided that country could be turned into a watchdog of its interests in southern Arabia.

. . .

The Western press has reported the U.S. intention to 'modernise' and strengthen the regime in Saudi Arabia for the old purpose of ranging it against the United Arab Republic. Late last year, the United States and Britain expressed readiness to supply Saudi Arabia with $400 millions' worth of arms, including American Hawk missiles, British jet planes, radar and means of communications and telecommunications.

The fratricidal war in the Yemen cost thousands of human lives. There was a steady flow of dollars and pounds sterling, and various British and American weapons into the royalist camp. It was a war of attrition. The

[1] Jordan actually withdrew from the intervention against the Yemeni Republic in February 1963, and on April 1, 1963, King Hussein officially announced that Jordan was suspending all aid to the royalist forces.
[2] These conflicts were largely the result of Anglo-American rivalries not only in Saudi Arabia but in the whole of the Arabian Peninsula, and also of the clash of interests between the Saudi monarchy and British imperialism in the south of the peninsula.

powerful coalition hoped to wear down the young republic, split the liberation front in the south of the Arabian Peninsula, eventually robbing the Yemeni people of their revolutionary gains and crushing the insurgents in Aden and Oman.

The fanning of the civil war in the Yemen was intended to help keep Saudi Arabia and Jordan in the wake of imperialist policy. The imperialists are also making great efforts to keep Tunisia, Kuwait and the Lebanon under their sway. Washington and London plan to turn these countries into a stable Right-wing grouping among the Arab countries. With this aim in view they attach great importance to economic levers. Saudi Arabian and Kuwait oil is so far almost entirely in the hands of the imperialist monopolies. The Lebanon and Kuwait are big banking and financial centres in the Arab East.[1] The financial and trading monopolies of Western Europe and the U.S.A. are well entrenched there. Among the countries of the Arab East small Jordan is in second place and the Lebanon third as regards the amount of American aid received. Tunisia is a country where the Right-wing bourgeoisie so far holds strong positions.

Kuwait's close ties with the Western monopolies determine its special attitude towards inter-Arab co-operation. In 1965, for instance, when the question of an Arab common market was on the point of solution, a serious obstacle arose: Kuwait's National Assembly refused to ratify the decision of the Arab Council for Economic Unity.

This step was the result of the influence exerted by the imperialist monopolies which hold first place in Kuwait's imports and were afraid of higher customs tariffs if Kuwait joined the Arab common market. It was also the result of the jealousy with which the Sheikh's suite and growing trading and industrial circles in Kuwait are guarding their somewhat exceptional position in the Arab East: owing to its enormous oil reserves, Kuwait has an unprecedentedly high average income per head of the population (over £1,000 a year).

Clearly, the special stand taken by Tunisia, on many issues, including sanctions against West Germany, is doing a great deal of harm to Arab solidarity. On the other hand, efforts are being made to revive projects for a Pan-Islam pact to disguise the intended union of reactionary forces.

The increased activity of the imperialist and the Right-wing forces in several Arab countries has damaged Arab anti-imperialist unity. The Western press was quick to note that friction and conflicts between the Arab countries would be an insuperable barrier to the convocation and work of the Casablanca conference.

At the same time, opposite forces and trends came into action. Having realised the gravity of the situation, the Arab peoples and their leaders

[1] Early in 1965, Kuwait's banks had accounts in London totalling some £150 million, while Kuwait's private depositors kept there some £100 million.

made fresh efforts to improve the political climate in the Arab East. The important agreement signed by the U.A.R. and Saudi Arabia on August 23, 1965, paved the way for a peaceful settlement and an end to hostilities in the Yemen.

Despite their virtually unlimited material and military resources, the interventionists found themselves in a difficult military situation and complete political isolation. Realising that they would be unable to impose a military solution of the Yemeni problem on the republicans, the royalists were forced to start cease-fire negotiations.

The pressure of the progressive anti-imperialist forces in Saudi Arabia also played its part.

The removal of King Saud from power was largely due to the pressure of the young forces: educated civil servants, technicians, intellectuals and the rising class of businessmen. These forces want domestic reforms and demand the end of domination by foreign oil monopolies led by the American ARAMCO; they want a rapprochement with the Arab countries, above all the U.A.R., as the country that has scored the greatest success in its struggle for political and economic emancipation. King Faisal, who replaced King Saud, is much more aware of these tendencies than his predecessor.

The main task of the national-liberation forces in the Yemen and the other Arab countries is to prevent the imperialists and the Right-wing reactionaries from wrecking the cease-fire agreement and using it as a cover to continue the fight against the republican liberatory forces in the Yemen. The Solidarity Pact adopted at Casablanca reinforced the Yemen cease-fire agreement, but practice will naturally be the test of both, particularly since the imperialists still hope to torpedo the agreement on the Yemen. The Western press is busy spreading rumours about the hopelessness of the conference between the royalists and the republicans which opened at the end of last year in Haradh and is foretelling a resumption of hostilities in the Yemen. The progress of the talks at the Haradh Conference is giving rise to justified anxiety in the Arab world.

Socio-economic relations inside the Arab countries and their foreign economic policy are now an important front in the anti-imperialist struggle.

The extensive reorganisation of the state and administrative apparatus in the U.A.R. last summer and autumn opens up new prospects for the country's advance along the non-capitalist way and gives it fresh possibilities for rapid economic development. It also gives the people more say in deciding the country's future. In the last five-year period, production in the United Arab Republic rose as much as 7·2 per cent a year.

.   .   .

Social and economic change in the other Arab countries is taking place in more complex conditions. Although the Right-wing Baathists suffered a defeat and were ousted in Iraq and Syria, this does not mean that the reactionary nationalist forces which campaign under the banner of Islam and slogans of Arab unity and even Socialism have laid down their arms. Over the last few years, a bitter struggle has been going on in these countries between the forces favouring deep democratic social reforms and transition to the non-capitalist way, and the reactionary nationalist forces striving to build up the positions of capital and preserve the 'traditional' ties with international financial and commercial capital.

In Iraq, where the positions of the imperialist oil monopolies are especially strong, the situation continues to be extremely difficult and unstable. The anti-imperialist forces there are divided, and the country's international positions have been greatly weakened as a result of the continuing reprisals against the democratic forces, and especially of the war against the Kurdish people which has now been going on for four and a half years. The Kurds' endeavour to obtain autonomy within the Republic of Iraq and to maintain and strengthen the state unity and integrity on the basis of democracy and anti-imperialism meets with obstinate reluctance on the part of reactionary sections of ruling circles in Baghdad to find a settlement of the Kurdish question. The normalisation of relations between Iraq and the U.A.R. and several other Arab countries is being greatly hampered by activities of pro-imperialist agents and the Right-wing forces, who fear the effect U.A.R. non-capitalist development may have on other countries.

In Syria, events have of late taken a different turn. In 1964 and 1965, a great number of industrial enterprises and all oil and mineral resources were nationalised. This strengthened the state sector, which now accounts for about 80 per cent of industrial output. Agrarian change is also being effected more rapidly.

The implementation of socio-democratic reforms demanded, as in the U.A.R., an extension for the democratisation process and greater possibilities for political and social initiative on the part of the working people and their parties and organisations. Progressive leaders, including Communists, were released from prison. The rights of the trade unions were extended, and administrative councils were set up at the factories to represent the Government, the Baath Party, the trade unions and the workers. Peasant unions are being organised in the countryside. A National Council, with the participation of workers, peasants and military men, was set up last August to work out a new constitution. The situation in Syria cannot be said to have been finally stabilised. However, it would be wrong to underestimate the significance of the socio-economic transformations and shifts for both internal development and the consolidation of democratic tendencies in Arab policy as a whole.

The progressive forces in Syria, including the Communists, support the incipient socio-democratic reforms, and insist on the consistent implementation of an anti-imperialist democratic line in domestic and foreign policy.

Saudi Arabia, Kuwait and the Lebanon show growing tendencies to economic independence. This finds expression, for instance, in the great attention Saudi Arabia and Kuwait, like all Arab countries in general, devote to the development of national oil production, which for the time being, exists alongside foreign concessions. The desire to solve this problem is also reflected in the activity of the Arab League's economic bodies.

What is typical of the present situation in the Arab East is that even in the areas where British imperialism still maintains political power and battles are still in progress, the problem of economic liberation and development becomes increasingly urgent.

In 1965, the Arab League set up a fund for the economic development of southern Arabia. Kuwait has a considerable part to play in this fund. The resources of this country are beginning to be used for the economic progress of the Arab countries[1] and not just for strengthening the financial power of the City of London. The economic development projects being drawn up for the struggling nations of the South Arabian Peninsula provide additional and weighty proof that victory over British colonialism is not far off.

Britain's political and even military defeat in the colonial war against the people in the south of the Arabian Peninsula has now become obvious even to the British Government. The semi-official press writes about 'Middle Eastern Viet-Nam' and London's decision to redeploy its forces from Aden to Bahrein. According to the British *Observer*, 'Under the plan for a withdrawal from Aden, Britain is expected to transfer part of the forces there to Bahrein, in the Persian Gulf.' The newspaper went on to say that 'the R.A.F. will move to Masira Island, off the east coast of Arabia',[2] where major British bases are being established.

By setting up the Federation of South Arabia and including Aden in it, London hoped to reinforce its positions, stifle the protest of the working class in Aden and muster against it the principalities, sheikhdoms and sultanates. Actually the working-class movement in Aden has now merged with the liberation and democratic movement in the south of the Arabian Peninsula. Even in such a tiny spot as the Sultanate of Quaiti

[1] Kuwait plays an important role in the Afro-Asian Bank. Its Government has set up a special economic development fund for the Arab countries called upon to help implement economic projects in Asia and Africa. It has granted economic development loans to the Sudan, Jordan, Tunisia, Algeria and the U.A.R.

[2] *Observer*, Aug. 1, 1965.

(which is hard to find on the map of the protectorate of East Aden), an Arab Socialist Party was formed last summer to fight for freedom, Socialism and the unity of southern Arabia, including the protectorates and islands.

The inertia of the medieval customs in the vast Arabian Peninsula has been exploded by the Yemeni revolution and the struggle of the volunteers and guerrillas in the south of the peninsula. The formidable strikes in Aden are clear evidence that this port is one of the largest centres where the industrial proletariat is maturing and Middle East international workers' solidarity is being forged.

The struggle for the liberation of southern Arabia is a most important stimulus for greater Arab unity as a whole, and specifically the class solidarity of the workers in the Arab countries.

.   .   .

Today, when the Arab peoples are opting for a way of development, and social and class contradictions have been aggravated and laid bare in the whole of the Arab East, the need for friendly co-operation between the world Socialist system and countries fighting for greater independence and progress becomes increasingly imperative.

The conflict between the United Arab Republic and West Germany, and U.S. economic pressure on the U.A.R. have shown once again that any economic aid from imperialism may at any time play the role of a mine laid under the national economy and independent policy of countries fighting for freedom from colonialism.

.   .   .

The Soviet Union and the other Socialist countries are co-operating with ten Arab countries. What this means can be seen if only from the fact that they are taking part in projects accounting for 40 per cent of capital investments under the U.A.R.'s Five-Year Plan (1965–1970).[1] There are, however, ample opportunities for further developing economic relations between the Arab countries and the Socialist world.

What is of interest in this respect is the question of co-operation between the Soviet Union and the oil-producing countries of the Arab East and also the problem of economic co-ordination between them.

Imperialist propaganda has more than once made a great noise about Soviet oil 'dumping' and has alleged that the Soviet Union's economic interests are incompatible with those of the Middle East oil-exporting countries. It is not the U.S.S.R.'s fault, however, that the economic situation in the Middle East is such that the area consumes only 2 per cent of the world's petroleum output, while possessing more than 60 per cent

[1] See *Al Gumhuria*, Feb. 3, 1965.

of its prospected oil resources. Western propagandists prefer to say nothing of the fact that this is the result of domination by imperialist monopolies. It is the Soviet Union and the other Socialist countries that are extending assistance to the Middle Eastern countries, for example, the Iraqi Republic, the Syrian Arab Republic and the United Arab Republic, in developing their national oil and chemical industries.

There is no doubt, that the general industrial upsurge in the Middle East countries (which is largely promoted by the economic support of the Socialist world) creates a stable domestic market for oil and oil products, thereby laying a sound economic foundation for their independence of the world capitalist market. It will eventually be possible to bring about a situation in which countries wishing to obtain Middle East oil will do so under conventional deals instead of through the plunderous exploitation of concessions.

. . .

The anti-imperialist democratic tendencies in the Arab East are strengthening, and this is of especial importance now that imperialism has adopted a tougher line in Asia, Africa and Latin America. What is decisive is the ever greater activity of the working people and the development of democratic thinking to counter reactionary nationalist and religious trends, on which the imperialists and the Right-wing elements are largely relying all over Asia and Africa. At the same time, the progressive national forces want the main anti-imperialist tasks to determine relations between the Arab countries.

International Affairs (Moscow), No. 3, March 1966.

2

Statement on the Situation in the Arab Countries
by the Arab Communist Parties, May 1967

The Communists of the Arab countries, meeting in May 1967, discussed the present situation in the Arab countries and the course of the struggle going on on the main front between imperialism, reaction and Zionism, on the one hand, and the Arab national-liberation movement, on the other. They also exchanged information on the peculiarities and perspectives of the development of the actual situation in the various Arab countries. In connection with all this the meeting also discussed the problems of links and unity between the Arab patriotic, progressive and revolutionary forces.

The meeting believes that the present situation in the Arab world is characterized by the extension and intensification of the national struggle against colonialism and neocolonialism, and by a deepening of the content of the national liberation movement. Large sections of the Arab peoples and influential social forces are increasingly becoming attracted to the slogan of socialism, which is the right way of development for our countries, for them to build their independent economies and do away with their backwardness.

The participants in the meeting note with satisfaction that the struggle of their parties over a long period, the sacrifices they have made and the light of socialist ideas, which have triumphed in the socialist world, have been, and will be, the most important factor in this development.

In such new free states as the United Arab Republic, Syria and Algeria, where deep-going social and economic changes have been effected, the Communists and other progressives see it as their task to uphold, consolidate and extend these gains, and to complete the job of providing the necessary political and social prerequisites of their countries' advance to socialism.

The Arab peoples are stepping up their fight against imperialism and its plans, against reaction and Zionism. Cooperation and solidarity between the newly-free Arab countries are becoming closer. Their policy of liberation and their progressive achievements play an important part in intensifying the struggle of the Arab peoples for freedom and progress and in carrying it deeper.

The national revolution of the peoples of Aden and the occupied south of Arabia against the British imperialists, for freedom and independence is gathering momentum. This sacred revolution involves the working class and all other patriotic forces. It is supported and assisted by all progressive and patriotic forces in the Arab countries and throughout the world.

The people of the UAR and their revolutionary, progressive and patriotic forces are increasing their resistance to the American and other imperialists, who are intent on changing the progressive policy line of the country. The UAR continues to develop its independent economy and to build important economic projects, first of all the Aswan Dam. It continues to extend fraternal support and assistance to the Yemen, which is defending its revolution and its republican system.

The Arab people of Syria have, thanks to the cooperation of their progressive forces, won an important victory over the oil monopolies by securing higher royalties. Syria foils all the conspiracies and threats of imperialism, Zionism and reaction directed against it, which intensified above all after February 23, 1966, and after Syria began to extract its oil by itself and to build economic projects of its own, primarily the Euphrates Dam.

In Algeria the main trend is to fight imperialism, and Algeria is carrying on this fight together with other newly-free Arab and African countries, in the face of attempts on the part of the reactionaries backed by the imperialists to do away with the political, economic and social gains of the Algerian people. However, the social forces opposing the road chosen by the people and trying to abolish the people's achievements have not laid down arms yet. To foil the schemes of the imperialists, defeat the home reactionaries, maintain and consolidate the gains of the revolution and raise the creative enthusiasm of the masses so that they may overcome the political difficulties facing the country by peaceful and democratic means it is necessary for the revolutionary, progressive and patriotic forces, both those participating in the present government and those not participating, to achieve unity and wage a joint struggle in accordance with the aspirations of the people.

In Jordan, after Israel's aggression against the village of Sumu, the people took vigorous patriotic action against the imperialists and the policy of the pro-imperialist regime. This action is evidence of the great revolutionary potentialities of the Arab people of Jordan and of their progressive and patriotic forces fighting for a national system that would side with the free area of the Arab world and ensure freedom and democracy to the people.

The Lebanese people are intensifying their fight against imperialism and reaction. By rallying their patriotic and progressive forces, they have succeeded in preventing a visit by the U.S. Sixth Fleet, which is used as an instrument of conspiracy and intimidation against the Arab liberation movement.

In Iraq the patriotic forces and the masses generally are fighting with increasing resolve to establish a democratic system opposing imperialism and its oil monopolies, taking steps to settle the Kurd question and leading the country to liberation and to social and economic progress.

We support the people of Iraq, the Iraqi Communist Party and the progressive forces of that country in their struggle and their effort to secure the release of thousands of Communists and other progressives who are tortured in Iraqi jails. The continued detention of these fighters for freedom, progress and socialism is a violation of human rights and a challenge to Arab public opinion and to the progressive forces.

In Saudi Arabia, the isolation of the feudal reactionary puppet government is increasing, and the struggle of the masses and their progressive forces against this regime and the American monopolies which plunder the people of their riches is growing in breadth and depth.

The people of Bahrein are opposing the imperialists and the oil monopolies. By consolidating their revolutionary front they are fighting for liberation and independence, against the British colonialists' plans for setting up a new military base in that country.

New steps are being taken in an increasing number of Arab countries toward cooperation and mutual support of the progressive, revolutionary and patriotic forces. There are objective and subjective conditions for this cooperation to become closer and to develop into a broad front in each Arab country, in keeping with the actual situation there, and in the Arab world as a whole.

In the Syrian Arab Republic, the Communists and Left Baathists are engaged in cooperation that yields important results. It is in the interest of progress in Syria to promote this cooperation.

In the Lebanon the front of the progressive and patriotic parties, forces and political leaders, which furthers the popular movement and influences developments in the country, is going from strength to strength.

In the Sudan the progressive and patriotic forces are closing their ranks. These forces are in the van of mass struggles in defence of democracy and the Constitution, against the reactionaries and the Rightists, who are trying to abolish democracy and the Constitution, taking advantage of the attempt to dissolve the fraternal Sudanese Communist Party.

It is a legitimate historic aspiration of the Arab peoples to achieve unity. A new conception of the idea of Arab unity is evolving, a conception prompted by the interests and the will of the masses, the new social content of the national liberation movement, objective conditions, the free expression of the will of each Arab country on an equal footing, and solidarity and cooperation against imperialism and reaction, for social progress. The experience of the struggle for Arab unity has helped to ascertain this new content, and our Communist parties have enriched it.

Relations between the newly-free Arab states and some other Arab countries, on the one hand, and the socialist countries, particularly the Soviet Union, the cradle of the Great October Socialist Revolution, a true friend of the Arab peoples, a bulwark of world peace, on the other, are growing and strengthening. These friendly countries render vast disinterested assistance to our countries in every field, which makes for the consolidation of their political independence and helps them to build up their independent economies and to combat backwardness.

The struggle of the progressive forces for full-fledged diplomatic relations with the friendly German Democratic Republic is gaining in scope. Imperialist and reactionary attempts to restore the relations between the Arab countries and the Federal Republic of Germany, which backs Israel, participates in supplying it with all that is needed for aggression, takes a provocative stand against the cause of liberation of the Arab countries and helps neocolonialism to strengthen its positions in the Arab world, fall through.

The imperialists, particularly the American imperialists, do all they can to prevent the progressive liberation movement in the Arab world from growing, to stop and eliminate it, to maintain their position and privileges, to continue plundering the Arabs of their riches, regain lost positions, and penetrate into various Arab countries by neocolonialist methods. The imperialists continue their feverish activity in support of the plan for a so-called Islamic pact, which is plainly intended to camouflage their criminal schemes in the Arab world. They bribe the home reactionaries in the Arab countries and help them to gather strength in the hope of re-establishing their rule in those countries.

The progressive patriotic forces are subjected to brutal repressive measures in Saudi Arabia and Jordan. Nineteen patriots were executed in Saudi Arabia. The prisons are filled with those who oppose reaction and American domination in the country. In Jordan the reactionary rulers have arrested Communists and other progressives, and hold rigged elections to impart a semblance of legality to their rule and to continue their policy of conspiracy.

The imperialists arm Israel, supply it with all that is required for aggression, and support its efforts to usurp the legitimate rights of the Palestine Arabs in their own country. They incite it to continuous sorties in the Arab border area aggravating the situation in that area and endangering peace. Israel committed its latest act of aggression against Syria last April. It showed itself once again to be a tool and the main base of imperialism in the area. The imperialists use Israel to combat the Arab liberation and progressive movement, to back reaction and rotten reactionary regimes, and to prevent the Arab peoples from using their riches and other resources to develop their countries.

In northern Iraq (Kurdistan), where the Kurd question has yet to be settled, the Iraqi rulers are committed to a policy which does not in fact lead to meeting the Kurd people's lawful demand for autonomy. The imperialists and reactionaries are trying to aggravate the situation in Kurdistan by refusing to recognize the legitimate rights of the Kurds, thwarting the armistice agreement and resuming the civil war.

In the Lebanon the imperialists instigate and encourage the reactionaries to provoke religious discord with an eye to establishing a reactionary regime that would take its cue from the imperialists and the Arab re-actionaries against the interests of the Lebanese people and the newly-free Arab states, primarily against fraternal Arab Syria.

The imperialists try to take advantage of border disputes between Arab states to aggravate the relations between them and to exhaust their strength.

In North Africa – in Tunisia, Algeria, Morocco – and particularly in the relations between Algeria and Morocco, the interests of the two brother peoples require that the two states should do all in their power to avoid violence and the use of arms, to make earnest efforts toward settling their disagreements through direct peaceful, fraternal talks. In this connection it is necessary to note that to bring about such a settlement, the progressive and revolutionary forces in both Arab countries must play a decisive role in uniting the Maghreb as an important step toward the unity of the whole Arab world.

The U.S. Sixth Fleet cruises in the Mediterranean and in Arab territorial waters, endangering the Arab national liberation movement and supporting Israel.

The military coup carried out in Greece according to the plans and instructions of U.S. intelligence agencies and directed against the vital interests of the Greek people should not be viewed in isolation from the conspiracies the U.S. imperialists hatch in the Mediterranean and the Arab world.

In a number of Arab countries whose rulers do not – primarily because of the struggle of the progressive forces – play the role played by the rulers of Saudi Arabia and of Jordan, the imperialists try to reinforce the reactionary elements and to crush the Communist, progressive and patriotic forces. They strive to establish territorial regimes there whose entire activity would serve imperialist interests and plans.

Everywhere the imperialists are out to undermine or prevent co-operation between Communists and other progressive and patriotic forces.

The aim of all this imperialist activity is to undermine the regimes existing in the newly-free Arab countries, deliver a blow to the Yemeni revolution, thwart the revolution in Aden and the occupied south of the Arabian peninsula, prevent the liberation and progress of other Arab countries, check the upward trend of the national democratic movement in the Arab world and strike hard at the whole liberation movement of the Arabs, so as to strengthen the shaken positions of the imperialists and to regain those of them that were lost, assure the continued plundering of our countries of their riches, primarily of their oil resources, and perpetuate the backwardness of our countries.

The meeting, exposing the plans of the imperialists, Zionists and Arab reactionaries and their acts of aggression, wants to reveal the immense danger threatening the Arab national liberation movement today, to contribute its share to the definition of the objects of the movement and to the planning of actions necessary for staving off this danger, and to defeat those from whom it emanates. We are certain that there is every opportunity of achieving this lofty goal.

In view of the fundamental contradiction existing in the Arab world, where the imperialists, Zionists and reactionaries are at one pole and

the peoples of the Arab countries, their patriotic, progressive and revolutionary forces supported by the forces of liberation, progress and
socialism throughout the world, and above all by the Soviet Union, at
the other pole, we consider that the chief method of countering the
impending danger is to promote the solidarity and cooperation of these
forces, join their efforts together in each Arab country and throughout
the Arab world despite certain differences, which should not be an obstacle
to joint action on the principal agreed issues.

The Communist, revolutionary and patriotic forces must cooperate to
beat off the furious attacks of the imperialists and reactionaries on the
Arab peoples, to eliminate colonialism and neocolonialism in the Arab
world, mobilize the masses against all imperialist intrigues, conspiracies
and blocs, and bring about the withdrawal of the U.S. Sixth Fleet from
the Mediterranean. They must cooperate to support the struggle of the
Arab countries to establish national anti-imperialist and progressive
regimes that would lead these countries to progress and prosperity.

The progressive and revolutionary forces must cooperate to maintain
the progressive achievements and changes won or being won in the
newly-free Arab countries, to strengthen these countries and develop
them with a view to encouraging the initiative of the masses and to
drawing them into creative endeavour in those countries. They must
cooperate to curb the enemies of progress who are operating and gathering strength and are supported from without, and to close all the loop-
holes in the policies and the economies of these countries that may be
used by imperialist and reactionary conspirators. They must cooperate
to ensure that the Arab peoples have all their natural resources, particularly oil, put at their complete disposal, and that these resources are used
wisely for developing the Arab countries and doing away with their
backwardness. They must cooperate to give the fullest moral and material
support to the revolution in Aden and the occupied south of the Arabian
peninsula, to support and strengthen the Yemeni Republic and end all
interference by the imperialists and by Saudi Arabia aimed at re-establishing the hated monarchic regime there. They must cooperate to step up
the fight against continual acts of aggression on the part of Israel, to
identify themselves with all progressive and patriotic groups and organizations fighting courageously in those countries whose governments
submit to an imperialist diktat, and to fight for an end to terrorism and
repression in those countries.

The Communists of the Arab countries are inspired by the ideas of
creative Marxism-Leninism. They are inspired by a high morale in the
fight against the imperialists and reactionaries, and are carrying on a
selfless struggle for social progress. Ever since their parties came into
being the Arab Communists have been fighting for the triumph of

socialism and for the deliverance of the masses from backwardness and exploitation, and they have always put the interests of their peoples above everything else. They earnestly and sincerely call on all patriotic, progressive and revolutionary forces in the Arab countries, irrespective of the parties or trends they may belong to, to rally together against imperialism, Zionism and reaction in order to fight for the complete liberation of the Arab world, for progress and the elimination of backwardness in any political, economic and cultural field, for a radiant future for their peoples, for Arab unity on a sound basis.

The road to these cherished aims and aspirations of the Arab masses lies through close relations between these forces, relations ruling out all discrimination against this or that trend and based on mutual respect, on fraternal, frank and principled exchanges of views. All this will make for an atmosphere of mutual confidence without which no cooperation can be fruitful.

The imperialists and reactionaries raise the banner of anti-communism as they strive to prevent the unity of the patriotic, progressive and revolutionary forces. Hence every attempt to split the progressive forces, bring confusion into their ranks, ignore or attack the Communist parties serves, as the sad experience of the past has shown, none but the interests of the imperialists and reactionaries and injures the national-liberation movement and progress, that is, the cause of the whole Arab people.

In the interest of the fight against imperialism, for progress, for the unity and cooperation of the progressive forces, all progressives must strive for the release of imprisoned Communists and other revolutionaries and champions of progress in Iraq, Algeria, Jordan or any other Arab country. Meeting this demand will go a long way toward closer links and cooperation between all progressive forces.

A very important task in this respect is to foster cooperation between the newly-free Arab countries and to promote their relations with other Arab countries through the fight against imperialism. This will weaken the positions of reaction and strengthen the progressive and patriotic forces of various trends.

The nature of the struggle going on in a number of Arab countries against continued imperialist influence and reactionary domination calls for the cooperation of the revolutionary and progressive forces and all other patriotic forces and for the rallying of all sections of the people interested in complete emancipation from imperialism.

.   .   .

Source: Information Bulletin, Documents of the Communist and Workers' Parties, No. 11 (99), Prague, 1967.

3

From Speeches by President Gamal Abdul Nasser in Damascus

March 13, 1959

. . .

Now come the enemies of Arab Nationalism whom you had housed and fed in your good country. Consumed with mortal rancour, Red rancour, they denied all the lofty principles of Nationalism.

They had not been able to let out steam while they were here in your country because the consciousness had prevailed everywhere. So, their leader fled when you decided upon the merger and raised the banner of Arab nationalism aloft.

When the revolution took place in Iraq, they went there, imagining that they might be able to realise in Baghdad what they failed to realise here in Damascus. Their leader, who had fled, returned to your city, thinking that the fruit was ripe and that Syria will yield to Communism, the agent. He forgot that these people have always defended their freedom, independence and nationalism and would, by no means hand over their lead to the agent. The Communists are agents. We all know that they are agents.

When their leader returned once more to your city, believing together with his followers – the agents – that the fruit was ripe, they were surprised to be faced by the awareness of the people who rose to defend their nationalism, nay, to defend their religion and faith, discarding atheism and red communism.

The people rose to defend their nationalism, so the Communists went to Iraq where the leaders and rulers of Iraq opened the gates of Baghdad for them in order that they may work against your Republic assuming that they would be able to establish a Communist 'fertile crescent' in which Baghdad would be used as a springboard for Communism.

They forgot, brethren, that Arab nationalism had faced persecution over the years at the hands of apostates and agents, but the heroic Arab people have always defended their nationalism.

Following the inception of the Iraqi revolution, and even after the concentration of the Communist agents in Baghdad, we took upon ourselves to endeavour, by every possible means, to maintain the unity of the Arab ranks and to restore the harmony with Iraq for there exists no reason why it should not be maintained.

. . .

The question, brethren, was not difference over doctrine, principles or mission. It was black and red rancour directed against you and your Republic for the achievements it scored and because your Republic preserved its independence, was able to remain outside the spheres of influence and remained the master of its own will.

We tried every means in order to secure the unity of the Arab rank, but the Communist plots blocked out attempts. The Communists had their plans to dominate Syria; but, upon failure, found consolation in the revolution of Iraq. The Communists immigrated to Baghdad in order to turn Iraq into a Communist state from which Communism will spread to the rest of the Arab countries thereby creating a Communist fertile crescent.

Their method was to sow dissension, disseminate rumours, forge documents, and plant hatred in the hearts of the Arab people in Iraq against the sons of the United Arab Republic.

. . .

Brethren,

These lies have been disseminated by the Communist agents, the false prophets of nationalism and democracy.

. . .

We in Cairo, brethren, know that the Communists are agents. We did not permit the establishment of a Communist party in Egypt because we were sure that the Communist party in Egypt does not act in conformity with its own will or work for the interest of its own country. We were sure that it received inspiration from abroad and worked for the foreigner.

The Communist party in Egypt used, since 1953, to receive directives from the Communist Party in Italy and carried out these instructions. The Communists are agents because they accepted to sell their country to the foreigner and carry out the foreigner's instructions.

The Communist Party here in Syria comprised agents who received their inspiration from abroad and even received funds from abroad.

We all know that Communists are agents. We will not accept, brethren, to have agents rule us, for when we took it upon ourselves to get rid of imperialist stooges we also sought to put an end to the reign of agents. The era of agents in our country exists no longer. We pray to God that the people of Iraq, who last year had risen to liberate their country of the stooges of imperialism and did actually rid themselves of them, would be able also to get rid of agents and enjoy freedom and independence.

These, brethren, are our principles.

. . .

When we prohibited the Communist party from functioning in our country, we did so because we were endeavouring to preserve all that which we held sacred, and to protect our nationalism.

It was clear to us, brethren, that if we allowed a reactionary party to work for imperialism, and a communist party to work for Communism, patriotism and nationalism would be lost; because these and the others would receive assistance from abroad – from the enemies of Arab Nationalism – and would try to defeat their own homeland. If the reactionaries won they would have liquidated patriots, and if the Communists won under the guise of false democracy, they would have proclaimed a dictatorship in order to liquidate patriotism and nationalism, in the same manner as patriotism and nationalism are being liquidated today in Iraq.

Fellow-Countrymen,

We speak frankly to each other. We know our way. We shall not hand the nation over to imperialism and the reactionaries, nor shall we hand it to Communism and dependence, but it will remain patriotic, nationalist, solely for the sons of the Arab nation.

. . .

Press Release P.R. 46/59, UAR Information Department, Cairo.

March 15, 1959

. . .

The Arab people's struggle had not stopped throughout those years.

. . .

But the Communists, the agents, who were at that time receiving their inspiration from outside their country, and who were receiving instructions from Communist parties abroad, were trying to exploit the struggle of the Arab people in Egypt for freedom and democracy, in order to turn it into red Communism bathed in blood and enveloped in terror.

The Communists, brethren, have tried all ways and means to infiltrate the Army in Egypt but we were aware of them as we were well aware of our own cause. We have never accepted Communism, neither before nor after the revolution, because we believed in an undying mission, the mission of Arab nationalism. We were unable to change our faith nor were we able to believe in atheism and dependence, because Communism – brethren – believes in atheism and believes in dependence.

The Communists tried before the inception of the Revolution in Egypt to embrace some members of the Revolution (to bring them into their fold) and I was one of them. The Communists tried by all means to convince me of joining their school and to share their principles, but –

brethren – I have accepted to do so for the simple reason that I was not able to believe, under any circumstances, in atheism or in dependence.

I was sure, fellow-citizens – and I know many of the Communists in Egypt – I was sure of their way, and I was equally sure of the course which they follow. I knew their inside secrets even before the Revolution. I knew the most intimate particulars about them, even before the Revolution I knew, brethren, that the mission of Communism is based on atheism and on dependence. I had some acquaintances from amongst the Communists, who endeavoured to exploit this acquaintance in order to bring me into the fold of Communism because they believed that, in so doing, they would achieve a great victory. But I staunchly believed in Arab nationalism and disbelieved atheism and dependence. I believed in Arab nationalism in the same manner as the whole Arab people in every Arab country did when they struggled for the sake of their fatherland and shed their blood. I held the same belief shared by the Arab people in every Arab country, the staunch belief in pure Arab nationalism. I also share with them their disbelief in atheism and dependence.

Today, brethren, as we face the events which are taking place in the Arab area, we cannot ignore our history.

The rancour of Arab Communists was concentrated upon us here in Egypt. They launched many campaigns against us but we faced them, we did not submit to their threats or to their pressure because we believed that our mission was the mission of Arab nationalism, freedom and independence. We believed that our mission was to rid ourselves of spheres of influence and dependence. It was the mission of ethics.

The Communists, brethren, endeavoured to exploit the revolution in Egypt and tried to use it in order to impose their domination, the domination of a small group over the overwhelming majority, indeed over the whole people. They wanted to set up a dictatorship based on blood under the guise of forged democracy, but the Arab people in Egypt realised that Communism is tantamount to atheism and dependence. The Arab people in Egypt had complete faith in their mission based on Arab nationalism. They defeated the Communists, and the few remained few; the minority was even isolated and rendered unable to disseminate its mission among the Arab people in Egypt.

. . .

Some Communists fled the United Arab Republic, though until that time, we had not taken any measures against them because we had declared that we were not going to call anybody to account for the past, but that we would judge by the future.

The Communists went out of Egypt weighed under their complete defeat following the proclamation of merger by the Arab people in Egypt and in Syria. The Communists went out of Syria too feeling the full impact of their defeat, because the Arab people had unanimously shown their staunch determination to uphold the unity. Their unanimity spelled out the people's will. It spelled out that the people were the masters of their will and their faith. It proved that these people were endeavouring once more to restore their past history through unity in order to liberate themselves and to face the machinations, ambitions and aggressions of the foreigners.

Communists went out of Syria; the Syrian people knew that Communists here did not in any way support unity for they believed unity would block their way.

. . .

We all know that Communists are first class opportunists. They are seeking opportunities to dominate Baghdad. They spread false slogans in Baghdad – slogans void of democracy. For what's democracy in Baghdad today? It is the democracy of terrorism, gallows, Communist street-courts and the murder of everyone who does not comply with their demands.

This is their type of democracy – the severest kind of terrorist dictatorship. This terrorist dictatorship of the Communists was proclaimed. In Baghdad who could raise his voice or give voice to his nationalism because murder will be his lot.

The Communists of Iraq, together with the Communists who fled from your country, launched one attack after the other against your Republic and mobilized the feelings in order to divide between the peoples of Iraq and the United Arab Republic.

. . .

Present-day Communists in Iraq are trying to liquidate all honest national elements, and endeavouring to sow discord between the people of Iraq and the Arab people so that they may render Iraq a Communist stronghold from which they would rush to set up a Communist fertile crescent in this part of the world. They relentlessly defend this objective for they recall that when they wanted to control you here, you dealt them a heavy blow, discarded them, even turned them out of your country for you preferred to stick to your religion, to adhere to your nationalism, your liberty and your independence.

Fellow-countrymen:

This is the situation we face today in the Arab world: Communists whose hearts are full to the brim with rancour in Egypt, Syria and every Arab country; Iraq's Kassem who suffers much from inferiority complexes, and feels that his role in the revolution of Iraq required him to rely on a faction to support him so as to be able to rule and to establish his rule; the false slogans used to mislead the Arab people in Iraq, and the Arab people in Syria. This is the situation in Iraq and in all other parts of the Arab world, and these are glimpses of our history and our struggle against Communism, atheism, dependence, and for upholding the mission of Arab nationalism.

. . .

March 20, 1959

Fellow Citizens,

. . .

Now, brethren, having emerged victorious from the battle in which we fought imperialism and its stooges, we face another battle – the battle against dependence, against Communism. Using the same weapons which helped us defeat imperialism and imperialist stooges, we can defeat Communism, agents and Communist parties.

Through our unity which enabled us to destroy imperialism and its stooges, we will, God willing, destroy Communism and dependence. There will be no new imperialism to replace the western imperialism from which we have liberated ourselves. No power on earth will be able to force us once more into spheres of influence.

We resolved to achieve our independence and to follow an independent policy, and succeeded in implementing that resolve.

We resolved to follow a policy of positive neutralism, and succeeded in putting into execution that resolve.

We resolved to pursue a policy of non-alignment, and succeeded in putting that policy into practice, too.

If, therefore, a small faction of heretics rises within the vastness of this Arab nation, making of themselves agents of the foreigner, advocating Communism and calling for dependence, we consider them as a schismatic faction, who betrayed their fatherland, their independence and the freedom of their country.

We, brethren, cannot in any manner allow this faction to work among us for the account of a foreign country or for the account of a foreign Communist party.

We will never accept either that a prime minister of a foreign country – the Soviet Union – should defend this faction.

We do not accept this protection, nor do we accept this sort of capitulations, for we had fought for the elimination of foreign protection and foreign capitulations.

If Khrushchev rises today to defend a small minority of the sons of our country who dissented from the unanimity of our Fatherland, saying that he is but defending Communism as a principle, we tell him that we do not consider this as defence of the Communist principle but as intervention in our affairs.

We do not interfere in the affairs of the Soviet Union, nor do we support a faction of the sons of the Soviet Union against another faction. So, if the head of the Soviet government intervenes today in order to support a small faction of the sons of our country against the unanimity of our people, we cannot accept that by any means.

We are free in our Fatherland to accept the principles which we consider in our interests and to reject the principles which represent dependence and atheism.

Press Release 50/59, UAR Information Department, Cairo.

4

From Nasser's speech to National Assembly members on May 29, 1967

. . .

The circumstances through which we are now passing are in fact difficult ones because we are not only confronting Israel but also those who created Israel and who are behind Israel. We are confronting Israel and the West as well – the West, which created Israel and which despised us Arabs and which ignored us before and since 1948. They had no regard whatsoever for our feelings, our hopes in life, or our rights. The West completely ignored us, and the Arab nation was unable to check the West's course.

. . .

Israel used to boast a great deal, and the Western powers, headed by the United States and Britain, used to ignore and even despise us and consider us of no value. But now that the time has come – and I have already said in the past that we will decide the time and place and not allow them to decide – we must be ready for triumph and not for a recurrence of the 1948 comedies. We shall triumph, God willing.

Preparations have already been made. We are now ready to confront Israel. They have claimed many things about the 1956 Suez war, but no one believed them after the secrets of the 1956 collusion were uncovered – that mean collusion in which Israel took part. Now we are ready for the confrontation. We are now ready to deal with the entire Palestine question.

The issue now at hand is not the Gulf of Aqabah, the Straits of Tiran, or the withdrawal of the UNEF, but the rights of the Palestine people. It is the aggression which took place in Palestine in 1948 with the collaboration of Britain and the United States. It is the expulsion of the Arabs from Palestine, the usurpation of their rights, and the plunder of their property. It is the disavowal of all the UN resolutions in favour of the Palestinian people.

The issue today is far more serious than they say. They want to confine the issue to the Straits of Tiran, the UNEF and the right of passage. We demand the full rights of the Palestinian people. We say this out of our belief that Arab rights cannot be squandered because the Arabs throughout the Arab world are demanding these Arab rights.

We are not afraid of the United States and its threats, of Britain and her threats, or of the entire Western world and its partiality to Israel. The United States and Britain are partial to Israel and give no consideration to the Arabs, to the entire Arab nation. Why? Because we have made them believe that we cannot distinguish between friend and foe. We must make them know that we know who our foes are and who our friends are and treat them accordingly.

If the United States and Britain are partial to Israel, we must say that our enemy is not only Israel but also the United States and Britain and treat them as such. If the Western Powers disavow our rights and ridicule and despise us, we Arabs must teach them to respect us and take us seriously. Otherwise all our talk about Palestine, the Palestine people, and Palestinian rights will be null and void and of no consequence. We must treat enemies as enemies and friends as friends.

I said yesterday that the states that champion freedom and peace have supported us. I spoke of the support given us by India, Pakistan, Afghanistan, Yugoslavia, Malaysia, the Chinese People's Republic and the Asian and African States.

After my statements yesterday I met the War Minister Shams Badran and learned from him what took place in Moscow. I wish to tell you today that the Soviet Union is a friendly power and stands by us as a friend. In all our dealings with the Soviet Union – and I have been dealing with the USSR since 1955 – it has not made a single request of us. The USSR has never interfered in our policy or internal affairs. This is the USSR as we have always known it. In fact, it is we who have made urgent requests of the USSR. Last year we asked for wheat and they sent it to us. When I also asked for all kinds of arms they gave them to us. When I met Shams Badran yesterday he handed me a message from the Soviet Premier Kosygin saying that the USSR supported us in this battle and would not allow any power to intervene until matters were restored to what they were in 1956.

Brothers, we must distinguish between friend and foe, friend and hypocrite. We must be able to tell who is making requests, who has ulterior motives, and who is applying economic pressure. We must also know those who offer their friendship to us for no other reason than a desire for freedom and peace.

In the name of the UAR people, I thank the people of the USSR for their great attitude, which is the attitude of a real friend. This is the kind of attitude we expect. I said yesterday that we had not requested the USSR or any other state to intervene, because we really want to avoid any confrontation which might lead to a world war and also because we really work for peace and advocate world peace. When we voiced the policy of non-alignment, our chief aim was world peace.

Brothers, we will work for world peace with all the power at our disposal, but we will also hold tenaciously to our rights with all the power at our disposal. This is our course. On this occasion, I address myself to our brothers in Aden and say: Although occupied with this battle, we have not forgotten you. We are with you. We have not forgotten the struggle of Aden and the occupied South for liberation. Aden and the occupied South must be liberated and colonialism must end. We are with them; present matters have not taken our minds from Aden.

I thank you for taking the trouble to pay this visit. Moreover, your presence is an honour to the Qubbah Palace, and I am pleased to have met you. Peace be with you.

5

Nasser: *Egypt's Debt to the Soviet Union*

.   .   .

The Middle East crisis: I do not want to go back to the circumstances which led to the Middle East crisis. All the details are known, starting with the premeditated aggression against Arab territory, to the imperialist collusion with the Israeli enemy, to the 5th June setback and its serious and sad results for our Arab nation. As you know, we lost the major part of our military power. We accepted the political solution experiment for several reasons. At that time we had no alternative to talking about a political solution; we had no armed forces to depend on. At the same time we are not advocates of war for the sake of war – not at all. If we can obtain our rights through political action, as happened in 1957, fine; if not, we have no alternative but to struggle for our rights and to liberate our land.

Furthermore, we want world public opinion to be on our side and really to know our position. At the same time, we must consider our present friends and our possible friends before we consider our enemies. A major part of the battle is taking place on an international level and under the eyes of public opinion throughout the entire world, which wants to live in peace.

We realised from the beginning, as we were trying a political solution, that it was a difficult and thorny road because the enemy was drunk with victory. We know that the principle of what has been taken by force cannot be regained by anything but force is a sound and correct principle in all circumstances. But we tried sincerely and are still trying sincerely on a basis from which we do not deviate. This basis is clear and definite in UAR policy: no negotiations with Israel, no peace with Israel, no recognition of Israel, and no deals at the expense of Palestinian soil or the Palestinian people.

.   .   .

With regard to a political solution, we will not in any way agree to give away one inch of Arab territory in any Arab country.

It is clear that Israel, which rejected the Security Council resolution, has many aims. The first is to achieve a political objective, because it won a military victory but did not achieve a political gain. Israel wants direct negotiations and wants a peace treaty signed. We reject this. Israel thus won a military victory but has so far been unable to achieve the political objective – signing a peace treaty with any of the Arab States surrounding it.

Therefore Israel will not withdraw. Why should it withdraw from the territory it occupied after achieving a crushing military victory? Israel, as they say, will remain in this territory hoping that conditions or regimes will be changed and replaced by regimes which will agree to the conclusion of a peace treaty with Israel.

How would the conditions change? Israel knows that the occupation burdens the hearts of all the sons of the Arab nation. Occupation represents fragmentation. Occupation is something out of the ordinary and is like a nightmare to all of us. Israel and the imperialist forces working behind it would be able to influence the domestic fronts and might be able to change the regimes and replace them with others which would agree to the conclusion of peace with Israel. As long as Israel knows that we have not yet attained a crushing offensive military strength, it will remain where it is, hoping to achieve political victory through a changing of regimes.

.   .   .

The fourth question is my recent visit to the Soviet Union and to Yugoslavia. Brothers, I mainly went to thank the leaders and people of the Soviet Union for everything they have given us and to discuss the situation. However, there is a fact which we must realise and know: Had it not been for the Soviet Union, we would now find ourselves facing the enemy without any weapons and compelled to accept his conditions. The United States would not have given us a single round of ammunition. It has given us and will give us nothing, but it gives Israel everything from guns to aircraft and missiles.

In reality, we have so far paid not one millieme for the arms we obtained from the Soviet Union to equip our armed forces. Actually, were it a question of payment, we have no money to buy arms. We all know the situation. We took part of the Soviet weapons as a gift and concluded a contract for the remainder for which we shall pay in the future in long-term instalments. Had it not been for the Soviet Union and its agreement to supply us with arms, we should now be in a position similar to our position a year ago. We should have no weapons and should be compelled to accept Israel's conditions under its threat.

At the same time, there exists a question which we must fully realise and understand: Why does the Soviet Union give us all these things? Why? We have one common aim with the Soviet Union – to resist imperialism. We do not want foreign influence in our part of the world. For its part, the Soviet Union is most anxious to oppose imperialism and to liquidate the imperialist concentrations to the south of its borders. Our ideological and national interest is against imperialism; the Soviet Union's ideological interest and strategy are against imperialism. I wish to tell you frankly and clearly that the Soviet Union has never tried, not even in our most crucial times, to dictate conditions to us or to ask anything of us. On the contrary, it has always been we who have asked.

Naturally, I did not pay my recent visit to the Soviet Union to express gratitude only, but to ask for things as well. After expressing my gratitude, I asked for things and after asking, I told them that I was ashamed. Do you not want anything from us? We ask you for things. But they answered: We have nothing to ask of you. I am actually telling this to you and to history so we may know who our friends and enemies are.

We went on asking for hours but they did not make one request of us. Even when I told them I felt ashamed that we were making many demands while they had asked nothing of us – I wish they had a request which we could fulfil – I asked if they had nothing to ask of us. They told us: We take this stand on the basis of our ideology – the ideology of national liberation and the peoples' struggle. We have nothing to ask.

The Soviet Union did not try to dictate any conditions to us. In our constant dealings with it, the Soviet Union has not tried to dictate any conditions – not even when we differed and we differed with the Soviet Union in 1959. At that time there was agreement on the first stage of the High Dam, the first industrialisation agreement and the arms deal agreement. Despite this, despite the difference which reached such extent that it was published in the newspapers, no attempt was made to apply pressure and no word of threat was uttered by the Soviet Union. Sincerity prompts me to say this.

There is another point. This is the element of the Soviet Navy and its appearance in the Mediterranean. I say that the States of the region, all the liberated States in the region, welcome the appearance of the Soviet Navy in the Mediterranean Sea as an element to balance the US Sixth Fleet, which sought to turn the Mediterranean into an American sea. The Soviet Navy did not threaten us. The Sixth Fleet is a strategic reserve for Israel, according to the Israeli Premier himself. When the US Navy leaves the Mediterranean, then those who wonder about the danger of the presence of the Soviet Navy will be able to speak and be heard.

On this occasion, I may make a quick reference to our attitude towards the United States. US policy has failed rapidly in this region. No one other than an obvious agent can openly declare friendship for the United States. The entire Arab world is aware of what the United States has done. We expected something different from the United States, or at least we did not expect all that has happened. However, that is the United States' business.

Giving arms to Israel while it is occupying Arab territory means that the United States supports Israel in the occupation of the Arab territory. Giving aircraft to Israel while it is occupying Arab territory means that the United States supports Israel in the occupation of the Arab territory. The complete US support for Israel at the United Nations and the adoption and defence of the Israeli point of view means that the United States supports Israel's occupation of the Arab territory. The US refusal to make a statement stipulating the need for the withdrawal of the Israeli forces to the positions they occupied before 5th June is proof that the United States supports Israel and, indeed, colludes with Israel in what it has done and is doing. Every member of the Arab nation is aware of this.

This matter is not confined to the Arab nation but also includes other States. Last year, it appeared that some CENTO member-States wanted to absolve themselves of CENTO, which was formerly called the Baghdad Pact. Yesterday we read that the Turkish students were throwing Sixth Fleet crews into the sea. Why? No sensible man in the United States asks himself why this has happened in the Arab world and in other States.

.   .   .

There is a big difference between co-operation and subservience. When we concluded the 1955 arms deal with the Soviet Union they said there was danger in the arms deal because it would drag us into subservience. They cited examples. When we began to conclude the High Dam agreement with the Soviet Union, they said Soviet experts would come to work at the High Dam and that this would lead to some sort of subservience. More than 5,000 Soviet experts came to the High Dam, but none of them interfered in our domestic affairs and none of them tried to convert any of the people of Aswan to communism. Nothing of the sort happened.

Today they are saying the same thing. For example, they say the Soviet experts in the Army mean domination of the army and subservience. I have said before that we asked the Soviet Union for these experts and that the Soviet Union was not receptive to giving us experts, saying it would expose us to attack. But in fact, after the 5th June events, anyone with insight who could evaluate things felt that we needed training and that we had a great deal to learn about war. Thus we asked for and got the military experts. They are helping us. We have, in fact, benefited from them; we have benefited from them in all fields.

What the psychological warfare suggested when we received arms in 1955 and when we concluded the High Dam agreement in 1960 may again be suggested this time.

Brothers, we feel that the entire Arab nation must feel grateful to the Soviet Union. Had it not been for the Soviet Union, as I have already said, we should now find ourselves with no arms in the face of the Israeli militarism, which has been blinded by its victory of June 1967. Egypt's independence – and I say this to all people – is not for sale, is not for anyone to buy and is not for mortgage. This will continue to be the case. It is this attitude that has placed us in the difficult situations we are experiencing.

. . .

From a Speech by President Nasser at the Arab Socialist Union Meeting on 16th Anniversary of the Egyptian Revolution, July 23, 1968.

6

Soviet Government Statement on the Situation in the Near East,
May 24, 1967

A situation giving rise to anxiety as regards peace and international security has been taking shape in the Near East in recent weeks. After the armed attack by Israeli troops on the territory of the Syrian Arab Republic on April 7 this year, Israel's ruling circles have continued to whip up military psychosis in the country. Leading statesmen, including the Foreign Minister Eban, have openly called for large-scale Israeli 'punitive' operations and the striking of 'a decisive blow' against Syria. The Defence and Foreign Policy Commission of the Knesset (Parliament) on May 9 granted the Government powers to carry out military operations against

Syria. Israeli troops deployed on the Syrian borders were alerted. Mobilisation was proclaimed in the country.

It is quite clear that Israel could not act in this way had it not the direct and indirect encouragement of certain imperialist circles which seek to bring back colonial oppression to Arab lands. These circles regard Israel under present conditions as the main force against those Arab countries which are pursuing an independent national policy and resisting imperialist pressure.

The Israeli extremists apparently hoped to take Syria by surprise and find her without support. But they obviously miscalculated. Showing solidarity with the courageous struggle of the Syrian people who are upholding their independence and sovereign rights, the Arab states – the United Arab Republic, Iraq, Algeria, the Yemen, the Lebanon, Kuwait, the Sudan, and Jordan – declared their determination to help Syria should it be attacked by Israel. The United Arab Republic, honouring its joint defence commitments with Syria, took steps to contain the aggression. Considering that in this situation the presence of UN troops in the Gaza area and the Sinai Peninsula would give Israel advantages for staging a military provocation against Arab countries, the UAR Government asked the United Nations to withdraw its troops from this area. A number of Arab states voiced their readiness to place their armed forces at the disposal of the Joint Arab Command to repel Israeli aggression.

As is known, in connection with the April 7 armed provocation, the Soviet Government warned the Government of Israel that it would bear full responsibility for the consequences of its aggressive policy. To all appearances, a reasonable approach has not yet been taken in Tel-Aviv. As a result Israel is again to blame for a dangerous aggravation of tension in the Near East.

It may be asked: what interests does Israel serve by pursuing such a policy? If they believe in Tel-Aviv that Israel will play the role of colonial overseer for the imperialist powers over the peoples of the Arab East, it is unnecessary to prove how groundless such calculations are in this age when the peoples of whole continents have shaken off the fetters of colonial oppression and are now building an independent life.

The Soviet Union for decades has given all-round assistance to the peoples of Arab countries in their just struggle for national liberation against colonialism and for the advancement of their peaceful economy. No one need doubt that should anyone unleash aggression in the Near East he will encounter not only the united strength of the Arab countries, but also strong opposition from the Soviet Union and all peaceloving states.

The Soviet Government firmly believes that the peoples do not want a military conflict in the Near East. The only people that may be interested in such a conflict are a handful of colonial oil monopolies and their hangers-on. It can interest only the forces of imperialism in the wake of whose policy Israel is following.

The Soviet Government keeps a close watch on Near East developments. It proceeds from the fact that the maintenance of peace and security in this area directly adjacent to the Soviet borders meets the vital interests of the Soviet people. Taking account of the situation, the Soviet Union is doing and will continue to do everything in its power to prevent a violation of peace and security in the Near East and to safeguard the legitimate rights of the peoples.

Pravda, May 24, 1967.

7

Statement by the Central Committees of Communist and Workers' Parties and Governments of the People's Republic of Bulgaria, the Hungarian People's Republic, the German Democratic Republic, the Polish People's Republic, the Union of Soviet Socialist Republics, the Czechoslovak Socialist Republic, the Socialist Federative Republic of Yugoslavia

On June 9, this year, leaders of the Communist and Workers' Parties and of the Governments of the socialist countries gathered in Moscow: from the People's Republic of Bulgaria – Todor Zhivkov, First Secretary of the Central Committee of the Bulgarian Communist Party, Chairman of the Council of Ministers of the People's Republic of Bulgaria, Zhivko Zhivkov, Member of the Politbureau of the Central Committee of the Bulgarian Communist Party, First Vice-Chairman of the Council of Ministers of the People's Republic of Bulgaria; from the Hungarian People's Republic – János Kádár, First Secretary of the Central Committee of the Hungarian Socialist Workers' Party, Jenö Fock, Member of the Politbureau of the Central Committee of the Hungarian Socialist Workers' Party, Chairman of the Council of Ministers of the Hungarian People's Republic; from the German Democratic Republic – Walter Ulbricht, First Secretary of the Central Committee of the Socialist Unity Party of Germany, Chairman of the Council of State of the German Democratic Republic, Willi Stoph, Member of the Politbureau of the Central Committee of the Socialist Unity Party of Germany, Chairman of the Council of Ministers of the German Democratic Republic, Hermann Axen, Alternate Member of the Politbureau of the Central Committee of the Socialist Unity Party of Germany, Secretary of the Central Committee of the Socialist Unity Party of Germany; from the Polish People's Republic – Wladyslaw Gomulka, First Secretary of the Central Committee of the Polish United Workers' Party, Jozef Cyrankiewicz, Member of the Politbureau of the Central Committee of the Polish United Workers' Party, Chairman of the Council of Ministers of the Polish People's Republic; from the Soviet Union – L. I. Brezhnev, General Secretary of the CPSU Central Committee, A. N. Kosygin, Member of the Politbureau of the CPSU Central Committee, Chairman of the USSR Council of Ministers, N. V. Podgorny, Member of the Politbureau of the CPSU Central Committee, President of the Presidium of the USSR Supreme Soviet; from the Czechoslovak Socialist Republic – Antonin Novotny, First Secretary of the Central Committee of the Communist Party of Czechoslovakia, Josef Lenart, Member of the Presidium of the Central Committee of the Communist Party of Czechoslovakia, Chairman of the Government of the Czechoslovak Socialist Republic; from the Socialist Federative Republic of Yugoslavia – Josip Broz Tito, Chairman of the League of Communists of Yugoslavia, President of the Socialist Federative Republic of Yugoslavia, Vladmir Popović, Member of the Presidium of the Central Committee of the League of Communists of Yugoslavia.

They studied the situation that has taken shape in the Near East as a result of Israel's aggression which is the outcome of a conspiracy against the Arab countries by certain imperialist forces, above all the United States. The participants in the meeting exchanged views on measures required to cut short the aggression and to avert its consequences which would be dangerous to the cause of universal peace.

The participants in the meeting deem it necessary to draw conclusions from the fact that Israel did not comply with the decision of the Security Council and did not stop military actions against the Arab states. The Israeli occupation of the territory of Arab states would be used to restore a foreign colonial regime.

On June 9, despite the cease-fire statement by the Government of Syria, Israeli troops started a new offensive on Syria's border, subjecting Syrian towns to barbaric bombing.

Struggling against imperialism for their freedom and independence, for the integrity of their territories, for the inalienable sovereign right to decide for themselves all questions of their domestic life and foreign policy, the peoples of the Arab countries are upholding a just cause. The peoples of the socialist countries are completely on their side.

The peoples of the UAR and several other Arab countries have scored historic victories in recent years in the winning of national independence and freedom. Important social transformations in the interests of the working masses were carried out.

We express confidence that these gains will be preserved, that progressive regimes will be consolidated despite the difficulties in the way of the Arab peoples.

At a difficult hour for the states of the Arab East, the socialist countries declare that they are in full and complete solidarity with their just struggle and will render them aid in repelling aggression and defending their national independence and territorial integrity.

The states participating in this meeting demand that Israel stop immediately military actions against the neighbouring Arab countries and withdraw all its troops from their territories behind the truce line.

It is the duty of the United Nations Organisation to condemn the aggressor. If the Security Council does not take the proper measures, grave responsibility will rest with those states which failed to fulfil their duty as members of the Security Council.

Resolute concerted action by all peace-loving and progressive forces, by all those who treasure the cause of freedom and independence of peoples, are necessary today as never before.

If the Government of Israel does not stop the aggression and withdraw its troops behind the truce line the socialist states which signed this Statement will do everything necessary to help the peoples of the Arab countries administer a resolute rebuff to the aggressor, to protect their lawful rights, to extinguish the hotbed of war in the Near East and restore peace in that area.

The just struggle of the Arab peoples will triumph!

Pravda, June 10, 1967.

8

A. N. Kosygin: *Aggressor's Troops must be withdrawn and Peace restored in Near East*. Speech at the Emergency Special Session of the UN General Assembly on June 19, 1967

Mr President,
Esteemed delegates,

Representatives of nearly all the nations of the world have gathered for the emergency special Session of the UN General Assembly to consider the grave and dangerous situation which took shape recently in the Near East, a situation which is causing profound anxiety everywhere.

True, hostilities are not in progress there now. The fact that a cease-fire was achieved is a definite success for the peaceloving forces. To a large measure the credit for this is due also to the Security Council though it failed to fulfil completely its duty in conformity with the UN Charter. The aggression is continuing. The armed forces of Israel are occupying territory belonging to the UAR, Syria and Jordan.

At any moment, as long as the Israeli troops continue their occupation of the territories they have seized, and until urgent measures have been taken to liquidate the aftermath of aggression, military conflict can erupt with new force at any minute.

Precisely because of this the Soviet Union initiated the convocation of an emergency Session of the General Assembly. We note with satisfaction that many states have supported our proposal. They have shown an understanding of the danger with which the situation is fraught, and a desire to strengthen peace.

The General Assembly has a responsible task – to adopt decisions which will pave the way to the restoration of peace in the Near East. This task concerns all states, irrespective of the differences in their social and political systems, philosophical views, geographical position or to what groupings they belong. The problem facing us can be solved only if the diversity and complexity of the contemporary world do not eclipse the common issues that unite states and nations and, above all, the need to avert a catastrophic war.

What problem is arousing the greatest anxiety among all nations today? We think that all the participants in the General Assembly will agree that the nations are anxious most of all about how to avoid this catastrophe.

No nation wants war. Today no one doubts that should a new world war break out it would inevitably be a nuclear war. Its consequences would be disastrous for many countries and peoples of the world. The more far-sighted statesmen of various lands, outstanding thinkers and scientists have from the first day of the existence of nuclear weapons warned of this.

The nuclear age has created a new reality in problems of war and peace, it has placed an immeasurably greater responsibility on the states in everything that is relating to these problems. No political or military leader can argue against that if he has not lost the ability to think soberly, the more so since military men have a better concept than others as to the consequences of a nuclear war.

However, in real life, international relations are crammed with facts which prove that certain states have quite a different approach to this. Attempts at interfering in the internal affairs of independent countries and peoples, at imposing on them political concepts and alien views on social systems from the outside have not ended. Everything is done to breathe life into military blocs. The system of military bases – the strongholds of aggression spread all over the world – is being modernised and improved. Navies are cruising thousands of kilometres away from their own shores and threatening the security of states throughout the entire regions of the world.

Even in those cases, when the aggravation of tension or the appearance of hotbeds of war danger is caused by conflicts between relatively small states, big powers quite often stand behind them. This is true not only of the Near East, where aggression has been committed by Israel, backed by bigger imperialist powers, but of other regions of the globe as well.

For nearly three years now the United States of America, having cast off all disguise, has carried out direct aggression against the Vietnamese people.

The war is being waged to impose on the Vietnamese people an order which is to the liking of foreign imperialist circles. It is no exaggeration to say that the world has condemned those who are to blame for this war. There is a way to settle the Vietnamese problem and it is a simple way: the USA must get out of Vietnam, must withdraw its troops. Above all, it must immediately and unconditionally stop bombing the Democratic Republic of Vietnam. No declarations about readiness to seek a peaceful settlement of the Vietnamese problem will sound convincing until this is done. The declarations the US leaders make must not be in contradiction to the real activities of the USA. It is necessary to take into account that the continuation of the war in Vietnam increases the danger of military conflict spreading beyond the limits of that region and is fraught with the ominous danger that this conflict could turn into a broad-scale military confrontation of powers. This precisely is the danger of the present course of the United States of America.

. . .

This is a far from complete list of events which keep international life at fever point and which sometimes lead to major aggravations and the emergence of hotbeds of war.

If we analyse the events in the Near East, we cannot but reach the conclusion that the war between Israel and the Arab states is not the result of misunderstanding or lack of understanding of each other by the parties concerned. Nor is it just a local conflict. The events which took place recently in the Near East in connection with the armed conflict between Israel and the Arab states must of necessity be considered within the context of the general international situation.

I do not wish to dwell on particulars, but it is necessary to speak of the main facts, in order to make a correct appraisal of all that has happened.

What did the last year demonstrate in relations between Israel and the Arab states? Continuous aggravation of tensions and attacks that grew in scope by Israeli troops on one or another of Israel's neighbours.

On November 25, 1966, the Security Council censured the Government of Israel for its thoroughly planned 'large-scale military action' against Jordan, committed in violation of the UN Charter, and issued a warning that should such actions be repeated, the Security Council would have to consider 'the further and more effective steps as envisaged in the Charter'. However, Israel refused to heed this lesson.

On April 7 of this year, Israeli troops attacked the Syrian Arab Republic. It was a major military operation involving aircraft, tanks and artillery. Following this Israel provoked new military clashes on the border with Jordan.

At the time, a number of states warned Israel once more that it would be held responsible for the consequences of the policy it was pursuing. But even then the Israeli Government did not reconsider its course. Its political leaders openly threatened 'broader military actions against the Arab countries'. The Prime Minister of Israel made it clear that the April armed attack on Syria was not to be the final measure and that Israel itself would choose the methods and the time for new similar actions. On May 9, 1967, the Israeli Parliament empowered the Government of Israel to carry out military operations against Syria. Israeli troops began to advance to the Syrian borders and mobilisation was effected.

At the time, information started to come to the Soviet Government, and I think not only to us, that the Israeli Government planned to strike a swift blow against Syria at the end of May with the aim of smashing it and then to transfer hostilities to the territory of the United Arab Republic.

When the war preparations had entered the final stage, the Government of Israel suddenly began to pronounce, both confidentially and publicly, assurances of its peaceful intentions. It declared that it did not intend to begin hostilities, and did not want conflict with its neighbours. Literally several hours before the attack on the Arab states the Minister of Defence of Israel swore that his Government was seeking a peaceful settlement. 'Let diplomacy work,' this Minister said at a time when Israeli pilots had already received orders to bomb the cities of the United Arab Republic, Syria and Jordan. What unprecedented perfidy!

On June 5, Israel launched war against the United Arab Republic, Syria and Jordan. The Government of Israel violated the UN Charter, the norms of international law and demonstrated that all its peaceloving declarations were utterly false.

Everyone knows what followed.

I shall remind you here, at the headquarters of the United Nations Organisation, only of how brazenly the aggressor ignored the demands of the Security Council for an immediate cease-fire.

On June 6, the Security Council proposed that all hostilities should end as a first step towards the restoration of peace. Israel expanded operations on the fronts.

On June 7, the Security Council established a deadline for the termination of hostilities. Israeli troops continued their offensive and Israeli aircraft bombed peaceful Arab cities and villages.

On June 9, a new categorical demand was issued by the Security

Council for a cease-fire. Israel ignored this, too. The Israeli army opened an offensive against the defence lines of Syria aimed at effecting a break-through to Damascus, the capital of this state.

The Security Council had to adopt yet another, and its fourth, decision, a number of states had to sever diplomatic relations with Israel and give a firm warning that sanctions would be applied, before the Israeli troops stopped hostilities. The major part of the territory of the Arab states, which is now practically under Israeli occupation, was seized after the Security Council had adopted the decision on the immediate termination of hostilities.

There is irrefutable proof to show that Israel bears the responsibility for unleashing the war, for all who suffered from it and for its consequences.

But if anyone needs further evidence that the war in the Near East was unleashed by Israel and that Israel is the aggressor, Israel itself has provided the proof. It is impossible to explain in any other way the refusal of the Israeli Government to support the Soviet Union's proposal to convene an emergency Session of the UN General Assembly. If the Government of Israel felt no guilt before the nations of the world, it would not fear our discussion and the decisions which the General Assembly is bound to adopt.

Israel has no arguments to justify its aggression. Its attempts to justify itself – like those of its advocates to whitewash its policies and actions – based on declarations that the attack on the Arab states was a forced step, that, allegedly, the other side left Israel no other course of action, are all false.

If Israel had claims against its neighbours, it should have come here, to the United Nations Organisation, and sought a peaceful settlement here, as it is authorised by the UN Charter. After all, Israel claims the right to use all the rights and privileges which accrue from being a member of the United Nations Organisation. But rights cannot exist without responsibilities.

More and more information is pouring in on the atrocities and violence being committed by the Israeli aggressors on the territories they have seized. What is happening on the Sinai Peninsula, in the Gaza area, in the western part of Jordan, and on Syrian territory occupied by Israeli troops, recalls the monstrous crimes committed by the fascists during World War II. The indigenous Arab population is being ousted from Gaza, Jerusalem and other areas. As, in its time, nazi Germany appointed Gauleiters in the regions it had occupied, so the Israeli Government is setting up an occupational administration in the territories it has seized and appointing its military governors there.

The Israeli troops are razing villages and destroying hospitals and schools. Civilians are being left without food and water, or any means of subsistence. The shooting of POWs and even women and children has been reported and ambulances with wounded have been burned.

The United Nations Organisation cannot ignore these crimes. The Security Council has already approached the Government of Israel with the demand that the preservation, safety, and wellbeing of the inhabitants in the regions it has seized be guaranteed. This resolution in itself is an indictment of the aggressor. The United Nations Organisation must force Israel to respect international laws. Those organising and carrying out crimes on the occupied territories of the Arab countries must be severely punished.

True to its principle of assisting victims of aggression, of supporting peoples who are fighting for their independence and freedom, the Soviet Union has come out strongly in defence of Arab states. We warned the Government of Israel, both before the aggression began and during the war, that if it decided to take upon itself the responsibility of unleashing a military conflict, it would have to pay in full measure for the consequences. We still firmly adhere to this stand.

There must be no political zigzags when we speak of war and peace and of defending peoples' rights. Of course, in order to settle one or another problem, states sometimes outline several possible ways. But in problems like this, which the emergency Session of the General Assembly is now considering, there exists no alternative for a resolute condemnation of aggression, and of those forces behind it, no alternative for the elimination of the aftermath of aggression. Otherwise it is impossible to end aggression, to discourage those who would care to launch such ventures in the future.

One may ask, why does the Soviet Union take such a resolute stand against Israel? No, gentlemen, the Soviet Union is not against Israel, but against the aggressive policies which are being conducted by ruling circles of that state.

Throughout the 50 years of its existence, the Soviet Union has treated all nations – big and small – with respect. Every nation has the right to create its own independent national state. This is one of the main principles of the policy the Soviet Union pursues.

It was this that determined our attitude towards Israel as a state when in 1947 we voted for the decision of the UNO to create on the territory of Palestine, a former British colony, two independent states – one Jewish and one Arab. Guided by this principle, the Soviet Union established diplomatic relations with Israel.

While supporting the right of nations to self-determination, the Soviet Union condemns, just as vigorously, attempts by any state to conduct an aggressive policy in relation to other countries – a policy of seizing foreign lands and enslaving the people living there.

What policy does the state of Israel pursue? Unfortunately, throughout the major part of its history, the ruling Israeli circles have conducted a policy of seizure and expanding their territory at the expense of the territories of the neighbouring Arab states, and ousting or even destroying the indigenous population of those lands.

It was so in 1948–1949, when Israel forcibly seized a considerable part of the territory of the Arab state, which was to be set up according to the UN decision. About a million people were driven out of their native land and doomed to hunger, suffering and poverty. All these years these people have lived like exiles, deprived of their motherland and means of subsistence. The acute problem of the Palestine refugees, which resulted from the policies of Israel, remains unsettled to this day, and tends constantly to aggravate tension in that area.

The same occurred in 1956, when Israel took part in the aggression against Egypt. At that time its troops invaded Egyptian territory as they have done now. At that time, too, Israel tried to retain the areas it had seized, but had to retreat beyond the armistice line under the powerful pressure brought to bear on it by the United Nations Organisation, by the majority of its members.

The members of the United Nations Organisation are well aware that throughout the years that followed, Israel has been committing acts of aggression against the United Arab Republic, Syria and Jordan. There has been no other issue about which it has been necessary to convene the Security Council so often, as that of conflicts between Israel and the Arab states.

As we can see, the aggressive war unleashed today by Israel against the Arab countries is a direct continuation of policies which the ruling extremist circles have imposed on their country throughout the entire existence of the Israeli state. It is against this aggressive policy that the Soviet Union has acted firmly and consistently, along with the other socialist and all peaceloving states. It is the duty of the United Nations Organisation to force Israel to submit to the demands of the nations. If UNO fails to do this, it will be failing to fulfil its highest duty, in the name of which it was created, and faith in the Organisation will be undermined.

Israel can establish its place among the nations of the world only by taking the path of peace, by abandoning its aggressive policies towards its neighbours.

We would not be consistent or fair in appraising Israel's policy, if we did not say with complete certainty, that, in its actions, Israel enjoys support from certain imperialist circles outside the country. More than that, these influential circles have made statements and indulged in practical activities which the extremists in Israel could interpret only in one way – as a direct encouragement to commit acts of aggression.

How else, for example, can we estimate the fact that on the eve of the Israeli aggression, a plan was being hurriedly worked out in the USA and Great Britain – and which was widely reported in the press – on establishing an international naval force to bring pressure to bear on the Arab states? How else can we estimate the military demonstrations of the 6th US Fleet off the shores of the Arab states and the increase in British naval and air forces in the Mediterranean and in the Red Sea area, or the stepped-up deliveries of modern armaments and ammunition for the Israeli army?

. . .

At present, the extremely bellicose circles in Tel Aviv are declaring that their seizure of Arab territories provides them with – as they brazenly state – the basis for making new demands on the Arab countries and nations. An unbridled anti-Arab propaganda campaign, supported by the press of certain Western countries, is being carried on in Israel. The force of arms is being lauded, new threats are being made against neighbouring countries, and it is being said that Israel will not heed any decisions, not even those adopted by the present Session of the UN General Assembly, if they do not conform to its demands.

The aggressor is in a state of intoxication. Plans devised long before to reshape the map of the Near East, are being brought to the fore. The Israeli leaders are declaring that Israel will not leave the Gaza area, or the western banks of the Jordan River. They are declaring that Israel intends to retain under its control the entire city of Jerusalem and say that, should the Arab countries not submit to Israeli demands, Israeli troops will simply remain where they are now.

What is the attitude of the governments of the USA and Great Britain to the Israeli claims? For all practical purposes, in this case, too, they are taking the stand of encouraging the aggressor. How else can the aggressor interpret their position in the Security Council which hampered the adoption of a proposal on the immediate withdrawal of the Israeli troops behind the armistice line? Declarations of support for the political independence and territorial integrity of the Near Eastern countries so lavishly made by the US representatives can have meaning only if those who utter them reject in no uncertain way the territorial claims of the aggressor and favour the immediate withdrawal of his troops.

By putting forward a programme of annexation, Israel completely loses all sense of reality and embarks on a very dangerous path. Any attempt to consolidate the results of aggression is bound to fail. We are confident that the United Nations will reject attempts to impose a settlement on the Arab peoples that might jeopardise their legitimate interests or humiliate them. Territorial conquests, if they were recognised by various states, would only lead to new and perhaps bigger conflicts while peace and security in the Near East would remain an illusion. Such a situation cannot be permitted to arise, and one can rest assured that this will not happen. Attempts to consolidate the fruits of aggression will in the long run rebound against Israel and its people.

By occupying UAR, Jordanian and Syrian territories, Israel is continuing to throw out a challenge to the United Nations and all peaceloving states. Therefore the main task of this Assembly is to condemn the aggressor and take measures for the immediate withdrawal of Israeli troops beyond the armistice line. In other words, the task is to clear all the territories of Arab countries of the Israeli invaders.

The Israeli aggression has resulted in paralysing the work of the Suez Canal, an important international waterway which has been transformed by the invaders into a front line.

The Soviet Union voices a categorical demand that the Israeli troops be immediately removed from the shores of the Suez Canal and from all occupied Arab territories.

Only the withdrawal of Israeli forces from the areas they have seized can change the situation in favour of a detente and the creation of conditions for peace in the Near East.

Is it not clear that unless this is done and the Israeli invaders evicted from the territory of Arab states, there can be no hope of settling other unsolved problems in the Near East?

Those who unleashed the war against the Arab states should not cherish hopes that they will gain advantages from this.

The United Nations, called upon to serve the cause of preserving peace and international security, must use all its influence and all its prestige to end aggression.

In its demand to condemn aggression and withdraw troops from the seized territories of the UAR, Syria and Jordan, the Soviet Government proceeds from the necessity to maintain peace not only in the Near East. It should not be forgotten that there are many regions in the world where there are bound to be those eager to seize foreign territories, where principles of territorial integrity and respect for the sovereignty of states are far from being honoured. If Israel's claims are not rebuffed today, tomorrow new aggressors, big or small, may attempt to overrun the lands of other peaceful countries.

.   .   .

There is another important aspect of the aggression perpetrated by Israel. The point is that this aggression was aimed at toppling the existing regimes in the UAR, Syria and other Arab countries, which by their determined struggle to strengthen their national independence and make progress have evoked the hatred of the imperialists and the solidarity and support of the peoples which have embarked on the path of independent development. Therefore, to permit the actions of Israel against the Arab states to go unpunished would mean opposing the cause of national liberation of peoples and the interests of many states of Asia, Africa and Latin America.

The Soviet Union does not recognise Israel's seizure of territories. True to the ideals of peace, freedom and independence of peoples, the Soviet Union will undertake all measures within its power, both in the United Nations and outside it, to eliminate the consequences of aggression and promote the establishment of a lasting peace in this region. This is our firm and principled course. This is our joint course together with other socialist countries.

On June 9, the leaders of Communist and Workers' Parties and governments of seven socialist countries declared their full and complete solidarity with the just struggle of the states of the Arab East. Unless the Government of Israel ceases its aggression and withdraws its troops beyond the armistice line, the socialist states 'will do everything necessary to aid the peoples of the Arab countries to deal a firm rebuff to the aggressor, to safeguard their legitimate rights, to quench the hotbed of war in the Near East and restore peace in that region.'

No state, however far removed from the area of the aggression, can remain aloof from the problem which is being discussed by the present emergency Session. The problem concerns war and peace. In the present tense international situation hours or minutes can settle the fate of the world. If the dangerous developments in the Near East, South-East Asia or any other place where peace is being violated, are not halted, if conflicts are permitted to spread, the only possible outcome today or tomorrow will be a big war, and no single state will be able to remain on the sidelines.

No state or government, if it is genuinely concerned about peace and the prevention of a new war, can reason that if some event takes place far from its borders it can regard it with equanimity. Indeed it cannot. A seemingly small event or 'local wars' may grow into big military conflicts. This means that every state and government should not only refrain from all actions that would bring about new complications, it must do all it can to prevent any aggravation of the situation, especially the emergence of hotbeds of war. Should they appear, however, it must try and quench them. This should be stressed especially in connection with the recent events in the Near East which have greatly complicated the already complex and dangerous international situation.

The Arab states, which fell victim to aggression, are entitled to expect that their sovereignty, territorial integrity, legitimate rights and interests, that were violated by the armed attack, will be restored in full and without delay. We repeat that this means, first of all, the withdrawal of Israeli forces from the occupied territories. This is the crucial question today, without which there can be no detente in the Near East.

Elimination of the consequences of aggression also means restitution of the material damage inflicted by the aggressor upon those attacked and whose lands were occupied. The Israeli troops and aircraft destroyed homes, industrial projects, roads and transport facilities in the UAR, Syria and Jordan. Israel is in duty bound to reimburse the full cost of all it destroyed and to return all captured property. It is in duty bound to do this within the shortest possible time.

Can the General Assembly measure up to the tasks that face it, can it cope with them? Yes, it can. The General Assembly should say its weighty word in favour of justice and peace.

The Soviet Union and its delegation are ready to work together with other countries, whose representatives have assembled in this hall. They are ready to work together with all other states and delegations in order to attain this aim.

Much depends on the efforts of the big powers. It would be good if their delegations also found a common language in order to reach decisions meeting the interests of peace in the Near East and throughout the world.

Guided by the lofty principles of the United Nations Charter and the desire to eliminate the consequences of aggression and restore justice as quickly as possible, the Soviet Government submits the following draft resolution to the General Assembly:

The General Assembly,

stating that Israel, by grossly violating the United Nations Charter and the universally accepted principles of international law, has committed a premeditated and planned aggression against the United Arab Republic, Syria and Jordan, has occupied a part of their territory and inflicted great material damage upon them,

noting that in contravention of the resolutions of the Security Council on the immediate cessation of all hostilities and a cease-fire of June 6, June 7 and June 9, Israel continued to conduct offensive military operations against the afore-said states and expanded the territory it had seized,

noting further that although at the present time hostilities have ceased, Israel is continuing to occupy the territory of the UAR, Syria and Jordan, thus failing to halt the aggression and throwing out a challenge to the United Nations and all peaceloving states,

regarding as inadmissible and illegitimate the presentation by Israel of territorial claims to the Arab states, which prevents the restoration of peace in the area,

1. Resolutely condemns Israel's aggressive actions and its continuing occupation of a part of the territory of the UAR, Syria and Jordan, which constitutes an act of recognised aggression;

2. Demands that Israel should immediately and unconditionally withdraw all its forces from the territory of the afore-said states to positions beyond the armistice lines, as stipulated in the general armistice agreements, and should respect the status of the demilitarised zones, as prescribed in those armistice agreements;

3. Also demands that Israel should restitute in full and within the shortest possible time all the damage inflicted by its aggression upon the UAR, Syria and Jordan, and their nationals, and should return to them all seized property and other material assets;

4. Appeals to the Security Council to undertake, on its part, immediate and effective measures to eliminate all the consequences of the Israeli aggression.

The Government of the Soviet Union expresses the hope that the General Assembly will make a decision that will be effective in ensuring the inviolability of the sovereignty and territorial integrity of the Arab states, the restoration and consolidation of peace and security in the Near East.

The convening of the General Assembly emergency Session is a fact of great international significance. Should the General Assembly prove incapable of reaching a decision in the interests of peace, this will be a heavy blow to the expectations of mankind regarding the possibility of settling major international problems by peaceful means, by diplomatic contacts and negotiations. No state, which is genuinely concerned about the future of its people, can fail to take this into consideration.

All peoples must feel assured that the United Nations is capable of achieving the aims proclaimed in its Charter, and of safeguarding peace on earth.

Pravda, June 20, 1967.

9

Decisions of the CC, CP of Israel (16th Plenary Session), June 22, 1967

The Central Committee of the Communist Party of Israel holds that the war which was started by the Eshkol-Dayan-Begin government on June 5, 1967, has caused the most serious harm to the national interests of the State of Israel and its international position. The war has not strengthened the security of Israel but has shaken it even more: it has not brought Israeli-Arab peace nearer but has put it off still further.

The war which was started by the Eshkol-Dayan-Begin government is an aggressive war, which was planned beforehand, together with the governments of the USA and Britain and with the support of the West German government.

. . .

The principal aim of the war was to bring about the fall of the anti-imperialist regimes in Egypt and Syria, to sever the connections of the Arab countries with the Soviet Union and the other socialist countries, and to protect the concessions of the foreign oil monopolies and the strategic bases of the Western colonial powers in our region.

The Central Committee warns: The security and future of the State of Israel demand an end to the aggression and to the plots with the American oil and armament magnates, whose hands are stained with the blood of the peoples of Vietnam and other countries.

The Communist Party of Israel has repeatedly warned the leaders of the Arab national movement that the declarations against the right of existence of Israel and the acts of terror on Israeli territory only serve the imperialists and Israeli militarists as a pretext to execute their aggressive plans against the anti-imperialist Arab countries, and cause harm to the anti-imperialist struggle and the struggle for the legal rights of the Palestinian Arab people.

. . .

The disentanglement of the State of Israel from dependence on the imperialist powers and the recognition by the State of Israel of the national rights of the Palestinian Arab people, and first of all of the rights of the refugees, is the road to Israel-Arab peace, and to the Arab countries' recognition of Israel and her national rights, including freedom of sea passage.

The Central Committee declares that all proposals for peace negotiations by the rulers of Israel under the conditions of continued Israeli occupation of Egyptian, Syrian and Jordanian territories are empty, demagogic proposals. These proposals, including the proposal for autonomy or the establishment of a Palestinian protectorate in the occupied territories, are not directed towards a peaceful solution but to the continuation of occupation.

. . .

The Central Committee warns against the danger of a military dictatorship in Israel. Only a united and militant struggle of all democratic forces can prevent the victory of fascism in Israel.

. . .

The Central Committee calls for a united struggle of the Jewish and

Arab workers in defense of their interests, against oppression and national discrimination, for equal national rights.

The Central Committee expresses its regret over the severance of diplomatic relations with Israel by the socialist countries – USSR, Czechoslovakia, Bulgaria, Poland, Hungary, Yugoslavia, and also by democratic Guinea. All the responsibility for this severance of Israel's relations with the socialist world falls on the Eshkol-Dayan-Begin government which launched an aggressive war.

The Soviet Union was and remains a faithful friend of the people of Israel and of all peoples. The severance of relations is not directed against the State of Israel, but against the policy of the government of Israel, which sacrifices the real national interests of Israel at the shrine of the interests of the Anglo-American oil companies in our region.

The Soviet Union did all in order to prevent war in the Middle East. Now the Soviet Union acts with all its might to liquidate the results of aggression and to safeguard peace and security in the region.

The experience of the period between the first and the second world wars proves that every capitulation to aggression, every appeasement of the aggressor will only increase his appetite, spread the flames of war and increase the danger of world war. The American imperialists who kindled, with the help of their local agents, the flames of war in Vietnam and the Middle East, are pushing towards a third world war. The cause of peace and people's independence, the cause of preventing a third world war, demands the liquidation of imperialist aggression everywhere.

The people of Israel are interested in peace in our region and in the world. The people of Israel are deeply interested in friendly relations with the USSR and all socialist and peace-loving countries.

The Central Committee warns against the danger to Israel emanating from the irresponsible national policy of its rulers, and urges withdrawal of the Israeli army to the armistice lines, for an end to the policy of force which relies on the imperialist powers for support.

·   ·   ·

Abridged.

10

Moshe Sneh: *From Victory in a War of Defence to a Durable and Just Peace*

Our Position during the Three Phases of the Crisis
In all the phases of the crisis in Israel-Arab relations with which we are still faced, our Israeli Communist Party has been guided in its policies by two unalterable principles: a strong desire for peace between nations –

and a solution to the conflict by means of an agreement which would guarantee the just national rights of all the peoples concerned.

a. During the prolonged period of heightened military tension between the Arab states we acted in accordance with the slogan: Anything to prevent the War! In face of the mounting wave of terrorist infiltrations across the Israeli borders, we fought in the Israeli society against the system of military reprisals and raids into Arab territories, and for an eminently defensive strategy of efficient and perfected protection of our borders and territories, in conjunction with a political offensive for a peaceful solution of the Israeli-Arab conflict as such, on the basis of mutual recognition of the legal rights of both sides. We condemned categorically any threats or use of force by any side. We warned the Israeli Government against the danger that imperialism may exploit any Israeli-Arab conflict for its own intrigues and plots. We approached influential sister-parties, both in socialist and capitalist countries, explained to them the whole complex problem of Israeli-Arab relations, and advised them, on the one hand, to exert their full influence on the Arab leaders to divert them from the crazy idea of destroying Israel, and, on the other hand, to take steps to draw the Israeli Government closer to the socialist camp and to move it from its one-sided orientation on the Western Powers, similar to the steps taken in the case of Pakistan, Iran, Turkey, etc. We did not limit our efforts to propaganda and information, verbal or printed, and we maintained direct contacts with numerous factors of public and ruling circles in Israel and abroad – because we were aware of the menace of military confrontation and wanted to prevent it, with all our heart and soul.

When the threat of war became imminent with the sudden expulsion of the UN Emergency Force from the Israeli border, after the concentration of powerful military forces on both sides of the frontier, and in particular after the aggressive step of imposing a naval blockade on Israeli shipping in the Straits of Tiran by the Egyptian Armed Forces, we intensified our activity to prevent war. We demanded of the Israeli Government to use all possible political action against the aggressive steps by the neighbouring countries, and to avoid all military reactions. We appealed to peace-loving factors in the world to exert their influence on both parties to the conflict and to request them to clear all obstacles on the road to peace, that is: mutual and gradual withdrawal of forces on both sides of the frontier; termination of terrorist activities by one side and of reprisal raids by the other side; cessation of threats of 'War of Liberation of Palestine and Destruction of Israel'; removal of the blockade on Israeli shipping in the Red Sea. And when we realized that the situation was deteriorating and likely to lead to a blood-bath in view of a lack of coordination between the great powers and the fruitlessness of political efforts, we broke the usual routine and approached certain addresses with the proposal to convene an international congress for a solution of Middle East problems, similar in its scope to the Geneva Convention of 1954 on South East Asia; had our initiative been followed, the war might perhaps have been avoided.

b. On the day of the outbreak of war, June 5, 1967, our Party was faced with the problem of assessing this military conflict and deciding what attitude to adopt towards it. We were guided by the well-known Leninist criterion, which bases the evaluation on the political aims of the two sides. Whereas the pan-Arabic coalition of Egypt, Syria, Jordan and Iraq, supported by the remainder of the Arab states, set as its premeditated, constant and declared military and political aim the destruction of Israel, the state of Israel, on the other hand, conducted a struggle for existence, security and independence. For this reason, this Central Committee decided on that date unanimously without dissenting or abstaining votes, that the Israeli Communist Party takes its stand together with the whole nation in this fateful struggle.

The magnificent victory of the Israel Defence Force, its commanders and men over the armies of Egypt, Jordan and Syria, and the fact of having occupied territories of these three countries, should not make us forget the grave danger to the existence of Israel with which it was menaced before this victory. I shall quote as an example the words of Ahmed Shukeiri, the Chairman of the Palestine Liberation Organisation, on June 2, 1967, reported from Amman by the *Morning Star* (organ of the British Communist Party), that the Jordanian or Palestinian Army may be the first to open fire and 'Will rush into the Palestine liberation war'; and answering a question what would be the fate of the Israelis in the case of an Arab victory, he added, 'We shall help to ship them back to their countries of origin', whereas Jews born in Israel 'those of them who still stay alive will remain in Palestine – but according to my estimates not one of them will stay alive.' . . .

Well then, if Frederic Engels was right in his letter to Bebel on October 24, 1891, that German socialists must fight for the defence of Germany in view of the threatening war with Russia, when he wrote 'If Germany is strangled, so shall we be, with her together' (quoted from the fourth Russian edition of Lenin's works, Book 12, page 335), – then we, the Israeli Communists, were right in saying: 'If Israel is strangled, so shall we be, with her together'. It is our good luck that the plot to strangle Israel was defeated in the Six Days War. The aim of not leaving one live Israeli was the goal not only of the 'Palestine Liberation' and its Chairman – this program was approved and supported by the Summit Meetings of

13 Arab kings and presidents, and only a few days before the outbreak of hostilities the President of Egypt, Nasser, declared that 'the final goal' of the 'general confrontation' with Israel was 'the destruction of Israel'. Even if we accept the interpretation given at a later date by Abdel Nasser, that he meant political and not physical destruction of Israel, that is, forcing on the Jewish people in Israel the rule of the Palestinian Arabs, even if we accept this evasive and confusing interpretation, even then Israel's war against this 'corrected aim' was a just defensive war, according to Marxist-Leninist theory. Lenin said: 'The socialists have recognized and do now recognize the legality, the progressive character and the justness of the defence of the motherland or of a defensive war only in the sense of throwing off the yoke of subjection by another nation' (Volume 23, page 19). We had here a war in defence of the Israeli motherland against a plot to impose on it the yoke of subjection by another nation, against the deprivation of the people of Israel of its right of national sovereignty. In 1948 the Arab League declared war with the aim of destroying the state of Israel at its birth – and now, in 1967 this was again the war aim of the pan-Arabic coalition, and therefore, this was on the part of Israel a continuation of the War of Independence of 1948.

Our attitude was courageous and independent. We did not hesitate to define independently our attitude to the military conflict and to demand from the Great Powers at the outset of the war not to take sides, but to act together for an immediate cease-fire and a peaceful solution to the advantage of both sides. In the midst of raging battles we appealed publicly to avoid any hurts to the civilian Arab population, we demanded the reparation of any wrongs committed, the taking of adequate measures to prevent in the future any incursion on the property, rights of honour of the Arab population, and the punishment of those responsible for any wrongdoings. We never ceased repeating during the hostilities, that our aim is peace and not the acquisition of territories.

c. After the military campaign came to an end, we continued the same political line which we followed before and during the war, that is, the line of striving for peace and for a solution of the Israeli-Arab conflict by means of agreement and justice. All these years we were for the right of self-determination for the two peoples of *Eretz* Israel, the Jews and the Arabs; all these years we believed in mutual recognition of the legal rights of the two peoples; we always underlined the moral and political need to solve positively and by agreement the problem of the Palestinian refugees. An opportunity has now been created to realize all these principles, to transform them from pretty slogans into a beautiful reality. We therefore have now to outline in public, in the press and in the Knesset, the broad lines of a peace plan – a peace without dictates by the victors and without surrender by the losers – and we presented this plan in contrast to the extreme nationalist circles in Israel, who see everything in the shape of annexation and territorial expansion.

.   .   .

We are Opposed to a Biased Attitude

To our deep regret, the attitude of the Soviet Government to the military conflict between Israel and the Arab states differs greatly from our attitude, as described above. The Central Committee of the Communist Party of the Soviet Union (in its resolution published in *Pravda*, June 21), takes as a point of departure the assumption, that this has been an 'Israeli aggression' as a 'result of a plot by the forces of the most reactionary international imperialism', against the progressive Arab states, which have taken the road of progressive social-economic changes in favour of the workers, and which follow an anti-imperialist policy'.

In our opinion there is no basis for putting the blame for aggression on Israel. The UN Secretary General, U Thant, reported to the Security Council that it was impossible to state which side started hostilities. The commander of the UN Emergency Force on the Egyptian-Israeli border, General Rikieh from India, declared in his leave-taking speech to his soldiers that 'both sides simultaneously opened an offensive against each other'. An operational order found by the Israeli Army in the HQs of Egyptian and Syrian brigades constitute irrefutable proof of in preparations for an offensive against Israel, timed for June 5, 1967. But Lenin taught us, that what matters is not who fired the first shot, but rather the political aim for which the shooting is being done. And the declared political aim of the Arab governments which have joined forces in the war against Israel was the destruction of Israel. It is, of course, possible to keep silent with regard to this vicious and incriminating conspiracy, but this silence will not change the facts. The continuous acts of sabotage and murder by infiltrators from the Arab terrorist organisations in Israeli territory can be ignored, but that will not change the facts. It is possible to disregard the Egyptian blockade in the Straits of Tiran, but this disregard does not cancel that act of aggression. One may overlook such an important factor as the attitude of Egypt and other Arab states, that the state of belligerence between them and Israel exists still and has existed all these years, but this important factor does not disappear through the act of being overlooked. In brief – the truth is, that Israel has repelled and defeated an aggression which threatened her very existence, and did not attack her neighbours.

We have shown on many occasions, that the coalition of the Arab states which had consolidated for war on Israel was not based on anti-imperialism and progress in favour of the workers. What kind of an anti-imperialism is this, which has as representatives King Hussein and King Faisal? And what kind of progress is this, if Colonel Aref is its standard bearer? Here is how the present regime in Iraq was described by no other than the representative of the Iraqi Communist Party (at the convention of the German Socialist Union Party in Berlin, April 1967): 'The Government continues its bitter fight against communism. Thousands of Communists and progressive persons still rot in prisons and undergo bodily and mental tortures. Others are barred from work for political reasons. The present rulers of Iraq deny the national forces their liberty. . . . A few months ago a worker's strike was suppressed by armed force. The chauvinist rulers have done nothing to solve the Kurdish problem. No vestige of goodwill is to be seen. The gates are wide open for foreign capital, and royalists and their agents are allowed to occupy important positions in the government apparatus. The rulers of Iraq mouth demagogic slogans of Arab solidarity, positive neutralism, and struggle against imperialism. But in their policies they try to reach a compromise with imperialism and re-action.' . . . This dependable communist evidence on the nature of the regime of one of the states which declared war on Israel, in conjunction with the irrefutable fact that the Israeli Army fought by itself, without the help of the United States or any other imperialist power, is enough to refute the spurious assumption that Israel is identified with imperialism and the Arab states with anti-imperialism. The common denominator of the military front against Israel is not anti-imperialism but rather pan-Arabism. And if a comparison would be made between the nature of the regimes in the countries of our region, the levels of their respective social economic, scientific and technical development, their democratic standards and the degree to which their working classes are organized – the outcome of such a comparison would not be detrimental to Israel. . . .

While the Arab national movement is, generally speaking, anti-imperialist, it is nevertheless like other movements of this type – infected by elements, symbols and vestiges of the stagnant past. Among other things, it is still infested by an extreme anti-Israeli chauvinism, which has been fostered during long years by imperialist intrigues. No example will be found in the whole world to compare with this attitude of the most progressive Arab governments, which refuse to accept the very fact of the existence of the state of Israel and of the need of co-existence with this state. How is it possible to overlook these roots of the conflict? This anti-Israeli Arab chauvinism serves – objectively speaking – the aims of imperialism and invites its intervention to a no lesser degree than the Anti-Arab Israeli chauvinism. A true, just and wise anti-imperialist policy in the Middle East requires therefore the removal of the Israeli-Arab conflict, the bringing of both sides to the mutual recognition of each other's rights; both sides should be directed towards the road of peace, progress and liberation from dependence on imperialist powers.

We – our people and our Party – refuse to listen to the counsel of various advisers, who tell us not to take seriously the threats of destroying Isreael, since they are nothing but 'verbal' threats, pure propaganda. No one will succeed in dulling the vigilance of the Jewish people, which has lost in this generation six out of ten million sons in Europe. No one can benumb the alertness of the survivors of our people, who have gathered here, in this region which saw during the present generation the extermination of other peoples – Armenians, Assyrians, Kurds. No one will allay our vigilance in the face of the extensive war preparations carried out in the course of recent years with the intention of realizing the 'propaganda' and 'verbal' slogan of destroying Israel, as for instance: the organisation, mobilisation and training of Palestinians in the 'Liberation Army' – which was endorsed by thirteen Arab states and received official blessing and material assistance from powerful popular China as well as from other sources; the forming of the 'Joint Arab Command' with the sole aim of war on Israel, since there has been – nor could there be – any other common goal (at the time Egypt and Saudi Arabia were fighting one another in Yemen); the network of Egypt's military treaties with Syria, Jordan, Iraq and faraway Arab states. . . .

We did not (and shall not) accept the advice to disregard the threats of destruction levelled against Israel, but neither was heeded our advice to institutions, conventions and authoritative factors in the camp of peace and world socialism – to repudiate openly, vigorously and courageously the slogans of 'destroying Israel', to condemn the economic, political and social boycott against Israel, the threats of a 'Palestine Liberation War' and the whole vile and stupid conception of the Israeli-Arab conflict as a conflict between colonialism and its victim. We have warned all those years that this will lead to war fraught with grave dangers not only to the security of the peoples of the region but also to the process of political and social progress in the Middle East.

Neither was our request accepted, that the world communist movement, the socialist states, and all the anti-imperialist camp adopt toward the Israeli-Arab conflict an attitude similar to the attitude adopted with regard to analogous conflicts, as between China and India, India and Pakistan, Ethiopia and Somalia, etc., that is to say – not siding with one party against the other, for a peace solution agreed to by both sides. To our deep regret, the Soviet Government adopted a one-sided attitude in favour of the anti-Israeli-Arab front, and has not, since many years, uttered one word of public disapproval of the aggressive utterances and actions of the Arab leaders against Israel.

The prejudiced approach to the Arab-Israeli conflict, which disregards the hard facts of reality, which absolves the reactionary anti-Israeli Arab chauvinism, heaps upon Israel baseless accusations and abuse, found its continuation on the subject of the military campaign of June 5–10, 1967, since the Soviet Government identified itself with one of the belligerent parties – with the Arab side, with the front of Nasser-Hussein-Attasi-Aref, finding no other comparison for the Israeli side than Nazi Germany. Small wonder if this campaign of condemnations, abuse and accusations heaped on Israel arouses anti-Semitic feelings, as we have learned, *inter alia*, from the speeches of the leaders of the Hungarian Socialist Worker's Party G. Kalay and Z. Komicin, who felt it necessary to warn against this disturbing symptom ('*Nepzabadszag*').

It is not enough to point out this attitude, this anti-Israeli campaign, nor is it enough to shake off all responsibility and connection with it – we must go to the root of this perversion.

The Root of the Perversion and the Chances to Remedy it

Apparently, some authoritative factors must have evolved the idea that pan-Arabic unity will be the force which will generate the anti-imperialist front in the Middle East, and that hate of Israel is the only cement capable of consolidating Arab unity. Useless to say that we oppose most strongly this vile idea, an idea which belongs to the school of thought of Mao Tse-tung and is quite alien to the Marxist-Leninist system of thinking. The trouble is that this authoritative factor apparently believes that in the competition for influence between the Soviet Union and China in the Arab world it is permittable and perhaps even desirable to adopt oneself the Chinese line and to imitate it. We reject categorically this theory as well. We consider it as part of the ill-advised general theory, which resulted in the collapse of the regimes of Kassem in Iraq, Ben Bela in Algeria, Nkrumah in Ghana, Soekarno in Indonesia, etc. . . . This is the conception of identification with the national anti-imperialist movement, instead of supporting only its progressive sides and conducting a struggle against its regressive sides, as Lenin taught us (Volume 20, page 18). This conception suffered a defeat in the very fact of the outbreak of the Six Day War, June 1967, and, naturally, in its repercussions.

And after the military campaign – what now? Just as Israel was faced – after its military victory – with the choice between annexations and a peace agreement – so are now Egypt and the rest of the Arab world faced with the fateful choice after their military defeat, to achieve an honorary peace with Israel or to prepare for a war of revenge. There is no third choice. We expect and we ask that the Soviet Union and all the world camp of peace and socialism, enlist their influence solely in the direction of agreement between Israel and the Arab states, on the basis of just and durable peace. Any other policy on the side of our international movement will only lead to further defeats. We in Israel have no need to have it repeated by the world, that we have a right to exist, but there is a definite need for all the states of the world to declare it unequivocally and loudly in the ears of the Arab leaders, so that they will finally understand that they must sit down to negotiate with the representatives of the state of Israel. Otherwise, how will peace be possible?

We have enumerated the differences of opinion existing between us and many and powerful factors in our international movement. But we, the Israeli Communist Party, are not at all alone. In particular, we must stress the attitude of the leadership of the Roumanian Communist Party and the Roumanian Government, who, after the Moscow conference of June 9, 1967, did not break off diplomatic relations with Israel, and which follows on the international political scene a policy which is not one-sided, but rather directed at inducing the two sides to negotiate on a peace agreement. In our opinion, this is the policy which, on principle, our international movement has been following in the case of all analogous conflicts, and there is no reason why an exception should be made in this particular case. We therefore hope and suggest that other socialist states and other communist parties accept the line adopted by the Roumanian comrades.

We are receiving reports on declarations by parties, youth movements, publications, personalities and circles belonging to the world movement of peace and socialism, including peace committees and leagues of friendship with the Soviet Union in various countries, whose attitude and stand are basically the same as ours.

We are convinced of the correctness of our stand. We are convinced that we know and understand well the problems of our region, and that the solutions which we put forward are in conformity with Marxist-Leninist principles, with socialist internationalism as well as with our socialist patriotism. The fact that there are differences of opinion between us and some important sister-parties is painful, but this is no reason for us to renounce our truth. All communist parties are independent, and obviously each party is qualified to decide on questions concerning her people and country.

It may be worthwhile to mention a certain deduction, which, like all deductions, contains both similarities and dissimilarities. At the outbreak of hostilities between China and India, the Indian Communist Party (except for a dissenting fraction) took the side of the Indian people against the Red Chinese Army – and up to this day this party (and not the fraction which seceded) enjoys the respect and recognition of the international movement. And yet the armies of Jordan, Syria and Egypt are by no means the Red Army – and, on the other hand, the Chinese Army never contemplated the destruction of India.

.   .   .

The definition of the character of a war (or of an armed conflict or of a military campaign) is a most difficult and complicated affair. In some instances the first definition had to be reassessed. Even in the case of a great war like the Second World War in its first stage (September 1, 1939 – June 22, 1941) the authorized international communist definition of this war was, that it was an imperialist war by both sides, in which the communists did not prefer any of the sides. Quite naturally, the communist parties in the countries invaded and occupied by the Nazis could not accept this preposterous definition. Quite naturally, Thorez and Duclos signed the appeal to the French working class and to the French people on June 10, 1940, to fight to the end against the Hitlerite conqueror, without waiting for a change in the definition of the war by the international authority. Similarly, Gomulka and his comrades founded the underground PPR to fight against Nazism, in contradiction to the authorized (but criminal) decision to disband the Polish Communist Party, and in contradiction to the authorized definition of the character of the war. It was only later that a correction arrived from far away, stating that the war had from the beginning a democratic and anti-fascist character, and the entry of the Soviet Union into the war only intensified this character.

We are convinced that with regard to the Israeli-Arab conflict and in particular the latest military clash there has been a distortion by the Government of the Soviet Union, which caused the mistakes of further socialist governments and communist parties. We are convinced that this distortion will be rectified, as was the case with earlier distortions on other subjects. We are convinced that the declaration made by the Soviet Ministry of Foreign Affairs on April 17, 1956, which expressed the willingness of the Soviet Union to aid – in co-operation with other factors in the UN – in the establishment of Israeli-Arab peace through a mutual agreement which would take into consideration the legal rights of all the peoples concerned, is valid to this day, and that this is the correct basis for Soviet policy in our region.

We are quite aware of the great disappointment and consternation in all circles of the Left, among all friends of the Soviet Union, in the Israeli public opinion. In the name of the Israeli Communist Party, we say to all of them: Do not identify a wrong and distorted but temporary political stand – with the Soviet Union as a general historical value, and even less with communist ideology, with the world-embracing significance of the Great Socialist October Revolution. And to those who steer Israel's policy we say and we repeat: all efforts should be directed at opening the bridge to the Soviet Union which has been wrongly closed to us, and let us beware not to burn this bridge, in the opening of which we are so interested.

Our Israeli Communist Party is at present confronted by a difficult struggle on two fronts: within Israel we fight against the craze of territorial conquests, and in the international communist movement we struggle against the identification with Arab anti-Israeli chauvinism. In each of these two campaigns we fight for peace and for justice for both peoples. And there where peace and justice are to be found, it will victoriously prevail.

Kol Ha'am, June 30, 1967. From a lecture at the 18th Plenary session of the Maki Central Committee.

II

On the Policy of the Soviet Union in Connection with the Israeli Aggression in the Near East: Resolution of the Plenary Meeting of the CPSU Central Committee. Adopted on June 21, 1967

Having heard and discussed the report of L. I. Brezhnev, General Secretary of the CPSU Central Committee, 'On the Policy of the Soviet Union in Connection with the Israeli Aggression in the Near East', the Plenary Meeting of the CPSU Central Committee resolves:

Fully to approve the political line and practical activities of the Politbureau of the Central Committee aimed at cutting short Israeli aggression, at supporting the United Arab Republic, Syria and other Arab states subjected to attack, and at averting the dangerous consequences of aggression to the cause of universal peace.

The Israeli aggression is the result of a collusion of the most reactionary forces of international imperialism, primarily the United States, against one of the detachments of the national-liberation movement, against the advanced Arab states which have embarked upon the path of progressive social and economic transformations in the interests of the working people, and which pursue an anti-imperialist policy.

In the conditions when the United States is continuing its predatory war in Vietnam the Israeli aggression in the Near East constitutes another link in the common chain of the policy of the belligerent imperialist circles which are trying to stop the historical advance of national independence, democracy, peace and socialism.

The Soviet Union, the other socialist countries and all progressive anti-imperialist forces are with the Arab peoples in their just struggle against imperialism and neo-colonialism, for the inalienable right to themselves decide all questions of home and foreign policy. Expressing the will of Soviet Communists and all Soviet people, the Plenary Meeting of the Central Committee vigorously condemns the Israeli aggression and declares its solidarity with the peoples of the UAR, Syria, Algeria and the other Arab countries.

The Plenary Meeting notes that the quick, resolute and joint actions of the Soviet Union and the other socialist states played an important role in stopping the military operations in the Near East. The position of our Party and the Soviet Government and their practical steps in connection with the events in the Near East have the full support of all Soviet people.

The Plenary Meeting of the Central Committee states with satisfaction that at the important point in the development of international events the fraternal socialist states that signed the Statement on June 9, 1967, acted together, shoulder to shoulder. It has been confirmed once again that the joint actions of the socialist countries are a powerful factor in the struggle against the aggressive intrigues of international imperialism.

The Plenary Meeting of the Central Committee fully approves the Statement of the Central Committees of the Communist and Workers' Parties and Governments of the Socialist Countries of June 9 this year and confirms that the Soviet Union, together with the other socialist countries, will do everything necessary to help the peoples of the Arab countries vigorously to repulse the aggressor, to protect their lawful rights, to abolish the hotbed of war in the Near East and to restore peace in that area.

The chief task today, when the forces of imperialism and neo-colonialism, taking advantage of the situation created by Israeli aggression in the Near East, encroach on the independence and territorial integrity of the Arab states, is to prevent the aggressor from profiting from the results of his treacherous actions, to get the interventionist troops withdrawn immediately and unconditionally behind the armistice line and have the aggressor pay for the damage caused to the UAR, Syria and Jordan.

In accordance with the basic aims of the policy of our Party laid down by the 23rd CPSU Congress and confirmed by the 1966 December Plenary Meeting of the CPSI Central Committee, it is necessary to continue the struggle against the bellicose forces of imperialism and their policy of interference into the internal affairs of other countries, continue to pursue the line of support of the Arab states in their struggle for freedom, independence, territorial integrity and social progress.

It is necessary in the future, too, to consolidate friendship and cohesion between the Soviet Union and Arab states, resolutely to rebuff imperialist scheming, expose its real, anti-popular aspect, conduct the struggle against the slanderous campaign and splitting activities of the Mao Tse-tung group aimed at disuniting the anti-imperialist forces, undermining confidence between the peoples of the Arab nations and the peoples of the socialist countries.

The Plenary Meeting of the CPSU Central Committee considers that the developments in the Near East emphatically stress the need of unity of action of the Communist and Workers' Parties, the international labour movement and the national-liberation movement of the Afro-Asian and Latin American peoples, all peaceloving and progressive forces, all who hold dear the cause of peace and independence of peoples, the cause of the struggle for world peace.

The Communist Party of the Soviet Union, translating into life the decisions of the 23rd Congress, will continue to conduct unflaggingly the struggle against the aggressive forces of imperialism, to maintain high vigilance of the Soviet people, to consistently implement the Leninist line of peaceful coexistence of states with different social systems, to fulfil its internationalist duty – to give all possible support to the peoples fighting for their freedom and national independence for social progress. Joint actions of the forces of peace, democracy and socialism, of the national-liberation movement can bridle the aggressor and avert a new world war.

The Plenary Meeting of the CPSU Central Committee calls upon Party organisations, all working people of the Soviet Union to exert fresh labour efforts aimed at the building of communism, at the further consolidation of the economic and military might of the country, to mark the glorious 50th anniversary of the Great October Socialist Revolution in a worthy manner.

Pravda, June 22, 1967.

12

From a Speech by Leonid Brezhnev at a reception for graduates of Military Academies in Moscow on July 5, 1967

The Middle East is one of the major areas of the national-liberation movement. Progressive Arab states – the UAR, Syria and Algeria – have chosen the non-capitalist road of development. In their foreign policy, progressive Arab countries pursue an anti-imperialist course.

International imperialism, above all American and British imperialism, refuses to reconcile itself to all this. For many decades the imperialists regarded that area as their own domain, and were accustomed to shape the destinies of the peoples living there as they pleased.

The interests of the oil monopolies, which make huge profits in the Middle East and are the main suppliers of crude oil and fuel to the NATO countries, are also of considerable importance for the imperialists. The Middle East holds 60 per cent of the world's oil resources. The Arab countries account for some 50 per cent of the world's oil trade. Almost one million tons of oil a day was supplied by the area to Western Europe.

The American monopolies make over $1,200 million a year on Arab oil and the British monopolies, $600 million. The investments of the American monopolies there are repaid in approximately 18 months as compared with 10 years in the United States itself.

As for the prime cause of Israel's anti-Arab aggression, it lay in the desire of the American and British imperialists to strike at the national-liberation movement in the Middle East, to stop the peoples' advance along the road of social progress at all costs, to force countries that have won freedom and independence at so high a price back into colonial bondage, and rob them of their wealth. Imperialist propaganda efforts to pass off this aggression as merely a result of Israeli-Arab national discord are aimed at concealing the true causes of the aggression, at camouflaging the class meaning of those events. The Middle East crisis is a confrontation between the forces of imperialism, on the one hand, and the forces of national independence, democracy and social progress, on the other.

The Soviet Union sees its task in foiling imperialist designs in the Middle East and in helping the Arab states to uphold their freedom and independence. We have long-standing relations of sincere amity and cooperation with many Arab countries, as well as with other countries that have thrown off colonial tyranny and are following the road of progress.

In the very first days of the Israeli aggression the USSR, acting in close unity with other socialist states and in constant contact with the Arab countries, took vigorous measures to stay the hand of the aggressor, protect the lawful interests of the Arab peoples, stop the armed conflict, and prevent it from increasing to proportions imperilling all of mankind.

As we now look back we can confidently say that in the crucial days of the Middle East crisis we did what was right.

Now that hostilities have ceased, it is necessary first of all, that the aggressor withdraw his troops from all the territories he has overrun. An aggressor must never be permitted to benefit from his treacherous attack, nor must aggression ever go unpunished.

The Middle East situation remains tense and everything must be done to prevent the flames of war from flaring up again. The Israeli government relying on the backing of its patrons – the USA, Britain and West Germany – is brazenly challenging the peace-loving states. The behaviour of Israel's overweening rulers on occupied Arab territory deserve the most emphatic condemnation.

The aggressors comport themselves there like brigands. In committing atrocities against the Arab civilian population, they apparently seek to imitate the crimes of the Hitlerite invaders.

At this new, political stage of the struggle to end the aggression and eliminate its consequences, we give every support to the Arab peoples. As you know, the emergency session of the UN General Assembly, called on Soviet initiative, was addressed by A. Kosygin, head of the Soviet Government, the heads of government of several other socialist countries present at the Assembly, and the representatives of many other states of the world, all of whom condemned the Israeli aggression and demanded the immediate withdrawal of the aggressor's troops behind the armistice line. The aggressive role of Israel and those behind its back was conclusively demonstrated and exposed at the session.

We would like to emphasize once again that the aggressor must get out of alien territory and compensate the peoples of the UAR, Jordan and Syria for the damage done to them. It is only fair that this should be done. The Soviet people and fair-minded men and women the world over demand that it be done.

The Soviet Union firmly and resolutely supports the Arab states in their struggle for freedom and territorial integrity and gives them every possible help. The other day, as you know, N. Podgorny, President of the Presidium of the Supreme Soviet of the USSR, paid friendly state visits to Cairo, Damascus and Bagdad. We attach great importance to those visits and to the frank and friendly exchange of opinions that took place with President Nasser, President Attasi and President Aref, and with other Arab leaders.

The exchange of opinions will, no doubt, promote our relations and the coordination of joint actions in the political struggle in defence of the rights and interests of the UAR, Syria and other Arab countries.

When they started the conflict in the Middle East, the imperialists aimed their main blow at the countries which have taken the non-capitalist road of development. They strove, first of all, to overthrow progressive regimes. But they failed.

From this rostrum we would like to tell our Arab friends that the Soviet people know very well that the Arabs are going through a time of stress. But then, in a liberation struggle there occur temporary failures along with victories, as the history of any nation shows. These failures cannot break a nation which has firmly embarked on the road of freedom and independence – they only strengthen its determination in the struggle.

The events in the Middle East have shown once again how treacherous imperialism is and how important it is to defend the gains achieved in the course of the national-liberation struggle. The cause of national and social emancipation is a just cause, and for its sake it is necessary to strengthen in every way the newly-free states, their defences and their unity, always to be ready to counteract the aggressive intrigues of imperialism.

It is our firm conviction that the just cause of the Arab peoples, who have risen to fight for national independence and social progress, will triumph. We are confident that the revolutionary forces of the Arab world will draw proper conclusions from the events which have taken place. In the struggle against aggression the Arab peoples are strengthening their unity.

At present the imperialists are operating their propaganda machine at full capacity pouring out falsehood and calumny in an attempt to weaken and isolate the Arab countries, to embroil them among themselves and to split the Arab countries, on the one hand, and the Soviet Union and other socialist countries, on the other. The imperialists are most particularly anxious to undermine the friendship of the Arab peoples and our Soviet country.

Our Arab friends see the meaning of this venomous propaganda. They realize that in the present situation it is particularly important to strengthen the united front of the Arab peoples and the peoples of the socialist countries.

In their talks with Soviet representatives, Nasser, Attasi, Zuayyin, Boumedienne, Aref and other leaders of friendly Arab countries emphasize that the peoples of their countries are aware of the support the Soviet state has been rendering them and that the Arabs will firmly safeguard their friendship with the Soviet Union against all encroachments.

. . .

The Moscow Statement of the socialist countries played a big role in ending the war in the Middle East. That action gave immense moral and political support to our Arab friends and had a sobering effect on the aggressor and his patrons.

The unity of socialist countries, life shows, is a great force. The Communist Party of the Soviet Union will always work unremittingly to further this unity.

The June meeting of the CC CPSU, having discussed the recent events in the Middle East, emphasized the need to continue the struggle against the bellicose forces of imperialism and their policy of interference in the domestic affairs of other countries.

In following its policy of peaceful coexistence, the Soviet Union is not going to indulge aggressors. The imperialists should learn it well that

Lenin's statement about just and unjust wars is as valid as ever and that the Soviet Union will resolutely oppose every intrigue of the war-mongers and support the peoples fighting for their freedom and national independence.

.   .   .

The FRG has made a substantial 'contribution' to the preparation of Israel for military ventures, and during the conflict in the Middle East it actually sided with the Israeli militarists. The aggression in the Middle East has all the sympathy of the militarist rulers of West Germany, who covet foreign territory and still cannot bring themselves to give up their dream of swallowing the German Democratic Republic, the state of the German working people.

.   .   .

Source: *Pravda*, July 6, 1967. English translation published in *Information Bulletin*, Documents of the Communist and Workers Parties, No. 14 (102), Prague, 1967.

13

Soviet Government Statement on the Middle East, March 30, 1968

The Middle East situation continues to be a focus of attention. Tension resulting from the crisis of last summer brought about by Israel's adventurist policy is not subsiding. Israel, an imperialist state, is continuing aggression against neighbouring Arab states, deepening the crisis and producing still more dangerous international consequences.

The Israeli Government is constantly organising military provocations against Arab states. This is confirmed by reports that in violation of the decision of the Security Council on the cessation of military actions, Israeli troops on March 21 carried out a new bandit attack on Jordan using large ground and air forces.

In the occupied areas Israeli troops are committing arbitrary acts and crimes, and conducting big punitive operations against the local population.

Certain steps are being taken, the aim of which is to incorporate indigenous Arab territories, captured as a result of the aggression, into the Israeli state. The Israeli Ministry of Internal Affairs officially announced on February 29 this year that the Sinai Peninsula, the Gaza area, the area to the west of the River Jordan captured from Jordan, the Golan heights in Syria henceforth 'will not be regarded as enemy territory'. By this illegal act Israel is attempting to turn the ceasefire line into its state border.

Even earlier the Israeli authorities had given permission to numerous groups of Israeli settlers to settle on occupied Arab lands, including the west bank of the River Jordan. Military settlements of so-called farmers-soldiers are being set up. The Arabs are being driven away from the lands taken over by Israeli settlers and their property seized or destroyed.

The number of Arab refugees is growing with every day. Israel is carrying out this policy of driving the Arab population out of Israeli-occupied territories in order to prepare conditions for annexing and colonising these lands.

Notwithstanding the unanimous decision of the United Nations General Assembly, Israel is continuing its acts of conquest against the Arab part of Jerusalem.

Israel, which has the support of the United States Government and international Zionism, by its present actions is seeking to delay as long as possible a political settlement in the Middle East, to impose its imperialist terms on the Arabs, to force them to surrender and to renounce their right to the territories they own. In this the Israeli leaders make use of the fact that their patron – the United States – is itself appearing in the role of an aggressor in Vietnam, of a state crudely flouting the principles of the United Nations Charter and of international agreements. Both in the Middle East and in Vietnam we see an attempt by aggressive imperialist forces to strike a blow at the national-liberation movement and its advanced detachments.

The colonialist policy of Israel and the forces of world reaction backing it gives rise to the present dangerous international tensions. As a result of this policy the Suez Canal, this major international waterway, has been closed for more than nine months now, inflicting considerable economic damage to states whose ships use it, to international trade in general.

Displaying goodwill, the Government of the United Arab Republic expressed its readiness to bring out of the canal zone ships trapped there as a result of Israel's aggression and to start preparatory work on clearing the canal so that it could be reopened to shipping as soon as possible. The Israeli authorities resorted to armed provocations and prevented this.

Consequences must ensue from Israel's continuing aggressive line. By adopting on November 22, 1967, its resolution on the Middle East, the Security Council set the states a clear task – to achieve a withdrawal of Israeli troops from all captured Arab territories and to take other measures necessary to achieve the speediest political settlement of that area's problems: The principle of 'the inadmissibility of the acquisition of territory by war' and the demand for 'the withdrawal of Israeli armed forces from territories occupied in the recent conflict' are given prominence in the resolution and are the main and imperative condition for the restoration of peace in the Middle East. Only on this basis can the recognised borders of states in the area be safely secured.

The Security Council's resolution on the Middle East is not a recommendation or an opinion that governments are free to follow or ignore. On joining the United Nations Organisation every state undertook without fail to fulfil all decisions of the Security Council adopted in accordance with the United Nations Charter. Not to fulfil these obligations means to oppose the United Nations Organisation, to challenge this organisation whose purpose is to maintain international peace.

The Arab states, which suffered most from the Israeli aggression, have officially informed the United Nations Organisation of their readiness to fulfil the resolution of the Security Council dated November 22, 1967, and to cooperate with the Secretary-General's envoy in the Middle East empowered to facilitate the implementation of this resolution.

Israel, on the other hand, has from the start pursued a line of obstructing the decisions of the Security Council and General Assembly on the Middle East. In its adventurism Israel has gone so far as to react to the appeals of the United Nations' member-states that the Organisation's principles and the decision of the Security Council be respected, with arrogant territorial claims against the Arab states, threatening them with new acts of aggression and resorting to the use of armed force.

The Israeli Government has been hindering in every way the activities of the United Nations Secretary-General's special envoy in the Middle East, Jarring, whose task it is to find the shortest way to a political settlement of the conflict on the basis of the decision of the Security Council, the United Nations General Assembly and its Charter. Israel would like to use Jarring's mission to distort the meaning of the Security Council's decision. Never by a single word voicing its readiness to withdraw troops from all Arab territories occupied during the recent conflict, that is, to withdraw them to the positions they held before June 5, 1967. Israel and those backing it, are trying to force the Arab countries to begin talks on conditions that are incompatible with their lawful national interests, with their sovereignty, and are trying to delude world public opinion.

Israel is following in the footsteps of the Hitlerite criminals. It will be recalled that fascist Germany also captured foreign territories and then tried to dictate to the victim of the aggression her own terms of 'settlement'. But such actions were branded by the peoples as banditry, while those who tried to apply them were condemned after the rout of Hitler's Reich as international criminals. Those who today covet the lands of others and want to interfere in the domestic affairs of states would do well to remember this.

The Soviet Union firmly declares its determination to press along with other peace-loving states, for an end to the Israeli aggression and the liquidation of all its aftermaths, for the return of all territories captured from the Arab states as a result of the aggression of 1967 to their legitimate owners, and for the achievement of the necessary political settlement in the Middle East on the basis of respect for the sovereignty, territorial integrity and political independence of every state in the area.

The Israeli Government must unreservedly comply with the November 22, 1967 resolution of the Security Council and first of all withdraw its troops from all occupied Arab territories. It should know that Israel's challenge to the interests of international peace and security through its torpedoing of the cause of a political settlement in the Middle East cannot go unpunished.

As long as Israel's leaders, who have outside support, stand on positions of annexing Arab territories, the USSR and other countries – friends of the Arab states, champions of a stable peace in the Middle East, will help the victims of aggression because thereby they are fulfilling their duty in accordance with the United Nations Charter and the interests of maintaining peace. This must become clear to everybody.

Pravda, March 23, 1968; *Moscow News*, March 30, 1968.

14

K. Ivanov: *Israel, Zionism, and International Imperialism*

It is becoming more and more apparent that Israel is a predatory imperialist state. Those who until June 1967, believed that the existence of the state of Israel was threatened by its Arab neighbours have had their eyes opened by recent events.

This last year has also dispelled various illusions about the Israeli state as a haven for Jews flocking to Mount Zion to realise the principles of the Old Testament.

The fall of Israel and its betrayal of social progress stem from the vices of imperialism, and it is becoming clearer and clearer that imperialism is the course on which Israel is set. The architects of the domestic and foreign policy of this small state have been trampling more and more often the rules of the comity of nations, and this disgraceful defiance of the rest of the world is the root of the calamities that have befallen Israel's neighbours and bodes ill for the Israelis themselves.

I

It is six months since Gunnar Jarring, special representative of the UN

Secretary-General, undertook his mission which involved finding a political settlement in the Middle East according to the Security Council resolution of November 22, 1967. The resolution speaks of the need for an unconditional withdrawal of Israeli troops from the occupied Arab territories, putting an end to the state of war, and recognition of the right to independent national existence within secure and recognised borders for all states in the Middle East.

Here is the situation as it appears from the reports of the world press. The U.A.R., Jordan and other Arab states whose interests are most affected by the crisis told Jarring of their readiness to fulfil the Security Council's resolution. The Israeli Government is unwilling to make such a statement, claiming that the resolution only indicates the questions on which talks between Israel and the Arab states should be conducted. The men in Tel Aviv have been especially careful to avoid any statements admitting the necessity of a withdrawal from the Arab territories.

Israeli statesmen, both 'hawks' and 'doves', have been vying with each other in saying that Israel will not withdraw from the occupied territories and will not abandon what it has won at the price of blood. Plans for the establishment of a 'greater Israel' are being strenuously advertised at home and abroad and are becoming an official policy of the Israeli state.

As early as June 11, 1967, Israel's Defence Minister Moshe Dayan declared in a radio and television interview that Israel had no intention of returning the Gaza strip to Egypt or the western bank of the Jordan to Jordan. A fortnight later, he urged that Israel should dig its claws into the areas it had occupied. In early September 1967, Prime Minister Eshkol declared that 'no better natural border can be found between Israel and the U.A.R. than the Suez Canal'. At about the same time, Minister of Transport Carmel brazenly asserted that the River Jordan must become a 'natural boundary' with Jordan.

At a congress of the Rafi party in December 1967, Moshe Dayan discussed the question of those Israelis who wanted to set up a 'greater Israel' to include the Gaza strip and the western bank of the River Jordan. He said that 'to reject this urge would mean ignoring the basis of the return to Zion'. A month later, in an unconcealed effort to blackmail the Arab countries, he said that, unless the latter accepted Israel's terms, Israel would have to remain where it was.

In the atmosphere of epidemic war hysteria in Israel, generally accepted concepts are turned inside out. For instance, there are organisations opposing 'territorial concessions by Israel as the price for peace' (the withdrawal of the occupation forces from foreign territory is called 'territorial concessions' by Israel). It is claimed that 'Israel has more right to the western bank of the River Jordan than the Jordanian Hashimite Kingdom'. Wild crowds at a meeting chaired by Rabbi Frenkel, shouted:

'Not a foot of our native soil'. Minister of Information I. Galili declares that 'talk of giving up the territories occupied in the recent war does not promote peace'. Organisations of the Movement for a Greater Israel are clamouring against a return of 'the territories, including Israel's Biblical lands and territories won during the Six Day War'.

What is more important, however, is that these irresponsible statements are backed up by the actions of the Israeli authorities. At the end of February, the Israeli Ministry of the Interior issued an order which provoked a wide international reaction: Israeli law was declared to apply to the occupied Arab territories. It was officially announced that these were no longer enemy territories, that restrictions on the entry of Israeli citizens and foreign tourists were to be lifted, as were customs and other barriers. Earlier it had been announced that the authorities were giving permission for Israeli settlements to be set up on the occupied Arab territories. The expulsion of Arabs from these lands and the destruction of their homes are continuing.

.   .   .

Israel's actions are openly aimed against the interests of the Arab people and of all the other peoples of the world. In January, for instance, the Israeli military authorities demonstratively prevented the release of foreign ships stranded in the Suez Canal. By hampering the creation of conditions for a resumption of shipping through the Suez Canal, Israel has inflicted substantial material damage on the countries of Europe, Asia and East Africa who normally make great use of the canal. Incidentally, this is doing the United States a good turn, for, in contrast to Britain, France, Italy or India, the United States stands to gain from keeping the canal closed, as this gives American shipping companies vast super-profits.

Israel's ruling clique appears to have no desire for a settlement at all. In mid-March, when the Jarring mission was making some headway, Tel Aviv launched provocative military operations against Jordan to nip any settlement in the bud and to throw up as many insurmountable obstacles as possible. In the course of this carefully timed aggression, the Israeli troops inflicted serious damage on several Jordanian villages, especially Karameh, Dahal and Safi. After a 15-hour battle, in which the Israelis suffered considerable losses and met with resistance from the Jordanian army, the Israeli forces pulled back to the other side of the Jordan.

The Israeli warmongers were not sobered by the angry reaction of world opinion, and in the following few weeks launched a number of armed attacks on Jordanian territory, grossly violating Security Council decisions to end military operations. The Tel Aviv adventurists tried to justify their piratical attacks by referring to their alleged right to launch punitive operations against Jordan and Syria as reprisals for the activity of El Fatah guerrilla detachments in the occupied territories.

All these facts clearly indicate the intention of Israeli ruling circles to annex the Arab lands. However, an absolute majority of countries have resolutely condemned in one form or other any territorial changes in the Middle East and the establishment of an intolerable precedent there in the seizure of foreign territories by armed force. The Security Council resolution of November 22, 1967, likewise said that annexations were inadmissible. The fearless militarists at Mount Zion pretend that they do not care and that Israel can ignore with more or less complete impunity the mandatory decisions of the Security Council and flout world opinion. This brazen extremist policy is capable of dealing a blow at the very foundations of the United Nations, and its authority and prestige. At present, Israel, the Portuguese colonialists and the South African racialists constitute a little group of states in the United Nations who ignore the rules of international law, the comity of nations and the decisions of high and authoritative international organisations.

With the support of the U.S.A., Israel has in fact made a bid at becoming an outright colonialist power. Prominent politicians in Tel Aviv have been making wild statements to the effect that they refuse to give up the territories they have won and that it would be absurd and dangerous to withdraw their troops from their present positions. There are some kinds of people in Western Europe who applaud these wild speeches. But the strange thing is that Israel has been clearly setting its mind on open campaigns of aggrandisement at a time when even the major imperialist powers – the U.S.A., Britain and West Germany – have not dared advertise their neocolonialist policy or risk any head-on collisions with the world of emergent nations in the former colonies and dependent countries.

.   .   .

The sorry politicians and strategists at Mount Zion, dazzled by their temporary and illusory victories and their imaginary right to sow death and attack their Arab neighbours, apparently refuse to see that they are taking their country into a current of events so tempestuous that they will be unable to anticipate them, or even survive.

Statesmen who are incapable of anticipating events for more than a few months ahead do not deserve the confidence of the people. Nations who entrust their future to such leaders are inviting a lot of trouble. Tel Aviv's ruling circles refuse to see that the current conflict between Israel and the Arab states is not purely regional, but has features which determine the arrangement of forces throughout the world. In this day and age of the collapse of the shameful colonial system, the question is how the contradictions of the modern world will be finally unravelled.

Support for the just liberation struggle of the peoples has become an international duty of the Socialist countries and of all the anti-imperialist forces. No person, whatever his nationality, creed, or ideology, can be indifferent to the fate of more than one-half of mankind, if he has ever given serious thought to the future and to world progress. Declarations about the equality of nations and human rights, unless backed up by direct, constant and effective support for the anti-imperialist liberation struggle of the oppressed peoples, are empty words.

Twenty years ago, when Israel was emerging to statehood and the colonial system of imperialism was falling apart, her banners bore the slogans of die-hard imperialism, with the sole difference that they were written in Hebrew. A bourgeois diplomat, in no sense a supporter of the progressive Nasser regime or of the present Syrian Government, made this just comment: 'We no longer know whether Israel is trying to guarantee its right to existence or its right to expansion.' The answer is contained in the question itself: the right to expansion is what the zealous Tel Aviv over-ambitious successors to the conquistadores are trying to reserve themselves.

It would be naive to assume that Israeli ruling circles lack political sense. Realising its possibilities, Tel Aviv decided on an expansionist policy against the neighbouring states, with the most active support of the imperialist circles of the West, and, you might say, in the same drive against the national-liberation movement of the peoples of Asia, Africa and Latin America. Imperialism and international Zionism are brothers and confederates, and their alliance implies a division of labour. Israel has become a military and political battering ram of the most aggressive forces of international imperialism in the Middle East, while Zionist organisations in various countries, helped by U.S. ruling circles, have become active in favour of Tel Aviv, providing it with credits, armaments, diplomatic and propaganda support, resorting to threats, blackmail and downright misinformation.

Back in May 1944, *The New York Times* said very plainly that the future of Palestine should be determined with an eye to America's oil and military interests. In 1956, Israel was a puppet of the imperialist states which started aggression against Egypt, and it is still playing that role. But this is only a part of the truth about Israel. The rest is that, in the brief period of its existence, the state of Israel has gone the full circle and has itself become an imperialist state.

. . .

In November 1957, the Indian weekly *Blitz* published secret material of the Israeli General Staff on plans to set up a 'Greater Israel' from the Euphrates to the Nile. The document, 'Strategic Plan of the Israeli Army for 1956–1957', was drawn up before the Suez crisis. Israel's General Staff set out all the grounds for a 'preventive war' by Israel against the Arab states in order to change the overall situation in the Middle East.[1] The plan was for Israel to occupy the Gaza area and the Sinai Peninsula and to reach the Suez Canal, to seize extensive territories in Jordan, Lebanon and Syria, up to the borders of Iraq and Saudi Arabia; it was also planned to change the borders of the existing Arab states.

Official Israeli circles hastened to deny the report in the Indian weekly, but current official propaganda and – what is even more important – Israel's actions and attempts to keep its troops in the occupied Arab lands, show that the denial was no more than a smokescreen.

The defeat of the tripartite aggression failed to sober up the Tel Aviv politicians. They slid further and further into union with the most aggressive forces of modern imperialism. There was a steady growth of their appetite and impudence and of their undisguised racialism towards the Arab peoples.

In *The Merchant of Venice* we find the following passage: 'Hath not a Jew eyes? Hath not a Jew hands, organs, dimensions, senses, affections, passions? Fed with the same food, hurt with the same weapons, subject to the same diseases, healed by the same means, warmed and cooled by the same winter and summer, as a Christian is?'

These same questions can now be put to the Tel Aviv politicians and nationalists who are displaying a racialist arrogance towards the peoples of Asia, Africa and Latin America, and to the 100 million Arabs above all.

Theirs is indeed a short-sighted policy, backward-looking and orientated towards the forces of evil and reaction.

II

The right to expansion, which the influential Israeli politicians are now trying to secure, is one of the aspects of the imperialist policy of their state, which has openly proclaimed its adherence to the West. There are facts, and they are only far too numerous, showing that Israeli ruling circles do not regard the future of their country otherwise than as the main hotbed of war in the Middle East, presenting as great a menace as West Germany does in Europe. This historical parallel is warranted by the loyal service given by both these states – the F.R.G. and Israel – to U.S. strategic aims. It can be said that the F.R.G. and Israel have become (each in its own area) the mainstay of the policy of aggressive U.S. imperialism.

---

[1] For the full text see K. Ivanov and Z. Schienis: *Gosudarstvo Israil.* Political Literature Publishers, Moscow, 1958, pp. 38–48.

The Soviet Government's statement of March 22 designates Israel as an imperialist state, and that was no slip of the tongue, but a precise definition based on Israel's actual economic and political development.

The tone in Israel's domestic life is set by big capitalist monopolies – international and local – and it will be recalled that the sway of monopoly capitalism is the essence of imperialism. Real power in Israel belongs to big financial capital – local and foreign. This power has been growing steadily.

. . .

Israel's rulers are in no way discountenanced by the fact that they are closely collaborating with revenge-seeking West Germany, whose leaders have laid virtually official claim to being the successors of the bosses of Nazi Germany, the men guilty of torturing and murdering millions of people, including 6 million Jews.

As Israeli ruling circles carried forward their collaboration with international imperialism, they engaged in the most unbridled racialism in respect of the Arab minority, whose condition has been worsened by the intolerance of Judaism towards Mohammedanism and Christianity, the religions of the Arab section of the population in Israel and the occupied areas. Wild chauvinist and Zionist propaganda, the fanning of war hysteria, and hostility and hatred for the Arabs are all weapons the Israeli ruling circles have borrowed from the Nazi arsenal.

In Israel, racial discrimination is practised not only against the Arabs, but also against Jews from the African and Asian countries. The immigrants from the European countries and the United States have a privileged position, and it is they who control the levers of economic and political power in the country. In Israel, national oppression is the direct outcome of class and social oppression.

As any other imperialist state, Israel has its exploiters and exploited working masses. The Soviet people's sympathies are on the side of the working people, who are downtrodden (this applies especially to those who come from Asia and Africa) and whose awareness in many cases is dimmed and poisoned by the current chauvinistic and military propaganda. The fact that the majority of the population allow themselves to be used as an instrument of the chauvinist imperialist policy of the ruling classes – as was the case in Germany under Hitler – is certainly not to the Israelis' credit.

But there are healthy forces in Israel. They are headed by the Communist Party and led by Wilner and Tubi, two courageous men. The Party stands firmly on internationalism and the struggle against imperialism, in the face of terror and persecution by the government and the nationalistic reactionary parties.

A resolution adopted by the 13th Plenary Meeting of the Israeli Communist Party's Central Committee, 'In Defence of Peace and Democratic Freedoms' (*Zu Hadereh*, December 21, 1966), says: 'The experience gained in the 18 years of the Israeli state shows that the traditional Israeli policy merely serves to isolate Israel in the international arena and puts off peace with the Arab countries.

'The Central Committee of the Communist Party of Israel is profoundly convinced that there is a way out of the crisis and of Israel's isolation, towards mutual understanding with the Arab peoples and the much desired peace. The way lies through changing official policy – repudiation by the Israeli Government of participation in the imperialist plans aimed against the Arab peoples and of interference in the historical struggle of the Arab peoples against Arab reaction and imperialism for their national and social emancipation. It lies in the readiness of the Israeli Government to recognise the legitimate rights of the Arabs in Palestine, above all the right of Arab refugees to choose between returning home and receiving compensation. Such a policy would change Israel's whole position in the area, help to create a different atmosphere in Israeli-Arab relations, pave the way for talks and Arab recognition of the state of Israel and its legitimate rights, and lead to a fair and peaceful settlement of the problem on the basis of mutual recognition of the national rights of both peoples.'

III

The ideological exposure and defeat of Zionism as a political trend acquires considerable importance today for the international working-class movement and for all progressive and peaceloving forces in the world. Back in 1903, Lenin emphasised that 'the Zionist idea is absolutely false and essentially reactionary'.[1] It took organisational and ideological shape at the end of the 19th century among bourgeois Jewish leaders in Germany, Austria and Russia, and later in France and the U.S.A.

From the outset, Zionism operated as an avowed and implacable enemy of Marxism and the international working-class movement. Zionism is based on principles contradictory to Marxism. Its aim is incredibly narrow. It is to 'gather' the Jews in the 'promised land', namely, Israel, which, according to the canons of the ancient Judaic religion, will have neither social nor political inequality. Instead of irreconcilable class struggle against the bourgeoisie and the landowners, the Zionists preach the unity of all classes inside a sort of class-free and supra-class Jewish community; instead of overthrowing the power of the bourgeoisie and establishing the dictatorship of the working class, they establish ties and collaborate with the most reactionary groups of exploiters,

[1] V. I. Lenin, *Collected Works*, Vol. 7, Moscow, 1961, p. 99.

who for various reasons support the immigration of Jews to Palestine.

The history of Zionism proudly boasts of the meetings which Zionist leaders had before the First World War with the Turkish sultan, who oppressed the Arabs, and representatives of the tsarist government, which staged Jewish pogroms. The cases of Kastner, Nossig and other Zionist leaders revealed that during the Second World War they even had ties with the Hitlerite authorities.

Instead of calling on the working people of all nations and nationalities to join in their common international struggle against imperialism and colonialism, the Zionist leaders preach rabid nationalism and spread the idea that it is not the business of the Jews to fight against national and colonial oppression and exploitation of man by man, but that the Jewish working people should isolate themselves from the working people of other nations, establish a 'class peace' with the big Jewish bourgeoisie, and unite round the only Jewish state, whose name is Israel.

Marxism and Zionism are irreconcilably hostile to each other. The former stands for Socialism and internationalism, the latter for imperialism and narrow-minded Jewish bourgeois nationalism. That is exactly how proletarian revolutionaries, including those of the Jewish working people, have always regarded Zionism. There has always been a sharp principled struggle between these hostile socio-political trends.

However, Zionism cannot be regarded statically, because it evolves. It would be wrong to ignore the great metamorphosis Zionism has undergone since becoming the ideological and political banner of Israel. Zionism has passed through the logical stages of development from the petty-bourgeois, anti-Marxist nationalistic groups of the Bund, which after the October Revolution slid down to the positions of the counter-revolution, through the patently nationalistic Zionist organisations, which even contacted with the Hitlerites in the years of the 'brown plague', to the present pirate bands of Moshe Dayan, committing bloody atrocities in the occupied Arab territories.

It is no accident that Zionism has nestled in the seats of die-hard reactionary, colonialist and big business monopoly capital in the U.S.A., Britain and West Germany. The tasks of international Zionism, which at many points of practical activity links up with the intelligence and subversive organisations of the imperialist powers, are now very clearly expressed: they are to use Jewish bourgeois nationalism in the interests of imperialism and neocolonialism.

Zionist leaders are trying to instil into the minds of Jews in various countries, including the Socialist countries, that they have a 'dual citizenship' – one, a secondary one, in the country of actual domicile, and the other, the basic, spiritual and religious one, in Israel. Those were the very tricks used by the leaders of the Third Reich in the interests of German imperialism. In this way the Nazis set up their 'fifth column' in other countries, and in the same way modern Zionism tries to secure international support for Israel and its aggressive expansionist policy.

Only people who are politically blind can fail to see the danger lurking in this concept of 'dual citizenship'. The imperialist intelligence services and psychological warfare agencies have been spending hundreds of millions of dollars to subvert and corrupt the international working class and anti-imperialist movement as a whole, and especially the fraternal militant community of the Socialist countries. In this context, the 'dual citizenship' concept and the 'bridge-building' policy are two sides of ideological and political subversion and indirect aggression designed for the ultimate restoration of capitalism.

. . .

The Soviet people are also well aware of the lying methods used by the Zionist imperialist agents who are trying to depict the exposure and prosecution of Zionism as a sign of anti-Semitism. From year to year, centres of psychological warfare against Socialism in New York and Tel Aviv have been spreading slander about an imaginary persecution of Jews in the Soviet Union. They call their malicious and shameless lies 'freedom of speech'.

However, everyone knows that it was the Soviet Army that, by its incomparable feats of arms in the Second World War, rescued the peoples of Europe, including the Jewish people, from fascist slavery and destruction. The Nazi plans for a 'new order' in Europe provided for the successive destruction of a number of peoples and nationalities, with the Jews near the top of the list. The victory of Socialism in a number of countries of Europe and the liquidation of their exploiting classes upset the plans of the imperialist cannibals and led to the establishment of truly equitable relations between nations and peoples in the Socialist countries.

But it would be dangerous to assume that Hitlerism and its attendant atrocities were some sort of freak of history. Indeed, they were not. Look at Viet-Nam and the ruins of the Negro districts in American cities, recall the murder of Martin Luther King and the assassination of President Kennedy, read the newspaper reports of Israel's policy towards the Arabs and you will realise that Hitlerism was no accident. It was the outcome and product of the organic and regular features of imperialism. It can happen again.

Like many European nations, the Jews suffered terribly from this imperialist barbarity. But imperialism has a stranglehold on men regardless of nationality. Hitlerism was not only an expression of the qualities of a German nation stupefied. It was an example of aggressive imperialism as such. In Israel the once persecuted have themselves become avid persecutors and villains. They applaud the current crimes of imperialism. There is a good reason for this: Zionism has made a close alliance with the most reactionary and aggressive force in the world today – U.S. imperialism.

The crisis in Israel's imperialist policy, the crisis in modern Zionism is closely bound up with that period of world history when the movement for the liberation of the oppressed nations and nationalities in Europe and for their equality went beyond Europe and became a world-wide movement. The colonial oppression of the countries of Asia, Africa and Latin America is essentially the same thing as Hitlerism, but organised on a world-wide scale by international imperialism. And when the question arose of liberating all nations oppressed by imperialism from every form of colonialism and neocolonialism, the Zionists and the rulers of imperialist Israel found themselves on the other side of the barricade, in the ranks of the enemies of Socialism and progress. The old ties of Jewish financiers and Zionist leaders with big monopoly capital, with the Rothschilds and Kuhn-Loebs, completed the vicious circle.

Marxists differ from bourgeois nationalist leaders in that they regard social phenomena from the class positions of the militant proletariat. From the history of the liberation struggle in Europe we know that the fine fighters against the 'brown plague' included the best sons of the Jewish people, who were profoundly hostile to imperialism and bourgeois nationalism. But how was it that some Jewish working people, whose objective interests cannot possibly lie in the same plane with those of the big profiteers and businessmen, found themselves accepting colonialist and imperialist ideas?

One of the reasons is the absence of a militant and offensive line against Zionism in all its manifestations among the organisations of working people of which Jews are also members. Another reason is the obvious shortcomings in the ideological work and internationalist education of the working people, including the Jews, and in the fact that tolerance was shown to those who were susceptible to bourgeois and Zionist influence. It is the presence of such defects that can alone explain the international response which is given in some sections of Jewish working intellectuals to the false slogans of U.S. and Israeli imperialism. Those appear to be the chinks through which the enemy is trying to penetrate.

IV

The Soviet people take a consistently Leninist and internationalist stand against aggressive imperialist policy and bellicose Zionism and make a clear-cut distinction between the struggle against all types of nationalism,

Zionism and great-power chauvinism, and the struggle for complete national equality and fraternal cooperation of all nations and nationalities in the Soviet Union, including, of course, the Jews. The struggle against Zionism in the ideology and policy of Leninism is organically and indissolubly bound up with the struggle against anti-Semitism, a product of the self-same bourgeois society.

Characterising that disgraceful social phenomenon of the imperialist system – anti-Semitism – Lenin said the capitalists are 'fomenting hatred against the Jews in order to blind the workers, to divert their attention from the real enemy of the working people, capital. Hatred towards the Jews persists only in those countries where slavery to the landowners and capitalists has created abysmal ignorance among the workers and peasants. . . . The enemies of the workers are the capitalists of all countries. Among the Jews there are working people, and they form the majority. They are our brothers, who, like us, are oppressed by capital; they are our comrades in the struggle for Socialism. Among the Jews there are kulaks, exploiters and capitalists, just as there are among the Russians, and among people of all nations. The capitalists strive to sow and foment hatred between workers of different faiths, different nations and different races. Those who do not work are kept in power by the power and strength of capital. Rich Jews, like rich Russians, and the rich in all countries, are in alliance to oppress, crush, rob and disunite the workers.'[1]

In one of his well-known works called 'On the National Pride of the Great Russians',[2] Lenin wrote that it was wrong for Socialists to ignore the immense importance of the national question. It is especially important to remember this today, in this age when the national-liberation anti-imperialist movements are mounting and Socialism has triumphed in one-third of the globe. Today, when a great number of nations, big and small, are awakening to life, when so many of them are laying the foundations of a new, Socialist system, it would be an unpardonable error for politicians to forget about their national feelings and their national pride.

The Soviet people take pride in the fact that they were the first in history to break through the chain of world imperialism and carry out the Great October Socialist Revolution, that in conditions of tremendous privation and fierce class struggle they defended and built Socialism, and are now marching in a broad front towards Communism. Lenin wrote: 'The interests of the Great Russians' national pride (understood not in the slavish sense) coincide with the *Socialist* interests of the Great-Russian (and all other) proletarians.'

The same can and must be said about the national pride of all other nations and nationalities of the Soviet Union, including, of course, the

---

[1] V. I. Lenin, *Collected Works*, Vol. 29, Moscow, 1965, pp. 252–3.
[2] V. I. Lenin, *Collected Works*, Vol. 21, Moscow, 1964, pp. 102–6.

Jews. Today, it is no longer the awareness of a vanguard alone, but of the overwhelming majority of working people in Socialist society, of all nations and nationalities in this great multi-national country of ours.

After my article in *Pravda* on September 24, 1967, called 'The Shame of Israel', I received a curious letter, which was unsigned, but of a clearly Zionist content, which tried to justify Israel's aggression. The letter ended with these words: 'Well, go on marching along the road of anti-Semitism, if you have no other.'

There is a lot of malice in these words but not a bit of reason. The author of this anonymous letter may perhaps fail to realise that Zionism and anti-Semitism are the products of one and the same bourgeois social system, that they are not antipodes, but twins born of the same womb. Both these phenomena are deeply hostile to Leninism and the Soviet system.

It is quite possible that our angry opponent, who may well hail directly from abroad (this is quite common nowadays), really fails to understand that the vast majority of Soviet Jews unite with the Soviet people in unconditionally condemning the piratical policy of the imperialist state of Israel.

In the 50 years since the October Revolution, not only nations, but nationalities as well, have undergone profound and all-round Socialist transformation. Honest Soviet people of Jewish nationality have become men and women of Socialist nationality; they are as profoundly instilled with the spirit of Socialism and internationalism in foreign relations as are people of all other fraternal nations and nationalities inhabiting the great, victorious and powerful Socialist Soviet Union. For the exploiting classes (and this applies to *all* nations and nationalities in this country) have been eliminated in the U.S.S.R. once and for all, the bourgeois mode of production has been supplanted by its opposite, the Socialist mode of production, and social ideals, which are quite different from those in the U.S.A., Israel or in tsarist Russia, have triumphed in every sphere of life. That is *the essence* of the Socialist transformation of all nations and nationalities which has taken place in this country in the 50 years of Soviet power. And that is also a source of the Soviet people's sense of legitimate pride and moral superiority.

International Affairs, June 1968.

15

Akhmad Chagouri: *'Baathist Crimes in Syria'*

Since their advent to power in Syria the Right-wing Baath have pursued an anti-popular policy. Enjoying no support among the people they maintain themselves in power through terror and repression. Dozens of patriots are held in prison. Many public personalities of varying political views, undesirables in the eyes of the government, are arbitrarily denied civil rights. Among them are Khaled Bagdash, General Secretary of the Communist Party, Akram Hourani, former leader of the Left wing in the Baath Party, Afif Bizri, former Chief of the General Staff, and many others.

Only recently the Baath committed yet another heinous crime. On January 28 the police agents arrested Abdel Kader Ykhwann, member of the regional committee of the Communist Party in Homs. Ykhwann died under torture. Seeking to cover up their crime, the murderers secretly buried their victim during the night.

The murder evoked indignation both in Syria and abroad. People everywhere protested: demonstrations were held all over the country, demanding that the culprits be brought to trial. The pressure was such that Prime Minister Amin Hafez had to instruct the Attorney-General to investigate the case, to tell the people the truth about the crime and call to account those guilty. The Minister of the Interior, who went especially to Homs to calm the population, was compelled to denounce the murder, qualifying it as a 'criminal offense'.

Subsequent developments showed, however, that the government's 'denunciations' were not worth much, for a few days later the Baath arrested in Latakia another progressive leader, Akhmed al-Fadel, who likewise was subjected to savage torture.

The Baath crimes expose the true nature of their rule, established behind the screen of the demagogic slogans of 'unity', 'freedom' and 'socialism'.

Right from the outset the Syrian Communists pointed out that the Baath rule would not solve the social and political problems confronting the country.

The coup d'état of March 8, 1963, which brought the Baath Party to power, was the result of a series of conspiracies engineered by the imperialists and home reactionaries who dreaded the spread of the democratic movement and the prospect of a powerful alliance of all the national forces.

The Baath Party is acting, through its Right (Aflak) wing, on direct orders from the imperialists and the jingo elements. Its main slogan is anti-communism. Baath, a hotch-potch of heterogeneous trends and currents, cannot be a consistent exponent of the popular will and lawful demands of the masses; this is borne out by the contradictory nature of the laws and decrees adopted under the Baath rule: those of them which are of a democratic character still remain on paper.

Posing as socialists, the Right-wing Baathists raised a hullabaloo over the relatively progressive amendments to the agrarian reform law. In actual fact, however, they not only refused to go further with the agrarian reform, but enabled the feudal lords to recover the land already given to the peasants. Thus, Dkham al Khadi – the biggest feudal bey – was encouraged to evict the peasants from the land they had been given under the Reform and to make short shrift of those who refused to obey.

The new trade union law is anything but democratic. Trade unionists in Damascus and Haleb addressed letters to the authorities demanding the repeal of the law. Its undemocratic character can be seen in that it entitles the authorities to interfere in the affairs of the unions. Point 3 of Clause 2 of the law says: 'Industries in which the workers can organize shall be defined by a decree.' Point 2 of the same clause forbids the workers employed in the defense industry to be members of a trade union. Courts shall have the right to dissolve the unions.

It is not only workers and peasants but the entire people who are affected by encroachments on democratic rights. Freedom of the press applies only to Baath publications. Intellectuals and office employees who are not members of the Baath are dismissed and replaced by Baath men.

Discrimination is practised against the Syrian Kurds. Blinded by nationalism, the Syrian rulers placed at the disposal of the Iraqi Baathists (then still in power) a regiment for operations against the Kurds.

The Syrian Communists have resolutely opposed the anti-national policy of the Right-wing Baathists who ignored the demands of the people for social and economic reforms and gave a free hand to the imperialists conspiring in Syria.

Pretending that they want order in the economy, the Baath widely publicized their new economic measures connected with the foreign-exchange policy. What is actually meant is establishing a foreign-exchange market parallel to government control over foreign currency. This is a concession not only to the home capitalists but also to the neo-colonialists. The newspaper *L'economie Arabe* made it clear that the issue of new foreign-exchange legislation was raised by the West German government during unofficial talks with the Baath.

Summing up the results of a year of Baath rule in Syria, it can be said that it has led on the one hand to unemployment and a rising cost of living, to a freezing of the agrarian reform law and disruption of economic life and, on the other, it has discredited the idea of socialism which in the Baath version is nothing but anarchy, economic crisis and constant retreat before the feudalists and the big bourgeoisie.

This policy has led to the isolation of the Baath Party and to a rise of the popular struggle for the overthrow of the regime. On their part, the imperialists and the home reactionaries, realizing that Baath rule is nearing its end, have stepped up their conspiratorial activity with a view to preventing the replacement of the regime with a democratic government.

The Syrian Communists declare that it is more urgent than ever for patriots and democrats, regardless of their political views and religious beliefs, to unite against the danger with which the country is threatened as a result of the policy of the Right-wing Baathists and the conspiracies of the imperialists. The Communist Party maintains that only an alliance of all the national and democratic forces in the framework of a united people's front can ensure Syria a national-democratic regime, stabilize the situation in the country and take it along the road of progress.

World Marxist Review, May 1964.

16

Khalid Bakdash: *The National Liberation Movement and the Communists*

We older communists who had the good fortune to attend the Seventh Congress of the Communist International have unforgettable memories of that occasion. Dealing a smashing blow at sectarianism and orienting the Communists on the struggle for the unity of the working class and of all democratic forces against fascism and the danger of war, on the unity of all patriotic forces in the struggle against imperialism, it was truly a historical turning point.

Although the situation today bears little semblance to that of thirty years ago, the decisions of the Seventh Congress have not lost their significance for Communist theory and practice.

The conditions differed from country to country, and each Party worked out its own tactics adapted to the national scene, but this did not prevent full agreement on a common strategy and common tactics for the entire international Communist movement. The unity of the movement was based not on coincidence of the tactics of the various parties but on complete identity of aims.

Today, when the question comes up of the relation between the tactics of the working-class and Communist parties in power in the socialist countries and the tactics of the proletariat and the Communist parties which still have to win power, we should bear in mind that this is no new issue, that it occupied a prominent place in the deliberations of the Seventh Congress. 'For us it is perfectly clear,' Togliatti said on this score in his report, 'that the aims of the Soviet Union's peace policy and the aims of the policy of the working class and the Communist parties of the capitalist countries are identical. There can be no doubt on this score in our ranks. We not only defend the Soviet Union in general, we concretely uphold the whole of its policy and each of its actions. But this identity of aims by no means signifies that at each given moment, in the course of each particular action and on all issues the tactics of the proletariat and the Communist parties which are still fighting to win power must wholly coincide with the concrete tactical steps taken by the Soviet proletariat and the CPSI (B) which already exercise power in the Soviet Union.'

Today there are two erroneous, and I would say, even dangerous, approaches to this question. The first ignores the specific position of the Soviet Union in the world arena as the main economic, political and military bastion of the socialist camp. The proponents of this view would like to see the tactics of the Soviet Union completely coincide with the tactics of every other Communist Party. More, they would subordinate the tactics of the Soviet Union and its entire foreign policy to the tactical requirements of the other Communist parties.

The second erroneous trend holds, on the contrary, that all the Communist parties should take exactly the same attitude as the Soviet Union and other socialist states towards the governments of the countries concerned. We have seen this view crop up in the case of some of the newly-free countries of Asia and Africa. The Soviet Union and the other socialist countries pursue a policy of alliance with these countries against imperialism and for peace and help them to achieve economic independence. But this does not mean that the Communist parties and the democratic forces generally in the latter must under all circumstances support their governments and renounce the fight for democratic freedoms, for the workers' and peasants' demands and against the negative aspects and deficiencies of their foreign policy.

Here one important point should be noted. The issue of democracy cannot be posed today as it was thirty years ago, when the Seventh Congress called for defending bourgeois democracy, or whatever remained of it, against the fascist offensive. Bourgeois democracy has suffered bankruptcy in many Asian and African countries. But this does not mean that just because some progressive measures have been carried out we should remain silent when workers and peasants and progressives generally are deprived of democratic rights. The Communists take a clear-cut class stand. They demand democratic rights, not for the feudal lords, the big bourgeoisie and other reactionaries, but for the fighters against imperialism and reaction, for social progress, and especially for the workers and peasants, for the Communists themselves, for all who truly believe in socialism and want to see its triumph in their native country.

If developments since the Seventh Congress have proved the soundness of its guidelines and decisions, this is above all because the Congress was guided not so much by emotion, or by transient, chance phenomena but because it defined its attitude towards the various strata of society, parties and individuals not on the basis of verbal declarations, official programs or any particular aspect of their policy, but on the basis of their class nature, on the basis of a profound examination of class interests. The Congress did not seek to justify a particular policy by artificially elevating a tactical position or tactical considerations to the eminence of universal theory; to have done so would have meant jettisoning the class approach and, consequently, sacrificing the basic principles of Marxism-Leninism.

Be the objective conditions in one or another country what they may, and no matter how weak numerically and poorly organized its working class, no other social group, no other class and no individual can take over the historical mission of the working class. A policy which does not take cognizance of this is doomed to fail. The only correct policy is that which sees the working class not only as it is today but which takes into account its quantitative and qualitative development in the future. This, of course, is not to say that the other classes and social groups as well as individual leaders play no role in the common struggle. Every social group and each class should be regarded in the light of the place they occupy in the objective process of social development.

Situations may arise when one or another social group or individual leader is carried to the fore on the tide of the struggle against fascism, imperialism, feudalism and, in some cases, also against the big bourgeoisie. When this happens the groups or individuals in question should be supported and an alliance formed with them. But we must be on guard against attempts to justify such alliances by spurious theories repudiating the role of the working class both now and in the future on the pretext of developing Marxism-Leninism to meet the new conditions.

The Seventh Congress, while putting forward the united front tactic, called for safeguarding the integrity of the Communist parties, preserving their independence and strengthening their ranks. Stressing the need for resolute effort to extirpate every survival of self-complacent sectarianism, Dimitrov warned against the dangers attendant upon any 'minimizing of the role of the Communist Party in the united front'.

We, too, are against sectarianism, and we do not consider it permissible to go so far as to deny the role of the Communist parties and to call for their dissolution. As a matter of fact, the whole point in combating sectarianism is to strengthen the Party. It is essential to underscore the fact that the call issued by the Seventh Congress to the Communist parties to preserve their identity and to carry on independent activities was addressed not only to the parties in the West but also to those in the colonies and semi-colonies. Is there anyone today who would venture to claim that experience has shown that proletarian parties have no place in the conditions prevailing in the newly-free African and Asian countries?

True, at the time of the Seventh Congress the national-liberation movement was a far cry from what it is today when in a number of countries the big bourgeoisie has suffered fiasco and leadership of the movement has passed over either to the working class and its Marxist-Leninist vanguard, or to nationalist elements from among the intelligentsia and military people representing the petty bourgeoisie who have effected important socio-economic changes. In order correctly to judge these groups and elements and to assess the nature and trend of the changes they have brought about it is imperative to adhere to the class approach by which the Seventh Congress was guided.

If an anti-imperialist, anti-feudal revolution which has not yet fully carried out its national-democratic tasks (for example, in the sphere of agrarian reform, inasmuch as big property has not been abolished, and in relation to imperialism, insofar as its grip has not been completely destroyed) embarks on measures transcending these tasks and begins to make inroads in the positions of the big bourgeoisie, does this warrant the conclusion that this is already a socialist revolution, or that the given country is moving towards socialism, regardless of the class nature of the governmental power and the existing system and irrespective of the role played by the working class and the masses generally?

Needless to say, only sectarians and dogmatists could argue that measures of this type carried out under other than proletarian leadership have little to do with socialism. At the same time there are no grounds for saying that they signify that the given country has taken the socialist way. To take this view would be tantamount to saying that the leading role in establishing socialism no longer belongs to the working class but has passed over to the nationalist groupings and the small bourgeoisie.

Some comrades believe that the far-reaching reforms taking place signify a change in the basis, and that this is bound to bring about corresponding modifications in the superstructure. This view underestimates or ignores the interrelation of basis and superstructure. The superstructure is not always subject only to the influence of the basis. On the contrary, international and domestic factors can cause sudden changes in the superstructure capable of influencing the basis.

We Syrian Communists hold that there is nothing to gain from hasty characterization of one or another form of development as socialism or in the direction of socialism without thorough examination of the nature of the prevailing relations of production and without taking into account the class nature of the governmental power and the social system. Experience shows that sudden changes in governments, in their composition and policy, can alter overnight the general trend of development and jeopardize whatever socio-economic changes have taken place.

Nationalization of enterprises owned by the big bourgeoisie in the newly-free countries is a progressive measure and as such should be supported, but it alone is not enough to judge of the nature of the particular system and its future prospects. Who will claim that socialism boils down only to nationalization and that the other socio-economic and political aspects of the life of society are of no consequence?

The nature of the state sector of the economy, its perspectives and future depend on the nature of the governmental power and the system. The Arab countries offer a multitude of examples bearing this out. For example, the Iraqi authorities nationalized some enterprises belonging to the big bourgeoisie, but what is this nationalization worth when the self-same rulers shelve the none too radical agrarian reform, grant benefits to the imperialist oil monopolies, hold thousands of Communists and democrats in prison, wage a dirty war against the Kurdish people, trample on elementary democratic rights, and give free reign to dyed-in-the-wool reactionaries, accomplices of Nuri Said, who are again returning to political posts in the government and the administration generally? Developments of this type threaten to make the nationalization meaningless. Our Iraqi comrades are calling for the overthrow of this regime and the Syrian Communist Party fully supports their stand.

The implementation of some deep-going socio-economic reforms is no justification for negating the role of the working class and its vanguard in safeguarding these reforms.

Socialism is indeed becoming the decisive factor in the development of human society. But the economic and political influence of imperialism has not yet been abolished.

The socialist world influences the development of human society generally, but this influence cannot take the place of the class forces destined to be the mainspring of social progress in the newly-free countries.

Yet there are those who say that the supporters of the so-called 'Arab', 'African' or 'Islamic' socialism will, eventually, discover that the only real socialism is scientific socialism. From this it would follow that the future of these countries depends on the extent to which the adherents of these credos become convinced of the correctness of scientific socialism.

But experience shows that this is not the case. The shaping of the future depends on the struggle between classes and on the outcome of this struggle.

We consider it essential always to underscore the class nature of state power because the petty bourgeois strata and groups generally, owing to their class nature and the numerous contradictory trends inherent in them, cannot carry economic and social changes to consummation, to consistent and radical socialist reconstruction. The experience of a number of newly-free countries and the changes in the positions of their governments show that this contains a constant threat not only to further progress but also to the achievements gained to date. The same cannot be said of the working class, which is destined, whatever its present status, to play the key role in the process of socialist reconstruction. Success in this reconstruction depends on the activity of the masses, above all of the working class, on the part they play in the life of society.

Agrarian reform and nationalization involve overcoming formidable objective difficulties of an economic, social and political order, as is the case in Algeria, the United Arab Republic, Syria and other countries. The machinery of state alone with its army and police cannot cope with these difficulties. Nor is the popularity of one or another leader enough, as events have shown. What is needed is an influential, authoritative revolutionary mass party enjoying the confidence of the people and hence able to rally the masses to overcome the difficulties and capable of correctly implementing reforms while effectively countering the machinations of the domestic reactionaries and foreign imperialists.

This is not to say that we Communists do not recognize the role of the other revolutionary forces advocating socialism. On the contrary, we call for the unity of all these forces in order to overcome the difficulties and to combat the intrigues of imperialism and the reactionaries at home. But this unity cannot be based on the disbandment of the Communist parties or their being dissolved in other parties.

The Syrian Communist Party holds that in order to overcome the difficulties and to rebuff the intrigues of the imperialists and domestic reactionaries it is necessary to achieve unity among all progressives – the Left Baathists, Arab socialists, independent socialists, Communists and all progressives – in a national united front or in some other form according with the conditions in our country.

The Communists are the standard-bearers of socialism. Nothing could be more absurd than the views adumbrated by those who say that with the agrarian reform and nationalization under way the Communists no longer have any role to play. Imperialist propaganda, which is echoed in some quarters, would make it appear as if we wanted a monopoly of leadership, as if we denied that others have a role to play and wished to oust them from the seats of power merely to take their place. All we want is that all progressives, the Communists included, should take part in ensuring the success of the reforms and charting the overall policy of the country. Only in this way can past achievements be consolidated and progress maintained.

The Communists are eager to place the wealth of experience they have accumulated, their loyalty and their capacity for self-sacrifice at the service of society – indeed, they have already done so where they have been given the opportunity – in order to ensure successful implementation of progressive changes and to create the socio-economic and political preconditions for socialism.

The march of events in our area and throughout the world makes it imperative to achieve not only unity of the progressive forces in each Arab country but also the unity of the revolutionary patriotic forces on the scale of the entire Arab world.

The Syrian Communist Party calls for the establishment of friendly, fraternal relations between Cairo and Damascus on the basis of equality and non-interference in each other's internal affairs. This, we are convinced, would strengthen the positions of both fraternal countries, vis-à-vis imperialism, Zionism and reaction in general, and would help to reinforce the Arab national-liberation movement as a whole.

Today the Communist parties are mature enough to need no supreme international body to organize and coordinate the activities of the international Communist movement. But the maturity of the Communist parties does not signify that we no longer need to be bound by any international discipline; it means that we have achieved a level when we are able voluntarily to submit to this discipline even though there is no higher body of the type of the Communist International.

U.S. imperialist aggression against the people of Vietnam, U.S. intervention in the affairs of the Latin American and African peoples, the naked aggression of British imperialism against the Arab people of Aden, the collaboration of all imperialist forces with Zionism with a view to preventing the Palestine Arabs from exercising their legitimate rights, and the revanchist resurgence in West Germany which is endangering peace in the heart of Europe – all lend urgency to the question of the unity of the Communist movement not only as a matter of principle but as a vital practical problem the solution of which cannot be put off until a third world war breaks out. This unity must be achieved now so as to prevent a new war, so as to safeguard the freedom and independence of the peoples and uphold peace throughout the world.

World Marxist Review, December 1965.

17

'The Policy of the Syrian Communist Party', after the events of February 23, 1966

Since 1965 Syria has been advancing along a road of progress which has already led to the nationalization of all big capitalist enterprises and the establishment of state control over foreign trade. Our Party directly supported these measures of the government and urged all progressive patriotic forces to follow suit. It also declared its readiness to cooperate in *all fields without exception* so as to ensure the success of these measures and to consolidate them, and also to defend the gains of the people and Syria's independence against the conspiracies of the imperialists and reactionaries.

Our Central Committee stressed already in its 1954 Manifesto addressed to the working class that in the present situation the Communists are called upon to play an important role in steering the country along a progressive road of development.

Despite difficulties and obstacles, the Syrian Communist Party has unswervingly pursued its line, which implies, on the one hand, ensuring a profound understanding of the role of the Party and, on the other, supporting every progressive initiative, whatever its source. All our Party is convinced of the correctness of this line and considers that its implementation fully conforms to the present situation in the country as well as to creative Marxist-Leninist principles.

In the effort to implement this line our Party had to overcome some erroneous trends.

First, the Right revisionist view that the Communist Party is no longer needed, that Communists have nothing to do in the process of progressive development, for there exist other, non-Communist forces which support and work for this development.

Second, the Left dogmatic attitude denying any importance of other progressive forces in the struggle for socialism and of progressive economic and social reforms if carried out by progressive nationalist, i.e., non-proletarian elements.

Third, the views expressed with hostile intentions (imperialist propaganda is their chief source), according to which the Communists' call for unity and mutual assistance is merely a maneuver to push aside all other progressive forces.

Our Party firmly adhered to its principles, openly acting in political life and before the masses as an independent patriotic and internationalist organization, as a class party inspired by scientific socialism. At the same time the policy of our Party, its positions, its practical activity proved the sincerity of the Communists' appeal for unity and mutual assistance with the sole aim of ensuring the success of progressive experience in Syria.

Subsequent developments and life itself convinced many progressive, Left Baathists included, that our appeal conforms to the interests of objective progress in the present-day conditions and that mutual assistance between progressive forces consolidates the internal situation and strengthens Syria's positions in the Arab progressive and popular circles as well as in the world arena.

Thus there began to develop, despite countless difficulties, cooperation between Communists and Left Baathists. But it cannot be said that we shall overcome these difficulties easily.

After the events of February 23, as a result of which several rightists (Aflak, Bitar and others) were removed from the Baath leadership, this cooperation materialized, though not in full, in the composition of the government formed at the beginning of March 1966.

The decision to take part in the government was adopted by our Central Committee unanimously and it was approved by all Party branches.

Our stand on this issue is clear. In keeping with its slogans, our Party considered it its duty to fight in *all sectors*, i.e., both in and outside the government, for the implementation of patriotic and progressive tasks, for the success of progressive experience in the Syrian Arab Republic.

This does not mean that our Party agrees with everything that is taking place in the country and unreservedly supports any initiative of the government. Nor does this mean that we automatically endorse any stand of the government on this or that issue.

For instance, we insist on all progressive forces sincerely devoted to socialism participating in the government. Mutual assistance between progressive forces should not be confined within governmental limits, it should be realized in every area of mass activity as well as in the different fields of political, economic and social life. In other words, the government in Syria should rely on an alliance of all the progressive and patriotic forces – Left Baathists, Communists, Arab socialists, independent socialists and all citizens not opposed to socialism as the goal and will of the masses. This alliance can take the form of mutual assistance within a broad progressive national front, or any other form conforming to the realities of the country. This alliance is an alternative which can effectively mobilize all efforts of the people to frustrate the conspiracies of imperialism and reaction, consolidate the successes achieved, and overcome the difficulties. It will enable us to advance confidently in the realization of the great task facing the country – to effect economic, social and political measures necessary for Syria's entry upon the road of socialist construction.

While campaigning for the popular front it is necessary to insist, at the same time, on respect for the dramatic freedoms of the workers, peasants, all working people and all progressive forces. This means freedom of the press, political associations, and meetings and free elections to trade union, peasant, student and women's organizations, which should not be the exclusive privilege of any one party.

We proceed, not from narrow partisan interests, but from a striving to secure success of progressive Syrian experience, to ensure a progressive and stable regime in the country.

Experience shows that we cannot adopt as universal the theory of one-party system in the period of transition to socialism, especially at the present stage of the country's development. States which embarked on socialist construction 20 years ago still have, along with Marxist-Leninist parties, other parties as well, such as the Peasant Party in Bulgaria, The Peasant and Democratic Parties in the GDR, etc., which possess the necessary facilities, print their newspapers, and so on. The French and Italian Communist parties, each of which is one of the biggest parties in their countries, have declared that they do not belong to the advocates of the one-party system in the period of transition to socialist construction. In the course of decades of historical process there have formed several progressive parties in Syria. It would be wrong and nonsensical to claim that the existence of some of them is not needed any longer or has become pointless.

The Rightist elements in the Baath party now removed from the government, such as Aflak, Bitar and others, realized that they alone cannot govern the country. Therefore they decided to 'turn face' to the other Right forces. It is a great credit to the Baath Left that it succeeded in thwarting this maneuver and that its representatives proceed, although very slowly, towards the establishment of cooperation with the Left. The Syrian Communists hail this line, which accords with the interests of progress in our country. The Communists would not like to think that there is even one upright progressive-minded citizen, whether Baathist or not, who considers this cooperation to be merely of a temporary tactical character due to internal or external circumstances. This opinion not only testifies to the short-sightedness of its proponents, but is also an obstacle to the achievement of their own aims, whether in or outside the country. The efforts of all the other Left forces in order to continue and extend the steps aimed at consolidating all progressive forces and to destroy all obstacles to this alliance, ignoring the howls heard from the camp of imperialism and reaction and the blackmail on its part.

Working patiently and purposefully for the establishment of a stable progressive regime in the country, the Syrian Communists at the same time fight for the earliest adoption of progressive economic and social measures which are the demand of the time.

The interests of the country call for the speediest completion of the agrarian reform. This can be achieved by hastening the distribution among the peasants of the already confiscated land of feudals and landowners. To prevent red-tape, the peasants themselves should take part in effecting the reform. The experience of the socialist countries shows that this method is correct.

The second top-priority task in Syria today is to strengthen and expand the state sector through the realization of new economic projects and above all the construction of the Euphrates dam, which can be done only with the help of the Soviet Union. It is necessary to work out and put into effect a plan for the development of the state sector in the economy. An end must be put to the situation when all enterprises, all factories are isolated from one another, do not maintain any production contacts and have no clear prospect as regards output and marketing even for a year in advance. Along with introducing scientifically substantiated planning, we shall also have to create conditions for encouraging the initiative of the masses. The working class must play an important role in managing industry.

The third pressing task facing Syria is to pursue a correct and judicious policy towards the petty bourgeoisie and other middle strata, who should be convinced by facts, not merely words, that the economic and social reforms directed against the feudals and the big bourgeoisie do not run counter to their interests.

Frustrating the conspiracies engineered by the American, British and West German imperialists, such as the Islamic pact, calls for the solidarity of all the anti-imperialist forces of the Arab world and for their coopera-tion with the forces of socialism and freedom all over the world, above all with the Soviet Union, their vanguard.

On the plane of ensuring inter-Arab solidarity, the Syrian and Com-munist Party urges first of all the establishment of friendly and fraternal relations between Damascus and Cairo on the basis of equality and non-interference in each other's internal affairs. This would help strengthen the positions of the Arab liberation movement as a whole.

Progressive experience in Syria can and must be crowned with success. This success will signify important progress in the development of the entire Arab world and promote the establishment of Arab unity on the principles of progress and democracy. Only such unity can be viable.

We Communists will do everything possible for this experience to succeed in the interests of the workers, peasants, revolutionary intelli-gentsia, all progressives.

Editorial in *Nidal al Shaab*, central organ of the SCP, beginning of April 1966. English translation, *World Marxist Review* (Canadian edition), No. 73, July 8, 1966.

18

'The Soviet Union will not remain indifferent'. Soviet warning to Britain, Israel, and the United States (May 1966)

'The Soviet Union cannot and will not remain indifferent to attempts to violate peace in the regions near the frontiers of the U.S.S.R.

'It can be seen that the neo-colonialists are not abandoning their plans for recovering lost positions in the countries of the Middle East and are seeking by all means to prevent the free development of those countries.

'The Government of the Syrian Arab Republic has approached the members of the U.N. Security Council about the present aggravation of the situation around Syria and in the Middle East caused by the increased activity of the forces of imperialism and reaction in this area. Syria's approach is being given careful consideration by the Soviet Union.

'The peace-loving peoples link the increase in subversive activity by the imperialist Powers and their reactionary allies in the Middle East with the fact that the number of Arab States which, as sovereign States, are pursuing an independent policy, is growing steadily. These States include the Syrian Arab Republic.

'A meeting of the CENTO military and colonial bloc was hastily held in Ankara recently, a conference of American Ambassadors accredited to Middle East countries took place in Beirut, and ships of the U.S. Sixth Fleet have again appeared in Lebanese territorial waters.

'It is also known that high-ranking U.S. officials recently held conferences with representatives of the Israeli Government and General Staff. Evidently, as a result of this, aggressive and extremist forces in Israel have begun activities spearheaded against neighbouring Arab States.

'Provocations by Israel on the borders of neighbouring countries have become more frequent. According to press reports, the Israeli Army has been put on the alert, leave for officers and men has been cancelled, and Israeli troops are being concentrated on the Syrian border.

'Rabin, the Chief of General Staff of the Israeli Army, is making provocative speeches against the Arab States, depicting matters as if Israel could lay down what policy her neighbours must pursue.

'According to information available, some reactionary quarters in Jordan and Saudi Arabia who are dissatisfied with Syria's policy – and who are backed by the USA and Britain – are also hatching plans against this Arab nation.

'These facts show that the aggressive circles of certain imperialist Powers and their agents are apparently beginning to forget the lessons of the disgraceful failure of the aggression against Egypt and also their other defeats in the Middle East.

'The neo-colonialists are obviously unwilling to give up their plans to recapture their lost positions in the countries of the Middle East and are striving by all means to prevent the free development of these countries.

'The peoples of the Arab States are well aware that the cause of peace and their independent development are endangered by the new intrigues of the imperialist Powers, their reactionary agents in the Middle East and the ruling quarters in Israel – in particular their attempts to meddle in the internal affairs of the Syrian Arab Republic.

'For its part the Soviet Union, of course, cannot and will not remain indifferent to the attempts to violate peace in a region in direct proximity to the borders of the Soviet Union.'

Broadcast on May 27, 1966.
Source: Jewish Observer and *Middle East Review*, June 3, 1966.

19

Khalid Bakdash: *Syrian Communists Call for Arab Unity*

The serious situation created in the Arab East as a result of the criminal imperialist zionist aggression gives the Arab peoples an important and fundamental task to accomplish, i.e.: to sweep the aggressor's forces away from our land and liquidate the consequences of the aggression.

The safest way to accomplish that task is to analyze calmly and objectively the events which have taken place and draw from that the proper teachings and correct conclusions which may contribute to fill the gaps and shortcomings in every field of our life – to provide the proper conditions to accomplish the supreme national task, i.e.: to liquidate the aggression and its effects, while strengthening the Arabs' positions and their power to defend their national independence and sovereignty against any imperialist plot and plan, whatever its form and method of execution may be.

Is there any change in the balance of powers on the international stage?

There is no doubt that a painful defeat was inflicted to the Arab liberation movement by that sudden and treacherous aggression planned by American imperialism and supported by Great Britain and West Germany. How can we explain what actually happened? Was that an expression of a change of forces on the international stage in favor of colonialist and imperialist forces – as some people wish to make the Arab masses imagine? Not at all! The balance of forces on the international battlefield actually remains in favor of the forces of socialism and national and social liberation, while imperialist positions are being undermined and disrupted by efficient and very powerful factors, the most important of which consist of the following facts: the peoples of the socialist countries successfully continue to build up their society; tremendous advance of the foremost socialist power – the Soviet Union, day after day and even hour after hour, in every field; continuous progress and expansion of the workers' world revolutionary movement; continuous progress, expansion and intensification of the national liberation movement. There also are other factors which weaken the positions of world imperialism – such as the serious oppositions and splits in the very midst of the front of world imperialism and its various economic and military blocs.

. . .

The aggression actually failed to achieve its basic political goals!

Since war actually represents the extension of some particular policy by resorting to different means – as that is confirmed by Marxism-Leninism, it is obvious that the fate of the Israeli war of aggression planned by imperialism had to be the same as the fate of the imperialist policy which preceded that war, which was nothing but another method to pursue that policy. That means that in spite of the temporary military success, the goals of that aggression – i.e.: the complete elimination of the whole Arab national liberation movement, the ruination of friendly Arab-Soviet relations and the overthrowing of Arab progressive regimes. The American newspaper, *New York Herald Tribune*, actually wrote: 'In spite of her "dazzling" military victories, Israel actually did not achieve any fundamental political purpose, since she did not succeed in overthrowing the existing regimes both in Cairo and Damascus.'

Imperialist propaganda tried to conceal the actual nature of the Israeli aggression and described it as the mere consequence of a 'clash between two nationalisms [or nationalities]'; that propaganda was widely spread and deceived many people throughout the world. However, the socialist countries and the communist parties of the West – especially the important French and Italian communist parties – strongly opposed and exposed that distortion of the actual situation. Even in Israel itself voices – such as the voices of the Israeli communist representatives, Tawfig Tubi and Meir Wilner, and their supporters – were raised to confirm to the workers of the world that Israel's aggression was the execution of an American imperialist plan. The Soviet Union played the most important part regarding the disclosure of the real nature of the Israel aggression on an overall international scale – both within and outside the United Nations.

. . .

Defeat is temporary, but victory and the future are ours!

. . .

... We also have to understand very well what the imperialists tactics are and we believe that they may be summed up as follows:

Before the aggression, Anglo-American imperialism was unable – in spite of all its efforts – to overthrow the progressive regimes from within and that is why it resorted to the Israeli aggression, to which it assigned the basic goal of overthrowing those regimes – but that military aggression failed to achieve that. Consequently, imperialism now tries to take advantage of the situation created by the military aggression itself to renew its attempts to overthrow the progressive regimes from within.

For that purpose, imperialism has undertaken various operations – creating divisions and disorders inside every Arab country; weakening and isolating Arab countries, while creating divisions between them; creating divisions and suspicions between Arab and socialist countries – especially the Soviet Union; encouraging reactionary movements, on one hand, and adventurous tendencies, on the other hand. All that has to be foiled and all the required means to do it are easily available; all there is to do is to secure them and know how to take advantage of them.

The first thing to do is to increase the power of Arab defense and the fighting power, generally speaking. That depends first of all on ourselves and secondarily on the consolidation of friendly relations with the Soviet Union and other socialist countries, since Soviet assistance in weapons, ammunitions and supplies – before, during and after the aggression – has played and still plays a fundamental and decisive part in the consolidation of the power of Arab defense. That is a well known and accepted fact, for everybody, which fills every Arab patriot with the deepest feelings of gratitude toward the most powerful socialist country.

At the same time, it is necessary to organize extensively the people's masses – especially workers and peasants at large – into battalions of the people's army or otherwise, so that people may participate in the defense of their fatherland – village by village, house by house, span by span.

The joint fight of the army and the people is the sure guarantee capable to repel and crush any imperialist aggression. The example given by the heroic Vietnamese people is a living indication of that and an actual proof displayed under the eyes of the whole world.

Importance of the political element in the battle:

In addition to that, we imperiously have to consider the importance of the political element – the importance of the political aspect of our fight – under the correct perspective. To overlook the political factor – the political element – is a terrible mistake, which may have most detrimental effects on the activity of the Arab progressive patriotic forces in the foreign field (as well in the internal field, as we shall see).

Let us consider, for example, the special session of the General Assembly of the United Nations. Some people say: 'What have the Arabs gained from that?' Such words – even though they may have been said very innocently – actually express simple-mindedness and even total incomprehension of the actual nature of the era in which we live.

The special session of the General Assembly of the United Nations –

held at the request of the Soviet Union, in spite of the desperate efforts made by America and Israel to prevent it from being held – was a tremendous political operation.

Before the aggression, Israel and her masters had launched a tremendous world-wide campaign revolving around the idea that the Arab countries were preparing an aggression, while Israel only wished to defend her right to exist as a 'peaceful' and 'democratic' state against countries known for their backwardness, 'chauvinism' and 'clannishness'; according to that propaganda, the Arabs were the successors of nazism and – like the latter – intended to destroy the Jews – and other lies. Subsequently – during and after the aggression, Israel and her masters launched a very extensive campaign accusing Egypt of having started the aggression and saying that Israel had to do whatever she did to defend her security and had to occupy some territories to guarantee that security.

However, the session of the General Assembly of the United Nations was subsequently held and blew the whole thing to pieces leaving no stone unturned, with the help of the joint efforts of the socialist and Arab countries. Consequently, it became obvious to many countries which had been deceived and to the world public opinion that Israel actually was the aggressor and that the aggression took place in accordance with plans made by America and international oil monopolies. It thus became clear that the main purpose of the aggression had been to overthrow the anti-imperialist progressive regimes bent on realizing deep social changes to open the way to pro-socialist evolution.

Consequently, a deep and important change took place in the world public opinion – especially among millions of workers in the West. Although the session of the General Assembly did not officially succeed in adopting any decision indicting the aggression and requesting the liquidation of its consequences, more than two thirds of the countries nevertheless requested the withdrawal of the aggressor's forces (although some of those countries made that depend on specific conditions, which made impossible the adoption of a decision specifying that by a majority of two thirds). On the other hand, 99 countries disapproved the annexation of the old part of Jerusalem by Israel.

For many years, Israel has deceived the world public opinion by using the sympathetic feelings which had been growing in Europe and the world at large since World War II owing to the Hitlerian slaughters of Jews. Now, the facts reported by the socialist and Arab countries regarding the atrocities committed by the Israeli troops against the Arab population have proved that Israel – and not the Arabs – is the real successor of Nazism and actually uses the same methods as the latter with reference to the population of the occupied lands.

All that actually was such an important gain in favor of the Arab peoples that an Israeli newspaper – commenting on the activity of the Soviet Union inside and outside the United Nations – actually wrote: 'The Soviet Union actually has withdrawn the red carpet from under our feet.'

What does that mean? That means that Israel is afraid of international isolation just as anybody may be afraid of cholera or plague.

We must admit here that many progressive Arabs – including ourselves, the Communists, once in a while – do not give due attention and consideration to the political factor and its international effect. Declarations often are made, slogans brandished and we adopt some position without thinking of its possible international echo and its influence on the people's masses in various countries of the world – including in friendly countries. Examples of that are the well known declarations made by Shukeiri – as well as others, which are absolutely empty of any feeling of responsibility.

We may be Arab patriots and progressives, but we should not get carried away by our positions and slogans just as if everybody in the world had to be an Arab or all the people in the world lived and understood the problems of the Middle East as we ourselves live and understand them. We should not forget that what may be obvious and taken for granted as far as we, Arabs, are concerned, may not be so with reference to other people in the various parts of the vast and wide globe.

Consequently, we should establish our slogans, specify our positions and make our declarations in a manner which may contribute to isolate our enemy on the international stage – instead of isolating ourselves. 'What is that for?' some people may ask, but that is a useless and refutable question, since the most powerful countries in the world never ignore the political factor and its international effect and actually take that into very serious consideration whenever they are about to undertake something important.

That applies even more so to a fight undertaken by a small people to defend its independence and freedom. Who could – for example – deny the tremendous part played by the vast world campaign to support the courageous Vietnamese people and expose the oppressive American aggression disguised under the veil of the fight against 'the communist peril'? The efficiency of that campaign was so great that it actually was reflected inside the United States of America and manifestations consisting of many thousands of Americans were organized in American cities to stigmatize loudly the aggression of their own government against the Vietnamese people and request with hue and cry the cessation of the war conducted against the latter, while describing Johnson as 'the executioner'.

We urgently need a wise and farsighted foreign policy!

We should never grow tired to repeat and stress that we need a wise foreign policy to isolate Israel internationally, more and more, and refute the pretense made by Israel to justify her aggression, i.e.: that Israel wishes to establish a state of peace in the Middle East whereas the Arabs do not want that – as Israel pretends – and that she committed and still commits her crimes only to defend her existence and entity, but not for expansionistic and imperialist purposes related to the plans of Anglo-American imperialism – although that actually is so. Such a policy would contribute to stabilize and also ease the international climate in favor of the Arab peoples, with reference to the battle fought to liquidate the effects of the aggression, foil and check all plans of imperialist aggression through and with the help of Israel. Many noticeable progressive and nationalist voices are raised in the Arabic newspapers – in Cairo and elsewhere – to advocate the adoption of such a wise policy and this question should be settled in a comprehensive and responsible manner.

As a matter of fact, the Arab countries urgently need a foreign policy based on farsightedness and due reflection, as well as on the study and objective analysis of the facts – both in this area and in the international field, in a precise manner. In this field – as in all other political fields – and even more – it is not permissible to be carried away by feelings, embark upon empty exaggerations and/or brandish slogans which cannot be put into practice either at the present time or in the near future. That actually would – on one hand – give the enemy some shields to conceal its crimes and the real nature of its goals from the world public opinion, while that would – on the other hand – create inadequate and unfavorable reactions in the Arab people's public opinion, when it becomes materially obvious that those slogans were not properly studied with reference to available resources – and that would give leeway to the agents of imperialism and resentful reactionaries to advocate capitulation in favor of imperialism under the pretext that there is no use to fight.

We must say here that the official propaganda undertaken in China by Mao Tse-tung's bloc plays a dangerous negative part in this field – a part which ultimately blends with the American imperialist goals. In Indonesia – for example – Mao Tse-tung's bloc largely and effectively contributed to incite the revolutionary forces to adopt a hostile attitude toward the Soviet Union, on one hand, and embark upon weird and amazing adventures, on the other hand. Consequently, a hard blow was struck at the revolutionary forces, Suharto's regime was established, imperialism regained many of its strongholds and many national and social gains, for the realization of which the Indonesian people had made tremendous sacrifices, were lost. That actually was what American imperialism wanted and had been trying to realize.

Now, what has Mao Tse-tung's propaganda done during the Israeli aggression?

It actually launched an outspreading campaign against the cease-fire and actually reached the lowest degrees of inanity in its attacks against the Soviet Union, because the latter approved that cease-fire – although the Soviet Union itself actually had the full approval of the Arab countries – victim of the aggression, in that respect. As a matter of fact, the Soviet Union did not only adopt that attitude at the United Nations, but also warned Israel very sternly – as well as America – against the possible consequences of Israel's rejection of the cease-fire. In that manner the Soviet Union played an important and even decisive part in the muzzling of the aggression, while stopping the criminal zionist invasion of Arab lands. On the other hand, the propaganda of Mao Tse-tung's bloc against the cease-fire actually amounted only to one thing, i.e.: to let Israel take full advantage of her aggression to occupy more Arab lands and even invade the Suez Canal – and that is precisely what American imperialism wants.

Furthermore – during and after the aggression, the Mao Tse-tung's bloc invited the Arab peoples to sever their relations with the Soviet Union and adopt a hostile attitude toward the latter. That is exactly what was and still is advocated by radio-broadcasts from Israel, Washington and London – since that was one of the main goals of American imperialism, when it planned that Israel aggression.

And what is Mao Tse-tung's bloc doing today? It now ridicules the political fight aimed at exposing and isolating Israel and her masters, while giving an opportunity to the Arabs to gather and coordinate their forces and strengthen their defensive power. All that is described by the propaganda of Mao Tse-tung's bloc as 'opportunism', 'deviationism' and loss of revolutionary spirit; in other words they would like the Arabs to embark upon adventures without any preparation and without taking into consideration the possible consequences of their action – and that is exactly what is wanted and hoped by the American imperialists and the rulers of Israel who are worrying about the important and active efforts made by Egypt, Syria and other countries to consolidate their defensive potential with the extensive help willingly, resolutely and unconditionally extended by the Soviet Union.

The propaganda of Mao Tse-tung's bloc tries to make the peoples of the world – including the Arab peoples – imagine that armed fight, regardless of circumstances, is the only road to liberation and that political fight is pure fiction and absolutely useless. That propaganda naturally plays with people's feelings and arouses people's emotions, although that is far from being objective and that actually is refuted by the peoples' own experiences. Armed fight itself requires specific conditions actually prepared by political fight and President Nasser was right when he said, during the speech which he delivered after the aggression for the commemoration of 23 July: 'There is no short cut; on the contrary, the road is long. On the other hand, there is not only one way, but there actually are various ways – all of which we have to follow – leading to the same goal.'

In other words, whatever cannot be done directly to the Arab peoples by imperialism, Israel and mercenary reaction actually is undertaken and done by the Propaganda of Mao Tse-tung and his bloc in the name of 'revolutionism'.

With reference to those who spread Mao Tse-tung's propaganda throughout the Arab world, they do not consist only of a few misguided patriots. As a matter of fact, many imperialist agents resort to that propaganda to conceal their own propaganda and mention Mao Tse-tung instead of mentioning Johnson – since what Mao Tse-tung's bloc advocates under the name of 'intensified revolutionism' actually serves the intentions of American imperialism.

However, Mao Tse-tung's bloc has failed in its attempts to influence the Arab revolutionary movement to any noticeable extent – and will continue to fail in achieving that in the future. As a matter of fact, Arab workers, peasants and revolutionary intellectuals – as well as most Arab progressive and patriotic politicians, regardless of their respective tendencies – are no children, as Radio Peking seems to imagine.

.   .   .

Consolidation of the united front between Arab and socialist countries:
One of the most important lessons of the battle undertaken by our country is that it is necessary to consolidate the united front between Arab and socialist countries. The united front between the national liberation front and the socialist countries – the main power of which is the Soviet Union – is the result of a positive fact. In other words, these forces confront a common enemy – world imperialism. This is precisely why the attempts of those who try to ignore or disregard that positive fact have failed and will continue to fail; those who try to hinder that united front are practically bound – whether they actually want it or not – to help the other side, i.e.: the imperialist side. That is why they must be forsaken sooner or later by the national liberation movement, since the evolution of positive facts is stronger than any attempt, subtle and misleading as it may be.

There is no doubt that the first thing to do is to depend on ourselves in the fight against imperialism and its aggression. No sincere and true patriot can claim that the socialist countries should fight in his stead, while he does nothing to prepare himself or use all the resources which may be at his disposal – and the peoples' masses understand that very well, thanks to their sound patriotic intuition.

However, 'to depend first of all on oneself' is one thing and 'to depend exclusively on oneself' is an entirely different matter. The advocation of the last idea actually amounts to disregarding the united front consisting of the national liberation front and the socialist countries – the main power of which is the Soviet Union – and that is precisely why it is wrong and ultimately serves – whether those who advocate that want it or not – the wishes and plans of imperialism. The people's masses also know that, thanks to their sound patriotic intuition. Consequently, the correct revolutionary slogan of the national liberation movement is: We must first of all depend on ourselves, while using – without any reluctance or reservation – any available help, regardless of its nature – political, military or economic – which may be obtained from the Soviet Union and other socialist countries. Why do we say, 'without any reluctance or reservation?' That is because the Soviet Union and other socialist countries have never had – and just cannot have – any expansionist or 'domineering' intentions, as the propaganda of Israel and her imperialist masters pretend that they have, among other things.

That actually is inherent to the actual nature of the socialist countries and the best proof of that is given by the history of the Soviet Union since the Socialist Revolution of October and up to this year during which progressive mankind celebrates the fiftieth anniversary of that glorious revolution. It would naturally be wrong for any progressive patriot to imagine that the socialist countries are nothing more than sources of economic and military assistance and that they just have to give such assistance to our peoples as well as other peoples who fight to liberate themselves and build up their new economic life. To imagine that the united front between the socialist countries and our own country is based on that concept would be a sign of narrow-mindedness and far from objective. As a matter of fact, one of the most important principles and tenets of the united front between our country and the socialist countries – and especially their main power, the Soviet Union – is that there exists mutual experiences and understandings in politics, in the political fight, especially with reference to whatever concerns the most important matters, which undoubtedly prove that our respective interests – in that respect – are similar and even exactly the same.

One of the main lessons of the battle undertaken by our country against the imperialist Zionist aggression is that it is necessary to consolidate the united front between our country and the socialist countries – and that it is necessary to ensure an increasing osmosis between our country and the Soviet Union in the political field as well as in every other field.

Consolidation and strengthening of the unity of the Arab fight:

There is no doubt that unity in fight, common action, coordinated efforts – especially in the military and political fields – between progressive

Arab countries – especially between Egypt and Syria – represent the basis and principal foundation of a victorious Arab fight against imperialism and Zionism. However, it is also necessary to incite all the Arab countries to fight – in one way or another and to any extent possible – to force the aggressor's forces to withdraw from the lands which they have occupied and consequently liquidate all the consequences of the aggression. It is not permissible to desist from any public Arab political action which might contribute – even to a very limited extent – to paralyze the maneuvers of imperialism, Israel and reaction to create scissions between the Arab countries or incite some of them – in some way or another – to surrender to the Anglo-American directives or keep pace with them.

.   .   .

All that is certainly not opposed to the fact that it is necessary to incite all the Arab countries to join the fight to clear out the consequences of the imperialist Zionist aggression.

.   .   .

While the unity of the Arab fight and the united front [between the Arab countries] and the socialist countries are of an extreme and decisive importance which is obvious to anybody and not contested by any sincere and alert patriot in the Arab world, the unity of the fight of all the progressive patriotic forces in every Arab country is also of a special and even decisive importance, today, under the circumstances created by the treacherous Israeli aggression.

.   .   .

It is true that there are – among us – some individuals who might be called 'the Versailles set', in memory of the members of the French upper bourgeoisie who had fled in 1870 before the Parisian workers' revolution (Commune of Paris) and taken refuge at Versailles – in the suburbs, while waiting for the Germans to arrive, crush the people's revolution and bring them back to power.

When those people converse among themselves, they do not conceal that they are sorry and worried because the Israeli aggression failed to entail the overthrow of the present progressive regime in Damasucs (and, of course, in Cairo). They perhaps expected another aggression, which they hoped would realize their dream. However, that group consists only of a few people whose insight was blinded and whose patriotic feelings were killed by class interests.

On the other hand, the vast majority of our people – workers, peasants, revolutionary intellectuals and all the multitudes of laborers of every sort, as well as officers, troops and patriots at large – want to liquidate the consequences of the Israeli aggression. They all want to defend their fatherland at any cost, preserve their social gains and retain the progressive patriotic policy followed by their country.

.   .   .

The huge quantities of food stuffs and other things which were sent unconditionally by the socialist countries (for example: 5,000 tons of sugar from the Soviet Union, thousands of tons of fats and many thousands of coverings and blankets from East Germany, Bulgaria and other socialist countries – in addition to arms, ammunitions and so forth), prove that the policy of the socialist countries toward our country is not based on profit. If the policy of a country is based on profit, the country in question would not offer such tremendous help in arms and food free of charge. All that is a categorical proof of the inconsistency of the arguments raised by some spokesmen regarding economic relations (when they say, for example, that all the Socialist camp is interested in – in dealing with us – is profit and so forth) to justify their tendency to maintain our commercial relations as they have been, i.e.: mainly with West Germany and other capitalist imperialist countries.

.   .   .

Task of the party at this stage:
During the battle, the communists have done their duty and fought in every field possible – among the masses, in the various people's committees, in the battalions of the people's army, in cities and villages, in civil defense and rescuing operations, and/or any field to which they were called by the voice of the fatherland, fight and struggle – and some of them died on the field of honor.

Wherever there was action and fight, the communists have been models of courage, abnegation and perseverance. As a matter of fact – in Qunaytrah and other places on the front lines, their conduct aroused the admiration of the people's masses and every progressive patriot.

Reference should actually be made to the extensive activity and vital importance which have characterized the activity of communist women and girls under the strenuous circumstances through which the country has gone before, during and after the aggression.

.   .   .

The first task to be undertaken today by our party is to fight, politically, on two fronts: against right-wing and reactionary activities aimed at taking advantage of the defeat to advocate surrender to imperialism and against extreme tendencies advocating risky adventures without duly taking into consideration their possible consequences with reference to

Syria itself and the Arab East as a whole. We must mention here that when the reactionaries saw that their propaganda in favor of surrender to imperialism was unsuccessful, they actually started to encourage the tendencies advocating risky adventures because they thought that they would ultimately lead to the same results which they had in mind.

Those who advocate risky adventures ignore the need for political coordination between Syria, Egypt and socialist countries. They also ignore the need for a mutual understanding among these countries regarding any action concerning the withdrawal of the aggressor's forces and the liquidation of the consequences of the aggression. Furthermore, they ignore the necessity to take advantage – at the present stage – of all diplomatic and political means, in spite of the fact that such means – even though we may grant that they ultimately might not be sufficient – would strengthen the Arabs' position and permit to pursue the fight, in various ways and under miscellaneous forms, to liquidate the consequences of the aggression.

The most important task of the party is to pursue the fight to preserve and consolidate the progressive social and economic changes and complete them adequately, with the participation and supervision of the people's masses. It is necessary to continue to act and fight for the purpose of mustering all the anti-imperialist and progressive forces and ensure unity of fight among them. It is extremely important that the communists continue, with perseverance and dynamism, to establish and consolidate close relations with all the progressives – regardless of their particular tendencies and at all levels, in order to realize unity of action and fight among them. It is necessary to act and fight to increase and extend trade-union liberties in favor of the workers, as well as democratic liberties also in favor of the workers, the peasants and all progressive patriotic forces.

In addition to their patient and unceasing activity among the workers' and peasants' masses, the communists must listen carefully to the voice of those masses and take their remarks into consideration. They must try to make the progressives – whether they are members of the government or not – understand that the remarks of the workers, peasants, revolutionary intellectuals and all other progressives should not be resented and should – on the contrary – be considered with interest and attention, while the various governmental agencies should concentrate on controlling and prosecuting saboteurs and agents of imperialism and reaction, instead of harassing the progressives.

In other words we, communists, must perseveringly and assiduously conform to the plan of the party, which was adopted unanimously. Under this plan, we must do whatever we can to ensure cooperation, realize unity of fight among all the progressives and show the independent aspect of the party – its national and international aspect, especially with reference to important political questions and the most important basic matters. We must also do whatever we can to defend untiringly the interests of needy workers, peasants and all the people's toiling masses.

In the field of mass activities and organization work, two basic tasks currently confront us – the Communists:

1) Actual efforts must be improved and/or increased, as well as the mobilization of forces, resources and energies, up to the level which corresponds to the difficult circumstances of the battle which our country is fighting. In other words we must discard the usual methods concerning ordinary or 'peaceful' agreements – if this expression is correct – and improve those methods to a much greater extent.

2) It is also necessary to strengthen, consolidate and improve the party's order to meet the level required by the strenuous circumstances which confront the country as well as the party itself. In the communist party, Lenin says, order must be – under ordinary circumstances – of a semi-military type; under special circumstances – such as a civil war, order must be completely military. It is obvious that Arab Syria is at the present time involved in a very difficult fight against the foreign imperialist Israeli aggressor – under circumstances which are not less difficult, critical and complicated than those which characterize a civil war against the rule of the upper bourgeoisie. We consequently need to do whatever we can to realize that level of order in the party – at all levels, to meet the conditions through which our fatherland and people are passing at the present time.

. . .

The wheel of history cannot be turned back! However things may evolve and regardless of any difficulty and trial, victory is bound to be in favor of the standards of social and national liberation in our great Arab fatherland!

Al Akhbar, Beirut, September 3, 1967.

20

'For the Defence of the Iraqi Republic and the Gains of the Revolution'

In the enlarged session of the C.C. of our Party held in September 1958, our Party defined the nature of the 14th July Revolution as 'national democratic'. On this basis the Party defined the basic forces of the revolution – the workers, the peasants, the petty bourgeoisie, the middle bourgeoisie (the anti-imperialist, national bourgeoisie). The Party also defined the aims of the revolution in the resolutions of the enlarged session. At the same time it dealt with the issue of state power as a national, anti-imperialist, anti-feudal power, although it did not represent the entirety of the national forces.

. . .

In the field of national independence, Iraq withdrew from the Baghdad Pact, abrogated the special agreement with Britain, abrogated the pact of mutual security with the U.S. and its military and economic supplements and repudiated the Eisenhower Doctrine and other imperialist obligations. Relations of our Republic developed with the Soviet Union, the rest of the socialist countries and with the Asian and African countries.

. . .

In spite of tension in the relations between Iraq and the U.A.R. caused by the insistence of the U.A.R. rulers on pursuing a policy of plotting and aggression against our Republic, Iraq persisted in the policy of Arab solidarity and backing the Arab liberation movements. Iraq's democratic steps found a deep response among her Arab brothers, who view Iraq hopefully and sincerely as a source of inspiration. Iraq's liberation policy and its democratic achievements have also won sympathy and support from millions of peoples all over the world.

. . .

Yet this struggle encountered many and increasing difficulties. The Iraqi revolution which destroyed the reactionary – colonial royal system was at the same time of a radical progressive nature which frightened reactionary circles in Arab and neighbouring countries. Because of the close links between the Iraqi revolution and the Arab liberation movement, Egyptian reactionary strata pushed their anti-democratic government to utilise Arab nationalist sentiments in Iraq in order to crush democracy and to annex Iraq to the U.A.R. This period witnessed feverish activity on the part of the rulers of the U.A.R. and their followers in Iraq. This activity was not only aimed at spreading the domination of the reactionary quarters in Egypt over Iraq, but it also aimed at defending their positions in their own country protecting their anti-democratic system and at checking the wave of democracy inspired by the Iraqi revolution, which was received by the Arab peoples with hope and confidence.

Egyptian reactionary circles were able to exploit Col Abdul Salam Aref and cliques of other rightist nationalists to work for their own ends. As for the bands of local reaction, feudalists and followers of the extinct regime, they started rallying their dispersed ranks and concealed themselves behind false nationalist slogans, marching behind Abdul Salam

Aref and his collaborators. While it was gradually attracting the rulers of the U.A.R., imperialism encouraged their endeavours and those of their followers in Iraq and waited for the opportune moment to strike a blow at the Iraqi Republic and restore their lost domination.

.   .   .

When the danger of these reactionary activities increased and attained the degree of plotting against the Republic, and in implementation of the resolution taken at the enlarged session on the necessity of contributing to the defence of the Republic, the C.C. of our Party held a session at the beginning of November 1958 and dedicated it to analysing the nature and characteristics of the activities hostile to our Republic and to approving measures which would secure the foiling of the conspiracy hatched by Abdul Salam Aref and his supporters against the Republican system. The C.C. concluded that any act which aims to overthrow the present political power cannot but be an imperialist conspiracy to resist which the Party would stand behind the national government. After the failure of Abdul Salam Aref's attempts, the Party proceeded in its plan and took up a firm stand against the conspiracy of Rashid Ali El Gailani, the military putsch of Col. Shawaf, the banditry in Rawandooz and other plotting activities. The firm struggle which was launched by all the forces concerned in protecting the Republic and its democratic course with the participation of the widest masses of the people and in close solidarity with the national government have given fruitful results in ensuring the security of the Republic and consolidating its revolutionary democratic course.

.   .   .

This ought not however to overshadow the great efforts dedicated by our Party to national cooperation. Even since the first days of the revolution when the Baath Party walked out of the United National Front and went on exploiting new circumstances to attain private gains at the expense of the revolution and the national movement in general, and when various national parties refused to work within the Front of National Unity and started minimising the necessity of national cooperation, our Party was the one which took the initiative in appealing to the parties to restore and reconstruct the Front of National Unity. It emphasised the principle of cooperation and solidarity among the various national forces, while the rest of the parties continued for a long period of time to take up to varying degrees a negative stand on this vital issue. The efforts of our Party in this field succeeded and the positive stand taken afterwards by the national parties helped in the resumption of the activity of the United National Front, which included, besides our Party, the National Democratic, Baath and Istiqlal Parties. Our Party also concluded a charter of cooperation with the United Democratic Party of Kurdistan which joined the Front later on. Important steps were taken in the field of protecting the Republic and backing the revolutionary government. At the enlarged session of the C.C., held last September, resolutions of the session attributed particular importance to the cause of national cooperation.

. . .

However the efforts exerted in this direction encountered increasing difficulties, for the upper strata of the Egyptian bourgeoisie, which falsified the concept of Arab nationalism, had started working from the first days of the Revolution to attain domination over Iraq. They exploited the existence of rightist nationalists inside and outside the Government for their private ends. As is known, these acts affected cooperation inside the United National Front, when the Baath Party, and to a lesser degree the Istiqlal Party, took up an obstructive stand on the activity of the Front. Consequently some elements of these parties stumbled blindly, together with other rightist nationalist sectors, into the ranks of the enemies of the Republic, which led them in practice to be outside the ranks of the National Front. But in spite of the hostile manifestations of their activity which we felt, we continued to comply with the obligations of the alliance with them inside the National Front, hoping to make them retreat from their erroneous path. We were concerned for our Party not to let the anger of the masses be directed against them but to be directed 'solely against those who insist on pursuing the path of plotting'. For those who committed mistakes we paved the way of return to the arena of national cooperation, if they desired to rectify their position and take up again the struggle for the safeguarding of the Republic.

After the withdrawal of the representatives of the Baath and Istiqlal Parties from the United National Front, we continued our endeavours with the National Democratic Party and adhered to the articles of the charter of cooperation which was concluded between our Party and the United Democratic Party of Kurdistan.

. . .

The Revolution made good progress during the few months which followed the 14th of July. Side by side with the major victories and achievements which were accomplished in spite of conspiracies and external and internal dangers, the energies of the people surged up and contingent after contingent of the popular masses entered the arena of struggle. Then came the Mosul conspiracy which added new momentum to the popular movement because of the amazing speed with which the conspiracy was crushed. Furthermore the crushing of this conspiracy consolidated the foundations of patriotic rule, due to the firm rallying of the masses around the revolutionary Government. This increased correspondingly with the Government's ensurance of the rights of the people and their granting of liberties in response to the people's will.

The period which followed the crushing of the Mosul conspiracy marked the peak of the upsurge in the national movement and particularly in the peasant movement. It also marked an unprecedented increase in the popularity of the Government and the national movement in general. On the other hand the external dangers which menace the Republic shrank to a certain extent. Strong blows too were struck at the reactionary forces and the anti-Republican plotting elements. These blows paralysed the ability of the hostile forces to cause general harm to the security of the Republic for some period of time.

.   .   .

During the pre-revolutionary period the national bourgeoisie was a weak class due to imperialist domination and the nature of feudal relationships in the countryside and the retarded development of the national industry in the cities. The political struggle of the bourgeoisie was at that time limited in spite of the radical character which identified it on some occasions as a result of its being oppressed and due to the limitation of its chances of participating in political life.

Although the economic bases of the national bourgeoisie are still weak, the nature of the patriotic regime after the 14th of July has provided it with new possibilities and influence and accorded them the chance to play a big political role in the life of the country.

.   .   .

In view of the intended cabinet reshuffle at that time, we took the initiative of putting forward the slogan of participation in the government. The enlarged session of the C.C. pointed out that cooperation of the political representatives of all national classes in 'a coalition government' is the best form of political power at this stage in the national democratic revolution. Current experiences of many countries have indicated that a coalition government is a good model for political power. Even in the period of transition, this issue gains special significance because of the existence of representatives of all national forces in the cabinet is an important factor in the struggle against counter-revolutionary activities and for safeguarding the Republic, consolidating the gains of the revolution and guaranteeing the interests of all anti-imperialist classes. All this was from the viewpoint of theoretical principles.

In practice, our demand to participate in the patriotic government was erroneous because it did not give consideration to the position and the relationships of the national forces in the country, nor to the conditions of development of the revolution in relation to the Arab and international situation at the time.

In the political circumstances which followed the revolution – where the revolutionary government had embarked upon an anti-imperialist and anti-feudal policy and was (and still is) a transitional government the elements of which were chosen by the leader of the revolution – in such circumstances raising the slogan (in isolation from the leadership of the regime) for participation in the government was an erroneous sectarian act which did not take into account the aforementioned realities of the revolution and the relationships of the national forces. This action was bound to harm unity of these forces and disturb their solidarity in defending the Republic.

Moreover, the mass method which was taken as a means to express this demand for participating in the government, was another factor which deepened the negative results in the situation. The Press campaign, our overlooking or encouraging the penetration of this demand to the masses (particularly during the May day demonstrations, when this slogan was shouted by hundreds of thousands of citizens), as well as the wide educational campaign – all this exaggerated the strength of our Party and distorted its intentions in the view of the government, of considerable sectors of the Iraqi and Arab bourgeoisie and of many moderate forces. As a result they became panicky at that demand although the policy of our Party with reference to the economic interests of the national bourgeoisie and political cooperation with it a clear and frank policy, founded upon objective study of the realities of the present stage in the history of our country.

In addition, the political situation which arose shortly after the crushing of the Mosul conspiracy (and which we previously mentioned), in which the patriotic regime was consolidated, was such as to cause a tendency for the national forces to shrink from the demand of Communist participation in the government.

The sweeping wave of imperialist and reactionary slander and intrigue played a considerable role in exploiting this panic and the reserve towards this demand on the part of some of the national forces, in order to increase the division of the national ranks, drive a wedge among them and incite some against others.

If we take into consideration the connection of this internal situation with the external situation of the Republic – which was characterised throughout the period of the past year by the desperation of the colonialist forces, at whose interest the revolution had struck a mortal blow, and by threats from the covetous circles and ruling reaction in Arab and neighbouring countries – we realise the dimensions of the negative consequences which could have resulted at that time for the security of the Republic.

Out of our concern to remedy this situation and to re-establish solidarity with the government and all the national forces, we took the initiative of halting the educational campaign and acting in order to mitigate some of the negative reactions among other political forces which resulted from that campaign.

. . .

However the rigid method which we pursued in handling this issue did not result from close solidarity with the patriotic government and forces and consequently led to impairing our solidarity with these quarters.

. . .

However, the nature and composition of this front and its announcement under circumstances of mounting differences did not help in attaining its hoped for aims; on the contrary, it contributed to intensifying differences and impeded the restoration and consolidation of unity with the patriotic government and cooperation among all the national forces in the country.

The sum total of these attitudes resulted – as we have already mentioned – from the erroneous assessment, which exaggerated our own forces and minimised the role of the patriotic government and the other national forces in safeguarding the Republic. As a result of this erroneous assessment too, the Party concentrated its efforts on mobilising the masses to defend the Republic and develop it along the path of democracy. This in itself was correct, but it took place on some occasions in isolation from another basic issue, namely the issue of maintaining strong solidarity with the patriotic government and forces, an issue which is of first importance in securing the unity of the masses in their struggle to safeguard the Republic.

. . .

The drawing up of our daily tactics and plans (which are linked with the necessity to defend the Republic), in isolation from the patriotic government and forces and in reliance on our own forces only and on arousing the enthusiasm of the masses led the policy of our Party to be influenced by the spontaneous movement and to take a wrong stand on the excesses of the masses. This does not mean that we never opposed such excess. Our comrades have stood firm on many occasions, particularly among the workers against strikes and tresspassings. Ittihad El-Shaab dealt in some cases with excesses, mistaken spontaneity and unguided slogans. In general, however, we did not make sufficient effort in this respect.

Though it dealt with these problems, Ittihad El-Shaab did not give them sufficient attention. Furthermore, it reflected in its method of handling events the spirit of mass excitement and handled accordingly our attitude towards many official and non-official quarters, through criticism coupled with rigidity and not through strong solidarity with these quarters and confining ourselves to suitable objective criticism. The result was that we alienated some quarters with whom relations of solidarity could have been maintained or who at least would not have been induced to adopt a hostile attitude. . . .

.   .   .

In addition to this, the Party did not resort during this period to the procedure of deep scientific analysis of the swift and intricate develop-ments in the situation. It adopted some of its tactics in the light of daily developments of events and dealt with such events in isolation from their class roots and their general connections. The swiftness with which some negative trends in the political situation attained prominence took our Party somewhat by surprise, led it to over-weight the situation and to take an unnecessarily strong stand towards the patriotic government and some representatives of the national forces. This was reflected in the rashness in putting forward the slogan of 'No deviation . . .' and in some stiff articles which were published in Ittihad El-Shaab intended to mobilise the masses against signs of deviation.

This stiff attitude resulted from our minimisation of the role and ability of the patriotic government to resist the dangers stemming from deviation in the policy of the Republic, for which imperialism was working with all its energy as a first step towards subverting our Republic. All this led to impairing the unity of the national forces which was the weapon of victory in all circumstances.

We ought to have made an accurate class analysis of the real meaning of the first negative activities of the national bourgeoisie. This would have enabled us to avoid unnecessary excitement and to lay down a flexible and far-sighted policy in the light of the new circumstances and attitudes arising within the national movement.

.   .   .

The imperialists continued to work skilfully and actively in this atmo-sphere charged with disputes among the national forces. It is well known that the imperialists have cunning methods in this field, methods which are characterised by consistent and many-branched activity to divide the national force, social class and religious or racial other, so that they can ultimately achieve their aim of subverting our Republic. The imperialists in general, and the British imperialists in particular, have much experience in this field. They have their network of spies and agents in the country, old contacts on a wide scale and vast experience of failure and success. In this respect they usually start by identifying the distinguishing features of each national force, social class and religious or racial group (whether with reference to their interests, concepts or demands). They attempt to push each of them to strengthen their activity within these distinguishing features, while concentrating on brushing aside what they have in common. For instance, they try to drive some sections of the bourgeoisie to contract their activity in the market and production, while feeding their fears of the mass movement. They attempt to drive workers here and there to make erroneous moves of an extreme class character. They work on the one hand among the Arab people in Iraq in order to get statements or actions which reflect nationalist arrogance or fanaticism, overlooking the rights of the Kurdish people. On the other hand they provoke fear and a spirit of isolationism and nationalist sectarianism among the Kurdish people. In the same manner, they work to feed the spirit of aggressiveness and enmity among Kurds, Turcomans, Assyrians and Armenians. Similarly attempts are made with the political forces and parties to frighten one of the other and to sow the seeds of discord and suspicion among them, just as they work to create a breach between the Army and the government and the people. Recently we have witnessed examples of this imperialist activity for the execution of which groups of local reactionaries have volunteered. Domestic reaction set about working with unprecedented activity to this end. Side by side with the intensification of imperialist and reactionary intrigue, suspicion was deepened to a dangerous extent between some national forces and the patriotic government. Meanwhile the imperialists were able to continue their hostile activity on a bigger scale.

.   .   .

The violations of the rights and liberties of citizens which were intensified recently drove some people to take up a negative attitude towards the patriotic Government and rendered them incapable of seeing the real danger, represented by imperialism, reaction and the enemies of the Republic. The continuous provocations of reaction and their going so far as to shed the blood of citizens and to violate their dignity and the deliberate neglect on the part of some reactionary elements, who were not purged from the state machinery, all this led the masses to embark in some places on rash and excited actions, resulting from the necessity of self-defence and their strong concern for their gains and for the Republic. However the actions which were carried out by the angry masses in this respect led in some cases to mistaken excesses and acts of repression which cannot be approved.

These mistaken excesses have causes which ought to be studied and remedied in order to limit their effect. This is to be achieved through consistent educational efforts to guide the revolutionary zeal of the masses into the right channels. Otherwise penal measures and rebukes cannot handle this problem correctly.

The revolutionary zeal of the Iraqi people is a positive feature, which had on all occasions and particularly in the Republican era, a great effect in destroying the old system, in paralysing the activities of the enemies of the Revolution and ultimately in securing the steadfast march of the Revolution along the path of victory and consolidation. This characteristic feature has its deep roots in the history of the Iraqi people. Throughout long decades people were subject to the worst forms of despotism, exercised by tyrants and invaders. This led to violent reactions, reflected in many revolts and uprisings which were often drowned in blood, crushed fiercely and brutally. As a result, the masses were inspired by a mixed longing for revenge on the reactionary forces and for freedom. Because too of the extremely oppressive rule and arbitrary reactionary laws, the masses used in the past to solve their problems through violence and violation of the law in a spontaneous manner. Throughout generations of terror and slavery, a vigorous and fierce revolutionary spirit took hold of the masses, who were living in conditions of oppression, which increased day by day and whose indignation mounted accordingly. When the day of salvation came on the 14th of July, this spirit broke loose with the force of a volcano.

The long years which preceded the 14th July permitted but very limited opportunity for instructing the masses and educating and training them in organised political action. Therefore it was impossible for any force to control the zeal of the masses, especially the politically backward sections, who suddenly joined in gigantic numbers in the political struggle. In such a case it was inevitable for unguided zeal to work its effect and to lend the activity of the masses some extremist features.

Moreover the fact that the victories and achievements won by the people (under the Republic) after a bloody and bitter struggle were so valuable that this made the masses highly sensitive towards any sign or attempt to subvert these victories and gains. This sensitivity increased due to the successive conspiracies against the Republic.

All of these factors, together with the passing of the Revolution through contradictions, complications and deep and swift revolutionary transformations had created a spitable ground for extremist rashness among the people and all the excesses, wrong actions and violations of the law that accompanied this.

.   .   .

In the post-revolution period, our Party exerted special efforts to remedy some manifestations of mistaken extremism in the actions of the masses, but they were not sufficiently firm, as we have already explained. It is likely that elements, infiltrating among the masses, have exploited this extremist zeal and directed it on some occasions towards subversive ends.

The use by some politically backward people of methods of dragging bodies, torturing detainees, looting and trespassing on the rights and liberties of some citizens is something which has no link with guided revolutionary struggle directed against the enemies of the Republic and it is diametrically opposed to the noble aims of our national movement and the original revolutionary features of our people and party.

Our Party, which has never participated in the responsibility of government, has less chance of preventing the acts of torture which were inflicted upon detainees, in circumstances of mutiny and plotting against the Republic. Under no circumstances does it approve such methods of treating accused persons.

The revolutionary principles (which guide a party like ours firmly against the enemy) are based upon the mass mobilisation of the honest will of the people, in guided political struggle. Even in cases of preparing to wage armed battle with the enemy, the principles of the Party do not approve wrong, inhumane acts. That is why we relied, even in the hardest times of tyranny, on guided revolutionary mass struggle and rejected the method of individual assassination, terror and torture of individuals and other such acts.

Our Party (which works for the happiness of the people and their tranquility and security and which longs for overall human happiness) firmly condemns any violation of the dignity of the citizen and the rights of the individual. Our Party, which takes the stand of backing towards and alliance with the revolutionary government, emphasises the necessity of respecting the laws of the Republic and resists every erroneous slogan or action which does not serve the unity of the national ranks.

. . .

From the report of the Central Committee of the Iraqi Communist Party, *Ittihad el Shaab*, August 23, 1959. English translation, *Iraqi Review*, September 6, 1959.

21

Documents of the 3rd National Conference of the Iraqi Communist Party (1967)

The 3rd National Conference of the Iraqi Communist Party notes, with a feeling of deep gratitude, the exemplary internationalist solidarity which the CPSU and other fraternal parties demonstrated after the fascist imperialist coup of February 8, 1963, in Iraq. This glorious internationalist solidarity played an important role and helped towards the revival of the Iraqi Communist Party as a major political force in the country.

The internationalist solidarity with the Arab peoples displayed by the socialist camp headed by the Soviet Union, and by the entire world Communist movement during the imperialist-Zionist aggression in June 1967 was the main factor that prevented the realization of the ultimate aim of the aggression – elimination of the Arab national-liberation movement and progressive regimes in the Arab world. Precisely such was the aim of imperialism and its creation, Israel. This noble internationalist stand strengthened the relations of friendship and cooperation between the Arab national-liberation movement and the socialist camp, the world Communist movement. The anti-communist and anti-socialist ideas and policies received a telling blow.

The negative phenomena with which the world Communist movement is confronted and which find expression in a split in its ranks have caused harm and continue to weaken its vanguard role and the effectiveness of the contribution of the world Communist movement to the world revolutionary process whose ultimate objective is abolition of the world capitalist system and the building of a new world, the world of socialism and communism.

The split in the world Communist movement is fully and wholly on the conscience of the Mao Tse-tung group, which has seized leadership of the Communist Party of China and obstinately proceeds with its divisive policies. This group has distorted Marxism-Leninism and departed from it, embarking on the path of dogmatism. As a result of its activities the CPC has been divorced from the world Communist movement and the gains of the Chinese people are jeopardised. The barbaric methods and means employed by the Mao group to suppress and remove all the leading and internationalist cadres of the CPC who disagree with the opportunist course of the Mao clique have been condemned by the entire world Communist movement.

The 3rd Conference notes the existence of a constant danger from the right. The right deviationists attack the basic principles of Marxism-Leninism, the theoretical foundations and principles of socialist revolution, militating with particular viciousness against the ideas of the hegemony of the proletariat and the leading role of the Communist Party. It is asserted that these ideas are not indispensable for the building of socialism and its development. At the same time, in other countries, the danger of dogmatism and isolationism is increasing [the danger from the left]. All this is aggravated by manifestations of extreme nationalism, which adds to the deviationist danger and increasingly complicates measures to correct the situation.

All these trends, which are alien to Marxism-Leninism and its internationalist essence, have a common social and class basis – petty-bourgeois ideas and notions characterised by narrowly-understood patriotism, chauvinism and intolerance, which includes a hostile attitude towards the Soviet Union and its glorious Communist Party, exaggeration of the role of national and regional aspects, and scorn for the principles and fundamentals of Marxism-Leninism.

The Iraqi Communist Party, demonstrating its adherence to the healthy and principled relations between Communist parties which are clearly set out in the 1957 and 1960 documents of the Communist movement, reaffirms that it is a contingent of the international proletarian army. This is indicative above all of deep awareness of common responsibility for the unity of the world Communist movement, for the preservation of its purity and for uniting efforts to achieve the principal aims which are common for all the contingents of the international Communist and working-class movement.

While understanding the importance and special character of relations between fraternal Communist and Workers' parties in the Arab countries, the ICP will at the same time strive to make, jointly with these parties, its positive contribution to the defence of the unity of the world Communist movement and the purity of its principles, especially as regards petty-bourgeois ideology, to the defence of democratic freedoms, to the development and consolidation of the struggle of the Arab working people for eliminating the consequences of the Israel aggression, for democracy, social progress and socialism. The ICP resolutely comes out in defence of the legitimate national rights of the Kurdish people.

Resolution on the Opportunist Splinter Group

In September 1957 the opportunist splinter group set about subverting the unity of the Iraqi Communist Party. It took recourse to arnachist and fraudulent methods, to individual terror. Its actions were undertaken after a campaign of malicious slander against the ICP and its Central Committee and were accompanied by divulgence of secret Party documents.

In its subversive work the splinter faction took advantage of the difficult situation in which the Party had found itself as a result of the faction's efforts to create ideological confusion. Factional activities were also facilitated by the insufficiently principled stand of the Party leadership and some Party organisations on matters of organisational work, and by the existence in the Party of opportunist elements who aggravated the ideological and organisational difficulties, contributed to the isolation of some organisations from the masses, and hampered the utilisation of the possibilities for mass struggle.

The Iraqi Communist Party has fought, and continues to fight, against right-wing opportunism, regarding it as the main danger. At the same time it is fighting against isolationist opportunism (the left deviation). This struggle became especially necessary when isolationist opportunism had found expression in the establishment of an anti-Party splinter centre, the pernicious ideas of this opportunism had begun to be spread, and subversive work had been launched against our Party and the revolu-itionary movement in Iraq.

The splitters concentrated fire on the CC ICP, seeking to weaken and isolate it from the Party. They planned to strike at the Party leadership, split the Party, pervert its basic aims and tasks and prepare conditions for seizing leadership of the Party.

Tolerance towards subversive activity against the Party leadership, and the attempts to discredit it, the setting of rank-and-file Communists against the leadership is incompatible with Communism, with the traditions of our Party. It creates a permanent danger to the Party. The disagreements of principle that may arise between members of the leadership or part of the Party are resolved in the process of work, with the help of legitimate methods. But tolerance towards a campaign to discredit the Party leadership is out of the question, for it breeds an unhealthy atmosphere, creates a harmful precedent and jeopardises the Party as a whole.

The new splinter group does not differ from all other splinter groups the Party has known. They were petty-bourgeois in class essence and rooted in opportunist ideas. The fate of the new splinter groups will be the same as that of its predecessors. But it has a distinguishing feature – anarchist methods, violence which it has practised since its emergence. This confirms once again the need staunchly and resolutely to defend the unity of the Party and its revolutionary policy. It is necessary strictly to abide by the Leninist methods and vigorously combat all liberal trends and the group spirit, for in the final count they lead to factionalism and split.

The 3rd Conference approves the measures the Central Committee took after its extraordinary meeting in September 1967 and its meeting in October 1967, thus carrying out its duty to defend the Party and its unity. Concrete principled decisions were adopted on expelling the leaders of the splinter group from the Party; its subversive divisive activities were condemned. These decisions are very important from the viewpoint of principle rather than of practical significance, for the factionalists had actually put themselves outside the ranks of the Party, which resolutely, from Leninist positions of principle, condemned their subversive anti-Party splitting activity.

The Walid-Ramzi group found an associate in the small 'Nadji' group and began openly to settle accounts, taking advantage of the complicated position in the Party in an attempt to impose its conditions upon the leadership. A characteristic feature of this bloc is its anti-internationalist attitude towards problems of the tactics and strategy of the world Communist movement. Its leftism stems from petty-bourgeois adventurism. The Conference supports the leadership's decisions on expelling the leaders of the 'Nadji' group from the Party.

The Conference expresses confidence that all Party organisations will continue to fulfil, resolutely and in keeping with principle, their sacred duty to eliminate the splinter bloc and root out liberalism in theory and practice: *firstly*, by waging a determined and consistent fight against the splinter bloc in the field of policy, ideology and organisation, against tolerance towards the splitters. It is necessary resolutely to clear the Party of liberal elements, to combat laxity and strengthen proletarian party discipline. *Secondly*, by condemning erroneous views which threaten to weaken the Leninist principles of inner-party life and are conducive to group and splinter activities (among these views, the following can be listed: a) 'pressure of the masses on the leadership', which is a distortion of the Leninist conception of mutual party control; b) artificial division of the Party and the leadership into 'revolutionaries' and 'opportunists'; c) artificial division of the Party and the leadership according to the social position; d) insistence on debates in the Party on all questions without exception. *Thirdly*, by continuing contacts and meetings with erring elements who have sided with the splinter groups because of class immaturity and insufficient experience of inner-party work and struggle, which should be conducted on the basis of principle and should not be allowed to be turned into personal or factional struggle. The principled resolute stand of the Party demands condemnation of splitting activity and unconditional dissolution of all opportunist factions. The question of sanctions against the members of these blocs should be decided by the Party. *Fourthly*, by observing the principles of our Party and pursuing its general line, maintaining the links with the masses and widely applying all forms of revolutionary mass struggle.

The 3rd Conference, adhering to a stand as resolute and principled as that of the majority of Communists and Party organisations, is positive that all forms of liberalism, which is alien to the principles of Leninism, will be eliminated in the name of strengthening the unity and organisation of the Party, enhancing its militancy, justifying the confidence of the people and achieving its aims, above all the establishment of a revolutionary democratic regime.

Resolution on the Situation in the Arab Region

After the aggression of June 5, 1967, the situation in the Arab region remains unchanged:

1. Israeli troops continue to occupy large parts of the territory of Arab countries. The imperialist-Israeli plans for eliminating progressive regimes in the newly-free Arab countries have not been abandoned. The threat of aggression being renewed has not been removed. The activities of reactionary forces, regimes and agents in the Arab countries are being stepped up. The difficulties and the situation resulting from the defeat facilitate the hostile forces' activities against the Arab national-liberation movement aimed at eliminating its gains and restoring colonial regimes.

2. But the Israeli aggression has not achieved its principal objective, that of overthrowing the progressive regimes in Egypt and Syria. The two fraternal countries were able to repel the Israeli attack, aided by world imperialism, thanks to resolute support on the part of the Soviet Union and other socialist countries. They have rapidly made good their military and material losses also owing to Soviet help. The extensive assistance the socialist countries provided to the Arab states and their vigorous international political activity have vastly facilitated the isolation of the aggressors and the preservation and consolidation of the Arab national-liberation movement.

3. The aggression failed to crush the Arab national-liberation movement. The struggle of Arab revolutionaries in occupied South Arabia that flared up in the days of the June defeat culminated in the expulsion of the British colonialists from that part of the Arab homeland and the birth of an independent People's Republic of South Yemen. The plans of the rightist and reactionary forces to seize power in fraternal Egypt fell through. Despite the intensification of the war against fraternal republican Yemen following the withdrawal of Egyptian troops, the republican regime repelled the attack of the enemies and safeguarded its gains. At the same time, fraternal Algeria foiled a conspiracy against its progressive regime, and Arab resistance was stepped up on occupied territories.

4. The defeat was unprecedentedly instrumental in exposing the aggressive essence of imperialism, the racist aggressive nature of Israel. The treacherousness of the reactionary and dictatorial regimes existing in the Arab world was also laid bare. Profound changes occurred in the conscience of the broad masses, fortifying their revolutionary will. The defeat demonstrated once again the tremendous importance of the alliance of the Arab national-liberation movement with the socialist world camp, and also the need for departing from the policy of balancing between the socialist and imperialist camps covered up by the motto of 'non-alignment'.

5. The defeat shook the very foundations of the entire system of regimes, policies and erroneous views which predetermined it. There surged a wave of serious criticism helping to rectify shortcomings in the ideological system of the political regimes in Egypt and especially in Syria. The conscious masses came to realise that petty-bourgeois notions and ideas had seriously influenced the policy of the leaderships of the two fraternal countries, weakening their defence potential:

a) the conditions that existed in the fraternal countries had enabled rightist bourgeois and reactionary elements to seize key posts in the military, political and administrative apparatus and play a dangerous subversive role which helped to bring on the defeat;

b) in this situation there appeared spurious ideological and political trends which manifested themselves both in the sphere of national policy and in inter-Arab and international relations;

c) a vanguard political party armed with Marxist-Leninist theory was not in existence or debarred from power, from ideological and guiding activity. In Syria, political activity was concentrated and restricted within the framework of the organisation. The same was true for the Arab Socialist Union in Egypt. The resulting weakness of political organisation prevented mobilising the masses prior to and during the aggression. The revolutionary theory of the working class and of a fighting people had been replaced by erroneous models of 'socialism', 'classes' and 'state power'. This principal element of the weakness of the regimes had disarmed the workers, peasants and soldiers, affecting the ability of the people to repulse the aggression.

6. The conscious Arab masses and their political vanguard forces consider that elimination of the consequences of the aggression and success in foiling the designs of imperialism, Israel and reaction demand cardinal changes in the structure, policy and ideology of the regimes in the newly-free Arab countries and especially in fraternal Egypt and Syria, which bore the brunt of the fight against the enemy. These countries have to restore and fortify their defence potential. Serious changes have to be made in the army command and other spheres in Egypt. All this is indispensable for recovery from the defeat. What has to be solved in the first place, however, is the problem pertaining to a cardinal change in the attitude towards the fighting people and revolutionary political forces – establishment of popular democratic revolutionary regimes.

The experience of all progressive-minded Arabs shows that the actions of the people are made effective by a political regime under which the working class, through its party, performs a truly leading role; it shows that the way to making good the defeat, beating the enemy and achieving progress is the socialist way. There is the urgent need for a political party armed with the theory of the working class, the need to accept scientific socialism (Marxism-Leninism) as a guide to action, as an all-embracing theory of reconstructing society and the state. The freedom of all parties and political revolutionary forces is essential for mobilising the revolutionary energy of the masses.

Under such regimes, it is possible to fight successfully against imperialism and Zionism on all political levels, in the economic, military and ideological fields; it is possible to build a national army equipped with a revolutionary theory, to strengthen the alliance with the friendly socialist camp and all the other freedom-loving forces of the world in the name of victory over the enemy and further progress along the road of freedom, social progress and national unity.

7. The way to the establishment of such regimes lies through the formation of coalition governments uniting Communist parties and other progressive national forces. Thus optimal conditions will be created for mobilising the masses to eliminate the consequences of the aggression and frustrate the designs of the enemy.

The establishment of democratic fronts of political and class alliances is a pressing necessity. It is demanded by objective Arab realities. What is needed for Iraq and other Arab countries is the formation of coalition governments uniting all forces of a democratic front based on a firm worker-peasant alliance.

8. Given such governments and fronts, a solid basis can be built for effective national solidarity which will help rally the national-liberation forces of the Arabs for recovering from the defeat and removing its consequences. This solidarity will enable the Arab national-liberation movement to beat off the attacks of imperialism, foil the Israeli aggressive plans, outline for the Palestinian people the way to restoring the rights of which it has been robbed, and help it exercise the right to self-determination in their own land. Furthermore, it will create prerequisites for various forms of federation of newly-free Arab countries, for progress towards ultimate Arab unity.

9. This development hinges principally on the establishment of popular and democratic political regimes and national alliances and front, the forging of Arab solidarity on the basis of popular struggle and alliance with the socialist camp, for this is the beginning of success in making good the defeat, eliminating the consequences of the aggression and repelling the onslaught of imperialism and other hostile forces. Later on it will be possible to launch a victorious struggle in the military, political and other fields.

Reducing the causes of the defeat to secondary factors would not help do away with its effects. Contrariwise, emphasis on a military or political solution alone bespeaks a lack of realistic appraisal of the situation and of a sense of responsibility for the destiny of the Arab motherland. The talk of a people's war as the only way, attempts by any Arab country to adopt a special attitude towards the matter of consolidating the efforts of all the Arab states can prejudice the actions of the Arab and other countries aimed at isolating the enemy and removing the aftermath of the criminal aggression.

The situation resulting from the aggression has so far been favourable for the hopes of the imperialists and Israel to proceed with their aggressive policy. The situation of Syria, Iraq, Jordan, Egypt and other countries depends in large measure on the situation in the Arab world that shaped up after June 5, 1967. Hence the need to criticise isolationist trends and expose the treasonous policy of the reactionary governments of some Arab countries and the demagoguery of the Iraqi dictators.

10. The struggle against the Israeli-imperialist enemy provided the dictatorial rulers of Iraq with a pretext for a propaganda ballyhoo which helped them distort the principles of national-liberation struggle, Arab solidarity and Arab unity.

Their chauvinistic aggressive policy weakened the Iraqi army, which had been sent to fight the Kurdish people. Thousands of patriotic-minded officers and soldiers were imprisoned as a result of their reactionary policy, which further weakened the army. And when hostilities started, only symbolic contingents were sent to take part in the fighting. Instead of mobilising the efforts of the entire people, the stress was laid on propaganda. By their policy the Iraqi rulers paralysed the will of the people; they suppressed demonstrations by force and did not allow the people to arm themselves and take part in the struggle. It was only pressure from the people that compelled them to adopt a negative attitude towards the countries that aided the aggressor. Their conduct and policy were dictated by hostility towards the people, by oblivion of the national interests, by their ardent desire to help the reactionary regimes in Arab countries and come to terms with imperialism and the rulers of the neighbouring reactionary regimes associated with imperialism. Moreover, they took every advantage of the difficulties experienced by two fraternal Arab countries, Egypt and Syria. Utilising the situation to strangle the will of the people, they launched an onslaught on the working people, raising the taxes, widely applying dictatorial methods and destroying national unity by their policy of violation of the national rights of the Kurdish people and suppression of the progressive forces. Those who are fighting against their own people cannot fight against the enemies of the people. Those who side with puppet reactionary regimes and cooperate with the imperialists and their agents exclude themselves from the national camp of struggle against imperialism and Israel, against all enemies of the Arab nation.

It was not a lack of mutual understanding with the imperialist countries but the force of circumstances that compelled the dictators to sever diplomatic relations with some imperialist powers or resort to a formal termination of the export of oil to them.

The oil agreement with a French company, the agreement on arms deliveries from France, the opening of the domestic market for French and Italian capital and other steps unmasked the real face of the dictators selling out national interests. It is legitimate and necessary, given support of the people, for an independent revolutionary country to exploit contradictions between imperialist powers, but it is abnormal for such a policy to be pursued by a weak dictatorial government divorced from the people, for this jeopardizes the independence of the country and opens the door before neocolonialism. The Iraqi rulers' policy of expanding cooperation with France and Western monopolies means capitulation before an imperialist state, it is indicative of a search for a master to embrace. And this instead of genuinely equal cooperation with the friendly socialist countries.

The regime in Iraq cannot hold out long. It is bound to be replaced by a coalition government of all patriotic progressive forces which will put an end to the shameful anti-national policy, destroy the traces of the dictatorial regime and enable Iraq to play a worthy role in the anti-imperialist strugggle against Israel and the forces hostile to the national-liberation movement. The continued existence of the dictatorial regime isolated from the people is a large gap in the Arab front of national-liberation struggle. Imperialism is not necessarily planning to come down directly upon Egypt, Syria or Algeria. It will utilize the smallest loophole to infiltrate, to breach and weaken the Arab front in the course of its general offensive against the Arab national-liberation movement, to depose progressive regimes in a number of Arab states. Success in eliminating the consequences of the aggression and in foiling aggressive plans against Arab states calls not only for changing and transforming the political regimes in the newly-free Arab countries situated on the front-line of the struggle against imperialism and Israel. As far as Iraq is concerned, it pre-supposes the rallying of all progressive national forces in a single front of struggle to free our country from the dictatorial regime and the establishment of a democratic coalition government. This will enable Iraq to form, together with all other Arab countries, a united front capable of fighting to recover the annexed lands, eliminate the effects of the aggression, victoriously repel imperialist attacks and foil plans of aggression.

Resolution on the Kurdish Question

The Iraqi Communist Party reaffirms its stand on the Kurdish question based on the Marxist-Leninist principle of the right of all nations, big and small, to self-determination, their right to fight against national oppression and for the creation of an independent organism uniting the entire nation.

The chauvinistic reactionary ideas on the solution of the Kurdish question which ignore the right of nations to self-determination and pervert the aims of the Kurdish liberation movement come not from the workers, peasants and other Arab working people, but from the reactionary ruling circles.

The imperialists, the oil companies, the imperialists' agents and accomplices in Iraq and neighbouring countries are doing their utmost to nourish and fan the chauvinistic sentiments and aspirations current among the Arab ruling classes and bourgeois liberal organisations, on the one hand, and nationalistic fanaticism and separatism among the Kurds, on the other. Some progressive nationalist Arab organisations have begun to adopt sound realistic positions with regard to the national rights of the Kurdish people, positions conforming to the interests of the Kurdish and Arab peoples. But some nationalist forces still continue to insist on their erroneous chauvinistic claims.

While fighting against Arab chauvinism our Party is at the same time fighting against the nationalistic fanaticism which is to be observed among the Kurds. It is fighting for greater unity and solidarity between the Arabs and Kurds and other minorities, proceeding from the principles of internationalist fraternity among all the working people of Iraq regardless of their nationality or religion.

Our Party consistently supports the road chosen by the Kurdish people in Iraq; a road of fraternal unity and struggle, jointly with the fraternal Arab people, against imperialism and reaction of all kinds, in the name of freedom and democracy for the Iraqi people, for Kurdistan's autonomy within the framework of the Iraqi Republic, for the liberation of the Iraqi working people – Kurds, Arabs and people of other nationalities – from all forms of exploitation, for the building of socialism.

The national-liberation movement of the Kurdish people is part of the revolutionary democratic struggle in Iraq, it is an ally of the Iraqi proletariat in the fight for immediate and long-range objectives. There can be no just solution of the Kurdish problem under the present dictatorial regime, which is hostile to the entire Iraqi people and rules with the help of police terror.

The national unity of Iraq cannot be ensured until a lasting democratic solution of the Kurdish problem is found. The unity of Iraq, just as that of other multinational states, derives strength from mutual recognition by the two main nationalities, the Kurdish and the Arab, of legitimate national rights.

Despite the failure of all its previous attempts to crush the Kurdish revolution by fire, bullet and fraud, the reactionary chauvinistic regime refuses to reinstate the Kurdish people in their legitimate rights and stubbornly continues its bankrupt anti-democratic policy which is pushing the country to the brink of a precipice. This policy is fraught with a resumption of hostilities. The Iraqi rulers want to seize the initiative and, at an opportune time, to launch a new armed attack. They cannot reconcile themselves to dual power in Kurdistan, where the power of the regime and the power of the rebels exist side by side. Seeking to re-establish their full control over Kurdistan, they resort to deception and bribery to weaken the revolutionary forces. They maintain troops there and support the rightist group which committed betrayal back in the summer of 1966 and became an obedient tool of the chauvinistic dictators, who are rendering moral and material assistance to it.

Hence the need for the Kurdish revolutionary forces and their leadership to be vigilant and ready to fight back a sneak attack.

The main source from which the revolution can draw strength and on which it can rely for support is our people and their tremendous energy. The revolution enjoys the sympathy and support of real friends abroad, but there is also the need resolutely to oppose the manœuvres of the imperialists and reaction aimed at weakening and subverting the liberation movement. Correction of the mistakes of the Kurdish revolution in Iraqi Kurdistan will help strengthen the Kurdish liberation movement in Iranian and Turkish Kurdistan. Then the progressive forces of Iraqi Kurdistan will be able to fulfil with honour their national duty in helping the struggle of their brothers in the neighbouring countries. Intensification of the revolution calls for eliminating the element of spontaneity, reconstruction of revolutionary organisations on the basis of a coalition of all forces taking part in the revolution, and elaboration, in the liberated regions, of an adequate system of government by democratically elected organs, which will normalise life, defend the interests of the peasants and other strata of the population of Kurdistan, confiscate the holdings of feudals and landlords collaborating with the enemies of the revolution and distribute land among the peasants and the families of those killed in action.

The interests of the revolution demand that no single party should have franchise on political activity, that possibilities should be created for the activity of all organisations and groups taking part in the revolution. To ensure unity of effort in ideological work among the masses and in combating the defeatism propagated by the enemies, no repressive measures should be taken against any organisation.

The establishment of a political union organised on a common progressive platform will become the axis linking our Party with the Democratic Party of Kurdistan, a powerful instrument of mobilising the energy of the Kurdish people, consolidating the revolution and guaranteeing its victory.

The revolution will be further strengthened when its organisations and armed groups are cleared from reactionary elements and all those who utilised their posts for self-seeking aims.

The 3rd Conference warmly greets the heroic Communists of Kurdistan, who hold high the banner of combat fraternity of the Kurds, Arabs and other nationalities. It expresses confidence that they will continue their tireless struggle for the democratisation of Iraq and for Kurdistan's autonomy. The Conference supports the appeal of the Party organisation committee of Kurdistan to the leadership of the Kurdish revolution touching upon some problems of the revolution and indicating ways of their settlement. The Conference warmly greets all fighters against imperialism, reaction and the dictatorial regime in Iraq, for the national rights of the Kurdish people. It reveres the memory of those who have fallen in the fight for the just cause of their people.

The Iraqi Communist Party reaffirms its support of the just liberation struggle of the Kurdish people and their determination to continue it shoulder to shoulder with the other forces which are making their contribution to the revolution, striving to prevent a new armed attack by the reactionary dictatorial regime.

If the dictatorial chauvinistic regime decides to restart the war of aggression, the broad masses in Kurdistan will rise to defend their revolution and inflict a decisive defeat upon the aggressor. In this struggle they can count on effective and many-sided assistance from the broad masses in all corners of Iraq, from Arab and world public opinion. Long live Arab-Kurdish fraternity! Long live the struggle of the Kurdish people for their legitimate right to autonomy!

Resolution on the National Front

At the present stage great importance attaches to the problem of building class national alliances. A political alliance of patriotic and progressive forces will be an effective weapon in the struggle against the present regime, which is the chief obstacle to the triumph of the will of the people, to the realisation of their democratic and national aims.

The new alignment of class forces since the revolution in July 1958 has assumed a particularly clear shape in recent years. Although the aims of the national democratic revolution were not achieved, great changes took place in the attitude of some groups of the middle national bourgeoisie. Some of them joined the reactionary camp, began to look for allies in it and set about working out a political programme oriented on social reforms in the spirit of 'free capitalist development' and liberal democracy.

The Iraqi Communist Party, employing the Marxist method of analysis, came to the conclusion that at the present stage of Iraq's development a worker-peasant alliance should be the cornerstone of the national front for whose establishment the struggle is being waged.

The attitude to the parties and political organisations of the various classes with which alliance has to be concluded is determined in the light of a clear understanding of the tasks of the present stage of the national movement and the tasks of the revolution, with due regard to the positions of the classes and their political organisations.

Our Party follows with great attention the development which is taking place in a number of organisations of the petty bourgeoisie and which is connected with the character of our epoch, with the change in the content and trends of the Arab national-liberation movement, to say nothing of the growth of the revolutionary consciousness of the broad masses of our people, the main factor in the process of noticeable positive changes in the positions of these parties and blocs. The latter applies particularly to some of their conceptions and their policy with respect to the Communists and democrats after the fascist coup of February 8. This evolution creates prerequisites for and facilitates rapprochement and alliance between the Iraqi Communist Party and these parties, progressive and national forces. In this instance our Party proceeds from the need for a policy of class and political alliances to mobilise the forces and energy of the people in the struggle against imperialism, reaction and the dictatorship.

Our Party considers that there exist favourable conditions for building a bloc of progressive national forces with a view to realising the objectives for which our people are fighting, above all such as the overthrow of the dictatorial regime and the establishment of a democratic national coalition government which will take the initiative in eliminating all vestiges and traces of the dictatorial regime, grant democratic freedoms to the people, in the first place the freedom of activity of parties, give general amnesty to political prisoners, restore the rights of all those who were deprived of their rights and subjected to isolation, and eliminate the aftermath of the war in Kurdistan. Steps must be taken to ensure the rights of the Kurdish people, their autonomy. It is necessary to annul the amendments which the reactionaries introduced into the agrarian reform law, undertake resolute steps to restore our rights usurped by the oil monopolies and establish an independent national oil extracting and processing industry; to strengthen solidarity with the newly-free Arab countries in the fight against imperialism, Zionism and reaction, for eliminating the results of the Israeli imperialist aggression, and in defence of the rights of the Arab people of Palestine; to broaden and strengthen relations of friendship and cooperation with the socialist camp; to grant democratic rights to all progressive national forces, work out a law on democratic elections, hold, on its basis, elections to a Constituent Assembly, and prepare the transition of the country to democratic constitutional life.

If the Iraqi Communist Party and the other progressive forces succeed in building this political coalition, abolishing the dictatorship and establishing a provisonal coalition government, the Iraqi Communists will unhesitatingly defend, both within and outside the framework of state power, the interests and rights of the working people, and resolutely insist on the solution of pressing problems and the mobilisation of the people in the struggle against the plans of imperialism and the onslaught of the reactionary forces. The implementation of immediate tasks will facilitate the solution of other problems, above all the establishment of an Iraqi Democratic Republic.

The Iraqi Communist Party is sincerely ready to strengthen cooperation with its allies, to overcome temporary contradictions in a spirit of good will, proceeding from the vital interests of the working class and all working people. It will march forward together with its allies from among the progressive forces which identify themselves with the interests and aims of the working people. It resolutely comes out against imperialism and reaction and fights for a democratic Iraq free from national oppression and class exploitation.

Abridged from *Tariq al-Shaab*, January 1968.

22

Reza Radmanesh: *The Policy of the Iranian Communists*

. . .

The October Revolution wrought a fundamental change in the destinies of colonial and dependent nations. Their struggle for freedom now went beyond national or local bounds and became part of the world revolutionary process. Lenin pointed out that the socialist revolution would not, in the main, be only a struggle of the proletariat against the bourgeoisie of each country, but a struggle of all colonial, oppressed and dependent nations against world imperialism.

And under the stimulating influence of the October Revolution and Lenin's analysis of the national and colonial problem at congresses of the Communist International, Lenin's theory of revolution took firm hold in the colonial and dependent countries. Communist parties were formed in some of them and worked out their revolutionary strategy and tactics in keeping with their specific conditions. The development of the national-liberation movement has been closely linked with the growth and strengthening of the Soviet Union, the birthplace of the socialist revolution and, after World War II, with the socialist world system and the workers' struggle in capitalist countries. The movement thus entered a new stage.

. . .

The October Revolution gave our people a new neighbour, a new friend and protector of their freedom and independence – Soviet Russia, a country ruled by a workers' and peasants' government.

In the very first months after the revolution, the Soviet government, headed by Lenin, annulled the Anglo-Russian Treaty of 1907 and all agreements which in one or another way restricted or impaired the Iranian people's right to freedom and independence.

The Soviet government also repealed the capitulations and anulled all public and private debts, totalling more than 100 million roubles; this enabled Iran to force the other powers to repeal the capitulations in 1928.

The October Revolution thus eliminated the danger to Iran's sovereignty and independence. It freed her of the yoke imposed by Tsarist Russia and created the necessary preconditions for breaking out of political and economic dependence on the imperialist powers. The most pressing task was to end British imperialist domination and give the country democratic government.

That was the aim and substance of the 1918–19 national liberation movement which spread to a large part of the country and, after the conclusion of the shackling 1919 treaty with Britain, grew into an armed rising which in 1920–21 engulfed the provinces of Iranian Azerbaijan, Gilan and Khurrasan.

The defeat of the movement was due to the relative weakness of our working class, disunity and strife within the movement itself, leftist deviations and adventurism of some of its leaders and, last but not least, direct intervention by British imperialism which, following the *coup d'état* of 1921, placed the country under Reza Khan.

Though the 1918–21 anti-imperialist, anti-feudal democratic movement was suppressed, it laid a deep imprint on Iranian life, and this was to play a definite part in subsequent events. The onerous treaty of 1919, which virtually converted Iran into a British possession, was annulled. Britain was compelled to end the military occupation and withdraw all her forces from Iranian territory. The 1921 treaty with the Soviet Union – Iran's first equal treaty with a great power – laid the foundations for independence, sovereign and territorial integrity.

The founding of the Communist Party in June 1920 was one of the high points of the 1918–21 movement and was largely inspired by it and the October Revolution. The Party became an active and independent factor exerting a strong influence on the movement for national freedom.

*

The suppression of the 1918–21 movement and the introduction of a reactionary regime prevented us from utilising the favourable situation created by the October Revolution. In common with other countries bordering on the USSR, Iran became an imperialist base, a link in the blockade-chain surrounding the first socialist state.

The vacuum in Iran resulting from the overthrow of the Tsarist regime was filled by British imperialism, not by the national patriotic forces. Her position thus strengthened, Britain proceeded to introduce new methods of exploiting the country and made certain structural changes in its government.

Anti-communism and opposition to democracy became the underlying principle of home and foreign policy. Communist activity was savagely suppressed; contacts with the USSR were cut to a minimum, though their political and economic advantages were obvious to all. The Communist and other progressive parties and trade unions were banned; the Mejlis was turned into a caricature of parliament. The ruling element, dutifully following policies laid down by the imperialists, renounced Iran's traditional neutrality and signed the Saidabad military pact.

The net result was that Iran, besides remaining an economic appendage of the imperialist powers, was turned into a staging ground for their military and political gambles. Militarisation of the regime and alliance with the reactionary imperialist forces – it was by this dual tactic that the Iranian government hoped to maintain itself in power.

Its fallacy was glaringly demonstrated in the critical period of World War II. The twenty-year dictatorship of Reza Shah, that tool of imperialism and reaction in the Middle East, began to crumble in the very first days of the war. Communists and other progressive elements, many of whom had spent years in prison and exile, founded the Iranian People's Party (Tudeh), the continuer of our people's revolutionary traditions. In a very short time it developed from a few small nuclei into an influential force and gave leadership to the popular liberation movement.

That movement spread to the entire country, reaching its zenith in 1945–46 with the armed rising in Iranian Azerbaijan and Kurdistan, where a democratic government was formed within the Iranian state. But this time, too, it was suppressed with the help of the US and other imperialists.

The victory of the Soviet Army and the emergence of People's Democracies in Europe and Asia projected socialism beyond the borders of one country and made it a world system. This changed the whole balance of world forces to the advantage of socialism and the disadvantage of imperialism. And the change strongly affected the political and economic situation in Iran, a country bordering on the Soviet Union, the bulwark of the socialist world system. Again our country became one of the most vulnerable links in the system of world imperialism and reaction. That was the background to the new upsurge of the liberation movement in 1951–52, culminating in nationalisation of the oil industry, severance of political ties with British imperialism and the Shah's flight from the country. Unfortunately, this time, too, as a result of collusion between Anglo-American imperialism and Iranian reaction and of differences within the national-liberation movement, the struggle ended in defeat. Another reactionary *coup* was staged in August 1953. This time the Iranian ultras were helped by direct British imperialist intervention.

The following basic conclusions can be drawn from these developments:

1. With the passage of time the influence of the October Revolution, far from diminishing, has steadily and rapidly increased. The process begun in 1917 gained momentum and led to the emergence of the socialist world system, which has become a decisive factor in the making of world history.

2. Iranian experience, notably the liberation movements of 1945–46 and 1951–53, clearly show that imperialism, particularly American, is the chief enemy of Iranian freedom and independence and the biggest obstacle to progress and meaningful reform.

3. With the changed alignment of forces in favour of socialism, the Iranian national-liberation movement has been growing in strength and scope, taking in ever new class and social strata and advancing more concrete democratic demands.

*

The 1921 *coup* was carried out after the victory of the October Revolution, in the first stage of the general crisis of capitalism and at the height of the liberation movement. Its obvious purpose was to suppress the movement, bolster the position of British imperialism and check the spreading influence of the October Revolution. The 1953 *coup* was staged at a time when the national-liberation movement had led to the nationalisation of oil, when British imperialism had quit the Iranian political scene and the position of US imperialism had been weakened. Understandably, it caused more damage than the 1921 *coup*, and our Party regards it as a tragic chapter in the modern history of Iran.

The regime imposed on the country after the *coup* nullified all the gains won by the people in years of hard-fought struggle. It factually cancelled the oil nationalisation law, abandoned neutrality, acceded to the Baghdad Pact (Cento) and turned the Iranian market over to the imperialist monopolies.

Far from resolving social contradictions, it aggravated them and plunged the country into a profound economic and social crisis. The government made certain concessions in an attempt to adapt itself to the changing relation of forces at home and internationally. Its most important measures in this respect were the agrarian reform and improvement of relations with the Soviet Union and other socialist countries.

However, all its measures were superficial and inconsistent. Besides, the agrarian reform was deliberately designed to promote capitalist relations in agriculture without encroaching on the basic interests of the big landowners. And while slightly revising its policy on political and economic relations with the socialist countries, the government has been careful to safeguard the basic interests of the imperialist monopolies.

Two factors were largely responsible for this change of Iran's policy, which continues to be oriented on the capitalist world system, but takes into account the existence of the socialist world system.

The first factor is the chronic economic crisis, non-fulfilment of the five-year plans, discontinuance of American 'aid'; mounting pressure by political parties and groups within the country and abroad. The second is the Soviet Union's policy of peaceful co-existence and its disinterested economic aid, splendid examples of which we see in Egypt, Afghanistan, Iraq and other countries; the changing alignment of world forces in favour of the camp of peace, democracy and socialism and to the detriment of imperialism.

The recent policy changes are doubtlessly a positive development. Our Party believes that, irrespective of the government's motivations, they help to strengthen Iran's political independence and her efforts towards economic independence. Accordingly, our Party has urged maximum improvement of relations with the socialist states.

Though the government has consistently upheld monopoly interests and has repeatedly vowed allegiance to the West, the US and British imperialists look askance at its economic co-operation with the Soviet Union and other socialist countries, and there has been a good deal of criticism by the Western press and radio. The great popularity in Iran of closer ties with the socialist countries, despite objections and criticism from some myopic politicians, is in itself proof that our Party is following a correct course.

In analysing the political and economic changes of the past few years, one must be careful to avoid two errors: first, categorical negation of the positive aspects of these changes, which could only isolate us from the people and their aspirations, for the realisation of which we are fighting. Another mistake would be to over-estimate these changes on the assumption that, though they do not affect basic landowner and monopoly interests, they represent a fundamental change in the government's anti-democratic and reactionary policy. That view has no justification in reality and can only mislead the people, indeed, encourage them to accept and support the regime.

*

A cursory survey of Iranian history over the past fifty years will show that the ruling element has consistently striven to prevent the spread of socialist ideas, and to shape home and foreign policy in total disregard of the world-wide influence of the October Revolution. In fact, at one time the government ignored the very existence of the Soviet Union.

Our Party has always stood at the head of the genuine national and democratic forces in combating that policy. It has gone through many ordeals, has made sacrifices and has always displayed courage.

Today, too, we firmly believe that revolutionary ideas know no boundaries. What socialism offers the people cannot be concealed, obscured or discounted by anti-Communist propaganda, war bases, prison or torture. It should be perfectly clear that Iran, like every other developing country, cannot cope with her numerous economic and technological problems without the generous assistance of the Soviet Union and the other socialist countries. And that is precisely why we take a positive view of the present government's efforts in this direction.

Our country sorely needs fundamental reforms in every field of public, economic and political life.

The national and democratic aims of the Iranian people can be attained only through democratisation, and the process should begin with a general amnesty, release of political detainees, return of political exiles, re-establishment of civil and social freedoms, including freedom of parties, trade unions and other public organisations. Reforms that have no support among the people and are not of a democratic nature are bound to be short-lived and cannot produce the desired and much needed radical changes.

There is one more important prerequisite for Iran's development, economic democratisation: a thorough agrarian reform in favour of the peasants, abolition of monopoly control of the economy, a larger and democratically administered public sector, restriction of the private sector to increase the national income and provide the necessary investment funds to assure high growth rates. All these measures can be carried out, but only if Iran follows a non-capitalist path. Otherwise, notwithstanding partial reforms, the obsolescent economic structure will remain and so will the country's backwardness, that evil legacy of flunkeydom to imperialism.

Foreign policy, too, should follow a democratic course that accords with the national interest. That can be achieved only by adopting neutrality, combating neo-colonialism, extending and strengthening ties with the socialist countries and promoting friendship and co-operation with the emergent nations committed to peace, freedom, democracy and progress.

The People's Party, inspired by the ideas of October and creatively applying Marxism-Leninism to Iranian conditions, continues to work for a free, prosperous, independent and progressive Iran. And such an Iran can be built, but only through deep-going change in the social, economic and political fields. Our Party firmly believes that dedicated effort and unity with other national and patriotic trends will enable it to overcome all difficulties and fulfil its great mission.

World Marxist Review, November, 1967.

23

Western Interference in the Persian Gulf

In the recent period the ruling circles of the United States and Britain have been hatching plans for knocking together, under the aegis of those states, a military bloc in the Persian Gulf zone in connection with the British government's decision to withdraw its armed forces from that area within the next few years.

Mr E. Rostow, U.S. Under-Secretary of State, Mr. E. Black, the U.S. President's personal representative, and Mr. Roberts, British Minister of State, Foreign Office, recently visited the capitals of a number of countries in the Middle East, where they tried to palm off different variants of a plan for establishing a so-called system of joint defence.

According to a statement by Mr Rostow, Iran, Turkey, Pakistan, Iraq, Saudi Arabia and Kuwait could become the core of this bloc.

In Washington there is open talk about the necessity for the United States' 'military presence' in that area. American warships have already been sent to Bahrein.

The initiators of this entire undertaking are posing as 'defenders' of the interests of the Persian Gulf zone, but they will not succeed in concealing their real neo-colonialist aims. And their aims are primarily: the preservation and strengthening of the positions of the capitalist oil monopolies which for years and years have been extracting thousands of millions of dollars in profits from shameless robbery of the natural wealth in the Persian Gulf zone.

The policy of the imperialists there, as well as in other areas of the world, is aimed at preventing the national liberation movement, which has justice on its side, from successfully developing, and at putting a brake on the process of strengthening the national independence of the states of the Middle East.

In these circumstances, applying the treacherous tactics of 'divide and rule', imperialist circles of the United States and Britain are trying to implant mutual suspicion and differences among the peoples and countries in that part of the world.

Naturally, the countries of the Middle East are themselves becoming increasingly aware of the danger of the plans hatched by imperialist countries. Calls for 'joint defence' cannot fail to give rise, among them, to a very natural question: What is the reason that states situated many thousands of kilometres from the Persian Gulf, cherish the ambition of playing the part of some sort of 'guardians' or 'representatives' of the interests of the states and peoples in that part of the world?

One can easily understand the anxiety felt by the countries of the Persian Gulf in connection with the attempts of the neo-colonialists to poison their relations with one another, to harm the unity of the Arab states, to set Iran against the Arabs, and to divert the attention of those countries from the most urgent problems of our day, and especially from the problem of removing the consequences of the imperialist aggression by Israel.

According to the information available, Iraq, Iran, Kuwait, Pakistan and Turkey have already rejected the proposals for establishing a so-called system of joint defence.

The Prime Minister of Iran, Mr. Hoveida, has come out against foreign interference in the area of the Persian Gulf and has stressed that 'Britain's withdrawal through one door should not lead, for example, to America entering by another door, or even to Britain returning in some new form.'

The Soviet Union, loyal to its policy of protecting the national interests of sovereign countries and peoples against the encroachments of imperialists and realising that these plans of neo-colonialism are directed against the security of the southern frontiers of the USSR as well, comes out resolutely against the new attempts by aggressive circles in the United States and Britain to interfere in the affairs of the countries in the area of the Persian Gulf and to dictate their will to those countries.

The peoples of those countries, and they alone, have the right to shape their destiny. The sooner an end is put to colonialism and neo-colonialism in that area, the more successfully will the task of transforming the

Middle East into a zone of lasting peace and international co-operation be accomplished.

Tass statement, March 3, 1968.

24

Y. Serbin: *The Navigation Regime in Black Sea Straits must be Adhered To*

The Turkish authorities recently informed the states adhering to the convention on the navigation regime in the Black Sea straits that the American frigate 'William W. Pratt' was planning to enter the Black Sea in September of this year.

In connection with this it is appropriate to recall the basic points of the convention signed by the Soviet Union, Turkey, Bulgaria, Rumania, Britain, France, Greece, Jugoslavia and Japan in Montreux (Switzerland) on July 20, 1936, and by Italy in 1938.

The convention established that the principle of freedom of transit and navigation (art. 1) must obtain in the Black Sea straits. This general principle applied to merchant vessels, warships and aircraft. The rules of transit for shipping and passage of aircraft were outlined in the appropriate sections of the convention. Moreover, free transit through the straits in peace time was established for all merchant shipping, irrespective of nationality. With regard to warships, however, things are different.

First of all, the convention laid down a number of general principles concerning transit of warships with due regard for the security of Turkey, through whose territory the straits run, and of other Black Sea states, too. One of these rules, for instance, makes it obligatory not only to give timely warning of the forthcoming passage of warships through the straits (art. 13), but also limits the total number and tonnage of these vessels. Distinct differentiation is also made between the transit of warships belonging to the Black Sea states and those of other countries. Whereas the Black Sea states are permitted to send large vessels with a displacement of over 10,000 tons (art. 11) and in certain cases, submarines, (art. 12) through the straits, other countries may not do so. Moreover, countries not included among the Black Sea states, are permitted to send through the straits only strictly defined categories of vessels, the armaments, displacement and period of navigation in the Black Sea of which must correspond to the rules laid down in the convention.

Thus, in keeping with art. 10 the convention, only light surface craft and auxiliary ships of the non-Black Sea states are allowed to enter the

Black Sea. Furthermore, the total tonnage of the warships which the above states may send into the Black Sea simultaneously is also limited. Also, irrespective of the aims of the voyage, they may not spend more than 21 days in Black Sea waters (art. 18).

Appendix 2 to the convention outlines definitely the standards of displacement and maximum armament of these vessels. Only those warships of the non-Black Sea countries having a displacement of not more than 10,000 tons and carrying guns of not more than 203 mm calibre, may enter the Black Sea. The entry of a vessel of a non-coastal country carrying guns of more than 203 mm calibre would, therefore, be illegal.

It goes without saying that all these measures are meant to some extent or other to protect the security of Turkey and other Black Sea states, as it is directly stated in the preamble to the convention.

It should be borne in mind that in modern conditions, when powerful rocket and nuclear weapons have made their appearance, the rules of the convention limiting the armament of warships of non-coastal countries wishing to make the passage of the Black Sea, acquire especial significance. At present, small warships, the displacement of which does not prohibit their entry to the Black Sea, may be armed with rocket and nuclear weapons. Therefore, only strict adherence to these rules of the convention can answer to the interests of all Black Sea states, their security, and prevent any actions of a provocative nature in this area on the part of any countries whose shores are not washed by this sea. Let us see, then, what the American frigate 'William W. Pratt' which intends to steam into the Black Sea this September, represents. Its official displacement is 4,700 tons, that is, not even half the maximum permitted by the convention. Therefore, at a first glance, the right of this vessel to enter the Black Sea would not seem to arouse any doubts. Apparently, no doubts on this score arose with the Turkish authorities who are responsible for adherence to all the rules of the international convention on the transit of warships through the Black Sea straits.

However, a glance at Jane's official British reference book which supplies basic information about the warships of all countries, suffices to show that the 'William W. Pratt' is armed with rocket weapons of the 'Terrier' and 'ASROC' type, the calibres of which equal 350 and 305 mm., correspondingly. As we know, the 'Terrier' type rocket is a universal weapon adapted for use against aerial as well as coastal and surface targets, while the ASROC anti-submarine rockets can be fitted with nuclear warheads. Thus the armament of this American ship exceeds the standards set by the convention in its firepower. Its entry to the Black Sea would be a violation of the above-mentioned rules and of the significance of the convention on the regime in the Black Sea straits, and cannot, therefore, be considered legal.

The urgency of the question of the illegality of the entry of the above-mentioned American rocket-carrier to the Black Sea, as well as of warships of non-Black Sea countries carrying nuclear weapons is due to the necessity of protecting the interests of the security of the Black Sea states, particularly, in the present tense international situation caused by the United States' aggressive actions in Vietnam.

The peoples of all countries situated along the coast of the Black Sea cannot remain indifferent to the type of warship entering the Black Sea or to the aims of their passage. It is all the more impermissible, therefore, that any 'demonstrations of strength' of a provocative nature be organised in the Black Sea and that warships of states having no relation to this sea should rattle their rocket or nuclear weapons there. The Black Sea straits may be utilised in the interests of strengthening friendship, but not to the detriment of the security of states situated in this area.

The Black Sea must always remain a sea of peace and friendship among nations. This is in the interests of all the Black Sea countries.

Krasnaya Zvezda, September 3, 1966.

25

A. N. Kosygin's dinner Speech in Ankara

. . .

This visit, which is made at Turkey's invitation, is a sound manifestation of the establishment of mutual understanding between the two countries. The absence of any question which is the subject of dispute between our neighboring countries is very significant. Together with this, it is clear that there is reciprocal desire for the establishment of trade exchanges and economic relations.

Questions of the mutual relations of our countries have always been a very essential part of their foreign policies. This also holds true today. Our present visit also serves as a manifestation of the interest of the government of the Soviet Union in the establishment of firm mutual understanding with Turkey.

We consider that there now are objective conditions for the development of Soviet-Turkish relations entering a new stage.

We note with satisfaction statements by Turkish Government leaders that they are striving for a further improvement of relations with the Soviet Union, and we regard these statements with trust.

For our part, we do not consider that this development should happen at the expense of a worsening of Turkey's relations with any other state.

There is no reason for such a confrontation. At the same time, our peoples should feel fully confident that the Soviet-Turkish frontier, both at sea and on land, is a frontier of peace and friendship, and that this state of affairs cannot change under the influence of any extraneous factors. The Soviet Union would be ready to take concrete steps to insure and consolidate this confidence in our peoples.

The Soviet Union advocates a peaceful solution of disputes in any region of the world wherever these problems arise. This also refers to such a problem as the Cyprus question, which attracts great attention here in Turkey. The Soviet Government has already expressed its views on this question. The Soviet Union consistently supports the independence, sovereignty, and territorial integrity of the Republic of Cyprus. We consider that foreign troops must be withdrawn from the territory of the island, and war bases liquidated. The Cyprus question must be solved by the Cypriots themselves, of course, peacefully, without the use of force as a means of solving a national problem. The legitimate rights of both national communities on Cyprus, Turkish and Greek, must be observed.

Strengthening of trust and, consequently, improvement of political relations between the Soviet Union and Turkey creates favorable conditions for the growth of trade and economic cooperation between the two countries. We believe that political and economic relations must be developed together, complementing each other.

We have no doubt that the wonderful Turkish people have all opportunities to go forward quickly, solving the tasks of their economic development. The industriousness of the Turkish people is well known. Turkey has great natural resources and is linked with convenient sea lanes with many countries.

We have a deep understanding for the Turkish people's striving for progress, for further development of their economy and culture. We believe that the peace-loving and prosperous Turkish Republic can and must be an important factor of stability and consolidation of peace in this area of the world.

In conclusion I would like to say that we are satisfied with our talks with President of the Republic Cevdet Sunay, Prime Minister Suleyman Demirel, Foreign Minister Caglayangil, and other Turkish statesmen. These were talks that were marked by frankness and good will. No one tried to impose anything on anyone else. We sought to understand each other better and find more points of contact, and we undoubtedly reciprocally succeeded in this.

. . .

Tass, December 22, 1966.

Index

Abdi, General, 96
Abdullah, Amer, 168n
Abshire, Dr. David, 4
Abu Dhabi, 38, 122
Acheson, Dean, 22
Aden, 40, 41, 108, 109, 116
  Soviet Union and, 109, 110
  Suez Canal and, 110
  Faisal and, 115
  see also South Yemen's Peoples Republic
Aden Protectorate, *see* Aden
Adil, Salim (alias Radawi, Husain), 95
Afghanistan, 161, 193
Aflaq, Michel, 86
Afro-Asian Conference, 72
Ahmad, Imam, 104, 105
Al Anwar, 168n
Al Badr, 105
Al-Baidh, Salem, 109
Albania, 119, 152, 157
Al Bizri, General Afif, 169
Alborran Islands, 152
Alexandria, 152
Alexius, Patriarch, 67
Algeria, 11, 12, 72;
  Soviet Union and, 71, 72, 138, 142, 157, 184, 186;
  F.L.N. in, 72, 156, 178;
  Yemen and, 108;
  oil companies and, 118, 125, 128;
  communism and, 163;
  'revolutionary democracy' in, 177;
Al-Hakim Amer, Field-Marshal Abd, 67, 70, 72
Al Khalifa, 114

Al-Kuzbari, Mamun, 84
Al Sa'igh, Daud, 167
Al-Tali'a, 171-2
Altin, Cetin, 165
Amash, 103
America, the, 154
Amini, Dr., 30
Andaman Islands, 156
Anian, General Bahram, 40
Ara, Hussein, 171
Arab-Israeli Conflict, 9, 10, 11, 23, 36, 45–47, 50, 52, 91, 92-3, 116, 182-3, 191-192;
  Soviet Union and, 10, 23, 45–62 *passim*, 91, 93, 101, 111, 112, 145, 151, 182-3, 186, 187;
  Turkey and, 23;
  Iran and, 36;
  events preceding, 50, 52, 92, 94;
  Boumédienne and, 58-9;
  East Europe and, 60-1;
  and Western communists, 61;
  oil industry and, 127, 128, 129;
  American Sixth Fleet and, 155;
  sinking of *Eilat* in, 158;
  Arab communists and, 179;
  and see Documents 8-14, 245-89
Arab National Movement, 116
Arif, Major-General Abdel Rahman, 61, 103, 104
Arif, President Abdel Salam, 100, 102, 168
as-Sadat, Anwar, 69
as-Sallal, Abdullah, 105, 106, 107
Aswan Dam, 64, 66, 73, 74, 75, 82, 89, 139, 143

Atassi, Nuredin, 61, 87
Atatürk, Kemal, 5, 6, 15, 165
Austria, 119
Aybar, Mehmet Ali, 165
Ayub, President, 111

Badeau, John, 67
Baghdad-Basra railway, 96, 103
Baghdad Pact, *see* CENTO
Bahrain, Iran and, 40–1, 112, 114;
    Khrushchev and, 114;
    'liberation fronts' in, 116;
    oil and, 122
Bakdash, Khalid, 87–8, 90, 169, 177;
    and *see* Document 16, 292–8, and Document 19, 304–16
Bandar Abbas, 113
Bandung Conference, 9, 173
Barazani, Mullah Mustafa, 98, 99, 100, 101
Ba'th Party, 85, 86;
    in Syria: 11, 85–8, 92, 93, 94, 138, 156;
    see also neo-Ba'th;
    Khuzistan and, 41;
    All Arab National Command of, 86, 87;
    in Iraq: 85, 86, 94, 100, 102, 103, 104, 168
Bazzaz, 100–1, 102, 103, 168
Beliaev, 59, 78
Ben Bella, 72
Bitar, Salah, 86, 87
Boumédienne, President Houari, 54, 58–9, 61
Brezhnev, Leonid, 30, 72, 93, 147, 148, 151, 159;
    and *see* Document 12, 270–4
Bulganin, Nikolai, 10, 174
Bulgaria, 35;
    Jewish emigration from, 46;
    communist radio station in, 104;
    oil and, 122

Castiella, 157
Castro, Fidel, 27, 72, 174, 175
Central Intelligence Agency (CIA), 53, 91, 108
Central Treaty Organization (CENTO), 10, 24, 27, 40, 99, 111
Ceylon, 121
Che Guevara, 93, 171
China, 91, 93, 110, 116, 171;
    Soviet Union and, 32, 71, 113, 150, 163, 179, 193, 194
Chou En-lai, 70

Churchill, Winston, 111
'Cleopatra' incident, 67
Communism in Middle East, 11;
    nationalism and, 162, 163;
    internal disunity of, 163–4;
    new concepts of, 173–80 *passim*;
    and see Document 2, 221–8, and Documents 20 and 21, 316–40
Communist International (Comintern), 6, 7
Communist Party:
    Cyprus, 156;
    Egypt, 11, 170–2, 177, 178;
    France, 156;
    Greece, 156;
    Iran, 164, 181;
    Iraq, 11, 95, 97–8, 132, 167–9, 178;
    Israel, 46, 165–7, *and see* Document 9, 256–8;
    Italy, 156, 157, 170;
    Jordan, 167, 177;
    Lebanon, 169, 178;
    Morocco, 156, 178;
    Soviet Union (C.P.S.U.), 11, 95, 178, *and see* Document 11, 268–70
    Sudan, 162, 172–3;
    Syria, 11, 86, 87, 162, 163, 169–70, 177, 178;
    Turkey, 17, 19, 164–5, 181
Constantinople, 5
Crimean War, 152
Cromer, Lord, 80
Cuba, 75, 93, 110, 119, 121, 147, 159, 163, 174, 175
Curzon, Lord, 113
Cyprus, 17, 20, 193;
    Czechoslovakia and, 22;
    American bases in, 22;
    Communist party of, 156
Cythera, 152
Czechoslovakia, 27, 122, 131, 190;
    1968 crisis in, 3, 60, 78, 150, 157, 159, 165, 166, 168, 178, 179;
    Slansky Trial in, 61

Dayan, Moshe, 57
De Gaulle, Charles, 190
Demirel, 18, 19, 20, 21, 23, 185
Dhabi, 112, 116
Dhufar, Liberation Front of, 116
Djahanbani, General, 30
Douglas Amendment to Mutual Security Act, 67

Druzhba (Friendship) line, 121
Dulles, John Foster, 10

Eastern Europe, 149, 181, 184, 195;
    Iran and, 30, 35, 36, 38, 39;
    Israeli war and, 60–1;
    oil and, 121–2, 131–2, 135;
    Egypt and, 140, 141–2;
    and see Document 7, 243–5
East Germany, 3, 16, 150, 164, 166
Ecevit, Bulent, 23
Eghbal, 29
Egypt, 10, 11, 52;
    and U.A.R., 11, 12, 59, 65, 68–9, 71,
        74–5, 105;
    'scientific socialism' in, 11, 171–2;
    communists in, 64, 66, 162, 163, 170–
        171;
    nationalization in, 67–8;
    Free Officers' Movement of, 68;
    and National Charter, 69;
    Arab Socialist Union (ASU) of, 72, 77,
        86, 156, 171, 172;
    Suez Canal, 74, 75;
    economy of, 74–5, 191;
    Muslim Brotherhood in, 79;
    oil revenues and, 125, 127;
    East European loans to, 140;
    Great Britain and, 8, 45, 142;
    Iran and, 29, 41;
    Israel and, 52, 54, 92, 107;
    Jordan and, 73, 111, 112;
    Persian Gulf and, 116;
    Saudi Arabia and, 73, 114–15, 116;
    South Arabia and, 107;
    Soviet Union and, 63–84 *passim*, 137,
        138, 139–40, 141, 142, 143, 152–3,
        156, 157, 158, 159, 179, 181, 182, 183,
        184, 185, *and see* Documents, 3–5,
        229–41;
    Syria and, 64, 73, 84, 92;
    United States, 67, 74;
    Yemen and, 73, 76, 105–6, 107
Egyptian Press,
    Al Ahram, 71, 72, 73, 80, 81;
    Al Tali'a, 76, 171, 172;
    Rose el-Yusef, 79;
    Al Kateb, 172
Eilat, sinking of, 158
Emani, Sharif, 29, 30
Engels, Friedrich, 5
Eshkol, Levi, 54
Eskadra, Soviet fleet, 153–4, 157

Euphrates Dam project, 89, 90, 140, 143

Faisal, King, 107, 114–15
Fakhri, Selim, 168n
Farouk, King, 9, 43, 45
Fayek, Muhammad, 79
Federation of Persian Gulf Principalities,
    115
Fedorenko, 55
Ferid, Abdel Magid, 79
Finland, 27, 161
Forutan, Gholam Hussein, 164
France, 10, 104, 128, 129, 133–4, 156, 157
Front de Libération Nationale (FLN), 72,
    156, 178

Gasteyger, C., 154
Gibraltar, 157
Gomaa, Shaarawi, 79
Gomulka, Wladyslaw, 11
Gorshkov, Admiral Alexandr M., 76, 152,
    153, 157
Great Britain, 10, 43, 97, 106, 113, 114,
    142, 154, 156, 190;
    Aden and, 40, 41, 108, 109, 110;
    Persian Gulf, 40, 41, 108, 113;
    oil and, 119, 127, 129;
Grechko, Marshal, 70, 76, 89, 93, 111
Greece, 20, 156;
    Soviet Union and, 24, 61, 119, 152 157
Griffin, Admiral, 154
Gromyko, Andrei, 18, 20, 156;
    Egypt and, 73, 74, 140
Gurov, 121
Gürsel, General, 14, 15, 19

Hadj Ali, Bechir, 173
Hadramaut, 109, 110
Hafiz, Colonel Amin, 85–7
Hagia Sophia, church of, 5
Hammamet, Gulf of, 152
Hashemites, 11, 43, 94
Hatoum, Colonel Selim, 91
Havana Tricontinental Conference, 169
Haykal, 71, 72, 73, 80, 81, 170
Hedjaz, 114
Hitler, Adolf, 8, 60, 152
Hodeyda, 36
Horn of Africa, 109
Howeidi, Amin, 79
Hungary, 35, 62, 122
Hussein, King, 53, 62, 111–12, 155

India, 10, 138
Indian Ocean, 113, 115, 155, 156, 184
Indonesia, 175
Inönü, Ismet, 14, 15, 16, 17, 18
International Monetary Fund, 75
Iran, 1, 6, 8, 21, 28-42 *passim*, 63, 115, 191;
  communists in, 28, 29, 32, 33-4, 35, 38,
    40, 162, 163, 164, 181;
  economic growth in, 28, 29, 30, 36-7,
    39, 191;
  United States and, 29, 30, 32, 37;
  reforms in, 31-4;
  oil and, 37-8, 39, 41, 118, 122, 123, 124,
    127, 135;
  Bahrain and, 40-1, 112, 114;
  Kurdish problem, 98, 99;
  see also, Document 22, 340-6;
  and Doviet Union and Iran
Irani, President, 107
Iraq, 8, 11, 15, 45, 64, 65, 66, 89, 94-104
  passim, 115, 122, 174;
  Hashemites and, 11, 15, 94;
  communists in, 11, 65, 94, 102, 103-4,
    132, 162, 167-9;
  and see Documents 20 and 21, 316-40;
  Ba'th Party and, 85, 94, 100, 102, 168;
  Kurdish problem in, 97, 98-101, 102,
    168;
  oil and, 118, 122, 123, 124, 125, 127,
    132, 133-4;
  see also Soviet Union and Iraq
Iraq Petroleum Company (IPC), 97, 103,
  123, 124, 125, 126, 132
Israel, communists in, 46, 162, 165-7;
  Egypt and, 52, 54, 55;
  Iran and, 29;
  Soviet Union and, 8, 10, 12, 43-62
    passim, 78, 111, 121, 139, 155, 157,
    158, 181-2;
  Syria and, 49-50, 52, 54, 55, 59, 69, 90,
    92-3;
  United States and, 47-9, 53, 189;
  and see Documents 9 and 10, 256-268;
  and Arab-Israeli conflict
Italy, 104, 129;
  Soviet Union and, 119, 122, 152, 157;
  communist party of, 156, 157, 170
Ivanov, K., 78, *and see* Document 14,
  277-89

Jaber, Mamduh, 89
Jadid, Salah, 86-7, 91
Japan, 119, 121, 122, 131, 134

Jarring, Gunnar, 57
Johnson, President Lyndon, 17
Jordan, 53, 73, 111-12, 177
Judaism without Embellishment 48

Kahn, E., 4
Kapnist, Count, 113
Karachi, 156
Kassem, General Abdel Karim, 64, 174;
  Mosul uprising and, 65;
  communists and, 94, 95, 97-8, 167-8;
  Soviet Union and, 96, 101, 140;
  foreign policy of, 96-7;
  Kurdish problem and, 98-100;
  fall of, 100, 101, 168;
  Ba'th and, 102, 103;
  IPC and, 124
Kemal, Mustafa, *see* Atatürk
Kennedy, John F., 67
Kerala, 174
Khrushchev, Nikita, 10, 15, 18, 29, 114,
  147, 148, 151, 174, 176, 177;
  Egypt and, 11, 64-6, 67, 69-71, 73, 78,
    170;
  Soviet navy and, 152, 156;
  Cuban crisis and, 147, 158
Khuzistan, 31, 41
Komsomol, 51
Kondrachov, 49
Koratürk, Admiral, 15
Kosygin, Aleksey Nikolayevich, 36, 92;
  Turkey and, 21-3, *and see* Document 25,
    350-1;
  Egypt and, 73-4, 92, 140;
  military policy of, 147-8, 159;
  and see Document 8, 245-56
Kurdish problem, 97, 98-101, 102, 168
Kuwait, 41, 97, 112;
  Soviet Union and, 113, 114, 115;
  oil and, 37, 38, 122, 123, 124, 127
Kuwait Neutral Zone, 122, 123, 124

Latakia, 152, 153
Lebanon, 8, 15, 116, 169, 178, 184
Lenin, Vladimir Ilyich, 2, 5, 112, 162, 187
Libya, 118, 122, 123, 125, 127, 128

Madras, 156
Maghreb, 193
Mahdawi, Colonel, 94, 95, 96
Majlis, 30
Makarios, Archbishop, 17, 20
Malenkov, G. M., 146

Malik, Jakob, 72
Malinovsky, Rodion, 72, 73
Malta, 151, 152
Mansur, Ali, 32
Mao Tse-tung, 11, 27, 110
Marx, Karl, 2, 5, 69
Mazurov, Kyrill, 61, 82
Menderes, Adnan, 12, 14, 15, 18
Middle East Oil, 118–19, 121, 122–36
   passim
  Abu Dhabi: 38, 116, 122–3;
  Algeria, 123, 125;
  Bahrain, 122;
  East Europe, 35–6, 118, 121–2, 131–2,
    133, 135;
  Egypt: 75;
  Iran: 28, 35–6, 37–8, 122, 123, 124,
    127;
  Iraq: 104, 122, 123, 124, 125, 127;
  Israel: 121;
  Kuwait: 37, 38, 122, 123, 124, 127;
  Kuwait Neutral Zone: 122, 123, 124;
  Libya: 122, 123, 125, 127, 191;
  Persian Gulf: 113, 117;
  Quatar, 116, 124;
  Saudi Arabia: 37, 122, 123, 124, 125,
    127;
  Soviet Union and: 28, 38, 96, 103, 118,
    130–6;
  Western Europe and: 12, 118, 125–30,
    133, 134, 135
Middle East Oil Companies, 37–8, 115,
   123–5, 128, 133, 134;
  AGIP (Italian), 123;
  Arabian Oil Company (Japan), 123,
    124;
  Aramco (American cartel), 123, 124;
  British Pwtroleum Company (BPC),
    123;
  Compagnie Française des Petroles, 123;
  ENI (Italian), 123;
  Gulf Oil Corporation (USA), 123;
  Iranian State Oil Company (NIOC),
    123;
  Iran Sovneft Oil Company, 28;
  Iraq Petroleum Company (IPC), 97,
    103, 123, 124, 125, 126, 132;
  Kuwait National Petroleum Company
    (USA), 123;
  National Oil Company of Iraq, 133,
    134;
  Royal Dutch Shell (USA), 123;
  Socony Mobile Oil (USA), 123;

Standard Oil of California (USA), 123;
Standard Oil of New Jersey (USA),
  123;
  Texaco (USA), 123
Mikoyan, Anastas, 66, 73, 96, 97
Mirsky, G., 69, 85, 175–6
Mogadishu, 155, 156
Molokhov, Admiral, 156
Molotov, V. M., 9, 113
Moskva, the, 154
Montesquieu, 194
Montreux Convention, 8, 15, 24, 157
Morocco, 156, 178
Mossadeq, Dr., 28, 32
Mount Athos, 151
Mubarak, Yusef, 169
mullahs 30, 31
Muscat, 112
Mussolini, Benito, 152

Nassar, Fuad, 167, 177
Nasser, President Gamal Abdel, 2, 10, 27,
  59, 97, 163, 179;
  communism and, 11, 63, 64, 170–2;
  Syria and, 50, 94;
  Soviet Union and, 51, 62, 64, 70, 71–2,
    73, 74, 80–1, 83–4, 140;
  Israeli war and, 52–4, 56, 59, 81;
  Jordan and, 53;
  Iraqi revolution and, 64, 96;
  UAR and, 65;
  Lebanon and, 64;
  United States and, 64, 67, 80, 83, 155;
  Khrushchev and, 64, 65–6, 67, 69–70;
  Free Officers Movement and, 68;
  political power of, 77, 80;
  Yemen and, 106, 107;
  King Faisal and, 107, 115;
  liberation fronts and, 116;
  speeches of, *see* Documents 3–5, 229–41
Neo-Ba'th, 2, 27, 50, 90, 91, 94n, 163, 169,
  178;
  1966 coup of, 47, 49, 87, 88;
  Soviet Union and, 88–9, 93, 138, 179;
  Arab socialists view of, 91;
  events preceding Six Day War and, 92;
  see also Ba'th Party
Nicobar Islands, 156
Nik-Khah, 164
Nigeria, 128
Nkrumah, Kwame, 72
North Atlantic Treaty Organization
  (NATO), 4, 23, 48, 157, 159;

Turkey and, 12, 15, 16, 17, 19, 22, 24, 189;
Soviet Union and, 23, 24
Nuri as Said, 11, 15, 140
Nuri, Bahaeddin, 168n

O.E.C.D., 25, 118, 126, 128
Oman, Liberation Front of, 116
Organization of Petroleum Exporting Countries (OPEC), 121
Ottoman Empire, 5; *see also* Turkey

Pachachi, Adnan, 103
Pakistan, 21, 28, 111, 115
Palestine, *see* Israel
Palestine Liberation Organisation, 73
Pan Arabism, 2, 6, 10, 40-1, 101
Panislamism, 6
Panslavism, 5
Panturanianism, 17
Panturkism, 6
Paul I, 151
Peoples Republic of South Yemen, 108-110;
National Liberation Front of, 108, 116;
and FLOSY, 108, 116
Persia, *see* Iran
Persian Gulf, 112-17, 122, 127, 193;
Britain and, 40, 41;
Soviet Union and, 36, 41, 113, 114, 116, 153, 156, 184
Peshmerga Army, *see* Kurdish problem
Podgorny, President, 18, 61, 93, 112
Poland, 3, 35, 60, 62;
Jewish emigration from, 46;
anti-Zionism in, 60-1, 166;
Soviet oil and, 122, 131
Political Trends in the Arab East see Document 1, 213-21
Port Said, 152
Potsdam Conference, 8
Primakov, 18, 59, 78
'Protocols of the Elders of Zion', 49

Qasemi, Ahmed, 164
Qatar, 116, 124

Radawi, Husain, *see* Adil, Salim
Radmanesh, Reza, *see* Document 22, 340-6
Ribbentrop, Joachim von, 8
Rivero, Admiral, 154-5
Romanovs, 5

Rostow, Eugene, 115
Rumania, 35, 36, 41, 131, 166;
Iranian oil and, 36, 122
Russia, *see* Soviet Union
Rybkin, Colonel, 148
Ryshov, 15-16, 20

Sabry, Ali, 70, 79, 172
Saratoga, 154
Sarper, Selim, 15-16
Sa'ud, King Ibn, 114, 123
Saudi Arabia, 41, 73-4, 106, 112, 114-16, 118, 127
Sayyids, 104
Sazonov, 113
Serbin, Y., *see* Document 24, 348-50
Shah of Persia, 31, 32, 33, 35, 40;
Soviet Union and, 29, 30, 115, 163, 164, 185
Shaker, Mustafa, 169
Shaqai, Abbas, 164
Shawi, Nikola, 178
Shelepin, Alexander, 72
Shukairy, Ahmad, 59, 73-4
Slavophils, 5
Smith, Gerald, L. K., 49
Sneh, Moshe, *see* Document 10, 258-68
Soiuznefteksport, 121
South Arabia, 104, 107, 108-10, 193;
Iran and, 40-1;
Soviet Union and, 106, 109, 110, 115, 156;
Faisal and, 107, 114-15;
NLF strategy in, 116
South Arabian Federation, 108, 109
Soviet-Iranian Cultural Relations Society, 30
Soviet Union,
'socialism in one country', 7;
anti-Westernism and, 8-9, 182;
'military socialism' and, 9;
Bandung Conference, 9-10, 173;
Jews in, 9, 43, 44, 45, 46, 48, 193;
'national democracies' and, 69, 71-2;
new approach to communism of, 173-177;
Arab communism and, 173-80, 184-5;
arms supplies for Middle East from, 46, 137, 142, 184;
and trade and aid, 137-44 *passim*;
military policy of, 145-9, 151-61;
naval forces of, 1, 24, 25, 76, 81, 151-8, 159, 182, 184;

Soviet Union (*continued*)
 oil and, 1, 11, 12, 38, 41, 90, 103, 118–
  136 *passim*;
 Aden and, 41, 109;
 Albania and, 152;
 Algeria and, 58–9, 71, 72, 138, 142, 157,
  178, 184, 186;
 China and, 7, 32, 71, 146, 156, 175, 176,
  178, 187, 193, 194;
 Cyprus and, 1, 17, 18, 20, 21, 22;
 Egypt and, 3, 9, 10, 12, 51, 52, 53, 59,
  63–84 *passim*, 152–3, 155, 156, 158,
  159, 179, 181, 182, 183, 185;
  Aswan Dam, 64, 66, 72, 74, 75, 82,
   89, 139;
  military aid to Egypt, 10, 75–6, 82,
   138, 142, 157, 182, 184;
  and trade, 56, 62, 138, 139–40, 141,
   143, 184;
  Egyptian port facilities for, 152–3;
  Egyptian communists and, 170–2;
  and see Document 6, 241–3;
 Greece and, 185;
 Iran and, 12, 28–30, 32–5, 36, 38–42, 124,
  133, 134, 138, 139, 181, 182, 185;
 Iraq and, 64, 86, 96–104, 133–4, 137,
  138, 140, 142, 168, 185;
 Israel and, 23, 43–62 *passim*, 78, 139,
  155, 157–8, 165–7, 178, 181–2, *and see*
  Documents 11–14, 268–89;
 Jordan and, 53, 111, 112;
 Peoples Republic of South Yemen and,
  109, 110;
 Persian Gulf and, 36, 41, 109, 113–14,
  116, 117, 155, 156, 184, *and see*
  Document 23, 346–8;
 Saudi Arabia and, 74, 114–15, 116;
 Somalia and, 5, 6, 179, 186;
 Spain and, 157;
 South Arabia and, 106, 109, 110, 115,
  156;
 Sudan and, 1, 142, 186;
 Syria and, 3, 9, 11, 12, 45, 51, 62, 84–94
  passim, 153–4, 155, 181, 183, 184–5;
  neo-Ba'ths, 27, 47, 49, 88, 91–2, 93,
   94, 138, 179;
  anti-Israel propaganda, 45–50, 57–59;
  Six Day War, 52–6, 59, 61;
  Ba'th Party and, 85–6, 87, 138;
  economic relations, 89–90, 137–8,
   139, 140, 141, 143, 184;
  military aid, 89, 137, 142, 182, 184;
  oil agreements, 90, 133;

 Euphrates Dam project, 89, 90, 140,
  143;
 Turkey and, 1, 5, 6, 7, 8, 9, 13, 15–28
  passim, 139, 157–8, 164–5, 181, 182,
  185;
  Montreux Convention, 8, 15, 24,
   157–8, *and see* Document 24, 348–
   350;
  Cyprus problem, 17, 20, 23, *and see*
   Document 25, 350–1;
  NATO and, 12, 24;
  Turkish communists, 15, 164–5, 181,
   185;
 United States and, 24–5, 121, 138, 146,
  147, 148, 149, 150, 159;
  spheres of influence, 150–1, 160, 166,
   183, 187–9, 193;
 Yemen and, 105–8, 137, 138, 142, 149,
  159, 184, 186;
 Press and Radio in:
  International Affairs, *see* Document 1,
   213–21, and Document 14, 277–89;
  Izvestia, 48, 49, 111;
  Komsomolskaia Pravda, 48;
  Krokodil 57;
  Pravda, 22, 48, 50, 57, 58, 59, 65, 68,
   70, 73, 79, 109, 132, 171, *and see*
   Documents 6–8, 243–56;
  Radio Moscow, 50;
  Tass News Agency, 107, *and see*
   Document 23, 346–8 and Docu-
   ment 25, 350–1
Soviet Union and the Middle East The
 (Laqueur), 1
Spain, 157
Sudan, 142, 162, 172–3, 186
Suez Canal, 10, 74, 75, 110, 126, 127, 155
Sukarno, President Achmed, 72
Sunay, President, 19, 22
Stalin, Joseph, 6, 9, 50, 146, 162, 173, 174,
 187, 188, 189;
 Turkey and, 16;
 Jewish question and, 44;
 Middle East trade and, 139;
 nuclear weapons and, 147;
 Soviet navy and, 152;
 Finland and, 159
Straits, the (Bosphorus and Dardanelles),
 5, 8, 15, 24, 25
Sweden, 119, 121
Syria, 8, 52, 84–94 *passim*, 113, 116, 125,
 132, 183;
 Security Council, 57, 93;

U.A.R. and, 11, 12, 73, 84, 138;
Six Day War and, 49–56, 92;
neo-Ba'th, 2, 27, 47, 49, 87, 88;
guerrilla forces in, 50, 92;
communists in, 64–5, 86, 87, 162, 163, 169–70;
Ba'th party, 85, 86–7, 177;
nationalization in, 86, 87;
Iraq and, 94;
Yemen and, 108;
Jordan and, 111, 112;
see Documents 15–19, 289–316;
see also Soviet Union

Tabriz, 37
Takitri, 103
Talib, Naji, 103
Tashkent, 116
Tass News Agency, 107
Tiberias, Lake, 92
Tito, Marshal, 11, 61, 73, 81
Tlas, Mustafa, 93
Togliatti, Palmiro, 71
Tripolitania, 8
Trotsky, Leon, 5
Tudeh party, 28, 32, 33, 34, 163, 164
Tuganova, O., *see* Document 1, 213–21
Tunisia, 73, 152
Turkey, governmental changes in, 14–19;
communism in, 17, 19, 27, 162, 165;
and Labor Party (TIP), 17, 19, 156, 165;
NATO and, 12, 15, 16, 17, 19, 23, 24;
Cyprus problem and, 17, 20–23, 27;
Demirel and, 18–19, 20, 21, 22, 23;
Montreux Convention, 8, 15, 24, 157–8, *and see* Document 24, 348–50;
Economy of, 25–6, 27;
Euphrates Dam project and, 89;
Kurdish minority in, 98, 99;
Persian Gulf and, 115;
Soviet Union and, 1, 5–6, 7, 8, 12, 15–28 *passim*, 139, 152, 157–8, 181, 182;
United States and, 15, 16, 17, 19, 24, 27
Tuval, 19
United Arab Republic (UAR), 11, 12, 59, 65, 84;
Soviet Union and, 65, 68–9, 71, 74, 78, 138;
economy of, 74–5;
Yemen and, 105
United Nations, Palestine and, 8;
Cyprus problem and, 21;

Arab-Israeli conflict and, 45, 46, 53, 55, 56–7, 60, 93;
Soviet Union and, 56, 67, *and see* Document 8, 245–56;
Security Council of, 46, 56–7, 60, 93;
peace-keeping force in Gaza and, 74;
Kurdish problem and, 100;
Cuba and, 119
United States, 10;
Lebanon and, 15, 184;
Turkey and, 15, 16, 17, 24, 139;
Israel and, 59;
Egypt and, 67, 74, 80, 183;
Yemen and, 106;
aid to Jordan from, 111;
Persian Gulf and, 113;
Faisal and, 115;
oil and, 121–6, 127, 129;
Soviet Union and, 138, 159;
arms race and, 146, 147, 148, 149, 159;
NATO and, 149;
spheres of influence of, 150–1, 160, 183, 187, 189;
Sixth Fleet of, 59, 151, 154, 155, 156, 157;
Spain and, 157;
Middle East policy of, 160–1, 188–90, 193;
Syria and, 183;
Vietnam war and, 53, 189;
Jews in, 193
USSR, *see* Soviet Union
Urgüplü, 18

Valone, 157
Venezuela, 119, 120, 121, 124, 126
Vietnam War, 53, 189, 194
Vinogradow, 80

West Germany, 129;
Israel and, 48;
Euphrates Dam and, 89;
oil and, 119, 121, 127;
Persian students and, 164
Wichmann, Mrs. C., 4
World Marxist Review, 64, 84, *and see* Documents 15–17, 289–302, and Document 22, 340–6
Yahia, Taher, 103
Yahya, Imam, 105
Yamani, Ahmad Zaki, 127
Yemen, The, 193;
Egypt and, 73, 76, 105, 106, 107;

Yemen, The (*continued*)
  Soviet Union and, 105–8, 110, 137, 139,
    141, 159, 184, 186;
  UAR and, 105;
  civil war in, 105–8;
  Saudi Arabia and, 106, 107, 115;
  South Yemen Peoples Republic and,
    108;
  FLOSY and, 109
Yon, 16

Yugoslavia, 35, 56, 61, 157, 163

Zakharov, Marshal, 112
Zaydi, 104
Zionism, 6, 8, 65, 69, 178, 183, 192–3;
  Palestine communists and, 43;
  Soviet Union and, 43, 47–8, 57, 149,
    162;
  Hussein and, 111
Zuayin, Yusef, 50, 87, 89, 92, 93, 94n

DATE DUE

DATE DUE			
MAY 5 7			
MAY 5 7			
OC 18 '81			
GAYLORD			PRINTED IN U.S.A.